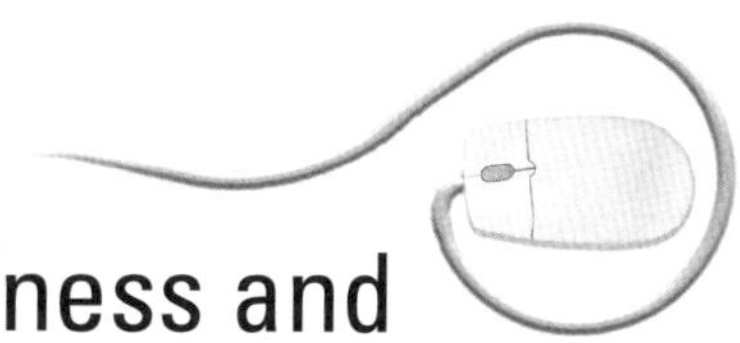

The Business and Information Technologies (BIT) Project

A Global Study of Business Practice

The Business and Information Technologies (BIT) Project

A Global Study of Business Practice

editors

Uday Karmarkar
University of California, Los Angeles, USA

Vandana Mangal
University of California, Los Angeles, USA

World Scientific

NEW JERSEY • LONDON • SINGAPORE • BEIJING • SHANGHAI • HONG KONG • TAIPEI • CHENNAI

Published by

World Scientific Publishing Co. Pte. Ltd.
5 Toh Tuck Link, Singapore 596224
USA office: 27 Warren Street, Suite 401-402, Hackensack, NJ 07601
UK office: 57 Shelton Street, Covent Garden, London WC2H 9HE

Library of Congress Cataloging-in-Publication Data
The business and information technologies (BIT) project : a global
study of business practice / edited by Uday S. Karmarkar and Vandana Mangal.
p. cm.
Includes bibliographical references and index.
ISBN-13 978-981-256-696-6 -- ISBN-10 981-256-696-1 (alk. paper)
I. Karmarkar, Uday S. (Uday Sadashiv) II. Mangal, Vandana. III. Title.

2006049624

British Library Cataloguing-in-Publication Data
A catalogue record for this book is available from the British Library.

Typeset by Stallion Press
Email: enquiries@stallionpress.com

Printed in Singapore by B & JO Enterprise

FOREWORD

Notwithstanding reports to the contrary, the size of the information economy in the United States has been steadily increasing from about 46% of the GNP in 1967 to about 56% of the GNP in 1992 and to 63% of the GNP in 1997 (Apte and Nath, 2004). In short, it has become a major part of the economy already, and will continue to dominate it for the foreseeable future making US truly an information economy.

The Internet phenomenon was primarily a matter of a fundamental change in information logistics, with the protocols of the web superimposed on a deregulating and increasingly competitive telecommunications environment. This story continues to play itself out.

However, there are new technologies and systems on the horizon, and it is most likely that a second slower wave of change based on infrastructure development, and then probably a third wave based on information processing, intelligent agents, and natural interfaces (as distinct from just the shipping and handling of information) will be observed. It is expected that all these technological and infrastructure developments will change the structure of firms in terms of organization and work process, will change information chains and inter-organizational relationships, and will alter the structure of industrial sectors, to the point that the traditional categories do not apply very well.

However, it is not clear how and when this will happen, or what will take its place. It is also not clear how lines of authority, responsibility and communication will be established in the new firm. One very basic change is occurring in the nature of the workplace. Most of the workers now face a screen for some significant period of time during work hours. The screen is a very different workplace from a desktop, since it is much better connected with places, people and processes outside the workplace. The screen (or interface) is also easily liberated physically from the desk and cubicle. It is apparent that the traditional notion of contemporaneous co-location as the core of an organization is ready to disappear.

Perhaps, the concepts of span of control and hierarchy will disappear in favor of some form of "just-in-time" and "only-on-demand" management.

The dot.com boom might have come and gone, but it has permanently changed the face of B2C relationships well beyond just the new phraseology. There is no question that sectors such as retailing, travel services, and financial services have been transformed, not just in terms of new entrants, but for the incumbents as well. For many consumer goods and services, the web is now a growing carrier of brand equity and customer recognition; it has become a new face for a company. The changes in the B2C layer are beginning to ripple back into supply and service chains. The impact on logistics, freight and delivery services is most easily seen, but many other equally dramatic changes are occurring inside and between firms, that are invisible to the casual observer.

The reduction in the costs of information logistics suggests obvious changes in business practice. As transaction costs drop, as large volumes of information can be reliably and quickly transported, there will be changes in the structure of business processes that exploit these advantages. Some of the consequences for B2B interactions have already been observed, although hype and overestimation have tended to distract from the very significant reality.

Perhaps, the most important issue today is the overall impact of these technologies on the structure of industry sectors and the economy as a whole. Many sectors are coalescing and converging. For example, newspapers, magazines, and broadcast organizations are all colliding on the web. Those sectors will fragment and reform into new alignments, which exploit their core strengths. The position that newspapers have held because of the economics of delivering information bundles to the door, is seriously threatened by online channels. For example, newspapers are not now or in the future, the strongest suppliers of "breaking" news, especially in multimedia formats. The television networks have the best collection and packaging systems for that task. Newspapers may hold on to criticism, commentary and review, though magazines could easily start to compete for that role. In turn, TV broadcasts will face challenges from web casts. Magazines will have to contend with web-based competitors, and go on the web themselves. Of course, these changes will not occur overnight. For a time, most media and publishing companies will have to think in terms of both sheets and screens.

There are very similar stories that can be told about other sectors, as well as about international trade. The point is that these changes are huge, and deserve to be followed closely. It is relatively easy to make broad brush comments about the changes that are underway, as we have above. However, hard information about the extent and distribution of these effects is lacking.

This book aims to capture the impacts of new information technologies on business and industry structure in various nations across the world. The potential for learning across these groups is vast. The nature of best practices in different countries varies widely. It is expected that several interesting local variations in business practices will be found, in addition to various impacts of technologies on business.

OVERVIEW

The BIT study documents the information technology driven changes that are occurring in business structure, business practice and sector structures across a wide spectrum of industry sectors in the United States and the rest of the world. The first step in the process was to do a base line study that established the state of this universe. Subsequently, the study is being repeated at appropriate time intervals to track the changes that are actually occurring, so as to provide hard information on what is really happening across the economic landscape as a result of changes in information technologies. The study will be across all sectors.

The BIT project is being conducted at a global scale. At the time of writing, the project has 12 partners in leading academic and research institutions around the world. The partners include USA, Argentina, Chile, Greece, India, Italy, Korea, New Zealand, Peru, Spain, Sweden, and Taiwan. The details of the BIT partners are in Appendix C.

Five of these teams (Italy, India, Korea, Spain, and USA) have conducted surveys during 2004–2005. It is expected that the BIT survey will eventually be conducted in perhaps 15–20 countries by research teams from those countries. This global perspective combined with the longitudinal view will provide a unique and comparative picture of technology and business practice across the world.

The potential for learning across these groups is vast. The nature of best practices in different countries varies widely. It is also not the case that the most developed countries are always the most advanced in technology use and penetration. For example, many countries are far ahead of the US in the degree of conversion to electronic banking and monetary systems. As an example, certain European countries have already closed their check processing facilities, since checks have almost passed out of use. India surpasses many countries in the extent of software project involvement and exports, despite a miniscule level of penetration of PC use or for that matter, phone usage. In many eastern countries, the use of wireless communications is rapidly outstripping traditional wireline systems. It is expected that several interesting local variations in business practices will be found.

This book brings together findings for the BIT survey for five of the countries partnering in the project. These are in Part I of the book. Part II of the book contains papers which either compare the BIT survey data from multiple countries or discuss findings from studies that look at specific sectors such as entertainment media and retail.

ABOUT THE AUTHORS

Alfredo Biffi is a Senior Lecturer and Director of Information Systems Department at the SDA Bocconi School of Management, Milano. He is also an Associate Professor in organization and information systems at the University of Insubria in Varese, Italy. His main research interests include information systems management, process management & reengineering, project management, and internet-based business trends. He is a Consultant for ICT-based organizational projects.

Anna Canato is a PhD candidate at Bocconi University, in the field of strategy and organization and a Research Assistant at the MIS department of the SDA Bocconi School of Management. Her research interests address the organization of innovative activities and strategic management. In her dissertation, Anna considers the role of organizational culture and identity during moments of profound transformation and their relevance for facilitating knowledge exchange in international organizations. Anna has past working experience as a change management consultant in international IT implementation projects.

Marco Cantamessa is an Associate Professor at the Department of Manufacturing Systems and Economics of the Technical University of Torino, Italy, where he teaches management of innovation and product development. His main research interest is on the impact that technological innovation has on product design, manufacturing systems, business processes and organizational models. He has authored or co-authored more than eighty scientific papers, of which nineteen have appeared in international refereed journals. He is a member of INFORMS, AITEM, The Design Society (where he serves on the Advisory Board) and has served on the Scientific Boards of a number of international conferences.

Jon Chang is a Graduate of the UCLA Anderson MBA program and participated in the AMR research project that led to his coauthored article in this volume.

Kai-Wei Chang is a Graduate of the UCLA Anderson MBA program and participated in the AMR research project that led to his coauthored article in this volume.

Sunil Chaudhary is the founding Principal of Riviera Partners. Prior to Riviera Partners, he was a co-founder in an enterprise search firm, CareerNet Consulting, in Bangalore India. He started the firm and within a short span of two years, CareerNet became recognized as one of the premier recruiting companies for early stage technology companies. He helped launch the innovative campus hiring service, which helped CareerNet place more than 250 graduating students from top engineering schools into technology companies. He also started the New Delhi office of CareerNet where he was responsible for putting in place the infrastructure, identifying and signing new customers, hiring new recruiters and daily management of the office. Prior to CareerNet, he worked as a software engineer for IBM Global Services.

Abhijeet Kumar Choudhary has rich experience in finance and IT consulting and is currently working with IBM, India. He has worked in consulting assignments for Oil major BP, Ineos to gain functional domain expertise in chemicals and petroleum business processes. He completed his Master of Management from the School of Management, IIT Bombay and B.E. (Honours) in Computer Engineering from the National Institute of Technology, Jaipur (formerly REC Jaipur).

Jason Chu is an MBA Graduate of the Anderson School at UCLA. He holds a bachelor's degree of economics from Trinity College in Hartford, CT. His professional experience includes international transfer pricing and financial planning in the biotechnology industry.

Atanu Ghosh joined the Shailesh J. Mehta School of Management in 1999 and brings with him rich academic and corporate experience after working with several organizations for more than 25 years. He was associated with several business schools as Visiting Professor and had taught courses in sales and distribution management, business marketing, international marketing, apparel marketing, and merchandising. He has developed a unique format for a course "Leadership, Vision and Entrepreneurship", that enables the final year students of the Master of Management program to learn about leadership in an innovative way. His areas of interest include strategic management, services marketing, relationship marketing, IT deployment by Indian business sectors, supply chain management, product launch, etc.

Michelle Green is an MBA Graduate of the UCLA Anderson School of Management. She holds a bachelor of science degree in mathematics with computer science from the Massachusetts Institute of Technology. Her professional experience includes implementing business intelligence systems in a variety of industries and business analysis and product management focusing in Internet banking for wholesale banking customers.

Uday S. Karmarkar is the LA Times Professor of Technology and Strategy at the UCLA School of Management in 1994. He previously taught at the Graduate School of Business at the University of Chicago (1975–1979) and the Simon School at the University of Rochester (1979–1994) where he held the Xerox Chair in Operations. He has published over 70 research papers and articles, has founded two academic journals and is on several editorial boards. His research interests include the information economy, service industrialization, technology management, manufacturing strategy, supply chain management, and service enterprise management. He has undertaken projects in operations and technology management, strategy, industrial marketing, and supply chain management with over 40 firms in the US, Europe and Asia. His teaching interests include management in the information economy, operations and technology strategy, manufacturing, and service management.

Hong-il Kim is a Doctoral Student of Korea University Business School. He got his MBA degree from Hanyang University.

Yunchong Lee is a Graduate of the UCLA Anderson MBA program. He participated in the AMR research project that led to his coauthored article in this volume.

Shilpa Madan is currently working as Sales Manager at Castrol India Ltd., part of BP Plc. She is a Gold Medalist from IIT Bombay, having completed her Masters in Management in 2005. She completed her bachelor's degree in technology (information technology) in 2003. She has been felicitated by several agencies for excellence in academics and marketing.

Harvinder Pal Mahey graduated from the Shailesh J. Mehta School of Management, IIT Bombay and holds a bachelor's degree in electronics & communications engineering from the National Institute of Technology, Jalandhar. He has several years of experience in the fields of Marketing and CRM consulting. At present he is working as a CRM Consultant with a leading Indian IT company. In his current role, his work on the implementation of sales force automation for a global logistics giant aims to automate the sales organization of his clients across approximately 220 countries.

Ramin Mahmoudi is a Graduate of the UCLA Anderson MBA program. He participated in the AMR research project that led to his coauthored article in this volume.

Andreina Mandelli is in the faculty of Business Economics at Bocconi University in Milan and is Senior Member of the Marketing faculty of SDA Bocconi, the business school of Bocconi university in Milan, Italy. She is a Visiting Professor at the University of Lugano, Switzerland. She is also a Senior Research Fellow at the Center for Digital Future, Annenberg School for Communication, USC, California. She has coordinated the BIT project in Italy since its launch. Her research interests are concerned with the network approach to markets and communication.

Vandana (Ann) Mangal is an Associate Research Director and Adjunct Professor at the UCLA's Anderson School of Management. In this position, she is involved in all activities of the BIT umbrella of projects' research cycle including fundraising, research and report and paper writing. She also handles activities related to the management of BIT and CMIE including budgeting, staff, managing relationships with partners and organizing conferences. In the past, she has worked as the Intel-HP Alliance Manager at Intel and as a Senior Business Analyst at Hitachi Data Systems and AE Business Solutions. She has also taught in the Information Systems Department at the University of Wisconsin-Madison's School of Business. She obtained her PhD from the Carnegie Mellon University and her under graduate degree in electrical engineering from PEC. Her research interests include technology management, organizational and technology changes, business processes, business continuity, market and survey research, financial services, retail and outsourcing.

Paolo Neirotti is an Assistant Professor at Politecnico di Torino, where he teaches Management Accounting and Management of Innovation. He obtained his PhD in Management, Economics and Industrial Engineering from the Politecnico di Milano Technical University. His main research interests include the governance of information systems investments in large enterprises, interdependencies between productivity trends, information technology and organizational changes, and the analysis on the growth of the ICT industry in European Union countries.

Kwangtae Park is a Professor of LSOM (Logistics and Service Operations Management) and Director of SLRC (Service and Logistics Research Center). He got his B.S. and M.S. both from Seoul National University and his PhD from the University of California, Berkeley. His research interests include quality management and service management.

Emilio Paolucci is a Professor at Politecnico di Torino Technical University, where he teaches Information Systems and Organizational Design for Management of Innovation. He is responsible for the post graduate Master's program in e-business. His research interests include the relationship between information technology and organizational models, IT governance and its effects on productivity, patterns of ICT adoption in the Italian economy, entrepreneurship and the creation of hi-tech start-ups. Such researches have been funded both by public institutions and private companies. He published many articles about these topics in international journals, and is an Associate Editor of the International Journal of e-business. Currently, he is a Member of the Board of Examiners of the "Innovative Enterprises Incubator" at the Politecnico di Torino.

Cinzia Parolini is a full Professor of Business Economics at the University of Modena and is a Senior Lecturer of Business Strategy at SDA Bocconi, Milan. Her research interests include the network approach to business strategy.

Marisol Pérez is a PhD student in Applied Economics at the Universidad Autónoma de Barcelona. Her research interests are knowledge economy, telecommunications and international economics. Writer of different articles in specialized magazines related to technology adoption and diffusion, she is currently the Research Assistant of e-business Center PwC&IESE.

Hosun Rhim is an Associate Professor and an Area Chair of LSOM (Logistics and Service Operations Management). He obtained his PhD degree from UCLA and both MBA and BA degrees from Seoul National University. His research interests include competition in service operations and service productivity.

Eulália Sanz holds a degree in Political Sciences and Public Administration and a degree in Media Communication, both from the Pompeu Fabra University. She is currently the Assistant General Manager of Barcelona Media – Innovation Center, whose main activity is the preparation, development and execution on R&D and innovation projects for communication companies.

Sandra Sieber is a Professor of Information Systems at IESE Business School. Her research focuses on implementation issues of information systems, IT-enabled innovation and knowledge management. She has widely published in both academic and business press and co-authored a book on information systems management. She forms a part of the editorial board of Information Technology and People, and she has served as a conference Chair for several conferences, including the 2002 IFIP 8.2 Working Conference and the 2003 European Conference on Organizational Knowledge, Learning, and Capabilities.

Josep Valor-Sabatier has a PhD in Operations Research from MIT, ScD in Medical Engineering and Medical Physics by the Harvard-MIT Division of Health Sciences and Technology. He is a Professor of Information Systems at IESE Business School in Barcelona, Spain. His current research interests include the impact of ITCs on competitiveness and industry structure. He has been the coordinator of the Task Force of the Spanish Prime Minister to propose a nation-wide strategy on information technology and for the impulse of the information society. His research has been published in the International Journal of Electronic Commerce, Knowledge and Process Management. He is in the editorial board of Information and Management. Dr. Valor served as the Conference Co-Chair for the 2002 International Conference on Information Systems (ICIS) in Barcelona.

Vicki Ting is an MBA Graduate from the UCLA Anderson School of Management. She holds a JD from Stanford Law School and a BA, with distinction, in quantitative economics from Stanford University. Her professional experience includes corporate and securities representation of high technology companies in Silicon Valley and regulatory and investor relations work for a major gas and electric utility.

Yan Zhao is the Vice President of Finance with China Agitech. Previously he was a Senior Analyst with Brean Murray Carret, Beijing office, covering US-listed Chinese companies. He holds an MBA from the UCLA Anderson School, and a BE from the University of International Business and Economics, Beijing, China. He is a Chartered Financial Analyst and a non-practising Member of the Chinese Institute of Certified Public Accountants.

CONTENTS

PART I

BIT (BUSINESS AND INFORMATION TECHNOLOGIES)

CHAPTER 1

THE UCLA BUSINESS AND INFORMATION TECHNOLOGIES (BIT) SURVEY — YEAR 2

UDAY S. KARMARKAR and VANDANA MANGAL

Summary

The UCLA Business and Information Technologies (BIT) Survey is aimed at understanding and tracking the impacts of technologies on business practices. This report presents the results of the second survey conducted in the US in 2004–2005.

The subject group of the survey consisted of organizations and sub organizations that make independent decisions with respect to the acquisition, implementation and the use of new technologies. The survey was sent to chief information officers and senior information systems managers as these individuals are most likely to be able to respond to the survey.

The survey addressed a wide range of business practices, including technology adoption, internal organization transformations, market facing activity, supplier and vendor relationships, and business results and performance consequences from the application of new technologies. Globalization and outsourcing/offshoring were also included.

The survey results indicate that businesses are changing internally as well as in terms of their interactions with their customers and trading partners. As might be expected, the rate of change is perhaps not as rapid as might be suggested by the "high water mark" examples which are described in the popular business press. However, the changes are without question both pervasive and on-going.

Some of the key results of the survey were as follows:

- The internal organization of companies is changing significantly in terms of both structure and workforce. Organizations are becoming flatter, with a wider span of control, more geographically distributed, and more "virtual". Teleconferencingteleconferencing is increasing, telecommuting is not as widely accepted.
- The workplace and work requirements are changing. Many employees face screens, many are being monitored for performance. Technical capabilities are becoming necessary. Executives are asking for more and better structured information.
- The degree to which outsourcing and off shoring are being pursued is still limited. IT services, payroll and market research continue to be the more widely outsourced business functions. Outsourcing is not considered to be causing workforce reductions.

- The technologies and systems that are the most widely adopted are wireless hardware and software and e-commerce tools and websites.
- Radio frequency identification (RFID) and identity management solutions are not being widely adopted at this time. However, many firms plan to purchase them in the near future, indicating that the interest in security is going up.
- Organizations are using multiple touch points for customer relationship management (CRM). These include online, mail, face-to-face and phone.
- Companies are collecting more data with online technologies. However, the use of this data for customer view integration is not as prevalent for marketing yet.
- The adoption of on-line sales has not as yet had a major impact on marketing strategy. In particular, there has not been a significant change in branding or positioning (across all respondents). However, there is substantial interest in having customers perform more self-service tasks while purchasing online.
- Technology adoption has caused internal communication costs and production costs to decrease. However, the costs of technology acquisition and implementation, and of consultancy and collaboration have predictably increased.

The most striking outcome of the survey is perhaps the organizational impact. It is clear that work life at the level of the individual, as well as firmwide organizational structures are changing. It is also clear that certain technologies and capabilities have been very widely adopted, e-commerce and active websites for internal and external communications are the most widespread. At the same time, there are some rather negative results: organizations do not say that they have expanded their reach on the market side very dramatically. The adoption of hardware-based technologies such as biometry and RFID appears to be slower than the software and communications side.

We note that since the survey is across all industry sectors, some finer analysis may reveal important local differences. This work is under way. In addition, the firm level surveys do not easily reveal sector level changes. Industry and sector studies that are being conducted by us and our research partners will help to understand those issues better.

This is the second survey in a series of surveys to understand the impacts of technologies on business practices. By comparing the results for the two years, we find that most patterns continue to remain the same. This shows the validity of the survey findings. Some trends that are emerging include the following:

- Some technologies that are beginning to emerge as the technologies for the future include wireless software and hardware, RFID and collaboration portal tools. ERP also continues to be popular for deployment in the near term.
- Continued investment of technology budgets into security hardware and software is observed. Although off shoring/business process outsourcing continues to be lower in the list of company technology budgets, it is seen to have an increasing trend.
- Outsourcing of IT services is increasing. Outsourcing is also not seen as the reason for reduction in jobs.
- The trend is towards the automation of all CRM functions. Partner relationship functions are also becoming more automated as supported by the strong increase in the adoption of e-payments and e-procurement.

- Technology is seen to be helping organizations understand their customers better in all strategic areas. However, although more data is collected with automation, businesses are not yet integrating the customer view significantly.
- Globalization is not seen to a great extent. However, the trend is towards increasing globalization to the Asian regions.

1.1. Introduction

1.1.1. *The BIT project*

Notwithstanding reports to the contrary, the information economy is alive and well. The study by Apte and Nath (forthcoming 2006) which follows earlier work by Machlup (1962,1982) and Porat (1977), puts the size of the information sector at about 55% of the value added to the GNP of the US in 1992. That was before the boom in online technologies and the web. Even a conservative extrapolation of the results of these studies would put the information sector at over 60% of the GNP today and is growing steadily. In short, it is the major part of the economy already, and will dominate it for the foreseeable future. The US can truly be called an information economy today.

The intent of the Business and Information Technologies (BIT) project is to study the impact of new information technologies on business and industry structure. The internet phenomenon was primarily a matter of a fundamental change in information logistics, with the protocols of the web superimposed on a deregulating and increasingly competitive telecommunications environment. This story continues to play itself out.

However, there are new technologies and systems on the horizon, and it is likely that a second slower wave of change based on infrastructure development, and then probably a third wave based on information processing, intelligent agents, and natural interfaces (as distinct from just the shipping and handling of information) will be observed. It is expected that all these technological and infrastructure developments will change the structure of firms in terms of organization and work process, will change information chains and inter-organizational relationships, and alter the structure of industrial sectors, to the point that the traditional categories do not apply very well.

One very basic change is occurring in the nature of the workplace. Most workers now face a screen for some significant period of time during work hours. The screen is a very different workplace from a desktop, since it is much better connected with places, people and processes outside the workplace. The screen (or interface) is also easily liberated physically from the desk and cubicle. It is apparent that the traditional notion of contemporaneous colocation as the core of an organization is ready to disappear.

However, it is not clear how and when this will happen, or what will take its place. It is also not clear how lines of authority, responsibility and communication will be established in the new firm. Perhaps, the concepts of span of control and hierarchy will disappear in favor of some form of "just-in-time" and "only-on-demand" management.

The dot.com boom might have come and gone, but it has permanently changed the face of B2C relationships well beyond just the new phraseology. There is no question that sectors like retailing, travel services, and financial services have been transformed, not just in terms of new entrants, but for the incumbents as well. For many consumer goods and services, the web is now a growing carrier of brand equity and customer recognition; it has become a new face for a company. The changes in the B2C layer are beginning to ripple back into supply and service chains. The impact on logistics, freight and delivery services is most easily seen, but many other equally dramatic changes are occurring inside and between firms, which are invisible to the casual observer.

The reduction in the costs of information logistics suggests obvious changes in business practice. As transaction costs drop, as large volumes of information can be reliably and quickly transported, there will be changes in the structure of business processes that exploit these advantages. Some of the consequences of B2B interactions have already been observed, although hype and overestimation have tended to distract from the very significant reality.

Perhaps, the most important issue today is the overall impact of these technologies on the structure of industry sectors and the economy as a whole. Many sectors are coalescing and converging. For example, newspapers, magazines, and broadcast organizations are all colliding on the web. Those sectors will fragment and reform into new alignments, which exploit their core strengths. The position that newspapers have held because of the economics of delivering information bundles to the door, is seriously threatened by online channels. For example, newspapers are not now or in the future, the strongest suppliers of "breaking" news, especially in multimedia formats. The television networks have the best collection and packaging systems for that task. Newspapers may hold on to criticism, commentary and review, though magazines could easily start to compete for that role. In turn, TV broadcasts will face challenges from web casts. Magazines will have to contend with web-based competitors, and go on the web themselves. Of course, these changes will not occur overnight. For a time, most media and publishing companies will have to think in terms of both sheets and screens.

There are very similar stories, which can be told about other sectors, as well as about international trade. The point is that these changes are huge, and deserve to be followed closely. It is relatively easy to make broad brush comments about the changes that are underway, as we have above. However, hard information about the extent and distribution of these effects is lacking.

The BIT study documents the information technology driven changes that are occurring in business structure, business practice and sector structures across a wide spectrum of industry sectors in the US and the rest of the world. The first step in the process is to do a base line study, which establishes the state of this universe. Subsequently, the study will be repeated at appropriate time intervals to track the changes that are actually occurring, so as to provide hard information on what is really happening across the economic landscape as a result of changes in information technologies. The study will encompass several sectors.

The BIT project is being conducted on a global scale. At the time of writing, the project had 13 partners from leading academic and research institutions around the world. The partners include Italy, India, Chile, Korea, Argentina, Greece, Spain, Taiwan, Peru, New Zealand, France, Sweden, Germany, and USA. The details of the BIT partners are in Appendix C.

Five of these teams (Italy, India, Korea, Spain, and USA) have conducted surveys in 2004–2005. It is expected that the BIT survey will eventually be conducted in, perhaps, 15–20 countries by research teams from those countries. This global perspective combined with the longitudinal view will provide a unique and comparative picture of technology and business practice across the world.

The potential for learning across these groups is vast. The nature of best practices in different countries varies widely. Nor are the most developed countries always the most advanced in technology use and penetration. For example, many countries are far ahead of the US in the degree of conversion to electronic banking and monetary systems. As an example, certain European countries have already closed their check processing facilities, since checks have almost passed out of use. India surpasses many countries in the extent of software project involvement and exports, despite a miniscule level of penetration of PC use or for that matter, phone usage. In many eastern countries, the use of wireless communications, is rapidly outstripping traditional wireline systems. It is expected that several interesting local variations in business practices will be found.

This project is complementary to the world internet project (WIP) originally centered at UCLA, and now at the Annenberg Institute of USC. That study consists of a panel survey of individuals, also conducted in parallel in multiple countries. The differences here are that we do not do a panel survey, the subject of our study is the organization (or a subset), and the survey can only be the starting point for deeper investigations of several industry sectors. Nonetheless, the WIP study was a model and catalyst for this project. Professor Jeff Cole, the research director and originator of WIP, has commented that a study like WIP should have been done for television in 1940, but never was. We would paraphrase that comment and say that a study like BIT might have been done to document the impact of the printing press, the telephone, the typewriter and the computer, on business organizations, but never was. Nevertheless, today we have the opportunity to do these studies as today's new technologies change both, the social and the work environments, as well as the larger economic picture in terms of industry sector structure, employment, and trade.

This report summarizes the results from the second BIT survey conducted in the US in 2004–2005 (the first US survey was conducted in 2003–2004). The hypotheses and the results are discussed in the following sections. The methodology used is described in

Appendix A. As we have mentioned, in addition to the survey itself, the BIT project also includes in depth studies of industry sectors and information chains, as well as studies of the changes occurring in the overall economy with respect to GNP, employment, and trade. These are reported elsewhere.

1.2. The Survey

The survey instrument was developed in close collaboration with our research partners in Italy and India. The lead investigators and collaborators from those teams were Professor Andreina Mandelli (SDA Bocconi, Milano), Professor Cinzia Parolini (SDA Bocconi, now at the University of Modena) and Professor Atanu Ghosh (SMSOM, IITB, Mumbai).

In developing the questionnaire, we first identified the most important and interesting issues which we hoped to investigate. We then framed the issues in terms of specific hypotheses capable of being supported or refuted by a survey. The hypotheses were then used to generate questions for the survey. The same survey instrument has been used for both years so that findings can be compared. The major issues and their relationship to questions in the survey are summarized below.

1.2.1. *Technology adoption/infrastructure and budget trends*

Question 1 — What technologies are organizations using currently or planning to use in the near future? What technologies are organizations not using and not planning to use in the future?

Question 2 — What technologies have organizations invested in (and not invested in) over the last three years?

1.2.2. *Organizational structure and workforce transformations*

Question 3 — How are organizations changing internally in terms of their workforce?

Question 4 — How are organizations changing internally in terms of their structure?

Question 5 — Are organizations outsourcing some of their business processes? Is business process outsourcing (BPO) more popular for certain functions in the organization such as accounting, marketing, IT and finance?

Questions 6 & 7 — What is the outsourcing budget for organizations for IT and nonIT functions? How much of the total outsourced business is offshore?

1.2.3. *Customer facing (CRM) interactions*

Question 8 — Are relationships with customers developed and maintained using multiple touch points? What are the most popular touch points?

Questions 9 & 14 — How is customer view integrated using certain technologies? What mechanisms are used by organizations to perform customer segmentation?

Questions 10, 11 & 12 — Are promotion and advertising budgets shifting towards online channels? Which online advertising methods have been adopted by organizations? In going online, are organizations creating a new face in terms of branding concept, slogan, logo and name?

Question 13 — For which functions is customer relationship management (CRM) becoming automated?

Questions 15 & 16 — Is the number of organizations selling products and services online increasing? How is online business different from traditional business?

1.2.4. *Trading partner (SCM) relationships*

Question 17 — What technologies are organizations using for communicating with their trading partners?

Question 18 — What IT-based channels and B2B mechanisms are organizations using for purchasing?

1.2.5. *Business results*

Questions 19 & 20 — What economic and operational business results are being impacted by technologies? What strategic areas are being impacted by information technologies?

1.2.6. *Globalization*

Questions 21 & 22 — Are organizations becoming more global? Is the geographic reach of organizations increasing?

1.3. Results

The survey was sent to senior information systems managers. The methodology is described in Appendix A. About 250 responses were received. The details of the sample are discussed in Appendix B. The results obtained by analyzing these responses are discussed below.

1.3.1. *Technology adoption/infrastructure and budget trends*

- Wireless hardware/software and websites/e-commerce technologies are the most deployed technologies.

- Radio frequency identification (RFID) and identity management solutions are not as widely adopted by organizations at this time. However, many plan to purchase them over the next few years.
- Budgets for security software and hardware and wireless technologies have increased. Budgets for offshore outsourcing/BPO and on-demand computing have not increased as much.

1.3.2. *Internal organization: workforce and structure trends*

- The demand for IT at all levels in the organization ranging from executive decision-making tools to skilled lower level staff and collaborative tools is increasing. The proportion of employees facing a screen is up as is the need for constant employee retraining.
- Outsourcing is not considered to be causing workforce reductions.
- Organizations are changing to hierarchies with flatter structures, fewer levels of control, and fewer middle level managers. Organizations are becoming geographically dispersed. Teleconferencingteleconferencing is on the rise although telecommuting is not as widely accepted.
- More organizations are monitoring the productivity of customer facing employees and are employing automated monitoring of workforce productivity. However, compensation is not based on these observations.

1.3.3. *Internal organization — offshoring BPO*

- IT programming, payroll and market research are the most outsourced business functions and processes. RFP bids and contract management, accounting, finance and order fulfillment are the least outsourced business functions.
- A slightly greater proportion of organizations outsource their IT functions compared to their nonIT functions.
- Organizations are beginning to offshore more of their business processes although the proportion of organizations currently reporting offshoring/BPO is still small.

1.3.4. *Customer touch points*

- Organizations use multiple touch points for CRM. Phone, e-mail, face-to-face, website — brochure ware and regular mail are the most used touch points, screen pops and phone text messaging are the least used.

1.3.5. *Customer view integration and customer segmentation*

- Customer view integration and segmentation of customers are currently employed by a small number of organizations. Statistical data mining, data marts/warehouses and demand forecasting are the most popular tools for customer view integration.

- For organizations segmenting their customers, segmentation by geography and use of portals are most popular.

1.3.6. *Online advertising and selling*

- Incentives in printed materials to drive customers to the company website is the most widely used online advertising mechanism. Advertisements or links on other websites to drive traffic to the company website, advertisements or links on search engines to drive traffic to the company website and web banners are other popular online advertising methods.
- Some organizations have changed their online image in terms of the branding concept, logo and slogan. Changing the name of the organization in going online is not as popular.
- Organizations have invested and plan to continue to invest in online advertising over the next few years. However, the organizations that are investing a lower percentage in online advertising plan to cut down their budgets slightly, while organizations that are investing a higher percentage in online advertising plan to increase their budgets over the next few years.

1.3.7. *CRM function automation*

- The most automated CRM functions include help desk, order placement, order tracking/fulfillment, and content management for websites. Sales calls automation is the least automated CRM function.

1.3.8. *Traditional versus online selling*

- Most organizations have traditional and online presence. No organization reported having only an online presence.
- The number of self-service tasks performed by customers and the data collected are higher for online selling, sales volumes and the number of products/services offered are higher in traditional selling.

1.3.9. *Trading partners relationships and purchasing mechanisms*

- Web-enabled communications, electronic data interchange (EDI), e-payments, and XML are currently the most popular communication technologies used among trading partners.
- Web-enabled communication, XML, e-procurements, and e-payments are the technologies of choice for future deployment in the next three years.
- Direct purchasing, long-term purchasing contracts and catalogues are the most used B2B mechanisms for purchasing; hubs and aggregators are the least used.

1.3.10. *Business results*

- Internal communication costs and production costs have decreased with technology adoption. Technology costs, and consultancy and collaboration costs have increased.
- Technology has increased the understanding of customer behavior in all strategic areas.

1.3.11. *Globalization*

- Organizations are increasing their geographic reach in terms of trade with other countries, the number of their production or service delivery bases in other countries and the number of countries in their supplier base.
- Organizations currently have or plan to have operations in Canada and Mexico (NAFTA), Western Europe and Latin America. Increasing globalization is observed in SE, East and South Asia as well as in Central and Eastern Europe. Increasing globalization in Asia and Central and Eastern Europe is expected over the next few years.

1.3.12. *Technology adoption/infrastructure and budget trends*

Question 1 — What technologies are organizations using currently or planning to use in the near future? What technologies are organizations not using currently (and not planning to use in the future)?

An overwhelmingly large number of organizations (94.8 and 93.1%) have deployed/plan to deploy wireless hardware/software and websites/e-commerce technologies. 79.4% have/plan to have collaboration and portal tools, 78.2% have/plan to have groupware and productivity tools such as Lotus Notes, 71% have/plan to have enterprise resource planning (ERP) and 66% have/plan to have surveillance tools. Among these technologies, collaboration/portal tools and ERP are on company budgets (about 25%) as the most popular technologies for adoption in the next few years.

RFID is currently adopted only by a very small percentage of organizations (10.5%). However, three times as many organizations (30.2%) plan to purchase the technology in the next three years. Similarly, identity management solutions are currently deployed by 19.8% of the organizations, but 30.2% plan to deploy them in the next few years. Business process modeling and business intelligence are also on the lists of about a quarter of the companies as planned purchases in the next few years.

These trends are shown in Fig. 1.1.

Codes for the trends are as follows:

1. Enterprise application integration (EAI) and middleware
2. Storage area networks (SAN) and network attached storage (NAS)
3. Operating system — Linux

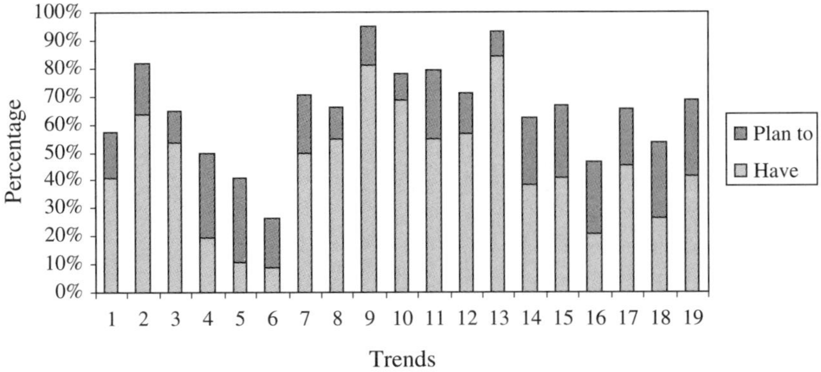

Fig. 1.1. Technology trends.

4. Identity management solutions
5. Radio frequency identification (RFID)
6. Biometrics
7. Third party authentication and verification
8. Surveillance systems
9. Wireless network connectivity hardware and software
10. Groupware/productivity tools
11. Collaboration & portal tools
12. Enterprise resource planning (ERP)
13. Website and e-commerce
14. Business intelligence
15. Business process modeling
16. E-learning
17. Enterprise instant messaging (IM)
18. Supply chain management (SCM)
19. Content management

Question 2 — What technologies have organizations invested in (and not invested in) over the past three years?

Security software (increased or increased significantly in 76.2% of the organizations) and security hardware (increased or increased significantly in 67.3% of the organizations) top the list of technologies organizations have invested in over the past three years. Wireless hardware and software (67.3%), software applications (62.1%), infrastructure (61.7%) and hardware storage (60.5%) budgets have also increased.

On the other hand, budgets for offshore outsourcing/BPO and on-demand computing (18.2 and 17.3%, respectively) have increased little in the past three years. These trends are shown in Fig. 1.2.

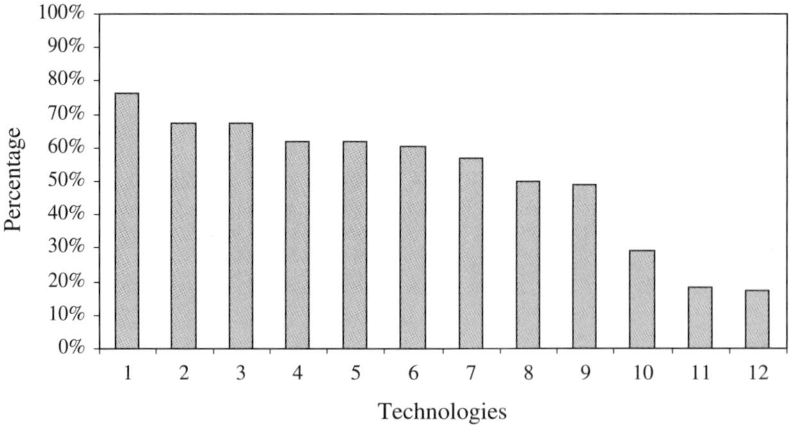

Fig. 1.2. Budget trends.

Codes for the trends are as follows:

1. Software: security
2. Hardware: security
3. Wireless hardware & software
4. Software: applications
5. Infrastructure
6. Hardware: storage
7. Disaster recovery & business continuity since 9/11
8. Intranets and extranets
9. Software: operating systems & networking
10. Service contracts ASP co-location application integration etc.
11. Business process outsourcing/offshoring
12. On-demand computing

1.3.13. *Internal organization*

Question 3 — How are organizations changing internally in terms of their workforce and the workplace?

The workforce is changing. The demand for decision support tools at executive levels is increasing tremendously. The proportion of employees facing a screen is increasing and workers need to retrain constantly. Teleconferencingteleconferencing is on the rise, workers are collaborating and the need for IT skills at lower levels is going up. However, telecommuting is not yet as widely accepted by organizations.

Outsourcing is not felt to be the leading to workforce reductions in organizations although and the role of automation in workforce reductions is not supported clearly one way or the other.

These trends are shown in Fig. 1.3 below.

Codes for the trends are as follows:

1. More employees are telecommuting
2. The use of teleconferencingteleconferencing is on the rise
3. The proportion of employees facing a screen is increasing
4. Automation of functions is leading to workforce reductions
5. Outsourcing is leading to workforce reductions
6. The need for IT skills at lower levels is going up
7. Collaboration between workers from the use of internet-based collaboration tools (such as net meeting) is increasing
8. Workers need to retrain constantly to keep up with changing technologies
9. The demand for intelligence in information at executive levels is increasing
10. The number of middle level managers is decreasing
11. The IT function is shifting from staff to line

Question 4 — How are organizations changing internally in terms of their structure?

The most significant trend is the increasing availability of new decision-making and online technologies, as reported by more than three-quarter (77.0%) of the organizations.

Organizations are becoming flatter, the number of direct reports to a manager is increasing and organizations are becoming geographically dispersed with direct reports to a manager not located at the same location as the manager.

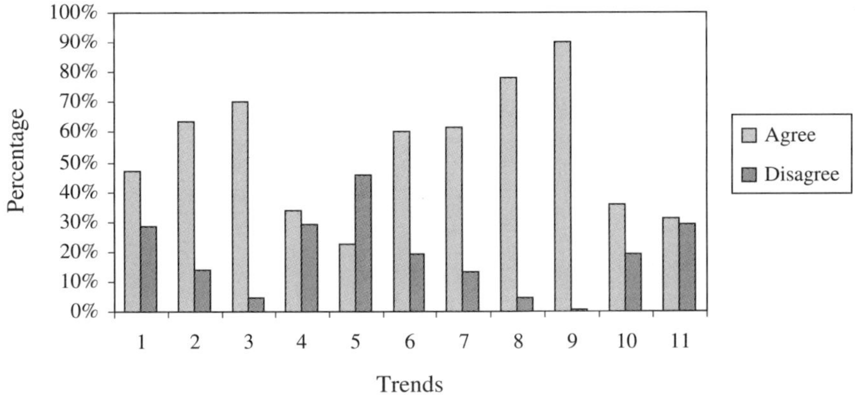

Fig. 1.3. Internal organization.

Although the number of organizations monitoring customer facing interactions is increasing, as is the number of organizations monitoring workforce productivity, incentives are currently not based on their productivity.

These trends are shown in Fig. 1.4 below.

Codes for the trends are as follows:

1. The span of control for most of the managers is widening (the number of direct reports to managers increasing)
2. The organization is becoming flatter (fewer levels in the organization chart)
3. The monitoring of customer-facing interactions is increasing (e.g. phone calls from/to customers)
4. Automated monitoring of workforce productivity is increasing.
5. Incentives are based on monitoring of productivity
6. The organization is becoming more geographically dispersed (e.g. direct reports to a manager located at different locations)
7. New decision-making tools and online technologies are increasingly becoming available.

Question 5 — Are organizations outsourcing some of their business processes? Is BPO more popular for certain functions in the organization such as accounting, marketing, IT, and finance?

The most often outsourced business processes are IT programming, payroll and market research. IT programming is outsourced (plan to outsource/significantly outsourced/partially outsourced) by 52.4% of the organizations, payroll by 46.4%, and market research by 44.4% of the organizations. RFP bids and contract management, accounting, finance and order fulfilment are not outsourced with 88.7, 87.7, 86.3,

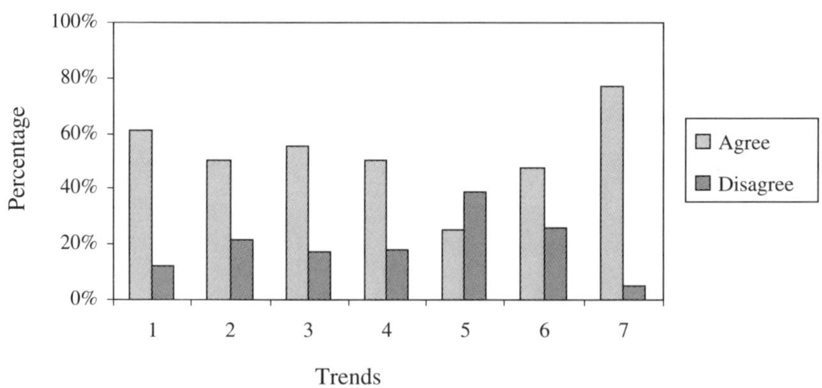

Fig. 1.4. Internal organization structure.

and 85.1%, respectively of the organizations not currently outsourcing these business processes.

These are shown in Fig. 1.5 below.

Codes for the business functions are as follows:

1. IT Functions: programming
2. IT Functions: data center operations
3. IT Functions: network management
4. IT Functions: data management
5. Customer contact
6. Payroll
7. Market research
8. Accounting
9. Finance
10. Order fulfillment
11. RFP bids and contract management

Questions 6 & 7—What is the outsourcing budget for organizations for IT and nonIT functions? How much of the total outsourced business is offshore?

The trends for outsourcing of IT and nonIT functions were measured as a percentage of the total sales revenue and are shown in Fig. 1.6. Almost one-third of the organizations (30.2%) outsource up to 1% of their IT functions and about one-fifth (21.8%) outsource up to 1% of their nonIT functions. Up to 5% of IT and nonIT functions are outsourced by 11 and 13.3% of the organizations.

These results are based on a smaller sample as close to half of the organizations did not respond or felt that it did not apply to them. This may also be interpreted that a large percentage of the organizations do not currently outsource or do not wish to talk about it.

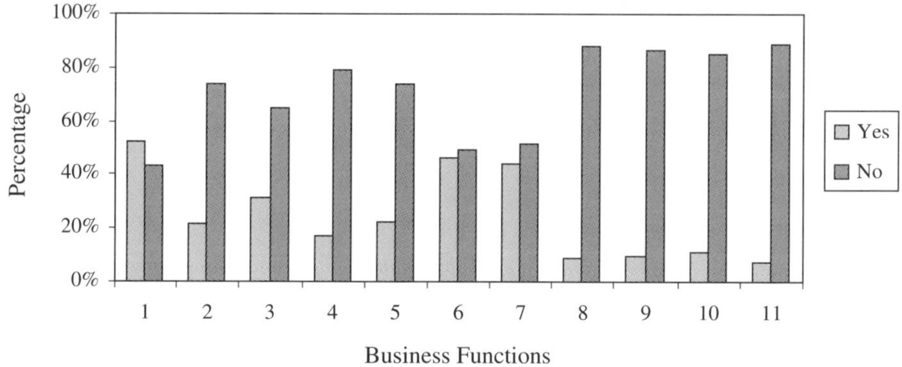

Fig. 1.5. Internal organization BPO.

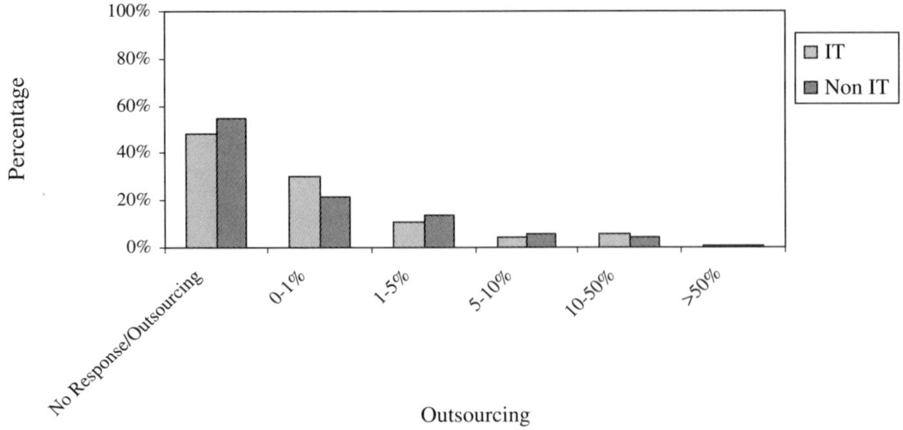

Fig. 1.6. Outsourcing as a percentage of sales revenue.

The survey instrument also contained a question on offshore outsourcing. Although a large percentage of the organizations did not respond, based on the ones that did respond, offshoring comprises 0–1% of the outsourcing budget for about 7% of the organizations and 10–50% of the outsourcing budget for about 6% of the organizations. These are shown in Fig. 1.7. This may indicate that offshoring is increasing dramatically in certain types of organizations and is still minimal for others.

1.3.14. *Customer facing interactions*

Question 8 — Are relationships with customers developed and maintained using multiple touch points? What are the most popular touch points?

Multiple touch points are used by organizations to interact with their customers. Phone (11.3%), email (11.2%), face-to-face (10.9%), company website — brochureware (10.4%) and regular mail (10.2%) are the most frequently used touch points. Screen

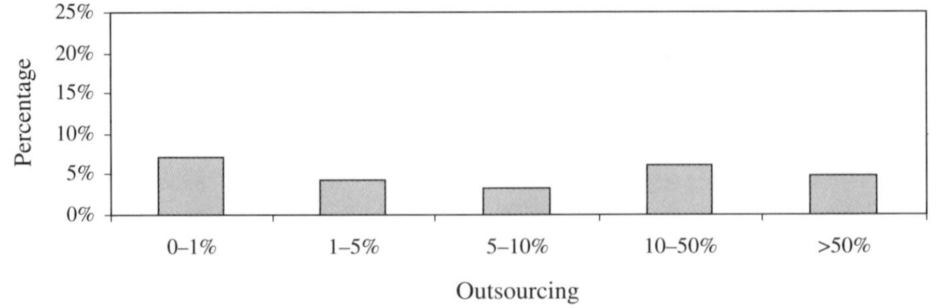

Fig. 1.7. Outsourced business that in BPO.

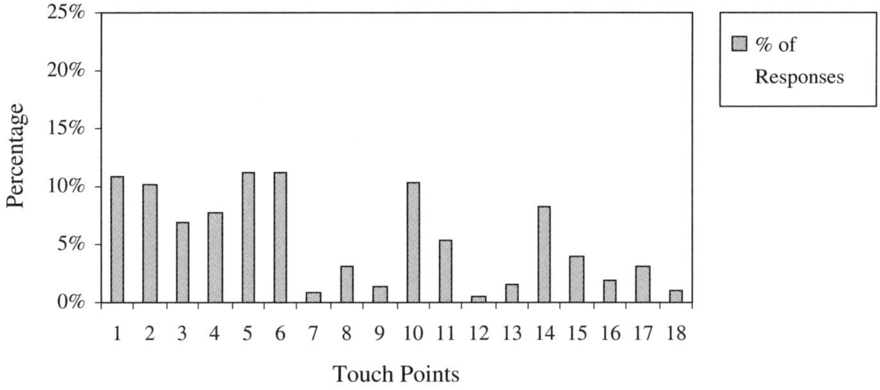

Fig. 1.8. Customer touch points.

pops (0.5%) and phone text messaging (0.9%) are the least used touch points by organizations. Refer to Fig. 1.8.

Codes for the touch points are as follows:

1. Face-to-face contact
2. Regular mail
3. Referrals
4. Fax
5. Email
6. Phone
7. Phone Text Messaging
8. Phone — Automated Interactive Voice Response (IVR)
9. Phone — computer telephony integration (CTI)
10. Company website — brochure ware
11. Company website — transactional including paying bills, online receipts, etc.
12. Screen pop
13. Online intermediary or third party
14. Printers/Flyers/Catalog
15. Radio
16. Kiosk
17. Extranet
18. Other

Questions 9 & *14* — How are customer views integrated into the organization using certain technologies? What mechanisms are used by organizations to perform customer segmentation?

Various technologies are used to integrate customer views into the organization.

Data mining/statistics is used by 16.3%, data marts/data warehouses by 15%, demand forecasting by 15%, and customer profiling by 13.8%.

Text mining (1%) and data mining with neural networks (1.9%) are the least used technologies for customer view integration.

These trends are shown in Fig. 1.9 below.

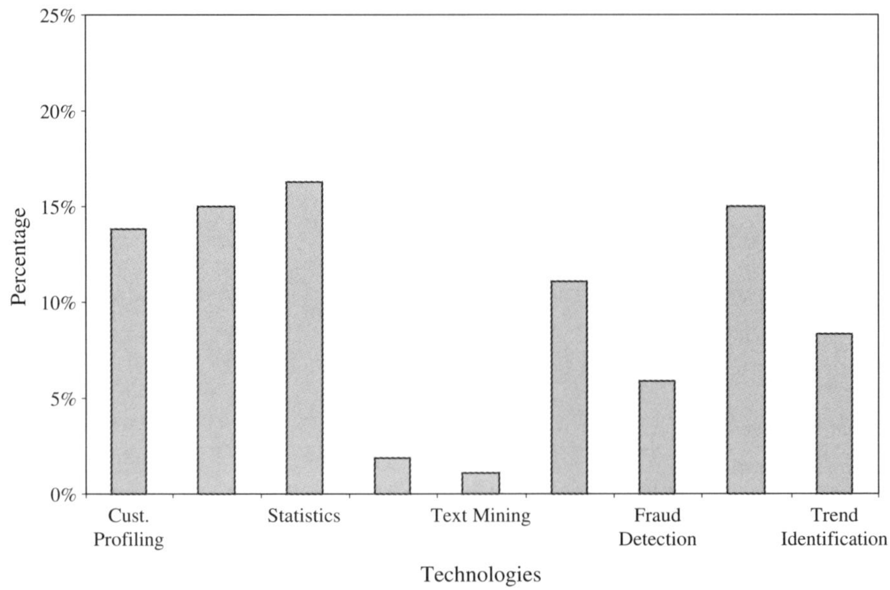

Fig. 1.9. Technologies for customer data analysis.

About a quarter (22.5%) of the organizations segment customers by geography and 16.3% use portals for segmenting their customers. The least used methods for customer segmentation are automated crossselling (e.g. using ATMs for banks) (2.2%) and developed user communities — in terms of channel management (5.4%).

These are shown in Fig. 1.10.

Codes for the mechanisms are as follows:

1. Personalize website by customer
2. Customized pricing
3. Geography
4. Access to online technology
5. Portals for customers
6. Developed user communities (in terms of channel management)
7. Automated cross-selling
8. Market Segment
9. Credit Scoring/previous history

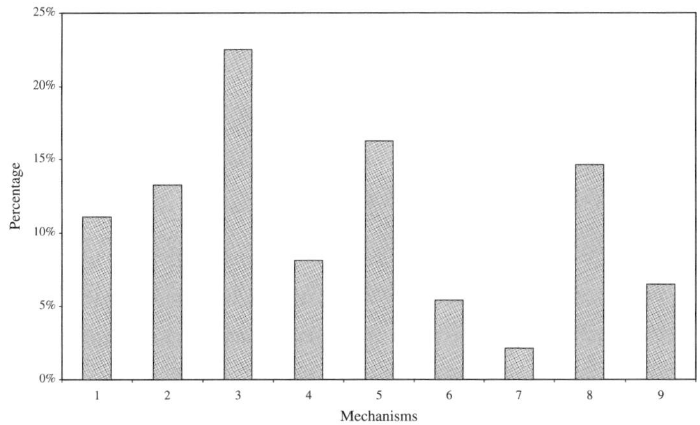

Fig. 1.10. Mechanisms for customer segmentation.

Questions 10, 11 & 12 — Which online advertising methods have been adopted by organizations? Are organizations getting a new face in terms of branding concept, slogan, logo and name in going online? Are promotion and advertising budgets shifting towards online channels?

Organizations use various channels for online advertising. Incentives in printed material to drive customers to the company website are used by about a fifth (19.5%) of the organizations, advertisements or links on other websites to drive traffic to the company website are used by 15.4% of the organizations, advertisements or placement in search engines to drive traffic to the company website are used by 11.8% of the respondents and web banners are used by 8.5%. These and other trends are shown in Fig. 1.11 below.

Codes for the mechanisms are as follows:

1. Personalize website by customer
2. Customized pricing

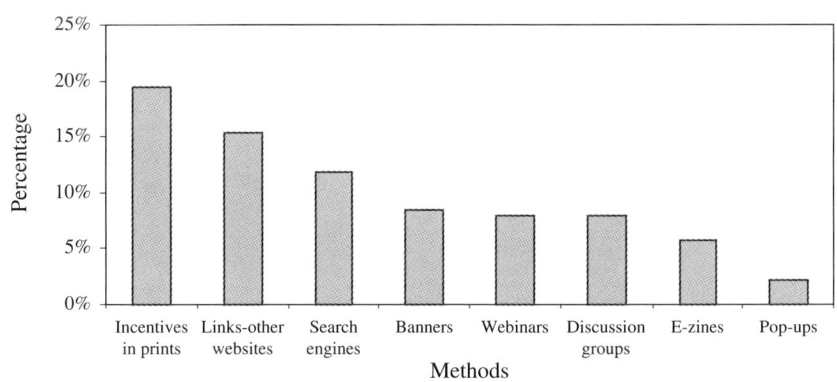

Fig. 1.11. Online advertising methods.

3. Geography
4. Access to online technology
5. Portals for customers
6. Developed user communities (in terms of channel management)
7. Automatic crossselling
8. Market segment
9. Credit scoring/previous history

About a tenth of the respondents invest 1–5% of their advertising budgets in online advertising with the percentage of organizations expected to decrease from 2002 to 2005. However, the number of organizations investing 10–50% of their advertising budgets in online advertising is expected to increase from 2002 to 2005. These trends are shown in Fig. 1.12 below.

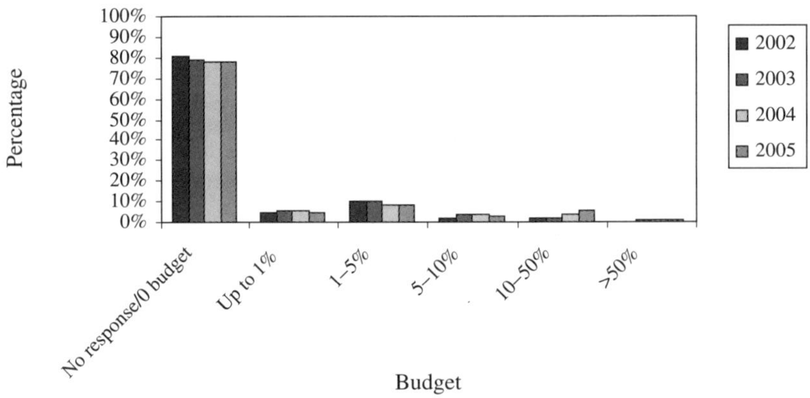

Fig. 1.12. Online advertising budgets as a percentage of annual advertising budget.

Less than a quarter of the organizations have changed their online image in terms of their slogan (23%), logo (23%) and branding concept (22.2%). Only a few organizations (8.1%) have changed their names, as shown in Fig. 1.13.

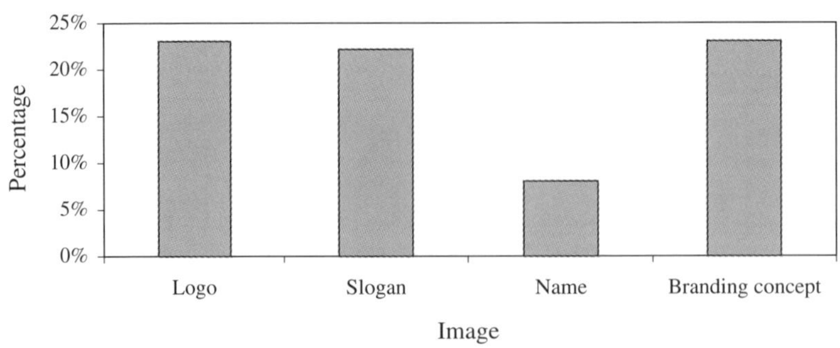

Fig. 1.13. Change of image in going online.

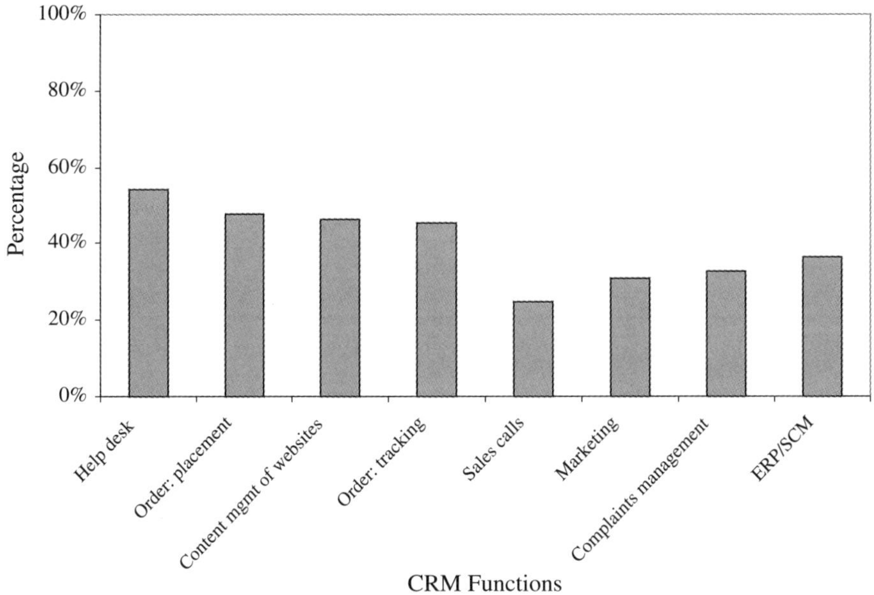

Fig. 1.14. Automation of CRM functions.

Question 13 — Which CRM functions have been automated?

Automated (either partially or completely) CRM functions include help desk, order placement, order tracking and fulfillment and, content management for websites. Sales calls and customer complaints management are the CRM functions that have been automated the least. As shown in Fig. 1.14, 54% of the organizations have automated help desk, 47.6% have automated order placement, 46.4% have automated content management for websites, and 45.6% have automated order fulfillment and tracking. Only about a quarter of the organizations have automated their sales calls (24.6%) function, 31% have automated their marketing and a third (33.7) have automated customer complaints management (Fig. 1.14).

Questions 15 & 16 — Are the number of organizations selling products and services online increasing? How is online business different from traditional business?

Close to half of the organizations (46.7%) offer Traditional as well as Online services and products, about 36% have traditional stores. No organizations reported having only online presence. These are shown in Figure 1.15.

Online business is compared with traditional business using several factors. Among these, sales volume, cost of products, products/services offered, data collected, and self-service tasks performed by customers are found to be different between online and traditional businesses. Figure 1.16 shows these differences. Lower and significantly lower responses are combined under the category of lower for online, higher and significantly higher responses are shown under higher for online. As shown in the

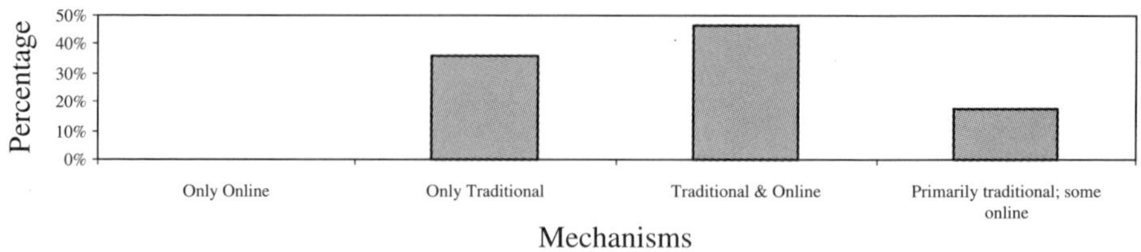

Fig. 1.15. Mechanisms used to sell products and service.

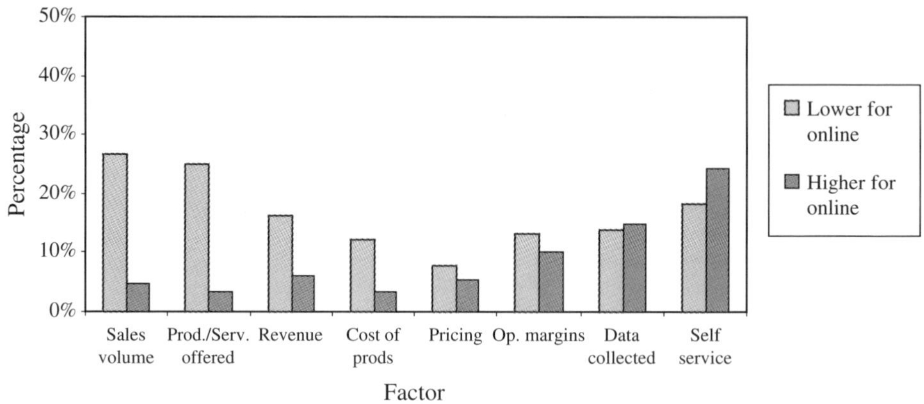

Fig. 1.16. Online versus traditional.

figure, online sales volumes are lower than traditional sales volumes for almost one-quarter (26.6%) of the organizations, and products/services offered are lower for online for 25% of the organizations. The number of self-service tasks performed by customers and the data collected are higher for online for 24.2 and 14.9% of the organizations, respectively.

1.3.15. *Trading partner relationships*

Question 17 — What application technologies are organizations using for communicating with their trading partners?

The most popular technology applications for communicating with trading partners (have or plan to have the application) used by organizations include web-enabled communications (48.8%), electronic data interchange (EDI) (44.8%), e-payment, (42.7%) and XML (41.9%). Overall, XML, web-enabled communications, e-payment, and e-procurement are the applications which are expected to be deployed increasingly over the next few years. Although almost all supply chain applications are expected to be deployed increasingly over the next few years, the use of e-compliance is not expected to increase as much.

These trends are shown in Fig. 1.17 below.

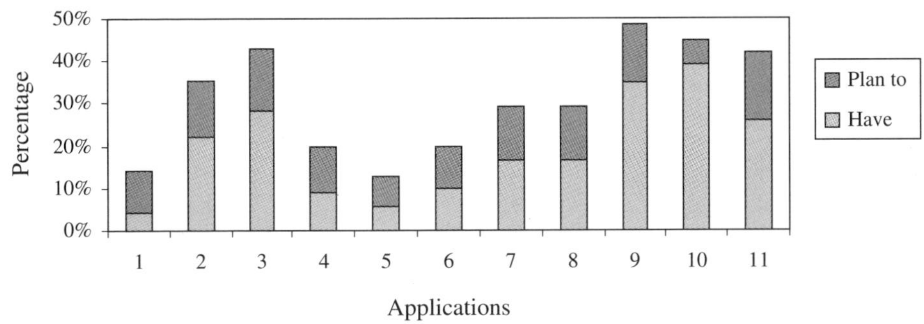

Fig. 1.17. Communication with trading partners.

Codes for the applications are as follows:

1. Partner relationship management (PRM)
2. E-procurement
3. E-payment
4. Collaborative forecasting
5. E-compliance
6. Collaborative planning
7. Demand planning and replenishment
8. Sourcing and procurement management
9. Web enabled communication
10. EDI
11. XML-based communications

Question 18 — What IT-based channels and B2B mechanisms are organizations using for purchasing?

Organizations are using direct purchasing (21%), long-term purchasing contracts (16.1%) and catalogues (12.8%) as B2B mechanisms for purchasing. Channels such as hubs (1.4%) and aggregators (2.4%) are the least used, as shown in Fig. 1.18.

Codes for the mechanisms are as follows:

1. Direct purchasing
2. Long term purchasing contracts
3. Catalogues
4. OEM links/hubs
5. Joint ventures and projects
6. Collaborative purchasing

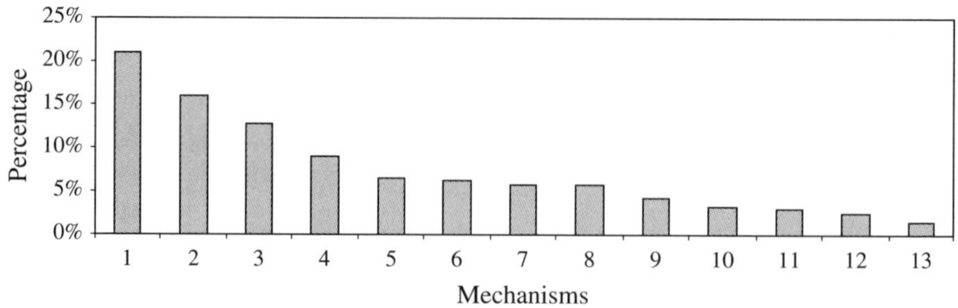

Fig. 1.18. Purchasing mechanisms.

7. Flexible, short-term contracting
8. Online marketplaces
9. Auctions/e-auctions
10. Buy side exchange or hub
11. Exchanges e-exchanges
12. Aggregators
13. Sell side exchange of hub

1.3.16. *Business results*

Questions 19 & *20* — What economic and operational business results and strategic areas are being impacted by technologies?

Various economic and operational results are impacted by technology. The highest cost reductions (decreased or significantly decreased) are in internal communications (36.7% organizations) and production (35.1% organizations). The costs have also decreased for customer service, human resources (HR), new product time to market (TTM) and market research.

The areas where costs have increased or significantly increased include technology (48.4% organizations) and consultancy and communication (24.2% organizations).

These business results are shown in Fig. 1.19.

Codes for the applications are as follows:

1. R&D costs
2. Production costs
3. Market research costs
4. Advertising and direct marketing costs
5. Promotional and customer loyalty costs
6. Commercial costs
7. Customer service costs
8. Technology costs

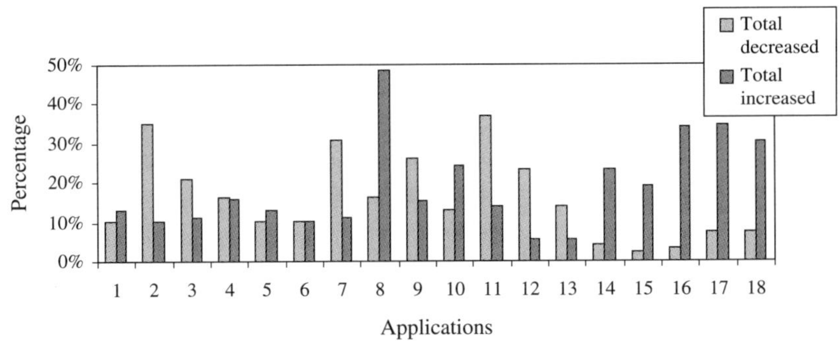

Fig. 1.19. Technology's impact on economic and operational results.

9. Human resources costs
10. Consultancy and collaboration costs
11. Internal communication costs
12. New product's time to market
13. New product's failure risks
14. Number of new products
15. Market share
16. Revenues
17. Profits
18. Margins

The technology has also impacted strategic areas in organizations. An understanding of customer satisfaction for current products and services, customer buying behaviour, knowledge of competitor's products and services, and understanding of future product expectations have all improved for about 40% of the organizations with technology deployment.

These are shown in Fig. 1.20.

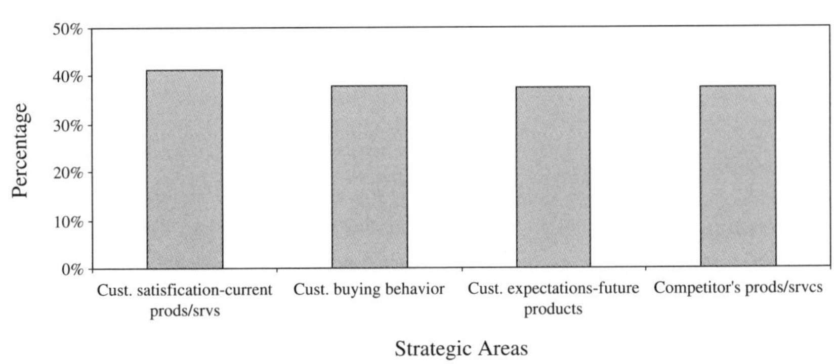

Fig. 1.20. Strategic areas impacted by technology.

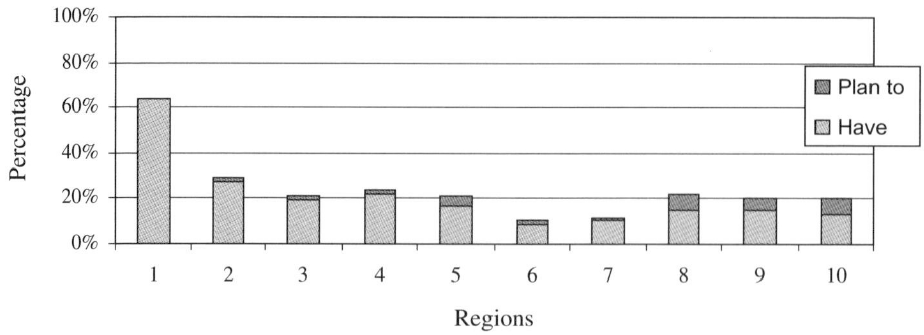

Fig. 1.21. Globalization regions.

1.3.17. *Globalization*

Questions 21 & 22 — Are organizations becoming more global? Is the geographic reach of organizations increasing?

Globalization in terms of the regions to which organizations have expanded or are planning to expand to is shown in Fig. 1.21. About 29% of the organizations currently have or plan to have operations in Canada and Mexico (NAFTA); about 24% in Western Europe; about 21% in Latin America and about over 20% in each of SE, East and South Asia. The three Asian regions also top the list of regions where organizations are planning to expand to the most, over the next few years. Increasing globalization is observed in SE, East and South Asia as well as in Central and Eastern Europe.

Codes for the regions are as follows:

1. USA
2. Canada and mexico (NAFTA)
3. Latin America
4. Western Europe
5. Central and Eastern Europe
6. Africa
7. Middle East
8. Southeast Asia
9. South Asian
10. East Asia

Organizations are increasing (or somewhat increasing) their geographic reach in terms of trade in other countries (29.4% organizations), the number of production or service bases in other countries (28.2% organizations), and the number of countries in the supplier base (23.8% organizations). Increased average distance to suppliers,

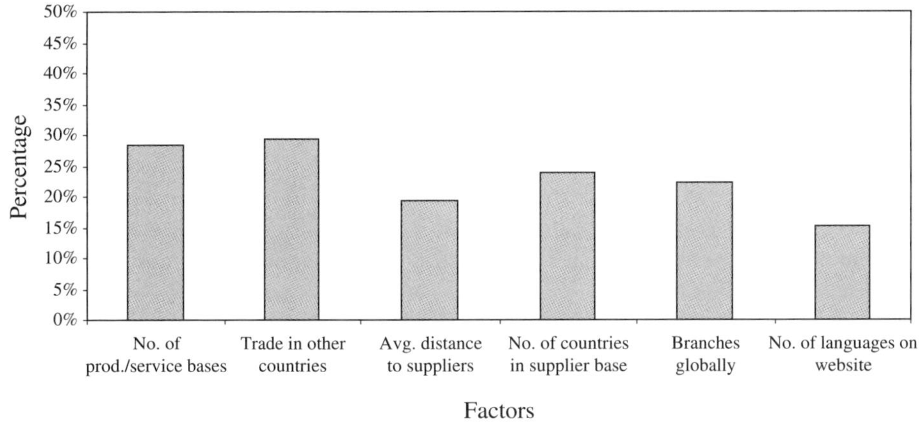

Fig. 1.22. Globalization trends.

increase in branches/distribution centers globally and the number of languages on the website and in brochures are the other factors that are considered.

These are shown in Fig. 1.22 above.

Acknowledgments

The support for the 2003–2004 BIT Survey has come from UCLA International Institute's Global Impact Research Program, UCLA Anderson School's Center for International Business Education and Research (CIBER), Applied Computer Research and UCLA Anderson School's Price Center for Entrepreneurial Studies and UCLA Anderson School's Entertainment Management Program. The authors would like to thank all these sponsors and supporters.

Bibliography

1. Apte, UM and H Nath (2006). The size, structure and growth of the U.S. information economy. In *Managing in the Information Economy: Current Research Issues*, UM Apte and US Karmarkar (eds.). Kluwer Academic Publishing, forthcoming 2006.
2. Machlup, F (1962). *The Production and Distribution of Knowledge in the United States.* Princeton, NJ: Princeton University Press.
3. Machlup, F (1980). *Knowledge: Its Creation, Distribution, and Economic Significance. Vol. I: Knowledge and Knowledge Production.* Princeton, NJ: Princeton University Press,
4. Porat, MU and MR Rubin (1977). The Information Economy (9 volumes). Office of Telecommunications Special Publication, 77–12. Washington DC: US Department of Commerce.

Appendix A: Survey Methodology

The second year survey for the BIT study was conducted as a survey mailed to target organizations in multiple industry sectors. Each subject in the study was an independent organizational entity that controlled its own information technology and information policy, and had a chief information officer (CIO) or similar management position within it. It is likely that since the subject organizations are able to make their own technology decisions (and investments), they also have profit and loss responsibility, although this is certainly not necessarily always the case. The surveys were addressed to the CIO (or similar position) as the person most likely to be knowledgeable about the subject.

One of the reasons to use a survey (rather than interviews, case studies or direct data collection) was to be able to address a large number of industry sectors. Understanding the impact of technology on a large number of sectors was important from the base line perspective so as to provide a more complete understanding of phenomena across the economy. Of course, the impact of information technologies is highly dependent on the underlying nature of each industry and the survey is being supplemented by studies at the sector level.

The major issues of interest were developed, which were then used to generate survey questions. The survey instrument was mailed to a database of over 25,000 individuals across all industry sectors in the United States. The data was acquired from an independent entity that collects corporate data. The CIOs (and related positions) were requested to complete the survey either by mail or online, where the survey instrument was also made available. Some face-to-face interviews were also conducted in the pilot phase of developing the survey.

The survey instrument (questionnaire) has seven major sections:

1. Technology adoption/infrastructure and budget trends — technologies adopted and budget trends.
2. Internal organization — changes in the internal organization's workforce, structure and in business process outsourcing due to technologies.
3. Customer facing interactions — changes in advertising, image, relationship management and other customer facing interactions due to technologies.
4. Trading partner relationships — changes in partner communications and purchasing mechanisms used due to technologies relationships.
5. Business results — operational and economic business results and strategic areas impacted by technologies.
6. Globalization — globalization of the organization due to technologies.
7. Organizational profile — the basic "demographics" of the organization.

Appendix B: Survey Respondent Sample Characteristics

About 250 responses were received. The sample characteristics were:

Titles of the respondents were as follows	
CIO and other C level executives	27.4%
Directors	29.0%
Managers	16.5%
VPs	8.9%
Officers	5.2%
No Response	12.9%
Size of organization in terms of	
Annual revenues	
Up to 100 million dollars annual revenues	31.1%
100 million to 1 billion dollars	34.7%
Over 1 billion dollars	10.1%
No response or Not Applicable	24.2%
Number of employees	
Up to 200 employees	8.1%
200 to 1000 employees	37.5%
Over 1000 employees	40.7%
No response or Not Applicable	13.7%
IT characteristics of organization in terms of	
IT Budget as a percentage of annual revenue	
Up to 1%	25.8%
1% to 5%	33.9%
Over 5%	16.9%
No response or Not Applicable	23.4%
Number of IT employees	
Up to 10 IT employees	25.4%
10 to 50 IT employees	33.9%
Over 50 IT employees	25.8%
No response or Not Applicable	14.9%
Sectors of organizations North American industry classification system (NAICS)	
Manufacturing (Metals, Machinery, Computer, Electronics electrical transportation Equipment, furniture, miscellaneous)	23.4%
Educational services	10.5%
Government	9.3%
Professional, scientific & technical services	8.5%
Wholesale trade	7.3%
Healthcare & social assistance	6.9%
Construction	5.7%
Information	2.8%
Manufacturing (paper, printing, petroleum, coal, chemical, plastics, rubber, nonmetalic mineral)	2.8%
Transportation	2.4%
Utilities	0.8%
Arts, entertainment and recreation	0.4%
Administrative & support, waste management & Remediation services	0.4%
No response	16.1%

Appendix C: Current BIT Partners

UCLA Anderson School of Management, **USA**
Uday Karmarkar, Research Director BIT, LA Times Chair Professor (Lead)
Dr. Vandana Mangal, Associate Research Director BIT (Lead)
Uday Apte, Professor, Naval Postgraduate School

IAE-Universidad Austral, **Argentina**
Lucio Traverso, Prof & Dir of IT, IAE Universidad Austral
Martín J. Muñiz, Research Assistant, IAE — Universidad Austral

Pontificia Universidad Católica de Chile, **Chile**
Sergio Godoy, Professor (Lead)
Theseus Institute, **France**
Craig Marsh, Professor, Human Resource Strategy (Lead)

Athens University of Economics and Business, **Greece**
Gregory Prastacos, Professor, Athens University of Economics
And Business (Lead)

IIT Mumbai, **India**
Atanu Ghosh, Associate Professor (Lead)
Deepak Phatak, Chair Professor

SDA Bocconi, **Italy**
Andreina Mandelli, Professor, SDA Bocconi (Lead)
Alfredo Biffi, Professor, SDA Bocconi
Cinzia Parolini, Professor, University of Modena
Emilio Paolucci, Professor, Politecnico di Torino

Korea University Business School, **Korea**
Kwang-tae Park, Prof & Dir, Service and Logistics Research Center (Lead)
Hosun Rhim, Associate Professor (Lead)

University of Auckland, **New Zealand**
Ananth Srinivasan, Professor, University of New Zealand (Lead)

Universidad, ESAN, **Peru**
Genaro Matute Mejia, Professor, ESAN (Lead)

IESE Business School, **Spain**
Josep Valor Sabatier, Professor (Lead)
Sandra Sieber, Professor

World Internet Institute, **Sweden**
Dr. Johan P. Bång, Director (Lead)

University of Lugano, **Switzerland**
Andreina Mandelli, Professor, University of Lugano (Lead)

National Sun Yat-sen University, **Taiwan**
Ting-Peng Liang, Prof & Dir, National Sun Yat-sen University (Lead)
Bing-Yu Chu, Prof & Dir, National Sun Yat-sen University

CHAPTER 2

THE ITALY BUSINESS AND INFORMATION TECHNOLOGIES (BIT) SURVEY*

ANDREINA MANDELLI, PAOLO NEIROTTI, ANNA CANATO, ALFREDO BIFFI, EMILIO PAOLUCCI, MARCO CANTAMESSA and CINZIA PAROLINI

Summary

The major intent of this project is to study the impact of new information technologies on industry structure, firms' practices and strategic results. Our research team, since 2002, has worked on this research agenda. The study that we present here builds on the results of the first Business and Information Technologies (BIT) study developed in Italy in 2002–2003 (see DeMattè *et al.*, forthcoming), which highlighted three important phenomena: first, the substantial difference in the rate of digitization of core processes, between firms of different sizes and information and communication technologies (ICT) governance complexity, which could be explained not only by different firms' capabilities, but also by the different role of technology in specific competitive contexts. Second, the different rate of digitization of different organizational processes: digital investments were much higher in the internal processes, and much lower in external relationships, with both customers and suppliers (e-commerce and e-procurement were not highly diffused). Third, the importance of cultural, social and organizational variables, not only as a precondition for the success of e-business projects, but also as a complementary "effect" of the projects themselves.

Our second survey built on these results, aims to collect more detailed data on the same critical areas:

(1) different and specific areas of adoption;
(2) the ICT governance processes;
(3) the organizational and social processes (capabilities and changes) related to ICT business impact;
(4) the general business results related to ICT innovation.

This report synthesizes the results we found with this 2004–2005 survey.

The Italian 2004 BIT dataset includes data collected through a survey of the chief information officer managers of a sample of the larger Italian companies, carried out

*This is the second BIT report from Italy. The first report was published in 2005, included in Apte and Karmarkar, (eds.), *Managing in the Information Economy: Current Research Issues*, New York: Springer Verlag (Kluwer Academic Publishing).

between October 2004 and April 2005. The respondents could fill in the questionnaire using the phone, the mail, and the web. The usable questionnaires were 214 out of 2326 invited answers (the response rate was 9.2%).

We have analyzed the results of the 2004–2005 BIT survey, focusing in particular on two areas of knowledge:

(1) the processes of ICT adoption and ICT governance;
(2) the relationship between firm's intangible resources and ICT processes and effects, at the organizational and business level.

In this survey, we found that:

- At this stage and for the type of firms considered (the larger firms), there is not any digital divide between Southern and Northern Italy in the spending for information technology (IT), despite of the economic diversity of the two areas.
- There is not any divide between Italian and foreign companies operating in Italy, since foreign groups doing business in Italy do not show higher spending rates for IT.
- The real divide, consistent with what we found in the previous BIT study, is related to the different IT investment efforts made by companies of different sizes.
- The nature of the industry helps in explaining the different IT adoption processes; the level of spending is significantly higher in the information intensive businesses of the service industries (financial services, consulting, and telecommunications).

With regard to the applications adopted and technology use:

- Corporate intranets and corporate websites represent the most diffused applications, while a minority of companies have explored e-procurement, e-commerce and other innovative frontiers in collaborative supply chains, in line with what we found in the first study, that is, that Italian companies have started to digitize internal processes more than external relationships, and communication processes more than commercial activities (Demattè *et al.*, forthcoming). This phenomenon is particularly interesting, if we consider the average size of our sample companies.
- The most innovative systems, radio frequency identification and e-learning platforms, still have a very limited diffusion, also confirming that the Italian companies tend to be late in the innovation cycle.
- It is also worth mentioning that the size of the company and the nature of the industry (more or less information-intensive) influence the type of activities performed online, and therefore the sophistication of the digital communication forms. Also, the organizational complexity and richness of the firm is important; our correlation analysis in fact showed that ICT adoption and ICT adoption trend are higher not only in companies distributed geographically (number of organizational units in Italy), but also in companies with a higher degree of organizational capital, market-based social capital, and innovation orientation.

With regard to the changes (strategic and organizational) induced in the organization:

- In the majority of firms, the number of employees who now use these new communication and information instruments has increased, the ICT function has become more integrated in the production processes, and there are more instruments to support employees in their decisions.

- New communication technologies have also started to change the way firms and people work, in the direction of what we call "digital enterprise", an enterprise connected and coordinated through digital communication (firms are now more geographically dispersed; in many of them videoconferencing has substituted business travels, and they use internet-based systems to coordinate employees).
- Despite these changes, the organizational impact of ICT investments is varied. Considering the perceived effect of ICT, in only a minority of firms the organizational structure seem to have become flatter, and employees are believed to have increased their power (components of what we call new organizational capital or new organizational capabilities).
- A richer explanation of how the ICT processes impact the organization can be derived by the analysis of the influence of the organizational and social capital on the ICT processes, and how the combination of these different resources with ICT can dynamically produce new capabilities and business advantages, beyond the organizational change called "digital enterprise". ICT adoption is in fact also correlated to significant changes in the organizational structure and capabilities.

With regard to the impact of ICT on firms' performance:

- The majority of the managers surveyed believed that their firms have achieved important results in the organizational and operational productivity areas, while it appeared more problematic in recognizing the benefits in terms of commercial efficiency, positive impact on successful new product development, and new strategic learning.

In conclusion we can say that, in general, the direction of ICT innovation in Italy has not much changed, even though the digital investments of firms seem to have increased (we cannot do a direct comparison because the two samples in the studies are different). There is still a divide related to the size of the firms and there is a tendency to invest more on internal communication and information processing than on the digitization of the external relationships and supply chain collaboration. This is particularly significant considering that we have surveyed some of the largest companies in the country. We know that this situation can draw a negative light on the Italian potential to explore the new frontiers of innovation and global competition. No country and no company can afford to consider itself protected and isolated in its local markets and capabilities.

Italian firms should learn and dare to explore the new frontiers of digital innovation in the awareness that ICT is not just a technology for doing the same things as before, in a more convenient and efficient way. ICT can become a strategic variable in firms, if it combines with new capabilities, new organization, and new pictures of the economy and the world.

2.1. Introduction

This report summarizes the results from the second Business and Information Technologies (BIT) survey conducted in Italy between the end of 2004 and the beginning of 2005. The results are discussed in the following sections.

The data used in this study represents the Italian country-level output of a broader international research project (the BIT project, coordinated by the Center for Management in Information technologies at the Anderson School of Management of UCLA) that investigates the impact of information and communication technologies (ICT) on business organizations in different countries of the world. We leave the detailed description of the entire project to other papers in this publication. We will focus on the characteristics of the project that deals with the issues addressed in this report.

The intent of the BIT project is to study the impact of new information technologies on business and industry structure. It is expected that new communication technologies "will change the structure of firms in terms of organization and work process, information chains and interorganizational relationships, and alter the structure of industrial sectors to the point that the traditional categories do not apply very well" (From the UCLA report).

The first important change is with regard to the form of work, work relationships, and organization (Mandelli, 1998). People will make decisions supported by rich sets of data and shared knowledge. The organization is likely to take a more networked, less hierarchical, and flexible form with the new communication opportunities offered by digital networks. Outsourcing and offshoring have already conquered the top of the agenda for not only technologists, but also for top managers.

Secondly, we are likely to see important transformations in the relationships with customers and suppliers, not only because there will be the use of electronic channels for commerce and procurement, but also in particular because the entire process of searching, building, and maintaining commercial relationships will become richer and more effective. The new information and communication logistics (which we called "cognitive logistics" in previous works, see Mandelli 1998) is likely to have a relevant impact on how people search for commercial information, compare offers' attributes, and make commercial decisions. It is also likely to change the intensity and frequency of commercial relationships.

But the product itself is going to become a new frontier of innovation. With the help of electronic communication, firms will improve and empower the process of product development, and they are also likely to transform the product itself. In all the sectors, we will see the predictions about "product augmentation" made by service management experts become true. This is likely to be particularly right for the information-intensive productions.

This drives us to the last and strategic point. It is likely that the new cognitive logistics will change the structure of business processes and global competition. Many sectors are becoming global networks of distributed resources and capabilities, and many of them are converging, since the changes in the information-based supply chains change both the competitive territory and competition rules.

Our research team has worked on this important research agenda, with the support of the Research Division of SDA Bocconi since 2002 and also of the Istituto Boella and the Politecnico of Turin since 2004. The first set of data was gathered in 2003 (for the results of this study see Dematte *et al.*, forthcoming). The results of this first study showed that it was difficult to draw simple conclusions about the e-business phenomenon in Italy. Both adoption processes and management perceived impacts that did not follow simple patterns and easy-to-interpret schemes. The analysis indicated a complex situation characterized by very different degrees and patterns of investments and very different perceptions about the results of these investments. These results could not be explained solely on the basis of the general time-lag of the Italian companies in the technological innovation process with respect to US firms.

This first analysis highlighted three phenomena. FIrst, the substantial difference in the rate of digitization of company core processes between firms of different sizes and ICT-governance complexity, which could be explained by different firms' capabilities and also by the different role of technology in specific competitive contexts. Second, the different rate of digitization of different organizational processes: digital investments were much higher in the internal processes, and much lower in external relationships, with both customers and suppliers (e-commerce and e-procurement were not highly diffused). Third, the importance of cultural, social, and organizational variables, not only as a precondition for the success of e-business projects, but also as a complementary "effect" of the projects themselves. This was interpreted as the intangible capital of the firms, that could make a competitive difference in the e-business innovation scenario.

Our second survey built on these results, try to collect more detailed data on the same critical areas:

(1) different and specific areas of adoption;
(2) ICT governance processes;
(3) the organizational and social processes (capabilities and changes) related to ICT business impact;
(4) the general business results related to ICT innovation.

This report synthesizes the results we found with this 2004–2005 survey.

2.2. The Italian 2004–2005 Study

The Italian 2004 BIT dataset includes the data collected through a survey of the Chief information officer (CIO) managers of a sample of the larger Italian companies, carried out between October 2004 and April 2005. The respondents could fill in the questionnaire using the phone, the mail, and the web. The usable questionnaires were 214 out of 2326 invited answers (the response rate was 9.2%).

The population under analysis was identified through the AIDA database (edited by Bureau Van Dijk). The criterion used for identifying large enterprise was exclusively the number of employees. Except for the tourist industry where the threshold considered was 50 individuals, enterprises with the number of employees higher than 250 individuals were considered for the other industries.

Some industries, such as mining, agricultural production and services, transportation, public health services, educational and social services, iron and steel production, metallurgical production, building industry, and real estate industry were excluded, given either the marginal weight information technology (IT) has in the core processes of these businesses or the difficulties in having reliable and complete data about the population of companies doing business in some of these industries (this was the case of the public organizations delivering health services in Italy).

Tables 2.1a and 2.1b show the distribution of the population and sample. The comparison between the sample and the Italian population of large enterprises demonstrates that the sample is not biased in terms of company size, kind of industry, and geographical localization. There was also a check for the presence of sample bias related to productivity indicators such as the added value per employee and the revenues per employee. Also, through the Kruskall Wallis nonparametric test, no bias was found in this case.

The data collection was based on a phone call made to each company within the population under analysis in order to collect CIO's main personal data, to describe our goals of the research, and to send the questionnaire to him/her.

Table 2.1a. The distribution of the population.

Industry		Size			
		< 500	500–1000	> 1000	Macro-industry
Food & Beverage (%)	5.48	71.09	15.63	13.28	
Textile (%)	6.81	79.25	16.35	4.40	
Printing & publishing (%)	2.91	66.18	14.71	19.12	Manufacturing
Chemical & pharmaceutical (%)	8.60	59.20	24.38	16.42	49.66
Mechanics, Electrics & Electronics (%)	20.93	67.89	18.81	13.29	
Automotive (%)	4.92	58.26	19.13	21.74	
Public utilities (%)	1.88	45.45	25.00	29.55	
Distribution (%)	12.24	69.93	15.03	15.03	Services
Tourism (%)	10.87	98.03	0.79	1.18	31.29
Logistic (%)	3.13	53.42	26.03	20.55	
Healthcare (private) (%)	3.17	79.73	16.22	4.05	
TLC (%)	0.64	26.67	6.67	66.67	Information services
Business services (%) (e.g. consultancy)	11.64	59.93	27.21	12.87	19.05
FInancial services (%)	6.76	27.22	16.46	16.46	
Total	100.00	66.65	17.42	13.18	100.00

Table 2.1b. The sample distribution by industry and size.

Industry	Size				
		< 500	500–1000	> 1000	Macro-industry
Food & Beverage (%)	3.74	75.00	25.00	0.00	
Textile (%)	6.07	69.23	30.77	0.00	
Printing & publishing (%)	1.87	50.00	50.00	0.00	Manufacturing
Chemical & pharmaceutical (%)	6.07	53.85	23.08	23.08	47.20
Mechanics, Electrics & Electronics (%)	22.43	62.50	25.00	10.42	
Automotive (%)	7.01	46.67	6.67	46.67	
Public utilities (%)	2.34	60.00	20.00	20.00	
Distribution (%)	13.08	71.43	10.71	17.86	Services
Tourism (%)	6.07	92.31	7.69	0.00	26.17
Logistic (%)	2.34	40.00	60.00	0.00	
Healthcare (private) (%)	2.34	80.00	20.00	0.00	
TLC (%)	0.93	50.00	0.00	0.00	Information services
Business services (%) (e.g. consultancy)	16.36	65.71	22.86	2.86	
FInancial services (%)	9.35	15.00	15.00	25.00	26.64
Total	100.00	60.28	20.56	12.62	100.00

After three weeks since the first contact, a recall was made to CIOs in order to collect the completed questionnaire. On the whole, at least one round of recalls was carried out for each company of the sample. All the companies that did not return the completed questionnaire to the research group after the third recall were eliminated from the contact list.

2.3. The Questionnaire

The survey questionnaire was designed taking into account the common knowledge needs of the international BIT project plus specific Italian-based research questions. The frame of the investigation is, in fact, similar for all the national surveys within the BIT network. The final purpose is to have a panel dataset about ICT innovation in businesses, which allows for longitudinal and crosssectional analysis. The focus of the common questions is on the processes and trends of ICT adoption, ICT-governance mechanisms (who decides what and how), and changes in the way the businesses are organized (within the business relationships and ultimately in the global design of the supply chain, great emphasis is given to changes in the organization — see the outsourcing and offshoring phenomena, in particular). Each country, indeed, is free to add new questions and to tailor them to the specific research interests of the teams and the local business environment.

When we started the study in 2003, we added to the Italian questionnaire, in particular, a few questions that made it possible to test the relationships between organizational and social capital (or capabilities), and both ICT adoption and organizational changes were added. We also added a few questions with the goal to collect data about the perceived business benefits of the ICT innovation processes (improved efficiency and competition-related processes). The rationale behind this is the general hypothesis that the ICT processes are strictly interconnected to the creation of new organizational and social-relational capabilities.

The will to access the impact of digital technology innovation processes within business organizations has been a common endeavor of management and IT scholars over the last decade. From a theoretical perspective, all these studies consider that ICT act as general purpose technologies, i.e. technologies whose rate of return increases when accompanied by complementary innovations (Brynjolffsson and Hitt, 2000). This is the economic rational for the huge impact that digital technology innovation processes have on the overall change of businesses. The phenomena like business process redesign, organizational transformation, and increased interaction with customer and suppliers that enable net-enabled business transformation (Straub and Watson, 2001; Barua, Konana, Whinston and Yin, 2004) are identified as complementary investments. These, together with the introduction of digital technologies, allow business organizations to increase their performance and efficiency in operations. The different contributions examine deeply the role of organizational capital in support to digitalization effort (Black and Linch, 1996, 2001; Brynjolfsson and Hitt, 2000; Brynjolfsson, Hitt and Yang, 2002; Bresnahan, Brynjolfsson and Hitt, 2002). They suggest that the "digital enterprise" is the firm that is able to leverage both organizational capital and investments in digital technology to reach a significant performance increase (see Brynjolfsson, Hitt and Yang, 2002).

While most of the studies focused only on organizational variables as complement to ICT investment, less research addresses on the role of other intangible resources, such as social capital. From a theoretical perspective, social capital is considered as a distinctive and difficult-to-imitate resource for organizations (Bourdieu, 1986; Adler and Kwon, 2002). Scholars suggest that there is a strong link between intangible resources and ICT investments, as ICT help improving the processes of communication and interaction with different stakeholders (Barua, Konana, Whinston and Yin, 2004).

We used this questionnaire in 2003 for the first time for face-to-face interviews with a sample of 66 Italian companies. The new version of the questionnaire includes the ameliorations suggested by the results of the first part of the study.

The final questionnaire is organized around the following areas of knowledge:

- Characteristics of the firms in the sample.
- Adoption and usage of digital technologies.
- Trends in the adoption and usage of digial technologies.
- The governance of digital innovation.

- Organizational capabilities and organizational changes related to ICT innovation.
- Business benefits related to ICT innovation.

2.4. The Sample

The questionnaire was sent to senior information systems managers of medium–large Italian companies of different industries, as per the sample construction explained earlier. The 214 responses are analyzed and discussed below.

Figure 2.1 shows the distribution of firms in our sample in terms of number of employees. Companies (19%) employ less than 250 employees, 29% occupy between 250 and 499 employees, 27% belong to the 500–1000 category and 25% are larger companies.

Of the firms surveyed, 50% are located in Northern Italy, the more economically advanced area of the country. The rest are located at the center and in the south of the country (Fig. 2.2).

We asked whether the firm was a part of the group, and in this case, if the managers in the firm had decisional power over the choices regarding ICT investments of other firms.

The descriptive statistics show that the majority of the companies in our sample are part of a group (43% are part of an Italian group, 23% of a foreign group). The firms

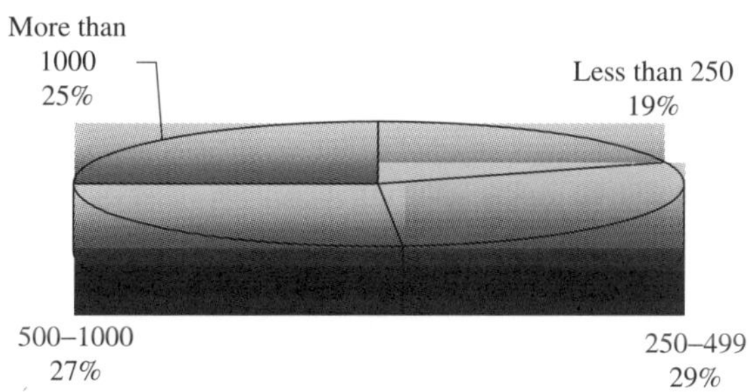

Fig. 2.1. Number of employees in our sample firms.

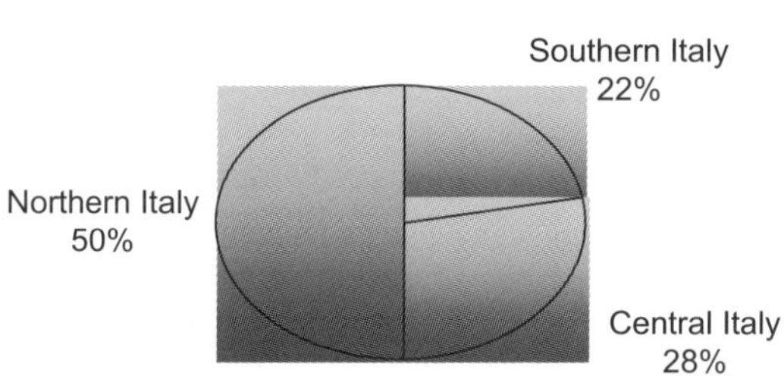

Fig. 2.2. Regional distribution of firms surveyed.

Table 2.2. Industrial groups and their role in ICT choices.

Is your firm part of an industrial group?	Respondents (%)	IF your firm is part of an industrial group, ...	Respondents (%)
NO	34	It does not control other business divisions /firms	40
YES, an Italian one	43	It controls other firms but plays no role in the decisions regarding ICT investments	10
YES, a foreign one	23	It controls other firms and plays a relevant role in the decisions regarding ICT investments	50

(50%) that are part of a group control ICT investments of other firms (Table 2.2). Thus, the complexity of the organizations which we have surveyed is particularly high. We will take this into account when we analyze the results regarding ICT and organizational innovation. This information about the complexity of the organizations surveyed is also confirmed by the geographical distribution of these firms. The companies (21%) have only one commercial or production site. Of them 51% have between two and ten sites. The rest are located in more than ten sites.

According to the collected data, the globalization of the larger Italian companies starts to be a relevant phenomenon. In the sample, 32% of the revenues are from abroad (13% extra-Europe). The firms (5%) anticipate that they will enter new Asian-Pacific markets. The global strategies are becoming more important for about half of these firms. It is particularly interesting to note that 42% of them have increased the revenues originated in foreign countries and 18% of them have increased the relevance of the activities outsourced in foreign countries (offshored). This data is particularly impressive, considering that in the 2003 survey what we called globalization of the firms was very low (Tables 2.3 and 2.4; Fig. 2.3).

Table 2.3. Trend about decisions concerning internationalization of business.

	Strong decrease (%)	Decrease (%)	Equal (%)	Increase (%)	Strong increase (%)
Number of operative units in foreign countries	5	2	75	16	2
Number of commercial units in foreign countries	7	1	68	22	2
Revenues from foreign activity	9	2	47	37	5
Internationalization of corporate website and brochure	2	1	79	17	2
Outsourcing in foreign countries	1	1	81	12	6

Table 2.4. Presence in international markets.

	We distribute our products/services (%)	We do not distribute our products/services but we plan to enter the market by 2007 (%)	We do not distribute our products/services and we do not plan to enter the market by 2007 (%)
Western Europe	64	2	34
Eastern Europe	54	5	41
North America	46	1	52
Central & South America	42	4	55
Africa	34	3	63
Asia, Australia and Pacific	43	5	52

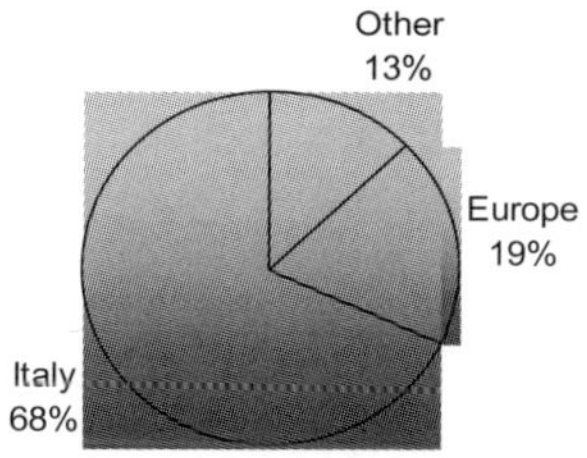

Fig. 2.3. Geographical sources of revenues.

But the globalization of the Italian companies becomes less evident when we pass from the commercial side (addressed when we looked at the percentage of revenue origin) to the supplier relationships. The majority of the Italian companies (79%) have relationships with national suppliers. Only 8% of them select business partners outside Europe (Fig. 2.4).

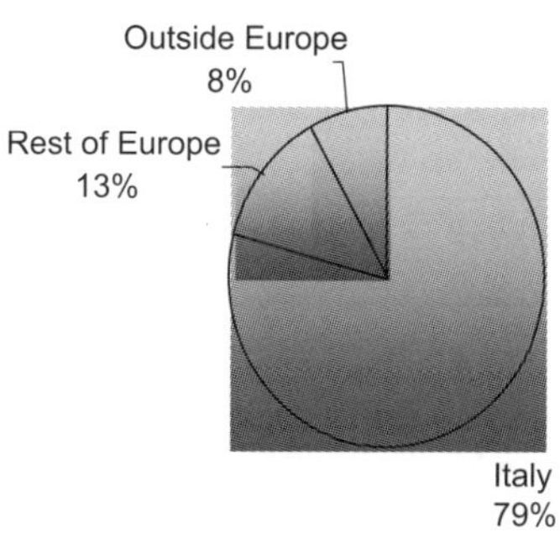

Fig. 2.4. Location of suppliers.

2.5. Information Technology Adoption

2.5.1. *The levels of IT spending*

The analysis on the adoption patterns of ICT in Italian large must be carried out by making three considerations:

- Recent international statistics point out a situation of delay of Italian companies in comparison with other European countries. OECD's estimates about IT expenditures in 2002 show that in Italy, the ratio between companies' IT investments and Gross domestic product (GDP) was equal to 5.2%, while the average for the top 15 European Union countries and for the US were, respectively, 7.0 and 8.2%.
- Small and medium enterprises largely prevail in the population of Italian firms; in 2004, 98% of the population of firms consisted of SMEs with more than ten employees (Istat, 2005). Therefore, the analysis of IT investments in large enterprises only represents a part of the Italian economy.
- There is a large economic diversity between the North and the South of the country, if we consider the contribution to the GDP stemming from these two areas as well as the number and the typology of companies operating in these regions.

In the sample, the analysis of the spending levels in IT confirms the delay of Italian firms in comparison with some of the main European Union countries. Table 2.5 shows that in 2004, the IT annual operating expenses (which include assets amortization, services acquired by providers and outsourcers, maintenance expenses and labour costs due to IT personnel) were about 2.5% of sales revenues on an average, whereas the budgets for new investments — which correspond to the expenditures in IT that can be capitalized and amortized — corresponded, on an average, to 1.21% of total revenues. The ratio between IT expenditures and value add is equal to 3.4%, if we consider only the budgets for new investments, while is equal to 5.7%, if we also consider the annual operating

Table 2.5. The level of investments in IT in 2004.

	IT investments sales revenues (%)	IT investments budget/value added (%)	Total IT expenditures/ value added (%)	IT annual operating expenses/sales revenues (%)
Mean	1.21	3.40	5.76	2.49
Median	0.45	1.42	4.00	1.08
5th percentile	0.05	0.20	1.19	0.23
95th percentile	5.40	14.27	18.25	10.00
1st quartile	0.17	0.59	2.26	0.58
Number of firms	159	151	128	178
Standard deviation	2.07	5.28	5.52	3.11

expenses in IT. This is the ratio that is quite close to the average level of investments estimated by the OECD in 2002 for the 15 European Union countries. Nevertheless, this estimate, being carried out only on large enterprises, may suffer from a bias, if we use it as an estimate for the entire population of Italian enterprises.

The analysis of the spending for IT, through nonparametric tests and ANOVA, shows that:

- there is no digital division between Southern and Northern Italy in the spending for IT despite the economic diversity of the two areas. At the same time, there is no division between Italian and foreign companies operating in Italy, since Italian subsidiaries of foreign groups do not show higher spending rates for IT;
- the spending rate for IT is positively associated with firm's size;
- the level of spending is significantly higher in the information intensive businesses of service industries (financial services, consulting, and telecommunications);
- neither the amount of budget for new investments nor the annual operating expenses significantly vary between companies that can be regarded as leaders in the adoption of new technologies and firms that can be regarded as followers in exploiting the opportunities given by emerging technologies.

These data on spending levels are important for comparing the attitudes of Italian companies to invest in IT with the trends occurring in other countries, but these Data provide a limited view on the main features of Italian firms' digitalization process. Besides the level of IT investments, it is also important to understand how expenditures for IT are allocated among investments on the infrastructure (IT platforms, middleware , enterprise application integration, databases, corporate LANs, etc.) and expenditures sustained for the introduction of new software applications which support the business need of the various organizational areas of the company.

2.5.2. *The integration of the IT portfolio*

Further analysis on the composition of the corporate portfolios of IT resources shows that the digitalization process of Italian enterprises has both negative and positive sides. One of the positive aspects is the increasing size of the portfolios of information systemsis (IS) held by companies: as Fig. 2.5 points out, the diffusion of software applications supporting the specific needs of the main organizational areas is relatively high, especially if we consider applications for production planning and control for administrative activities (such as billing, payroll, etc.), which show adoption rates superior to 90% of the sample. However, as Fig. 2.6 shows, in a relevant part of the sample these tools are not integrated with the IS of customers and suppliers, hampering the electronic exchange of data and the share of information (about production plans, bills

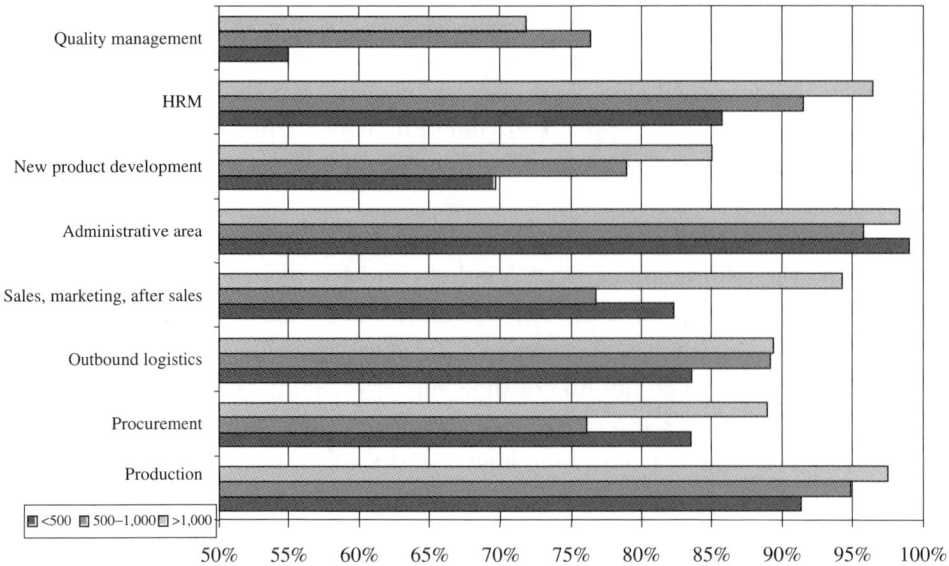

Fig. 2.5. Adoption of IT applications in the main organizational areas of a firm.

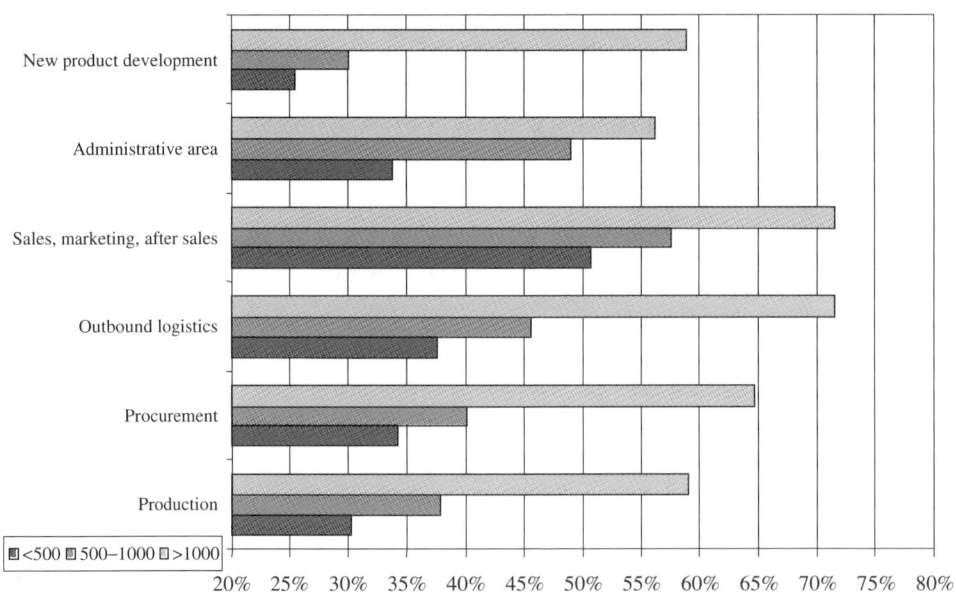

Fig. 2.6. Adoption of applications integrated with suppliers and customers' information.

of materials, invoices, etc.) among the supply chain. This is one of the main negative aspects in the diffusion processes of IT.

But integration problems do not only concern collaboration models among firms operating in the same supply chain. In fact, in several companies, the level of integration among the single applications that compose the corporate IT applications portfolio is still very low. The lack of integration in the different components of the applications portfolio is not necessarily the cumulative effect of a long series of managerial errors in planning IT projects, but it is in part explained by the rapid evolution IT had over the last three decades. During the different technological waves of this evolution path, the IT market offered new applications that were able to provide companies with new features, but with a limited degree of compatibility with preexisting systems. This has led several companies to introduce software applications that were not compatible with the IS previously introduced. Thus, the growth of the applications portfolio required companies to develop interfaces allowing communication among different IS. The efforts sustained for the introduction of the interfaces among the applications available in a company were intensive, just as the number of applications available was high. Therefore, in the short-run, several companies obtained poor results from the growth of their applications portfolio because of the additional efforts required to consolidate their IT portfolio.

But in large companies that lack the integration among IS, it is also due to the level of centralization in the IT management and in the authority for the most strategic technology decisions about the design and the implementation of an IS.

Literature on IS shows how in the 1970s and 1980s, firms alternated between models in which the IT management was centralized (and thus the authority for the majority of IT decisions was located in the corporate IT group) and models based on decentralizing authority for most IT decisions in divisional or functional IT units. Decentralized models were prevalent in the first half of the 1990s and had their rationale in improving business units' flexibility and customer orientation, by allowing them to define data standards and design their IT infrastructure according to their needs. However, this model hampered a disciplined growth of the applications portfolio in the time, exploited the synergies in IT management, and increased the costs sustained at the corporate level for the control on IT expenses.

Today, as data from the survey show, most of the firms are coming back to centralize IT governance and decisions about new IT investments. Therefore, business units or functions today are less autonomous in technology decisions with respect to the past: as Table 2.6 shows, this is occurring especially for decisions related to hardware and software architectures, master data standards for customers, products, suppliers, and intranet and extranet design and implementation. This choice has been carried out with the expectation of obtaining a better exploitation of business synergies related to IT, reducing duplications, establishing standards, improving the control on

Table 2.6. Trends in centralization levels in decisions about IT investments.

	With respect to 2000, the level of centralization...			
	Has diminished [single business units/functions are more autonomous in their IT decisions] (%)	Is the same (%)	Has increased [single business units/functions are less autonomous in their IT decisions] (%)	Total (%)
Hardware and software architecture	3.62	28.99	67.39	100.00
Data standard for customers and products	3.62	39.13	57.25	100.00
Intranet and extranet design and implementation	3.62	34.06	62.32	100.00

IT expenditures and planning a more disciplined growth of the corporate IT infrastructure in the time.

2.5.3. *The fields of investments*

The data available through the survey on the different fields of investments in IT do not allow for an investigation of how problematic it was for companies to continuously innovate their IT portfolios and to what extent companies were able to overcome the lack of integration among their applications. At the same time, we only get a partial view on how investments impacted the IT infrastructure and further investments on software applications.

For example, the adoption rates of middleware and enterprise application integration technologies (which are, respectively, 24.5 and 47.3%) are positively associated with firms' size and show higher rates in the information industries. This suggests that problems related to the lack of internal integration in the applications portfolios is still a problem for several companies but is more diffused in smaller enterprises.

ERP systems are adopted by 60% of the sample (the adoption rate in manufacturing industries is 74%); the adoption of these systems, as well as the diffusion of other technologies is positively associated with firms' sizes (Fig. 2.7).

Corporate web sites have a broad diffusion, but on an average, e-commerce capabilities are provided only in 37% of the sample web sites. These of online distribution channel shows a discontinuity in companies with more than 1000 employees (in this cluster, 52% of the firms have these web sites with e-commerce features).

The data warehouse technologies and data mining software follow a diffusion pattern that is quite similar to the one for ERP systems. Furthermore, Chi square analysis shows that there is a positive association between these technologies.

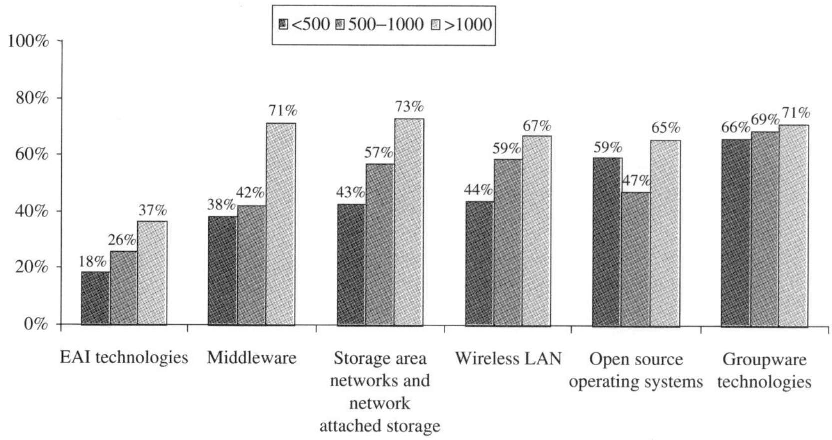

Fig. 2.7. IT adoption rates.

Conversely, radio frequency identification (RFID) systems and e-learning platforms still have a limited diffusion (equal to 11 and 23%, respectively, in the entire sample). The adoption rate of e-learning technologies shows a strong discontinuity in companies with more than 1000 employees (47%, versus the adoption rates of 14 and 18% in companies with less than 500 employees and firms with a number of employees between 500 and 1000) and is higher in information industries (in this cluster of industries, the adoption rate is estimated to be 43.8%). Obviously, RFID technologies have a higher diffusion in manufacturing companies and in service industries doing business in the logistics or in the large-scale retail distribution. However, their overall diffusion was still very low in 2004.

As for RFID technologies, the diffusion pattern of computer telephony integration is not associated with the firm's size, but rather with the industry: in service and information industries, the estimated adoption rates are, respectively, 33.3 and 38.8%, while in the manufacturing industries this rate is equal to 17%.

Corporate intranets represent the most widespread technology, adopted by about 85% of the sample. However, the modalities of the use of corporate intranets vary significantly among the sample, depending on the size and the industries of the companies. The companies with more than 1000 employees are more likely to use these technologies for synchronous or asynchronous activities to support team working (chat, instant messaging, etc.) or for document management activities (Fig. 2.8). Thus, we can conclude that in information industries, the impact of these technologies on the organization of work and on internal coordination mechanisms is more pervasive as the firm's size increases.

Conversely, the use of intranets for the communication of "institutional information" about the company and its internal procedures (e.g. corporate bulletins,

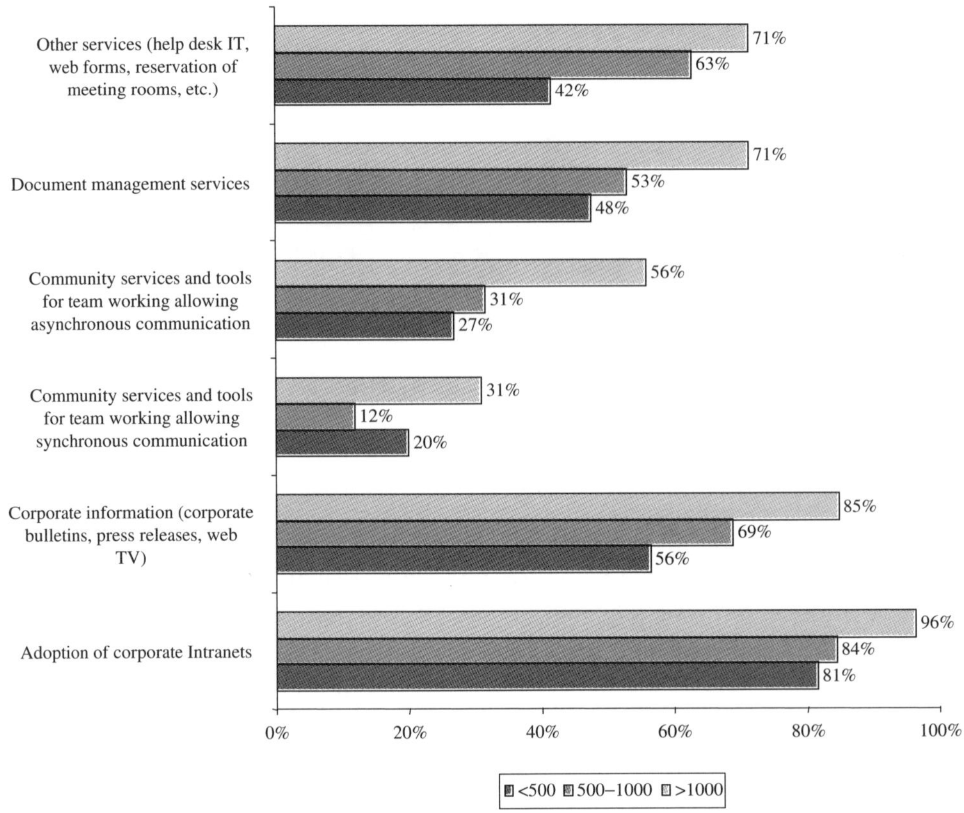

Fig. 2.8. Models of use of corporate intranets.

press reviews and releases) follows a diffusion pattern without any regard to the company size.

More evidence supporting the hypothesis on the limited degree of integration of IS along supply chains is the fact that a percentage of lower than 15% of the sample population uses IT for collaboration with suppliers for new product development activities or for production planning, demand forecasting, or inventory management (Fig. 2.9). Moreover, 35% of the companies analyzed do not use IT in procurement or collaboration activities. The use of IT for sourcing activities or for managing entirely online the transactions of procurement activities is diffused in 35.2 and 41.4% of the sample, respectively.

The analysis of IT expenditures trends shows that for most of the firms in the sample, the expenses for security hardware and software, business continuity systems and disaster recovery plans, and hardware devices for the storage of data show a general pattern of growth, while the expenses for IT outsourcing projects, end users training on IT contents, and consulting services related to IT show a more stable trend (Table 2.7).

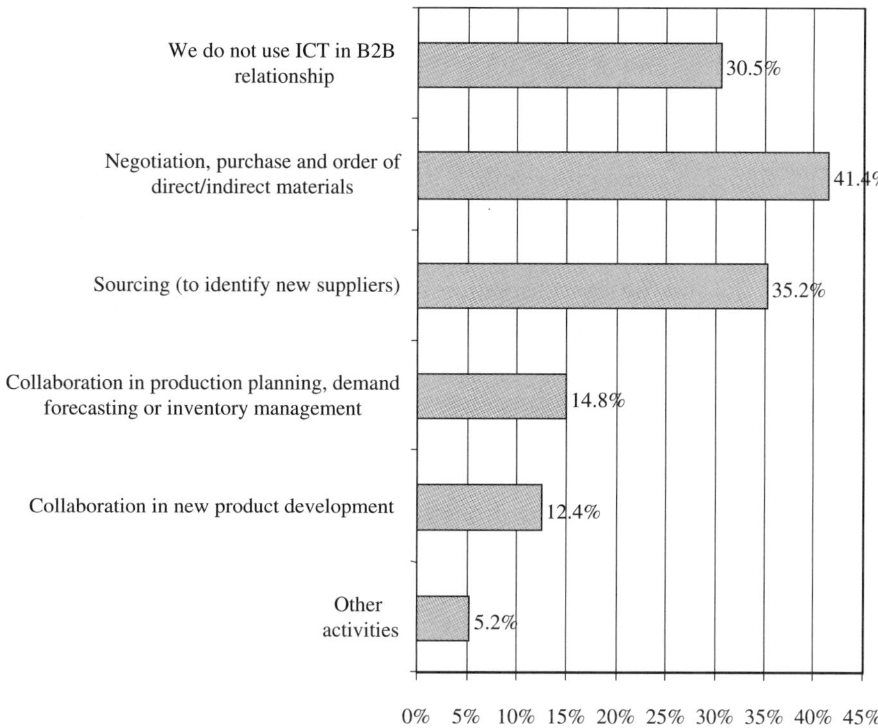

Fig. 2.9. The use of IT in business-to-business (B2B) relationships.

Table 2.7. Budget trends for IT expenditures between 2000 and 2004.

IT expenditures	Never invested in this area (%)	Decreased (%)	Unchanged (%)	Increased (%)
Hardware: storage	8.0	5.5	20.5	66.0
Hardware: security	2.0	1.5	18.5	78.0
Software: operating systems & networking	0.0	7.8	50.5	41.7
Software: security	1.0	1.5	15.7	81.9
ASP and hosting	33.8	10.9	33.3	21.9
IT outsourcing	32.8	7.0	30.3	29.9
Intranet e extranet	6.9	2.5	31.5	59.1
Wireless hardware & software	33.3	2.0	17.4	47.3
End users training on IT contents	10.0	7.0	49.5	33.5
IT consulting	4.0	14.4	47.0	34.7
Business continuity and disaster recovery	16.6	0.5	24.6	58.3

2.6. ICT Governance

Beyond the structural features of companies, the speed of the digitalization processes must also be considered in relation to the capabilities of managing innovation in the corporate portfolio of IT resources. Managing IT investments leads companies to cope with higher difficulties in comparison with managing other production inputs, given the need to integrate IS with the organization of business processes, the rapid rates of technological change in the IT market, the increasing size and complexity of corporate applications portfolio, and the transformations in the nature of competition and markets. In the background of these difficulties, managing innovations in the companies' IT portfolio requires firm-specific knowledge, a long-term and disciplined view, and a square focus on achieving the company's most fundamental goals. In more concrete terms, IT management requires reliable investments selection and prioritization methods, "make or buy" choices about information systems which must be in line with firms' core processes, and a way to share the authority and responsibility for IT investments among executives, IT managers, and service providers that enables alignment between these technologies and business needs. This explains why IT implementation and management usually continues to be kept in-house, despite companies doing less IT work "in house," when compared to 20 years back.

The difficulties to manage IT investments is confirmed in our analysis by the data which shows that 18% of the companies analyzed have obtained disappointing results by the IT projects undertaken between 2000 and 2004, at least once.

The most common reasons for the failure of IT projects are primarily related to the lack of top management's commitment, the resistance to change of end users, the lack of an adequate planning process for these investments, and the misalignment between the results foreseen by IT vendors and the results actually obtained (Fig. 2.10). Very seldom, the disappointing outcomes have been regarded as related to the extent of the budgets devoted to IT expenditures. This bolsters the main importance of managerial skills on the success of digitalization processes over IT spending levels.

These causes of failure for IT investments point out that the highest critical IT management capabilities are related to the following aspects.

- the planning process of IT investments, the IS department management autonomy in determining budgets for IT investments and the methods used to guarantee the process of integration and alignment between the IS department and the other firms' business functions. The importance of these factors requires companies to identify reliable criteria to prioritize IT investments proposals and methods to evaluate *a priori* costs and returns of IT projects proposals;
- top management's commitment towards IT investments and the C-level officers' recognition of the value of these technologies for company's competitiveness;

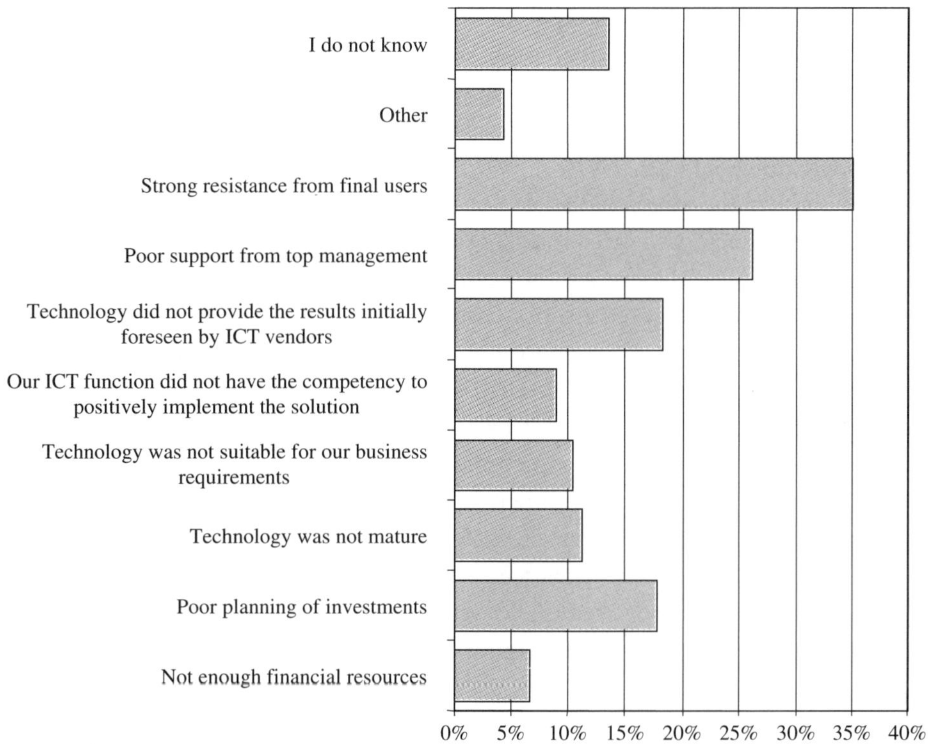

Fig. 2.10. Reasons for poor results from IT investments.

- the involvement of the CIO and the IS department in the company's strategic planning process;
- the level of centralization in the allocation of authority on strategic IT decisions;
- make or buy decisions in the management of IT; and
- the ability to work with IT vendors to develop appropriate systems and infrastructure, to manage relationships with outsourcing partners. Similarly, the IT planning process must be coordinated with the investments made by the most important suppliers. Regarding this point, we must consider that in some industries, such as the automotive, the IT adoption processes have been favored in the past by the role played by large enterprises which urged their suppliers to adopt ERP systems integrated with their IS in order to enhance collaboration processes along the supply chain.

Together with these features, the level of IT management capabilities is related to the availability of technical skills in the IS department and to the level of end users' skills on IT applications. This can be considered as highly correlated with firms' capability to adjust their human capital to the features of the technologies introduced.

In the survey, IT management capabilities available in each company were measured by asking the CIOs to indicate the extent to which they agreed or disagreed with a series of statements describing a situation in which some of the factors described above were well rooted in their companies. A 5 level Likert scale was used ($2 =$ strongly agree; $-2 =$ strongly disagree) (Fig. 2.11).

We found that the larger is the size of the company, the higher is the level of capabilities in the three size categories considered. Among the most critical factors, the analysis pointed out the limited use of appraisal methods regarded as adequate in evaluating *a priori* costs and returns of IT investments. The analysis also pointed out that only 40% of the sample systematically uses appraisal methods to evaluate costs and returns of IT investments. Another critical factor that emerged from the analysis was the limited importance attributed by top and middle management to training on IT contents for end users. However, end users' skills on IT applications do not represent an item of the IT management capabilities where large Italian companies show a particularly negative position. The situation for the technical skills owned by IS specialists employed in the IS department is not worrying as well.

At the same time, the coordination between the IT department and business functions' managers for expressing IT emerging needs in the IT planning process is not perceived to be particularly critical.

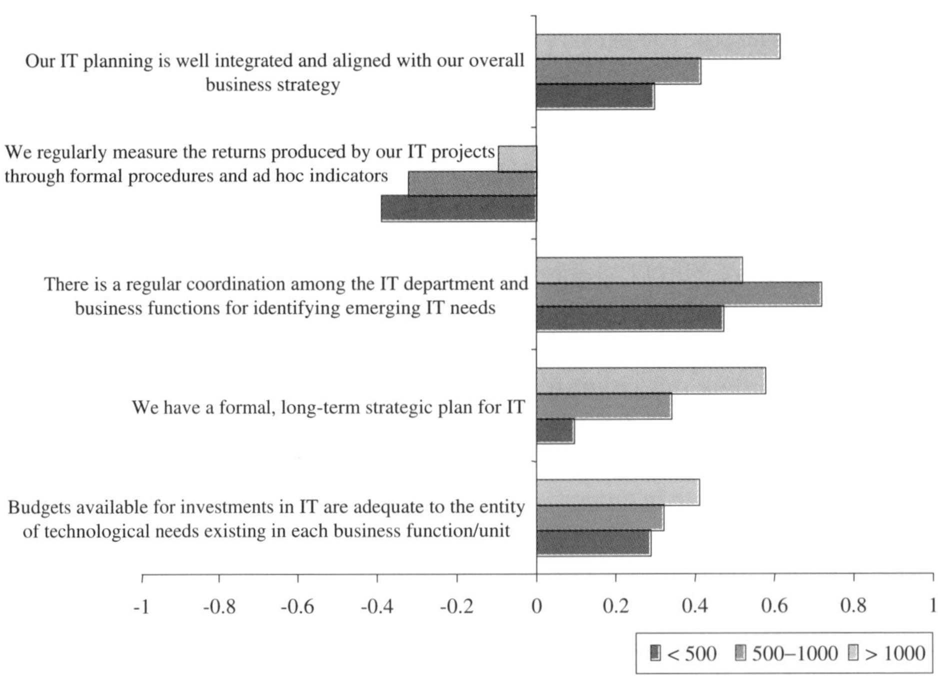

Fig. 2.11. IT management capabilities in Italian large enterprises.

Therefore, the main challenge for IT executives as emerging from this analysis is the definition of more reliable evaluation methods for IT investments proposals; this is a challenge which is in part hampered by the limits of traditional quantitative methods (such as the net present value or internal rate of return) in the field of IS.

2.7. Organizational Capabilities, Organization Change and the New Relationship Networks

In our survey, we collected information about the role of intangible resources such as organizational and social-relational capital in the digital technology innovation process. We argue that the creation and the availability of social and organizational resources enable a firm to develop new technological capabilities, and new organizational and strategic resources are also created in the processes. Indeed, the relevance of social capital for digital innovation processes has enormous implications on management of innovation. If ICT effectiveness requires new organizational and social capabilities, then it is likely that firms that will fail to invest in this direction will fall in to a considerable disadvantage, which will be difficult to overcome in the future and that the ability to exploit the complementariness between organizational capital, social capital, and technology investment will constitute a higher-order, dynamic capability of the firm (Amit and Shoemaker, 1993; Makadok, 2001).

2.7.1. *Old and new capabilities related to ICT innovation*

The contributions on the impact of ICT on organizations stress the more complex role of both ICT and organizational and cultural variables in the process (Robey and Boudreau, 2000; Fiol, 1991; Brynjolfsson and Hitt, 2000), and organizational learning (e.g. Cohen and Sproull, 1996; Fiol and Lyles, 1985). These contributions highlight that, in order to network, the organization needs to leverage knowledge and company relationships, which requires changing the ideas of the firm, the market, and the organization. In short, it is like saying innovation does not require special structures; it requires special resources and capabilities (Demattè *et al.*, forthcoming). That is why a specific part of the questionnaire was dedicated to investigate the organizational features and practices that can have relevant implications for ICT adoption and performance namely, information sharing, team-working, decision delegation, organizational communication, and human capital management. In this paper, we address the descriptive results of this part of the survey, trying to evaluate how developed these capabilities are in the Italian companies (at least in the larger companies surveyed in our study) and whether the adoption of digital innovation can be linked, in the perceptions of the IT managers, to organizational changes and the development of new organizational and strategic resources.

2.7.2. *Organizational and social capital in the surveyed firms*

Our results do not drive to easy conclusions about how developed the organizational capital is in our sample companies (Table 2.8). While knowledge-sharing and team-working culture is spreading significantly, it does not seem so for the organizational practices reflected in the willingness to build a more participatory model of work. According to the responses, in 69% of the firms in our sample there is an information-sharing culture, in 79% of them employees are often involved in team activities with colleagues from different functions/firms: about 70% of the firms adopt policies that assign a strategic role to the quality of the human resources. In more than half of them, there is a clear communication policy toward the employees. But the number lowers much when we look at another important organizational feature related to, what in the literature is called, "organizational capital" (Brynjolfsson and Hitt, 2000). In fact, there is a strong delegation policy in only 22% of the firms.

2.7.3. *Organization and supply chain change*

Also, the organizational impact of ICT adoption is complex, even though it is clear that digital innovation has driven important organizational changes. In 75% of the firms, the number of employees who now use these new communication and information instruments has increased, and this, of course, poses competence-related challenges to the organizations (in 77% of cases). The ICT function has become more integrated in the production processes (68%), and there are more instruments to support employees in their decisions (62%) (Table 2.9).

New communication technologies have also started to change the way firms and people work, in the direction of what we call "digital enterprise", a network-based enterprise connected through digital communication. 38% of firms are now more geographically dispersed. In 39% of firms, videoconferencing has substituted business travels, while 35% use internet-based systems to coordinate employees. Management of 74% of the firms showed increasing need to perform business intelligence and in 47% of the firms, individual and group performances are assessed more often.

Despite these changes, the organizational impact of ICT investments is varied. Only 29% of the firms have decreased the number of employees after their automation and outsourcing innovations. Only in less than 20% of the cases, the number of middle managers is decreased and employees are believed to have more power, even though 34% of the respondents said there is now a flatter structure. In several cases, middle managers (41%) and employees (46%) have increased their responsibilities.

2.7.4. *Dynamic capabilities in the ICT processes*

These results show that the organizational impact (organizational change and creation of new organization capabilities) of digital innovation varies in different companies.

Table 2.8. Organizational features (level of agreement).

	Strongly disagree (%)	Disagree (%)	Neutral (%)	Agree (%)	Strongly agree (%)
We are used to sharing information with employees	1	12	19	59	10
Employees are often involved in team activities with colleagues from different functions/firms	1	8	13	65	14
We are used to delegating decisions to employees who do not have managerial status	12	42	24	20	2
Management make an effort to formulate and communicate corporate mission and philosophy to employees	4	10	32	46	8
Strategic decisions are clearly communicated to employees who need to make operative decisions	3	12	29	50	7
There is an increasing use of incentives linked to individual and/or group performance	8	14	27	41	10
Management participate actively in the selection of new personnel	2	5	21	60	12
Management considers employee training crucial to business	1	8	23	48	20

Our hypothesis, consistent with the dynamic capabilities theoretical framework, is that there can be a correlation between organizational and social resources on one side and this impact on the other side.

In order to perform this correlation analysis, we built scales to reduce the number of the variables included in the analysis (see the Appendix).

The results of the correlation analysis support the hypothesis that there is a significant relationship between organizational/social variables and ICT adoption processes as well as between organization change and the creation of new organizational capabilities (see Table 2.10). ICT adoption and ICT adoption trend are higher not only in companies distributed geographically (number of organizational units in Italy), but also in companies with a higher degree of organizational capital, market-based social capital, and innovation orientation. ICT adoption is then correlated to signin the organization, in particular, the creation of what we have called the digital enterprise, the creation of new organizational capabilities, and the reorganization of the supply chain through the formula of outsourcing. We did not find any relationships between digital innovation and offshoring; the degree of use of this organizational formula is only correlated to being a part of the group and the number of organizational units in Italy.

Table 2.9. Changes in organization due to ICT introduction (level of agreement).

	Strongly disagree (%)	Disagree (%)	Neutral (%)	Agree (%)	Strongly agree (%)
The number of employees that use ICT instruments has increased	4	10	12	51	24
We increasingly use videoconferencing as a communication tool that substitutes business travels	18	19	24	27	12
Automation and outsourcing have decreased the number of employees	12	32	27	23	6
Personnel need more IT competencies to perform their tasks	2	7	15	59	18
We increasingly use Internet-based system to coordinate employees (e.g. Net meeting)	13	23	29	30	5
Employees are trained more often on IT contents	3	26	39	31	1
The percentage of middle managers (on the total number of employees) has decreased	5	33	46	14	2
Middle managers have more responsibilities	4	15	40	39	2
The ICT function is more integrated and more involved in production processes	4	7	20	56	12
Management have increasing need to perform business intelligence	3	8	15	52	22
Organization structure is flatter, with fewer hierarchical levels	5	24	36	28	6
Individual and group performances are assessed more often	4	17	32	39	8
Employees have an increased number of activities (job enrichment)	3	15	36	44	2
Employees have increased decisional power (empowerment)	5	29	46	18	2
Geographical dispersion has increased	8	25	29	31	7
We have more instruments to support employees in their decisions	0	9	29	57	5

2.8. Outsourcing Extent and Rationale

The digital communication technologies foster the creation of newly distributed organizational models. Several strategic and operations management scholars have focused on the redesign of supply chains, linked to the development of new network-based organizations (Kamath and Liker, 1994; Bensaou and Venkatraman, 1995; Nishiguchi, 1994; Dyer and Singh, 1998). While in the past firms could either make a product or service themselves or buy it through the market, now they have a third alternative: a

Table 2.10. Correlation between ICT adoption and organizational change.

	Number of organizational units in Italy	Part of a group	Information intensive industry	Organizational capital	Industry reputation	Market social capital	ICT adoption
Number of organizational units in Italy		0,128*					0,15*
Part of a group	0,128*						
Information intensive industry							
Organizational capital						0,142*	0,298**
Industry reputation							
Market social capital				0,142*			
ICT adoption	0,15*			0,298**			
ICT adoption change				0,155*		0,181**	0,214**
Innovation style				0,237**		0,120*	0,159*
Digital enterprise	0,214**	0,253**			0,127*		0,351**
Neworgcap		0,194**			0,229**		0,187*
Degree of outsourcing	0,236**	0,170**	0,115*	0,197**	0,184**		0,257**
Offshoring	0,158*	0,195**					

	ICT adoption	ICT adoption change	Innovation style	Digital enterprise	Neworgcap	Degree of outsourcing	Offshoring
Number of organizational units in Italy	0,15*			0,214**		0,236**	0,158*
Part of a group				0,253**	0,194**	0,170**	0,195**
Information intensive industry						0,115*	
Organizational capital	0,298**	0,155*	0,237**			0,197**	
Industry reputation				0,127*	0,229**	0,184**	
Market social capital		0,181**	0,120*				
ICT adoption		0,214**	0,159*	0,351**	0,187*	0,257**	
ICT adoption change	0,214**		0,183**	0,19**	0,163**	0,146**	
Innovation style	0,159*	0,183**		0,237**	0,182**		
Digital enterprise	0,351**	0,19**	0,237**		0,38**	0,220**	
Neworcap	0,187*	0,163**	0,182**	0,38**			
Degree of outsourcing	0,257**	0,146**		0,220**			
Offshoring							

long-term relationship with suppliers, more in terms of a "partnership" than in the form of a market transaction. "Lean manufacturing" (Womack *et al.*, 1990) and outsourcing have become a new frontier of supply chain management.

Outsourcing becomes offshoring toward new developing countries when productions are labor-intensive, or transportation costs are not relevant as in the information-intensive industries (Vestring *et al.*, 2005). This new organization of the supply chain builds on the development of new technological networks, since only digital infrastructures set the boundaries of the new ventures and collaborations (Karmarkar, 2004).

Consistently with this scenario, outsourcing has started to become a relevant phenomenon also in Italy, according to the data collected in our survey. In general, the ICT and information-intensive activities (ex. SW and payroll), and the specialized services (ex. market research) have been more affected by this phenomenon than the communication-based tasks (ex. customer support and procurement). This is consistent with the hypothesis (Karmarkar, 2004) that the new information-based supply chains will reorganize according to the new geographical distribution of specialistic capabilities and cost-related efficiencies.

This idea is confirmed by the results we found when we asked why firms outsource. There are many reasons why companies adopt these new formats. The majority of these firms want to gain access to capabilities that are not present in their companies. These strategic objectives are complemented by productivity-related goals and the willingness to create a more flexible organization (Figs. 2.12a and b).

This idea is confirmed by the results we found when we asked why firms outsource. There are many reasons why companies adopt these new formats. The majority of these firms want to gain access to capabilities that are not present in their companies. These strategic objectives are complemented by productivity-related goals and the willingness to create a more flexible organization (Fig. 2.13).

2.9. Business and Marketing Relationships

2.9.1. *Changes in the number of suppliers and geographical scope*

A good portion of the companies in our sample (32%) has not adopted digital technologies dedicated to the area of supplier relationships (Fig. 2.14). Even among the others, the impact of this innovation has been varied. Our results very interestingly show that in the majority of firms the number of suppliers is not increased due to the use of ICT, contrary to all the predictions made by the digital frictionless economy paradigm (see Mandelli, 2003 for a review). The relationships have costs also in the digital economy, and transaction costs still impact organizational and supply chain models, even though in different ways (Mandelli, 2003). In fact, according to our results, when ICT technologies enabled the selection of

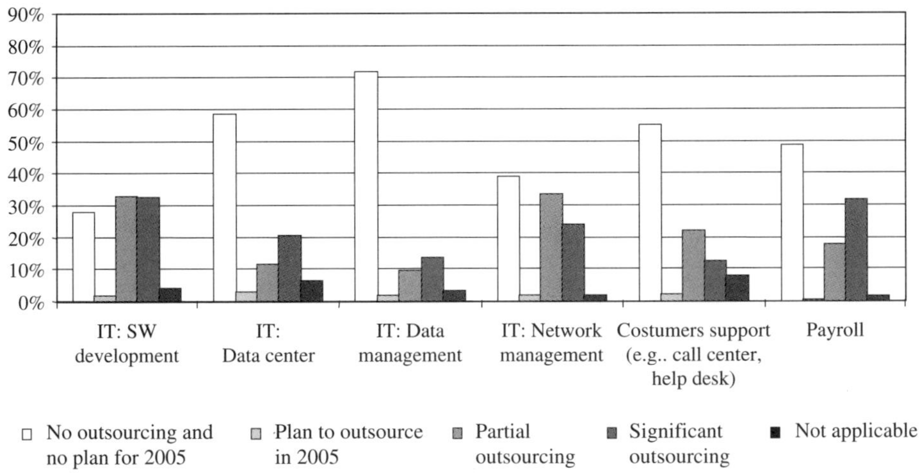

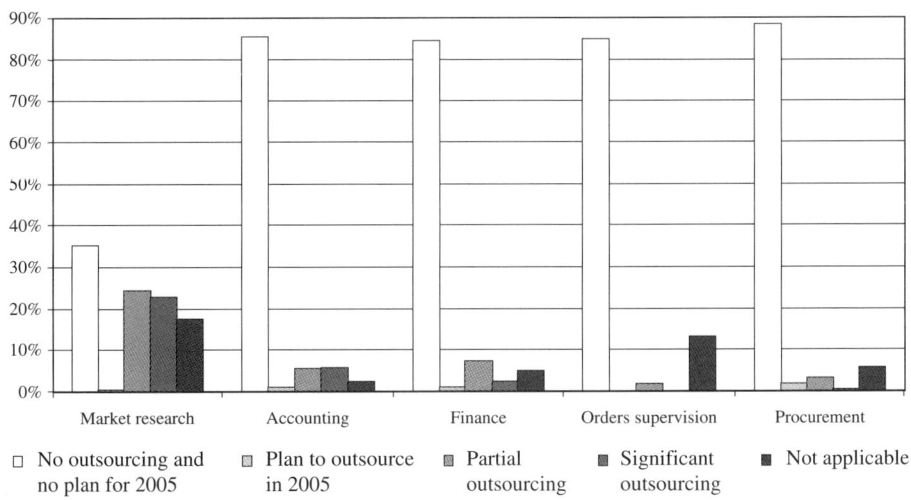

Fig. 2.12(a) and (b). Level of outsourcing for different activities.

new suppliers, the reputation of the supplier, access to strategic competence, and the already established relationships were more important than just geographical proximity (Fig. 2.15).

2.9.2. *Technologies for supply chain management*

Italian firms use digital technologies in the supply chain area mostly for supporting the selection and the supplier negotiation activities. But electronic channels are just starting to replace traditional supply relationship models. Only about one-third of the companies use electronic catalogs and EDI technologies, and a very few use the different forms of electronic markets (Fig. 2.16). It is very interesting to note that

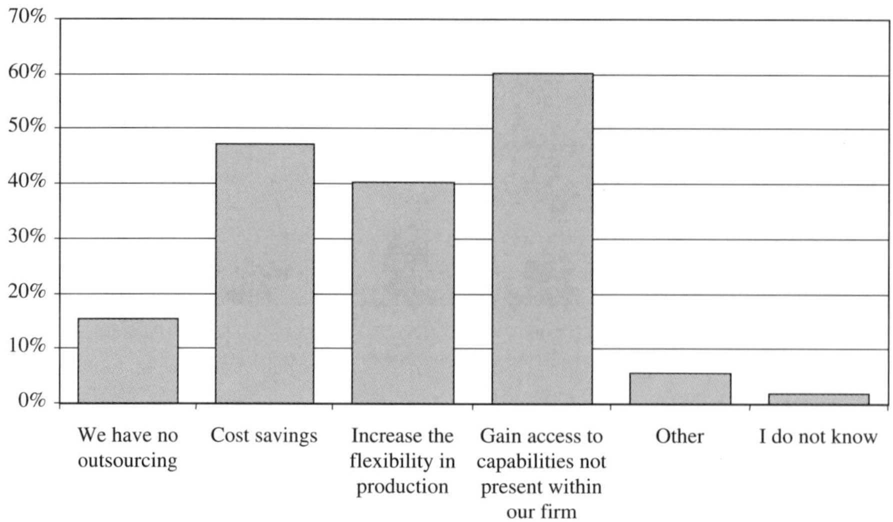

Fig. 2.13. Reasons for outsourcing.

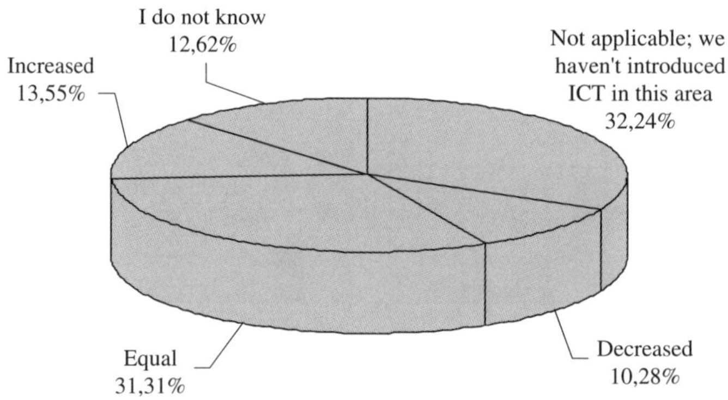

Fig. 2.14. How has the number of suppliers been modified, thanks to the use of ICT?

almost nobody uses public exchanges, in line with the hypothesis about the social costs and social embeddedness of business relationships that hamper the creation of many and diverse relationships (Mandelli, 2003).

2.9.3. *Interaction with customers (B2C only)*

This section of the survey was submitted only to firms that are active in B2C markets. The data refer to the 133 firms (62% of the entire sample) that answered this question.

The internet has changed the way we do commerce. No longer there is a need to have face-to face contact with a company representative to purchase goods, when this

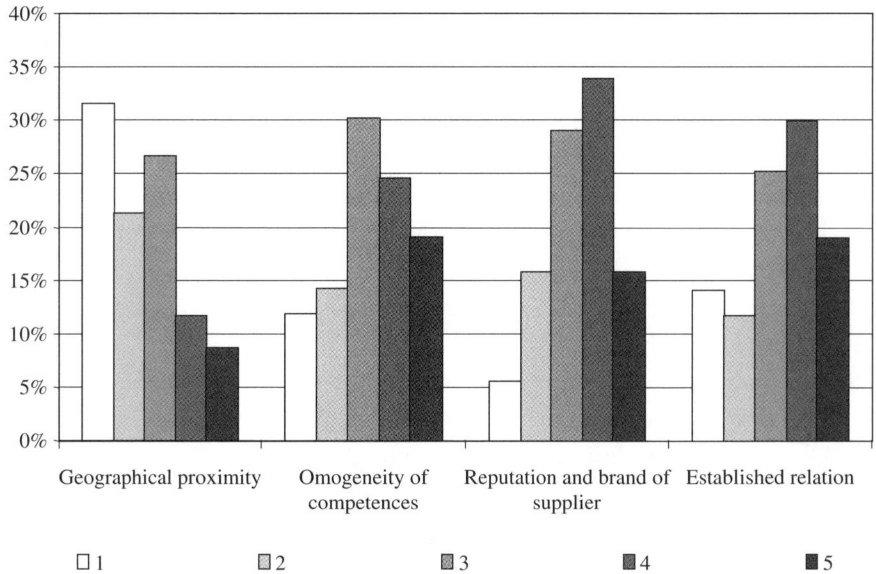

Fig. 2.15. When ICT enabled the selection of new suppliers, how important were the following factors? (scale from 1 to 5).

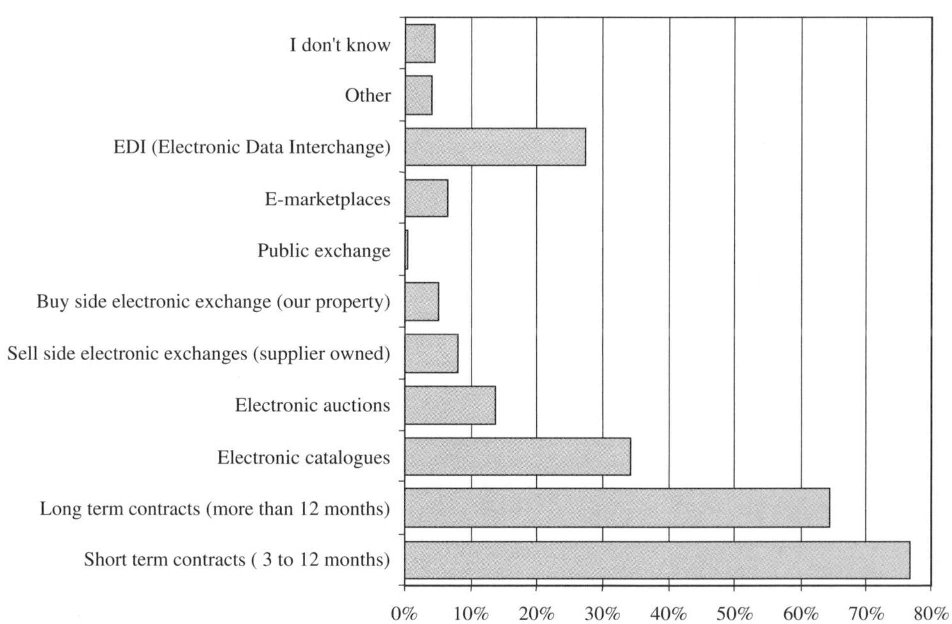

Fig. 2.16. Methods of interaction with suppliers.

can be done with the click of a mouse. The "brick and mortar" companies are being pressured to respond to these competitive threats. Many innovative companies have created strong online brand recognition, provide good customer service, and are open 24 h a day, 7 days a week, and 365 days a year. Some of them even give customers the option of customization and allow them to communicate with other customers through consumer communities. The quality of customer service allows customers to build a relationship with the company while providing important market information to the sellers. The physical stores can provide a better product-related service to their customers, but they cannot compete with the convenience and easy accessibility of purchasing online (Fig. 2.17).

In order for traditional companies to remain competitive in their industries, they have to learn on how to best utilize the internet for customer relationships (Chan and Pollard, 2003). Creating a website alone is not enough. The companies must ensure that they have the right value proposition and business model and that their online venture becomes a synergistic channel for them to promote their products to a wider customer base and to build better services for the existing clients.

A very important result from our survey is the one concerned with how companies include the internet in a multichannel strategy (Fig. 2.18). Less than half of the Italian firms surveyed use only offline channels, so this means the majority of firms have adopted, at least partly, e-commerce solutions. Another important result is the one concerning the different channel strategies. Only a very few companies, in fact, have an internet-only policy. The integrated and the multi channel strategies are the most diffused, in line with an idea of e-commerce defined not as a mere channel-substitution

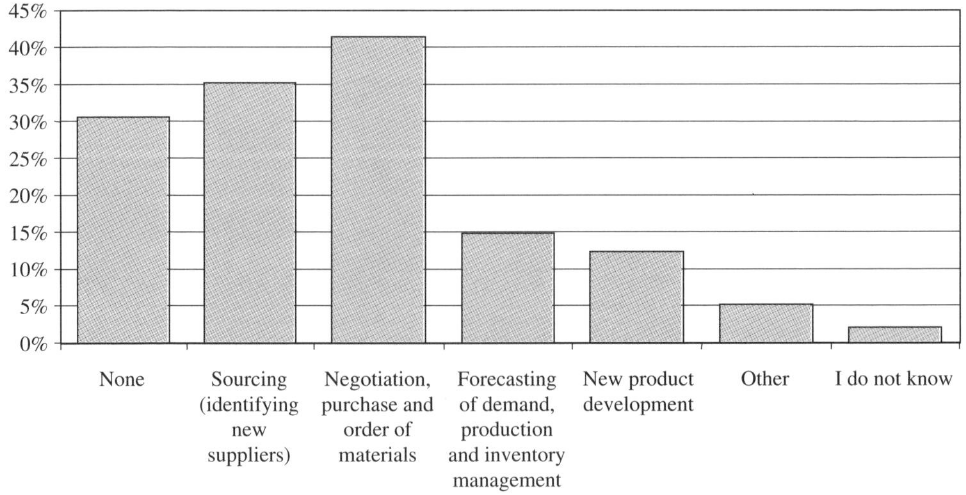

Fig. 2.17. Activities with suppliers that exploit Internet-based solutions.

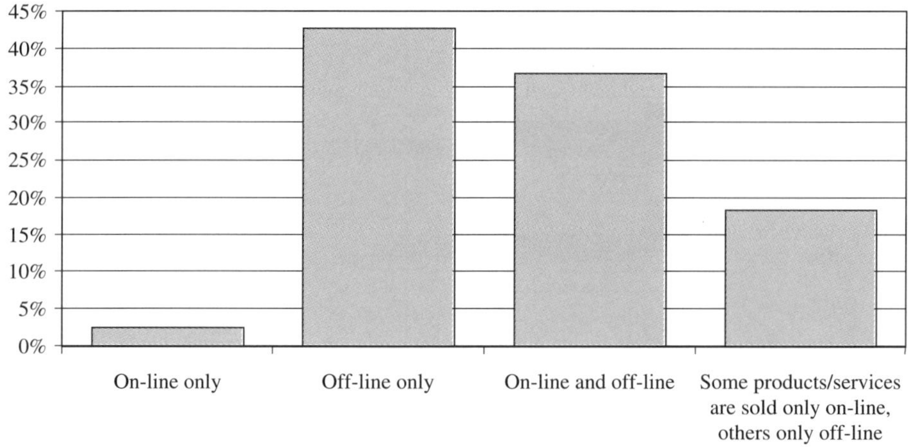

Fig. 2.18. Channel employed for B2C offering.

or disintermediation phenomenon, but rather as a strategy which firms can use to increase their service-level and value-centered relationships with customers. This is also confirmed by the data regarding the diffused automation of the customer service functions (Fig. 2.19).

E-commerce changes the nature of commercial offers (Fig. 2.20). In many cases, the prices can not only be dynamic (personalized), but also lower than offline, also because the companies report cost-savings due to the online channel. Also, the vendor–client

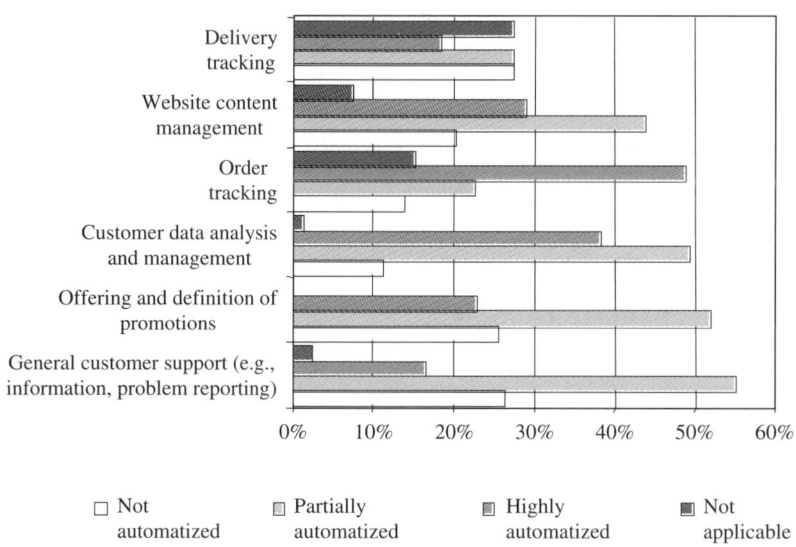

Fig. 2.19. Automatization of customer support activities.

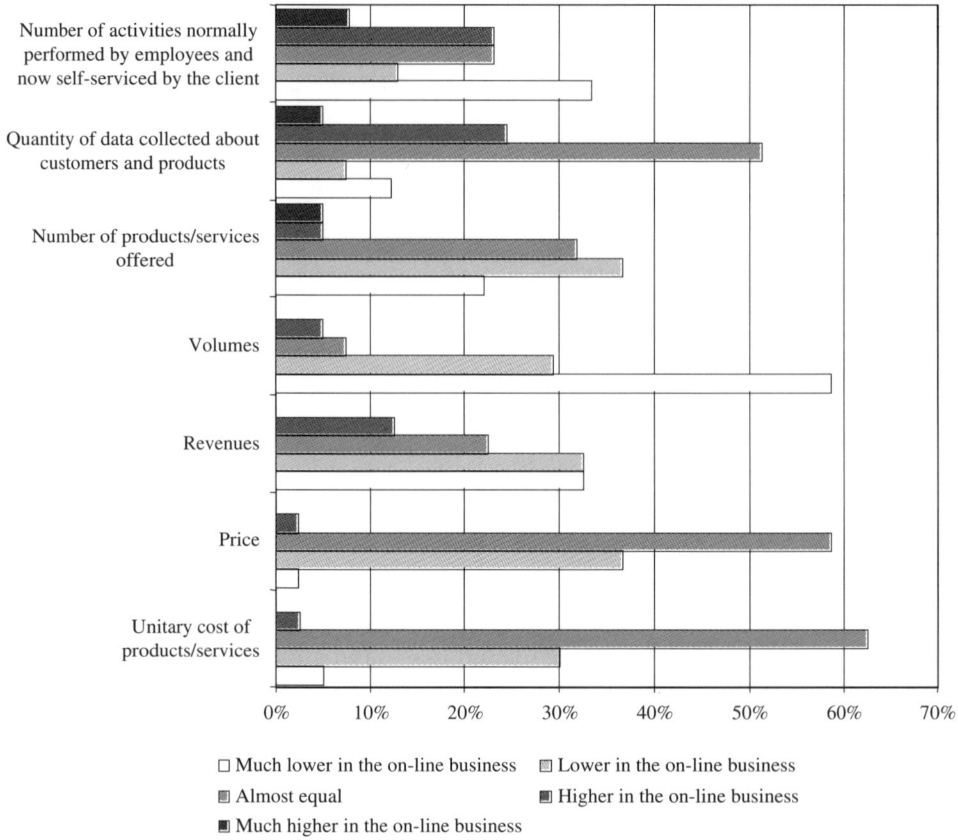

Fig. 2.20. Difference between online and offline offering (only for firms that have online offering).

relationship is innovative. Customers are required more often to become active in the selection and conFiguration of the products and services (self-service), while vendors can accumulate more knowledge on their clients, unit the one-to-one logistics of digital commercial channels.

2.10. Impact of ICT on Business Results

Our survey also investigated the perceived business benefits of ICT investments.

The importance of trying to link ICT investments and firm performance is clear, if we consider that companies tend to invest more on digital technology and when they are convinced they will have important economic returns on these investments. But this link is not so clear and not so easy to analyze. Tippins and Sohi (2003) write that there is not much empirical evidence in this area and that even "... [E]merging empirical evidence has shown that technology does not necessarily create a competitive advantage and there is no significant direct connection between IT and performance" (Tippins and Sohi, 2003, p. 747). But also that "... [T]he advantages of IT can be protected by embedding it in an organization through complementarity and co-specialization" (Tippins and Sohi, 2003, p. 747).

According to the resource-based view of management and the dynamic capabilities approach, the creation of intangible resources in the form of knowledge and relationships can make a difference in the competitive arena and create an advantage easier to protect from competitors.

This is why we analyzed both the tangible and intangible IT impact. We found (Fig. 2.21) that the majority of the managers surveyed believed their firms have achieved important results in the organizational and operational productivity areas, while they found it more difficult to recognize benefits in other domains (despite the dominant opinion they expressed that ICT has provided important competitive advantages (Fig. 2.22)). 60 to 70% of firms have reduced costs for internal communication and administration and also have increased efficiency in operations Fewer companies have increased commercial efficiency (transactions costs with suppliers, research of new customers and suppliers, cross-selling capabilities, customer support), and their ability to develop new, successful, and timely products (Fig. 2.21).

An important result is concerned with the impact of ICT on the learning capabilities of the firms. The ability to obtain information about markets and customers helps to ensure that firms are more attuned to changes in the environment, and it can result

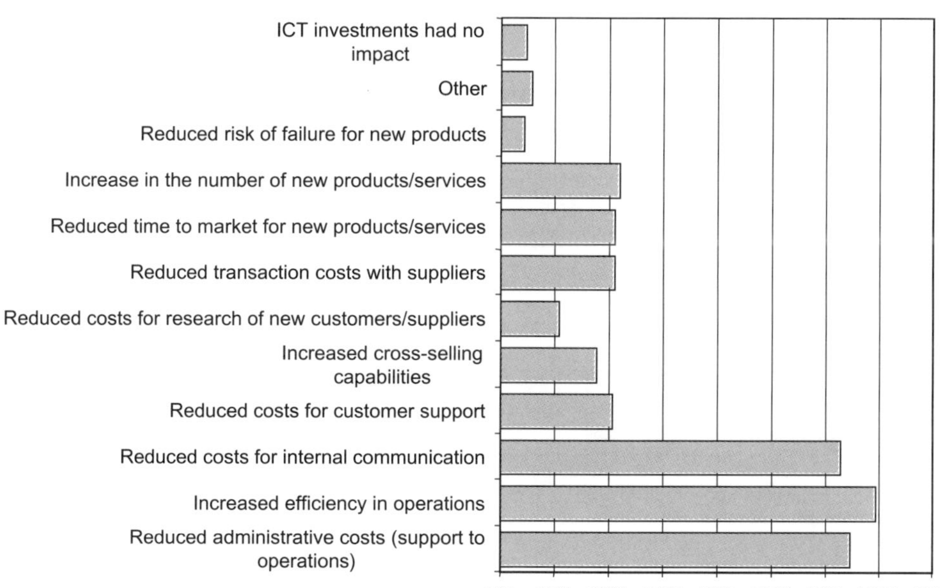

Fig. 2.21. Benefits derived from ICT introduction.

in a competitive advantage on slower, ill-informed competitors (Tippins and Sohi, 2003).

The majority of respondents in our survey recognized that ICT has positively influenced the strategic resource in different market-related areas, about half of the companies have increased knowledge about customer purchasing behaviour, customer expectations, and customer satisfaction. But less than 30% have increased their knowledge about consumers' lifestyle and competitors' offers (Fig. 2.23).

These results can be explained by considering that, digital technology makes easier and cheaper the access to the structured knowledge, that is, the type of knowledge related to customer relationships (expectations, behaviour, and satisfaction), while the

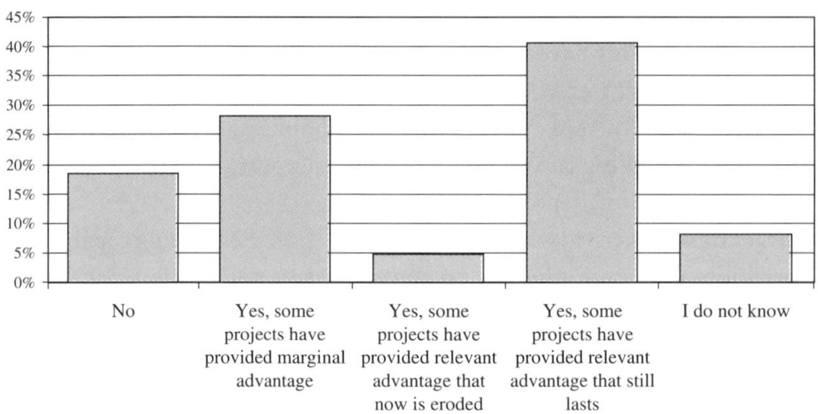

Fig. 2.22. Do you think ICT investments provided your firms with advantages towards competitors?

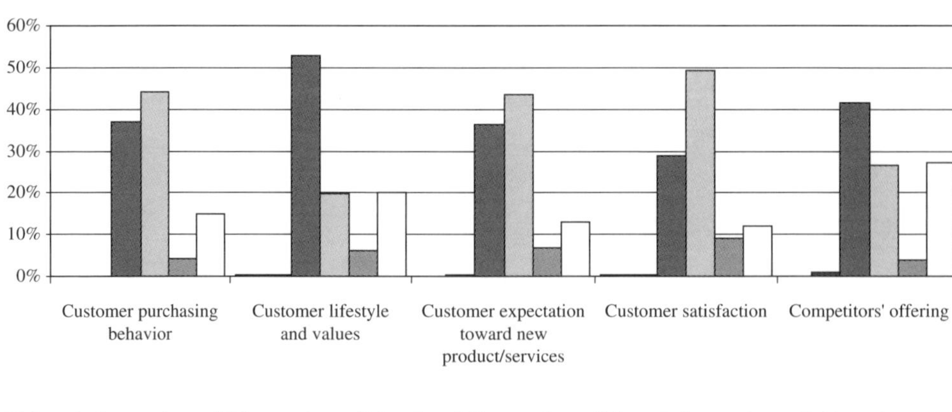

Fig. 2.23. How have ICTs modified your knowledge? (Trend 2000–2004).

impact on the access and creation of more complex knowledge is not very soon. It is to say that for the creation of complex resources, we need complex capabilities.

2.11. Conclusions

We have analyzed the results of the 2004 BIT survey in Italy. Focusing in particular on two areas of knowledge:

(1) the processes of ICT adoption and ICT governance and
(2) the relationship between firms' intangible resources and ICT processes and effects, at the organizational and business level.

Here we synthesize our results and point out their managerial implications. It can be useful to refer to our starting which is what we had concluded in our previous 2003 report, since it is interesting to compare the present situation to the one which existed two years ago:

The available data highlight three phenomena whose particular relevance is due to their strategic impact:

(1) the importance of cultural, social and organisational variables, not only as a pre-condition for the success of e-business projects, but also as a complementary "effect" of the projects themselves. This means that the existing intangible capital in the firms makes a competitive difference in the e-business scenario;
(2) the "lateness" of the Italian companies in the digitalization of company core processes (logistics, purchasing, collaborative product development), which can create a country-level digital competitiveness gap;
(3) the substantial difference in the rate of digitalization of company core processes between firms of different sizes. This can create "digital competitive divide" within the country (Demattè *et al.*, forthcoming).

In the second study, we found that, at this stage and for the type of firms considered (the larger firms), there is not any digital divide between southern and northern Italy in the spending for IT, despite the economic diversity of the two areas at the same time, there is not any divide between Italian and foreign companies operating in Italy. Since foreign groups doing business in Italy do not show higher spending rates for IT, the real divide, consistent with what we found in the previous BIT study, is related to the different IT investment efforts in companies of different size.

The nature of the industry helps explain the different IT adoption processes; the level of spending is significantly higher in the information intensive businesses of the service industries (financial services, consulting, and telecommunications).

Corporate intranets and corporate websites represent the most diffused applications, while fewer companies have explored e-procurement, e-commerce, and other innovative frontiers in collaborative supply chains, in line with what we found in the first study. The Italian companies have started to digitize internal processes more than external relationships and communication processes more than commercial activities (Demattè *et al.*, forthcoming). This phenomenon is particularly interesting if we consider the average size of our sample companies. The most innovative systems, RFID, and e-learning platforms still have a very limited diffusion, and confirming that the Italian companies tend to be late in the innovation cycle.

It is also worth mentioning that the size of the company and the nature of the industry (more or less information-intensive), influence the type of activities performed online, and therefore, the sophistication of the digital communication forms. Also the organizational complexity and richness of the firm are important; our correlation analysis, in fact, showed that ICT adoption and ICT adoption trend are higher in companies distributed geographically (number of organizational units in Italy), also in companies with a higher degree of organizational capital, market-based social capital, and innovation orientation.

In the majority of firms, the usage of new communication and information instruments by the employees has increased, the ICT function has become more integrated in the production processes, and there are more instruments to support employees in their decisions. New communication technologies have also started to change the way firms and people work in the direction of what we call "digital enterprise", an enterprise connected and coordinated through digital communication (firms are now more geographically dispersed in many of them, videoconferencing has substituted business travels, and they use internet-based systems to coordinate employees).

Despite these changes, the organizational impact of ICT investments is varied. Considering the perceived effect of ICT, the organizational structure seems to have become flatter and employees are believed to have increased their power (components of what we call new organizational capital or new organizational capabilities) only in a minority of firms.

A valied explanation of how the ICT processes effect the organization can be derived by the analysis of the influence of organizational and social capital in the ICT processes, and how the combination of these different resources with ICT can dynamically produce new capabilities and business advantages, beyond the organization change called "digital enterprise". ICT adoption is in fact also correlated to significant changes in the organization structure and capabilities.

The majority of the managers surveyed believed that, their firms have achieved important results in the organizational and operational productivity areas, while it seems more problematic to recognize benefits in terms of commercial efficiency, positive impact on successful new product development, and new strategic learning.

Looking, at the results of our study, also considering what we found two years ago, we can say that, in general, the direction of ICT innovation in Italy is not much changed, even though the digital investments of firms seem to be increased (we cannot do a direct comparison because the two samples in the studies are different). There is still a divide related to the size of the firms and there is the tendency to invest more on internal communication and information processing than on the digitization of the external relationships and supply-chain collaboration. This is particularly significant, we have surveyed some of the largest companies in the country, we know that, this situation can draw a negative light on the Italian potential to explore the new frontiers of innovation and global competition. No country or company can afford to consider itself, protected and isolated in its local markets and capabilities.

Italian firms should learn how to explore the new frontiers of digital innovation with the awareness that ICT is not just a technology for doing the same things as before in a more convenient and efficient way. ICT can become a strategic variable in firms, if it combines with new capabilities, new organization, and new pictures of the world.

Bibliography

1. Adler, PS and SK Kwon (2002). Social capital: prospects for a new concept. *Academy of Management Review*, 27, 17–40.
2. Amit, R and P Shoemaker (1993). Strategic assets and organizational rent. *Strategic Management Journal*, 14, 33–46.
3. Apte, UM and US Karmarkar (eds.) (forthcoming). *Managing in the Information Economy: Current Research* Issues. New York: Springer Verlag (Kluwer Academic Publishing).
4. Barua, A, P Konana, AB Whinston and F Yin (2004). An empirical investigation of net-enabled business value. *MIS Quarterly*, 28, 585–620.
5. Bensaou, M and N Venkatraman (1995). ConFigurations of interorganizational relationships: a comparison between U.S. and Japanese automakers. *Management Science*, 41(9), 1471–1492.
6. Black, SE and LM Lynch (1996). Human capital investments and productivity. *American Economic Review*, 86, 263–267.
7. Black, SE and LM Lynch (2001). How to compete: the impact of workplace practices and information technology on productivity. *Review of Economics and Statistics*, 83, 434–445.
8. Bourdieu, P (1986). The forms of capital. In *Handbook of Theory and Research for the Sociology of Education*, JG Richards (ed.), pp. 241–258. New York: Greenwood Press.
9. Bresnahan TF, E Brynjolfsson and LM Hitt (2002). Information technology, workplace organization, and the demand for skilled labor: firm-level evidence. *Quarterly Journal of Economics*, 117, 339–376.
10. Brynjolfsson, E and LM Hitt (2000). Beyond computation: information technology, organizational transformation and business performance. *Journal of Economic Perspectives*, 14(4), 23–48.

11. Brynjolfsson E, LM Hitt and S Yang (2002). Intangible assets: computers and organizational capital. In *Brookings Papers on Economic Activity Macroeconomics*, 1, 137–199.
12. Chan, PS and D Pollard (2003). Succeeding in the dotcom economy: challenges for brick & mortar companies. *International Journal of Management*, 20(1), 11.
13. Cohen, MD and LS Sprull (eds.) (1996). *Organizational Learning*. Sage.
14. Demattè, C, A Mandelli, A Biffi and C Parolini (forthcoming). Networks and business in Italy (draft title). In *Managing in the Information Economy: Current Research Issues*, US Karmarkar and UM Apte (eds.). New York: Springer Verlag (Kluwer Academic Publishing).
15. Dyer, JH and H Singh (1998). The relational view: cooperative strategy and sources of interorganizational competitive advantage. *Academy of Management Review*, 23, 660–679.
16. Fiol, CM. (1991). Managing culture as a competitive resource: an identity-based view of sustainable competitive advantage. *Journal of Management*, 17, 191–211.
17. Fiol, CM and LM Lyles (1985). Organizational learning. *Academy of Management Review*, 10, 803–813.
18. Istat (2005). http://www.istat.it.
19. Kamath, R and J Liker (1994). A second look at Japanese product development. *Harvard Business Review*, 72, 154–170.
20. Karmarkar (2004). Will you survive the services revolution? *Harvard Business Review*, 82(6), 100–107.
21. Makadok, R (2001). Toward a synthesis of the resource-based and dynamic-capability views of rent creation. *Strategic Management Journal*, 22, 387–402.
22. Mandelli, A (1998). *Internet Marketing*. Milan: McGraw Hill.
23. Mandelli, A (2003). Exploring the origins of new transaction costs in connected societies. In *Trust in Knowledge Management and Systems in Organizations*, ML Huotari and M Livonen (eds.), pp. 200–247. Idea Publishing Group.
24. Nishiguchi, T (1994). *Strategic Industrial Sourcing The Japanese Advantage*. New York: University Press, Inc.
25. Robey D and M Boudreau (2000). Organizational consequences of information technology: dealing with diversity in empirical research. In *Framing the Domains of IT Management: Projecting the Future Through the Past*, RW Zmud (ed.), pp. 51–63. Cincinnati, OH: Pinnaflex.
26. Straub, DW and RT Watson (2001). Research commentary: transformational issues in researching IS and net-enabled organizations. *Information System Research*, 12(4), 337–345.
27. Tippins, MJ and RS Sohi (2003). IT competency and performance: is organizational learning a missing link? *Strategic Management Journal*, 24, 745–761
28. Vestring, T, T Rouse and U Reinert (2005). Hedge your offshoring bets. *MIT Sloan Management Review*, Spring 2005, 46(3), 27–29.
29. Womack, JP, DT Jones and D Roos (1990). *The Machine that Changed the World*. New York: HarperCollins.

Appendix

For our correlation analysis, we had to build scales in order to reduce the number of variables considered. Here, we list the components of the scales.

In our study, the notion of organizational capital has been operationalized following the same dimensions proposed by the MIT studies (Brynjolfsson and Hitt, 2000; Brynjolfsson, Hitt and Yang, 2002; Bresnahan, Brynjolfsson and Hitt, 2002), and that are listed in the following questionnaire item.

Please tell us how do you agree on the following statements (with a 5 point scale, from completely disagree to completely agree):

Information sharing among the employees is common.
Often the employees are involved in multifunction/multidisciplinary work teams.
The management puts a relevant effort in the formulation and sharing of the corporate mission.
There is a clear and systematic communication of the strategic decisions to the employees that play a decisional role.
In thc last few years, the use of incentives linked to individual or group performance has increased.
The management participates actively to the selection and hiring of the employees.
The management considers employees' training important for firm's competition.

On the basis of the contributions from the literature, we consider social capital as a complex concept built around different types of relationships. In the survey, there are a few questions concerned with the quality of relationships between the firm and external actors.

We list the questions here:

Please tell us how do you agree with the following statements (with a 5 point scale, from completely disagree to completely agree):

The firm is well-known and has a good reputation in the industry.
The corporate brand is more well-known than the competitors'.
The product brand is more well-known than the competitors'.

According to the factor analysis results and the reliability of the scale, we consider two types of social capital, one based on customer and brand-based relationships, and a second one based on industry reputation (Reputational capital in Fombrun's 1996 words).

We needed also a scale which measured the degree of ICT adoption. We built a scale after controlling for the presence of the same factor in different components and testing for reliability, adding the answers to the following questionnaire questions:

Please give the appropriate answer for the following items:

Hardware and Software applications	Adopted	Planned adoption	Not adopted and not planned	DK
EAI (enterprise application integration)	[]	[]	[]	[]
Middleware (es. Microsoft ADO, IBM CICS)	[]	[]	[]	[]
SAN (storage area networks) NAS (network attached storage)	[]	[]	[]	[]
Wireless LAN	[]	[]	[]	[]
Operatine systems open source (es Linux)	[]	[]	[]	[]
Groupware e workgroup productivity software (es. Lotus Notes)	[]	[]	[]	[]
Enterprise resource planning (es. SAP R/3)	[]	[]	[]	[]
Website with e-commerce capabilities	[]	[]	[]	[]
Website with supplier collaboration capabilities	[]	[]	[]	[]
Datawarehouse, datamart (es: SAS/IML®), data mining (es: SAS® Enteprise Miner)	[]	[]	[]	[]
Radio frequency identification (RFID)	[]	[]	[]	[]
Computer telephony integration	[]	[]	[]	[]
E-learning	[]	[]	[]	[]

The scale regarding ICT adoption trend is built adding the answers to the following questionnaire questions:

Please give the appropriate answer for the following items:

Investment area	Never invested	Strong decrease	Decrease	No change	Increase	Strong increase
Hardware per l'archiviazione dati	[]	[]	[]	[]	[]	[]
Hardware per la sicurezza informatica	[]	[]	[]	[]	[]	[]
Software: Sistemi operativi	[]	[]	[]	[]	[]	[]
Software per la sicurezza informatica	[]	[]	[]	[]	[]	[]
Contratti di ASP e hosting	[]	[]	[]	[]	[]	[]
Outsourcing di singoli servizi IT (es.: gestione sistemistica, database administrator, ecc.)	[]	[]	[]	[]	[]	[]
Intranet e Extranet	[]	[]	[]	[]	[]	[]
Strumenti hardware/software per connettività wireless	[]	[]	[]	[]	[]	[]
Formazione agli utilizzatori ICT su contenuti informatici	[]	[]	[]	[]	[]	[]
Consulenza esterna su hardware e software	[]	[]	[]	[]	[]	[]
Sistemi di Business Continuity* e piani di Disaster Recovery*	[]	[]	[]	[]	[]	[]

Then, we built a scale for the concept digital enterprise, constructed by adding the answers to the following questions:

Please tell us how you agree with the following statements (5 item scale from completely disagree to completely agree), considering the consequences of ICT adoption between 2000 and 2004:

The number of employees who use ICT has increased.
The use of videoconference in substitution of the business trips has increased.
The use of the internet-based tools (ex-net meeting) for the work coordination has increased.
The frequency of tech training has increased .
The ICT function is more integrated in the production processes.
The necessity of business intelligence has increased in the management activities.
The firm can measure more frequently the individual and group performances.
The availability of decision support tools for the employees has increased.

The new organizational capabilities is a scale built by adding the following answer items:

Please tell us how you agree with the following statements (5 item scale from completely disagree to completely agree), considering the consequences of ICT adoption between 2000 and 2004:

The area of the middle managers' responsibilities has increased.
The organizational structure has become flatter, with less hierarchical levels.
The number of tasks assigned to employees (non managers) has increased.
The decision power of the employees (non managers) has increased.

CHAPTER 3

THE INDIA BUSINESS AND INFORMATION TECHNOLOGIES (BIT) SURVEY

ATANU GHOSH, HARVINDER PAL MAHEY and SHILPA MADAN

Summary

The UCLA Business and Information Technologies (BIT) Survey is a baseline study aimed at understanding and tracking the impacts of technologies on business practices. This report presents the results of the first survey conducted in India in 2002–2003. The subject group of the survey consisted of organizations and suborganizations that make independent decisions with respect to the acquisition, implementation and use of new technologies. The survey was undertaken by information system managers or chief information officers of the various organizations or subdivisions. The survey comprises of a varied set of questions covering diverse business practices, technology adoption, transfer, outsourcing and its impact on the organizational structure.

The survey indicates that the Indian businesses are changing, requiring more effective solutions to deliver better value to the customers and maintain their position in a fiercely competitive scenario. Indian businesses during 2002–2003 were definitely at an inflection point in terms of deployment of information and communication technologies, ready for a quantum leap in few years to come.

A few of the key results of the survey were as follows:

- The number of employees facing the screen is increasing across all sectors and the need for retraining to keep abreast with the latest technologies is being felt increasingly.
- The span of control is increasing with the organizations becoming flatter. The demand for executive decision-making tools is increasing across all the sectors.
- ERP, website, e-commerce, groupware and security tools form the most commonly deployed technologies by the Indian businesses. Also, third party authentication and verification, wireless networks, content management and collaboration tools have been identified for near-term purchase.
- Security is becoming a major concern with all the organizations and the importance of disaster recovery and business continuity is being realized. Even with this trend, advanced techniques like biometry still have to gain a strong hold in the Indian business sector.
- Radio frequency identification is also not widely adopted yet there is no significant inclination to purchase it in the near future also.

- Outsourcing is limited to market research in nonIT and programming, network management, etc. within IT. Functions like payroll and finance and accounting are largely being performed in-house.
- Organization websites are largely being used as platforms to provide information, except for in the financial sector, where transaction processing services are also made available through the website.

3.1. Introduction

According to World Information Technology and Services Alliance (WITSA) biennial study, "Digital Planet: The Global Information Economy," ICT spending is expected to grow faster than the global economy at approximately 8 per cent a year from 2003 through 2007. The data projects Asia to be a powerhouse of global growth in ICT spending by 2007. Asia will grow at a compound annual rate of 9.3 per cent from $568.2 billion in 2003 to $811.1 billion in 2007.

The domestic IT spending in India is at an inflexion point and there are numerous opportunities in the domestic sector, which can help catalyze growth in the next two to three years. India's technology spending has zoomed from $1.8 billion in 1993 to $7.1 billion in 2001 — at a compounded annual growth rate (CAGR) of 18.7 per cent. (Nasscom 2004) The spending on information technology includes a country's spending on hardware, software, software services and IT office equipment (like photocopiers and printers).

The key drivers for growth in the domestic market include[a]:

- Opportunities in verticals such as energy, BFSI, manufacturing, education, telecom and government.
- Increased penetration of computers in the household and SOHO segments.
- Increased investments in IT by the central and state governments in e-governance initiatives.
- Rapid adoption of broadband.
- Increased usage of nonPC devices, especially cell phones.
- Increased focus of small and medium-sized software companies on domestic market.

E-commerce activity during 2002 was estimated to be in the region of around US$ 300 million, almost half that of China. B2B e-commerce implementation was low, except in certain verticals such as the automobile sector and banking and finance.[b]

A recent survey by IDC on the Indian e-commerce transactions market showed that B2C e-commerce is expected to grow to Rs. 2 300 crore by the end of 2006 at a

[a] http://www.nasscom.org/download/indian_IT.pdt.
[b] http://www.nasscom.org/artdisplay.asp?cat_id=321.

CAGR of 79 per cent. These are the kind of changes happening in the Indian business with respect to deployment and usage of ICT.

The intent of the Business and Information Technologies (BIT) project is to study the impact of new information technologies on business and industry structure. The internet phenomenon was primarily a matter of a fundamental change in information logistics, with the protocols of the web superimposed on a deregulating and increasingly competitive telecommunications environment.

The BIT study documents the information technology driven changes that are occurring in business structure, business practice and sector structures across a wide spectrum of industry sectors in the United States and the rest of the world (Karmarkar and Mangal, 2004). The first step in the process is to do a baseline study that establishes the state of this universe. Subsequently, the study will be repeated at appropriate time intervals to track the changes that are actually occurring, so as to provide hard information on what is really happening across the economic landscape as a result of changes in information technologies. The study will encompass several sectors. The BIT project is being conducted at a global scale. At the time of writing, the project had nine partners in leading academic and research institutions around the world. The partners include SDA Bocconi (Italy), SOM-IITB (India), Theseus Institute (France), The World Internet Institute (Sweden), EIM (Germany), IESE (Spain), PUC (Chile), Korea University (Korea), and CEIBS (China).

This report summarizes the results from the first BIT survey conducted in India in 2002–2003. The hypotheses and the results are discussed in the following sections. The organizations in the sample have been broadly categorized into three verticals namely, financial, manufacturing, and service organizations. (For the sample profile, please refer Appendix B). While financial sector races ahead of the other two in deploying ICT, manufacturing and services both seem to be ready for the leap in the usage of ICT given the increasing pressure on margins and competition.

The methodology used has been described in Appendix A.

3.2. The Survey

The first phase of the study involved designing the instrument comprising of the trends/patterns to be studied, followed by pretesting and determining the relevance, reliability and validity of the questionnaire keeping in mind the present Indian business context. The major issues in the questionnaire are as discussed below.

3.2.1. *Technology adoption/infrastructure and budget trends*

Questions 1 & 2 — What technologies are organizations using currently or planning to use in the near future? What alternatives are being used for disaster recovery and continuity?

Question 3 — What technologies have organizations invested in (and not invested in) over the last three years?

3.2.2. *Internal organization*

Question 4 — How are organizations changing internally in terms of their workforce?

Question 5 — How are organizations changing internally in terms of their structure?

Question 6 — Are organizations outsourcing some of their business processes? Is business process outsourcing (BPO) more popular for certain functions in the organization such as accounting, marketing, IT, and finance? What is the outsourcing budget in organizations for IT and nonIT functions? How much of the total outsourced business is offshore?

3.2.3. *Customer facing interactions*

Question 7 — Are relationships with customers developed and maintained using multiple touch points? What are the most popular touch points?

Questions 8 & 12 — How is customer view integrated using certain technologies? What mechanisms are used by organizations to perform customer segmentation?

Questions 9 & 10 — Are promotion and advertising budgets shifting towards online channels? Which online advertising methods have been adopted by organizations? In going online, are organizations creating a new face in terms of branding concept, slogan, logo and name?

Question 11 — For which functions is customer relationship management (CRM) becoming automated?

Questions 13 — Is the number of organizations selling products and services online increasing? How is online business different from traditional business?

3.2.4. *Trading partner relationships*

Question 14 — What technologies are organizations using for communicating with their trading partners?

Question 15 — What IT-based channels and B2B mechanisms are organizations using for purchasing?

3.2.5. *Business results*

Questions 16 & 17 — What economic and operational business results are being impacted by technologies? What strategic areas are being impacted by information technologies?

3.2.6. *Globalization*

Questions 18 & *19* — Are organizations becoming more global? Is the geographic reach of organizations increasing?

3.3. Findings

The survey was sent to senior IT managers or chief information officers in the various organizations and subdivisions. About 75 responses from various industry sectors were received. The details of the sample have been discussed in Appendix B. The results obtained by analyzing these responses are as given below:

3.3.1. *Technology adoption/infrastructure and budget trends*

ERP, website, e-commerce, security tools, groupware form the most used technologies across all business sectors. However, there is a greater thrust on third party authentication and verification and surveillance systems by the financial institutions.

Wireless networks, collaboration tools, content management and e-learning are being considered for near-term purchase.

The spending on storage hardware, security software and hardware and infrastructure has increased across all the business sectors. The budgets for operating systems/networking, offshore outsourcing have not increased substantially.

3.3.2. *Internal organization: workforce trends*

The number of employees facing the screen has increased and is expected to rise further across all the three business sectors.

Teleconferencingteleconferencing is increasingly becoming most popular in financial services sector, but manufacturing and services are also ready to catch up. Automation is definitely taking its toll on the employee count, but only financial services and manufacturing organizations predominantly think that outsourcing is leading to a reduction in headcount.

There is an overwhelming agreement in all the sectors that need for IT skills in lower levels of the organization is going up. There is a consensus in the financial services sector that all workers need to retrain themselves to keep up with changing technology, services follows closely in sharing this thought.

3.3.3. *Internal organization: structure trends*

There is a clear trend that the organizational structure of Indian organizations is changing. The span of control under each manager is increasing and organizations are becoming flatter.

The organizations are becoming increasingly more conscious about monitoring of customer facing interactions and are also using automated monitoring of productivity.

Organizations across the sectors are becoming geographically dispersed and decision making and other tools are becoming available online.

3.3.4. *Internal organization: BPO*

The increasing trend of outsourcing the network management function across the sectors, payroll processing still being done house in approx. 60% of the organizations are studied.

Most of the organizations plan to outsource market research, in part or in whole; in the near future however, accounting, finance, order fulfilment, RFPs, bids and contract management are typically performed in-house and are indicated to remain so over the next few years.

3.3.5. *Customer touch points*

The use of several channels to be in touch with the customers is on a rise, with organizations across all sectors widely deploying face-to-face contact, regular mail, e-mail and phone. While financial services organizations have started providing phone text messaging and IVR, very few manufacturing or service organizations do so.

3.3.6. *Customer view integration and customer segmentation*

Customer profiling, trend identification and statistical data mining are the most popular tools for customer view integration.

Dynamic pricing and geographic segmentation form the most widely adopted customer segmentation strategies across the manufacturing and service sectors.

3.3.7. *Online advertising and selling*

Web banners, advertisements or links on other websites to drive traffic to the company website, advertisements or links on search engines to drive traffic to the company website are the most popular online advertising methods across all sectors.

Less than one-fifth of the organizations have changed their identities in terms of logo (17.6%) or name (12.2%) when going online.

3.3.8. *CRM function automation*

Order tracking and fulfilment, order placement and help desk support from the CRM functions are automated most often, while sales calls and marketing are the least automated CRM functions.

3.3.9. *Traditional versus online selling*

The data collected and self-service tasks performed by customers are higher for online selling while sales volumes, cost of products and the number of products offered are higher for traditional selling.

3.3.10. *Trading partners relationships*

Web-enabled communication and e-procurement are the most widely used methods for communicating with the trading partners. E-payment and collaborative forecasting and planning are the technologies that many organizations wish to adopt in the near future.

3.3.11. *Purchasing mechanisms*

Direct purchasing, long-term purchasing, and catalogues are the most used B2B mechanisms used for purchasing. Exchanges/e-exchanges, buy-side exchanges/hubs, sell-side exchanges/hubs and aggregators are the least used purchasing mechanisms.

3.3.12. *Business results*

Production costs, commercial costs, internal communication costs, and service costs have decreased with technology adoption, while technology costs have increased.

The technology has also played a role in strategic areas including the understanding of customer satisfaction for current products and services, competitor knowledge, and customer buying behavior.

3.3.13. *Globalization*

Over half the organizations surveyed are increasing production/services bases in other countries, trade in other countries, and distributors/branches around the world. Over a third reported an increase in the number of countries in the supplier base.

Organizations are planning to increase base in USA, Central and Eastern Europe and Canada and Mexico. The most established bases include USA, South Asia, Western Europe, and Middle East.

3.4. Technology Adoption/Infrastructure and Budget Trends

Questions 1 & 2 — What technologies are organizations using currently or planning to use in the near future? What alternatives are being used for disaster recovery and business continuity?

90.6% of the organizations across all business sectors either have or plan to have websites and e-commerce tools within the time span of next three years (Fig. 3.1). 73% of the

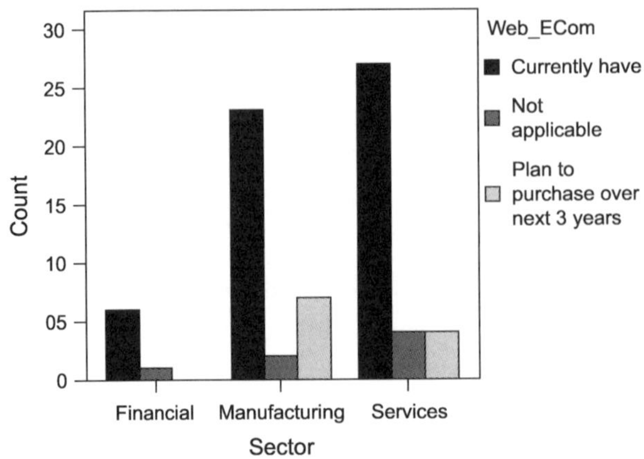

Fig. 3.1. Website and e-commerce adoption.

organizations already operate an ERP solution or are planning for one, 70.2% have/plan to have business intelligence tools, 78.3% have/plan to invest in collaboration tools in the near future, 66.2% either have an enterprise wide instant messaging system or are planning to have one.

Biometry has largely been adopted by the financial sector (57.1%) vis-à-vis manufacturing (12.5%) or services (8.6%). The same holds good for third party authentication and verification with 85.7% of the financial sector organizations being certified vis-à-vis manufacturing (12.5%) and services (14.3%) (Fig. 3.2). On the other hand, ERP dominates in the manufacturing sector (85.7%) as compared to financial sector (57.1%) or services (51.4%) (Fig. 3.3).

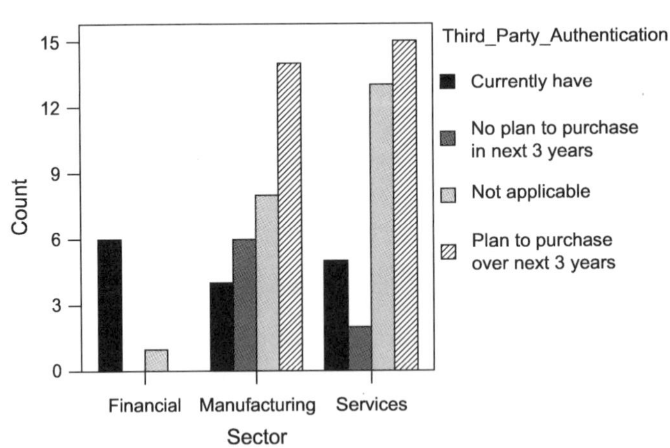

Fig. 3.2. Third party authentication and verification adoption.

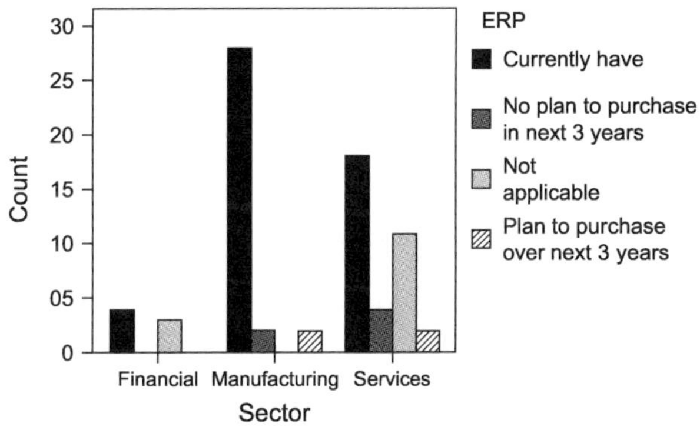

Fig. 3.3. ERP adoption.

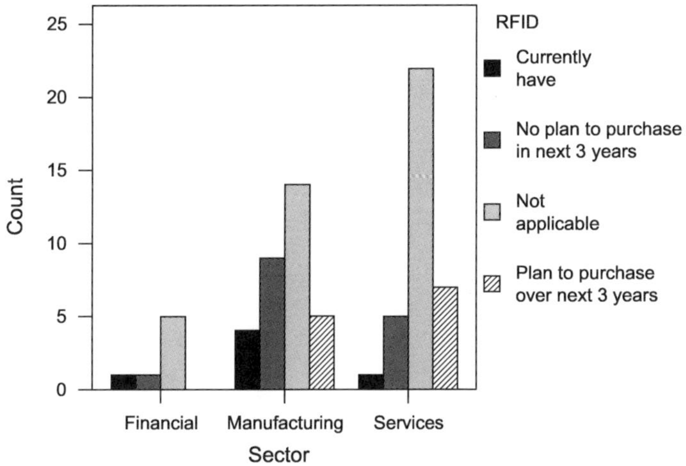

Fig. 3.4. RFID adoption.

Among these technologies, third party authentication and verification (39.2%) and enterprise application integration (33.8%) are the two most popular technologies on company budgets and slated for adoption in the next three years, followed by storage area networks (32.4%) and business process mapping (31.1%) (Figs. 3.1 and 3.2).

The technologies that fewer organizations plan to purchase in the next three years include ERP (5.4% have/plan to have, while 8.1% of the organizations do not plan to have) and biometry (10.8% have/plan to have, while 21.6% do not plan to have) (Figs. 3.3 and 3.4).

Radio frequency identification (RFID) is currently adopted only by a very small percentage of organizations (8.1%). However, 23% of the organizations plan to purchase the technology in the next three years (Fig. 3.4). Also, Linux is currently being

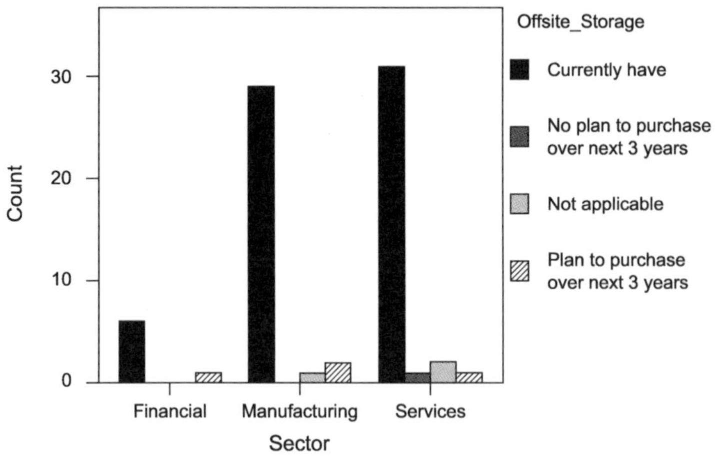

Fig. 3.5. Offsite storage adoption.

used by 39.2% of the organizations with almost 23.0% planning to buy in the next three years.

An overwhelming 89.2% of the organizations use offsite data storage for disaster recovery and business continuity, followed by mirroring (33.8%). About a quarter of the organizations surveyed planned to acquire cold sites (23.0%) and mirroring (23.0%) in the near-term future (Fig. 3.5).

Question 3 — What technologies have organizations invested in (and not invested in) over the last three years?

An overwhelming 70% of all the organizations surveyed indicated an increase in security expenditure since last year. Enhancing hardware security is a priority with almost 66% of the organizations (Fig. 3.6); however, improving application security is more important

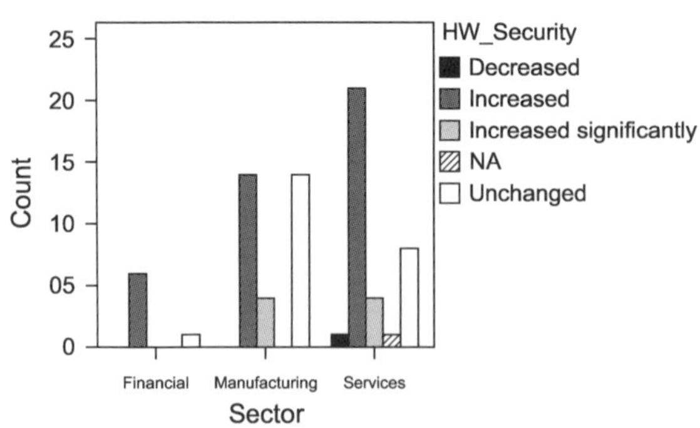

Fig. 3.6. Hardware security budget trends.

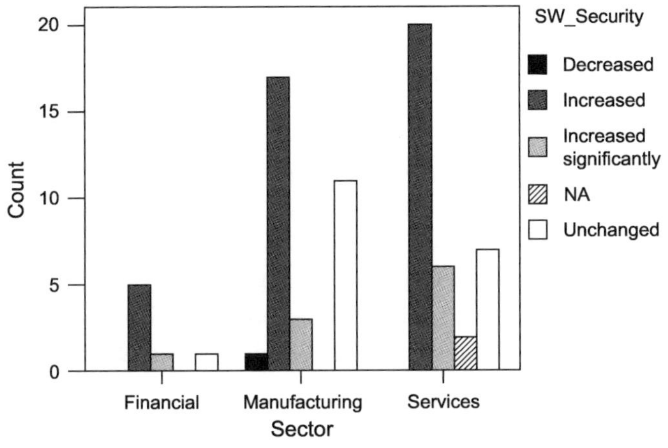

Fig. 3.7. Software security budget trends.

at 81%. Here also, we see a greater emphasis on security issues by the financial service providers (87.5%) vis-á-vis manufacturing (57%) and services (67%) (Fig. 3.7).

Disaster recovery and business continuity planning have become a part of the board room agenda at least for the financial services sector with over 88% of the respondents indicating an increase in expenditure in the next three years. Offshore outsourcing still does not seem to be a lucrative option for Indian companies with only about 19% indicating an increase in their outsourcing expenditure. Although only 12.5% of the corporates in the financial services claim to have considerably increased expenditure on outsourcing, around 19% of the organization in the manufacturing sector claim increased expenditure in the last year (Fig. 3.8).

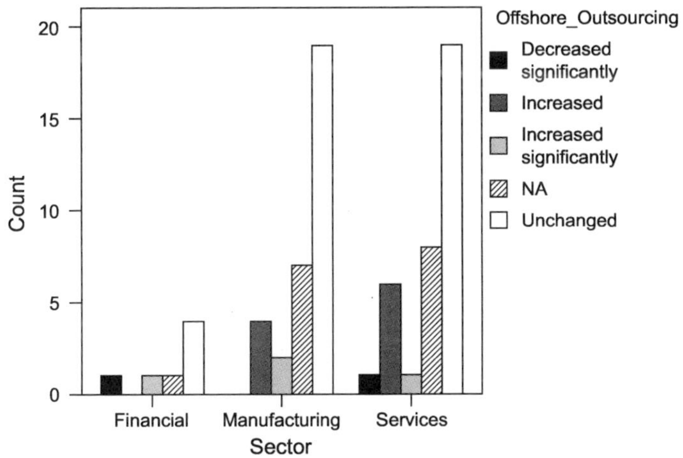

Fig. 3.8. Offshore outsourcing budget trends.

3.5. Internal Organization

Question 4 — How are organizations changing internally in terms of their workforce and the workplace?

The number of employees facing the screen is increasing not only in the proverbial financial (62.5%) and services (85.3%) sector, but also manufacturing (93.9%) (Fig. 3.9). As the organizations get geographically dispersed, the need for measures like teleconferencingteleconferencing and telecommuting is on the rise (Fig. 3.10).

The use of collaboration tools between the employees like netmeeting is also increasing. The demand for decision support tools for the executives is increasing. While there

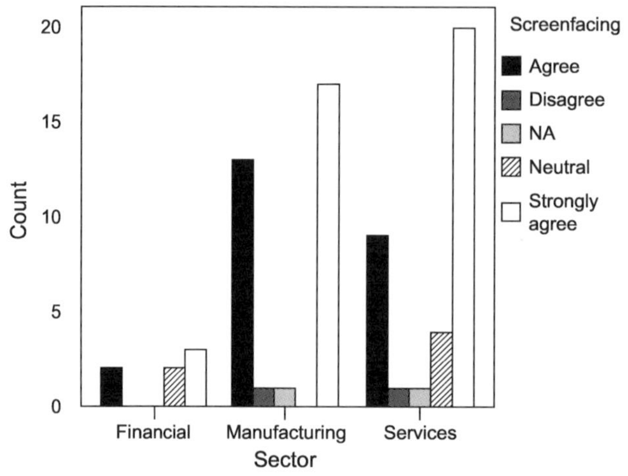

Fig. 3.9. Proportion of employees facing a screen.

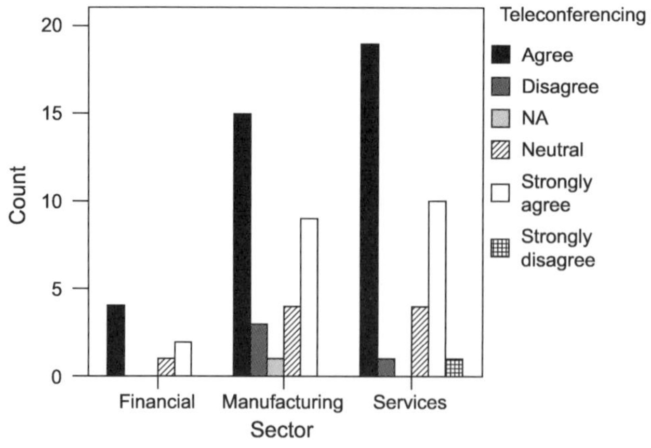

Fig. 3.10. The use of teleconferencing.

is a general consensus that automation is leading to workforce reduction, 62.5% of the financial organizations feel that outsourcing is leading to workforce reduction, vis-á-vis manufacturing (51.2%) and services (44.1%) (Fig. 3.11). This however, has not led to a reduction in the number of middle managers with only 12.5% of the organizations in the financial sector, 33.3% in manufacturing and 26.5% agreeing to this phenomenon.

An overwhelming 90% of the organizations surveyed agree that the need for IT skills at lower levels is going up and that retraining is essential to keep in pace with the changing trends (Fig. 3.12).

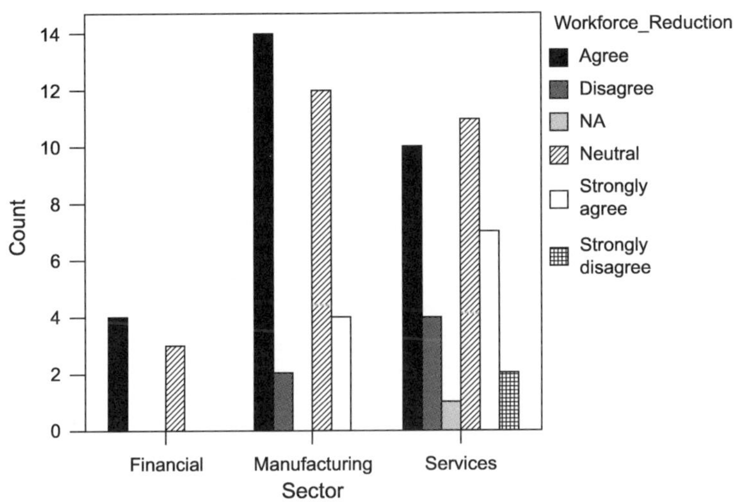

Fig. 3.11. Trends in workforce reduction.

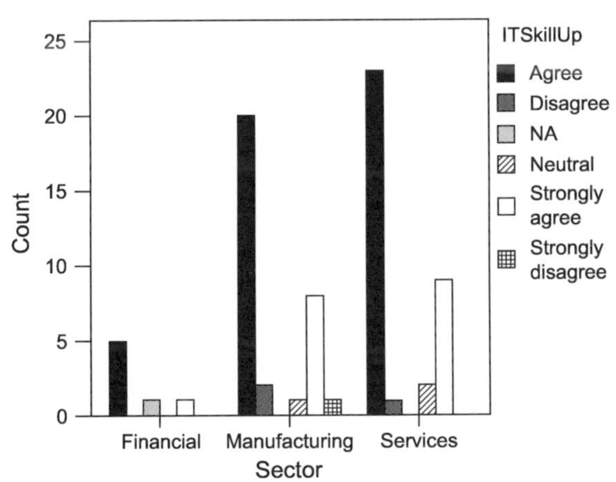

Fig. 3.12. The need for IT skills at lower levels.

Question 5 — How are organizations changing internally in terms of their structure?

While 56% of all the organizations surveyed support that organizations are becoming flatter, only 25% from the financial services agree to this, while the proportion for manufacturing (72.7%) and services (88.2%) is much higher (Fig. 3.13). The span of control for the managers is on the rise with 61.4% of the organizations agreeing to this.

Geographically dispersed organizations are becoming common across all the three sectors (financial services — 87.5%, manufacturing — 75.7% and services — 67.7%) (Fig. 3.14).

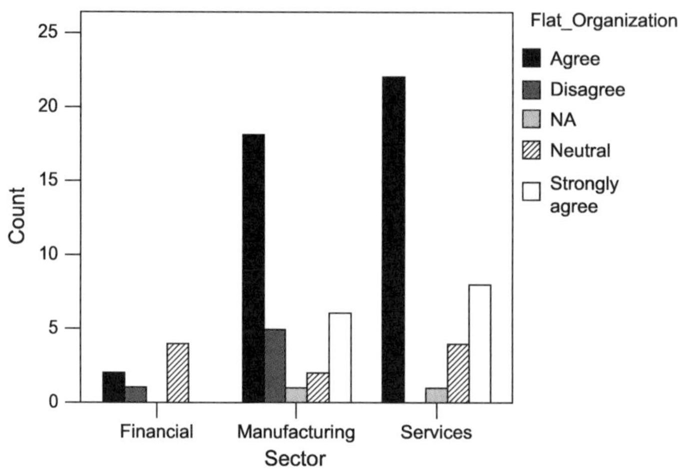

Fig. 3.13. Organization structure trends.

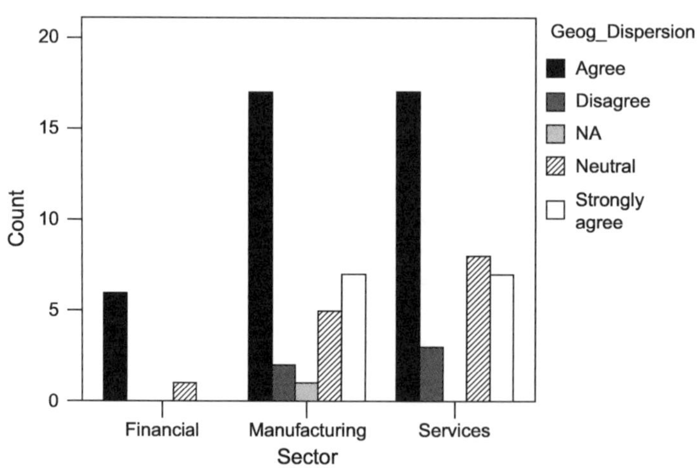

Fig. 3.14. Geographical dispersion trends.

The monitoring of customer facing interactions is on the rise across all the three sectors (77.0%), while automated monitoring of productivity is most common in the services sector (Fig. 3.15). Over half the organizations surveyed agree (70.3%) that incentives are based on productivity.

Another significant trend observed across the board is the availability of new decision-making tools and technologies being made available online as reported by 84% of the organizations (Fig. 3.16).

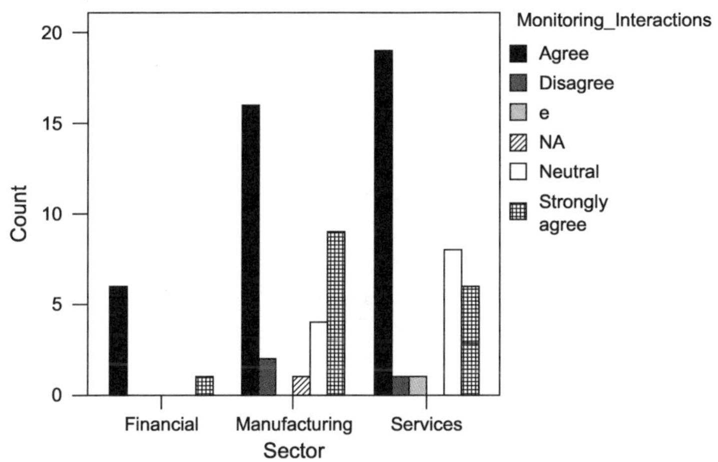

Fig. 3.15. Trends in monitoring customer facing interactions.

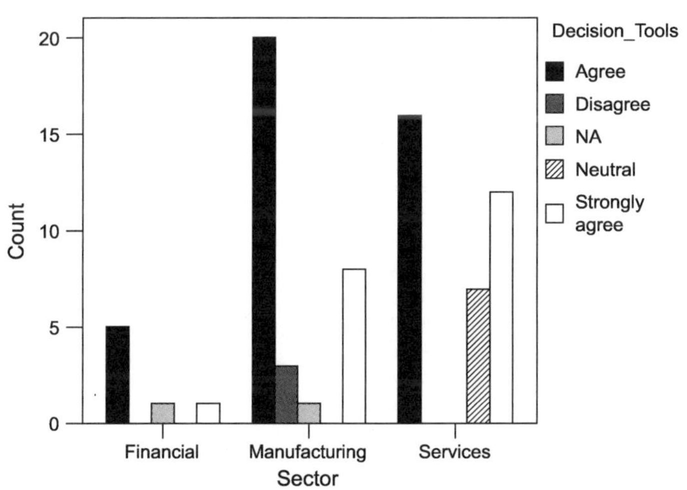

Fig. 3.16. Trends in the availability of decision-making tools.

Question 6 — Are organizations outsourcing some of their business processes? Is BPO more popular for certain functions in the organization such as accounting, marketing, IT, and finance?

Mundane activities like payroll processing are still being done in-house in almost 58% of the organizations across all sectors. However, 10% of the manufacturing organizations and 15% of the service organizations are looking forward to outsourcing this in the near future (Fig. 3.17). Accounting and finance do not form a part of the portfolio of the activities being outsourced with 77 and 68% of the organizations surveyed performing it in-house and not planning to outsource over a three year horizon (Fig. 3.18).

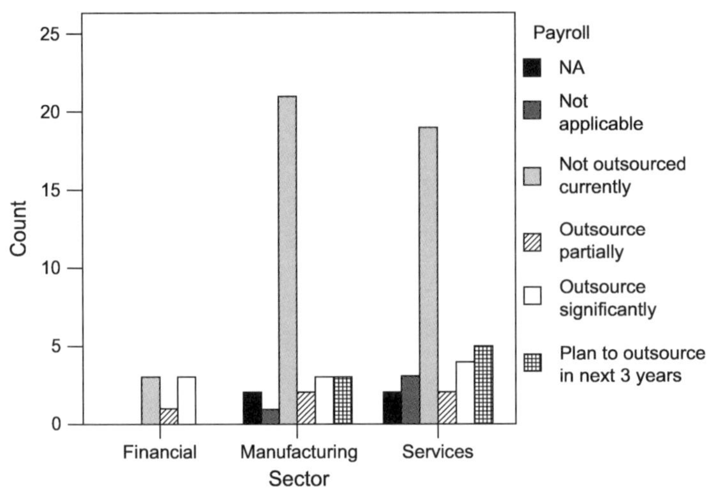

Fig. 3.17. Payroll outsourcing trends.

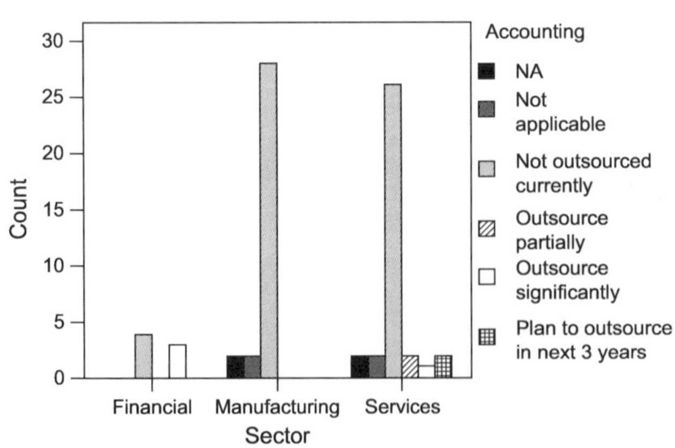

Fig. 3.18. Accounting outsourcing trends.

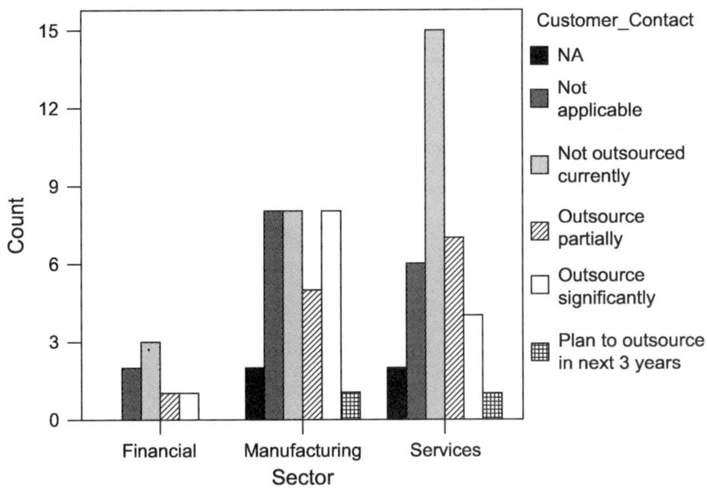

Fig. 3.19. Trends in customer contact outsourcing.

While 88% of the financial sector organizations outsource programming jobs, only 59% of the manufacturing and 35% of the service sector do so. The results indicate that over 60% of the organizations in the service sector do not outsource network operations and have no plans of doing so in the near future. However, voice-based customer service/call center outsourcing is being utilized by 37.5% of the banks, 40% of the manufacturing enterprises, and 35% of the service organizations interviewed (Fig. 3.19).

3.6. Customer Facing Interactions

Question 7 — Are relationships with customers developed and maintained using multiple touch points? What are the most popular touch points?

Several touch points are being used by organizations across all sectors to keep in touch with their customers across all sectors, including face-to-face (93.3%), regular mail (84.0%), e-mail (94.7%), and phone (92.0%) (Fig. 3.20). The financial sector has pioneered in the use of phone text messaging (37.5%), interactive voice response (50.0%) and computer telephony integration (37.5%) to serve its customers, and the penetration is increasing (Fig. 3.21).

A significant number of organizations (85.3%) across all the sectors use their websites as a tool to provide information to the customer, while the organizations in the financial sectors have also started providing transactional services through their websites (Fig. 3.22). Screen pops (9.3%) are the least used methods of keeping in touch with the customer.

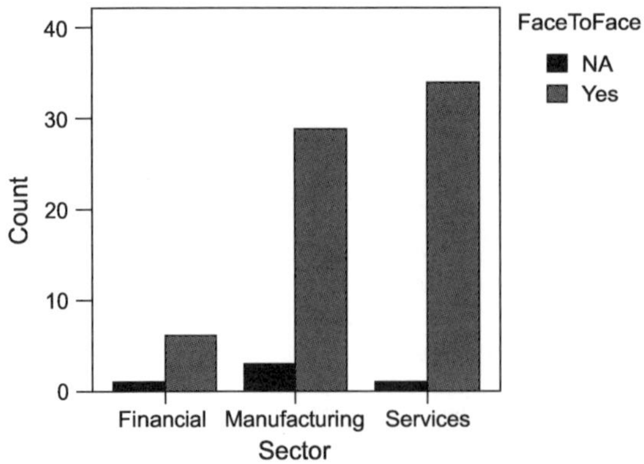

Fig. 3.20. Usage of face-to-face contact.

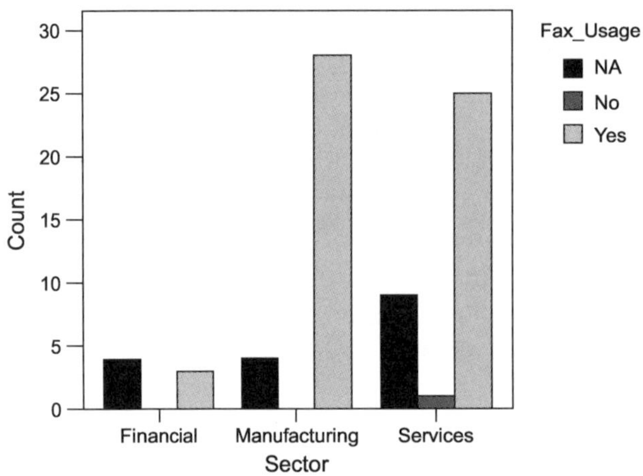

Fig. 3.21. Usage of fax for customer contact.

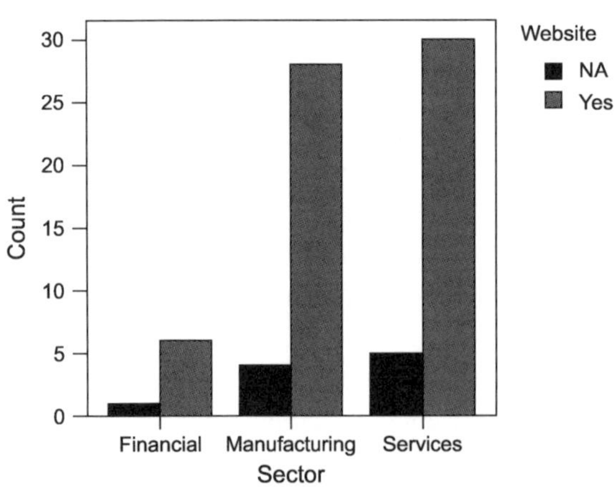

Fig. 3.22. The use of websites for customer contact.

Questions 8 & 12 — How is customer view integrated using certain technologies? What mechanisms are used by organizations to perform customer segmentation?

Across sectors, customer data analysis is more heavily used by financial and services sectors including customer profiling (75.0% and 73.5%, respectively, vis-à-vis 45.5% in manufacturing), data mining using statistics (37.5 and 47.1% vis-à-vis 27.3% in manufacturing) (Figs. 3.23 and 3.24).

The techniques like neural networks for customer segmentation are yet to make their presence felt with only 2.7% of the organizations using it. Fraud detection is a priority with financial sector at 37.5%, while about 18% of the manufacturing and service organizations use the same (Fig. 3.25).

Demand forecasting is largely used by the manufacturing sector (57.6%), while the count for financial sector and services sector stands at 12.5 and 38.2%, respectively.

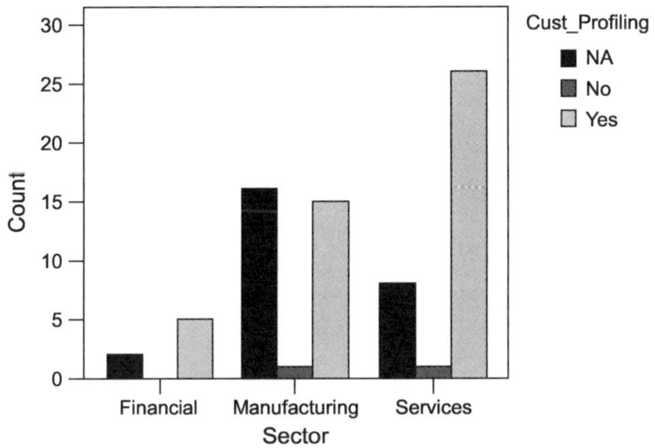

Fig. 3.23. Trends in customer profiling.

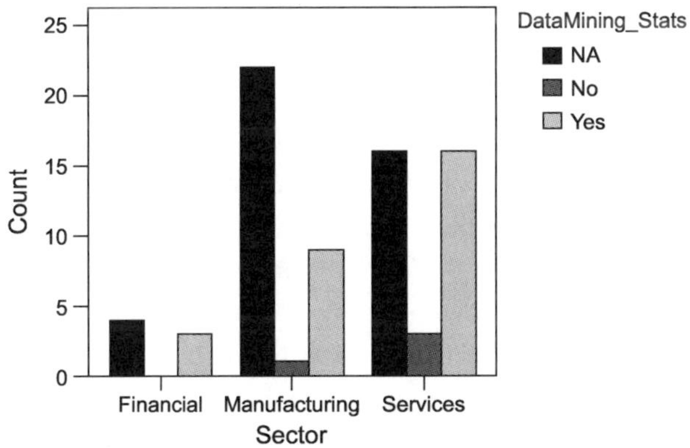

Fig. 3.24. Trends in data mining: statistics.

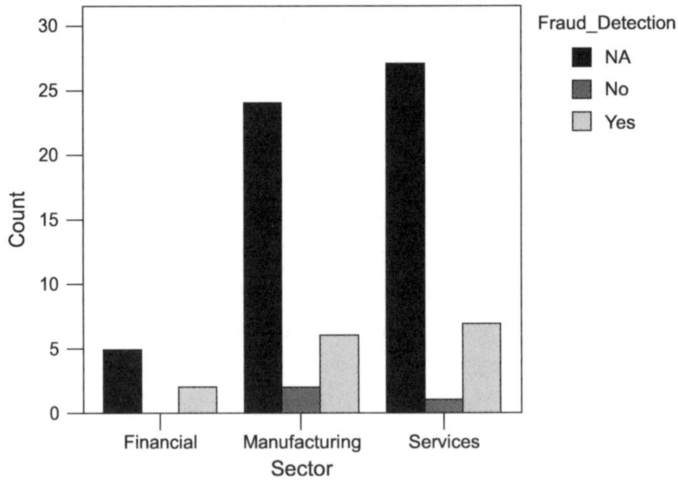

Fig. 3.25. Trends in fraud detection.

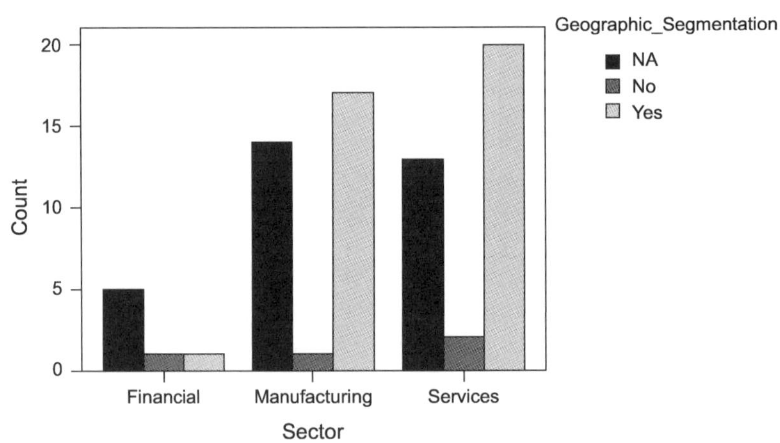

Fig. 3.26. Trends in geographic segmentation.

While automated crossselling is the most widely used mechanism in the financial sector (42.9%), dynamic pricing and geographic segmentation are popular in the services and manufacturing sectors at 45.7, 43.8, 57.1%, and 53.1%, respectively (Fig. 3.26).

Overall, the least used methods for customer segmentation include automated crossselling (10.8%) and by access to online technology (14.9%).

Questions 9 & 10 — Are promotion and advertising budgets shifting towards online channels? Which online advertising methods have been adopted by organizations? In

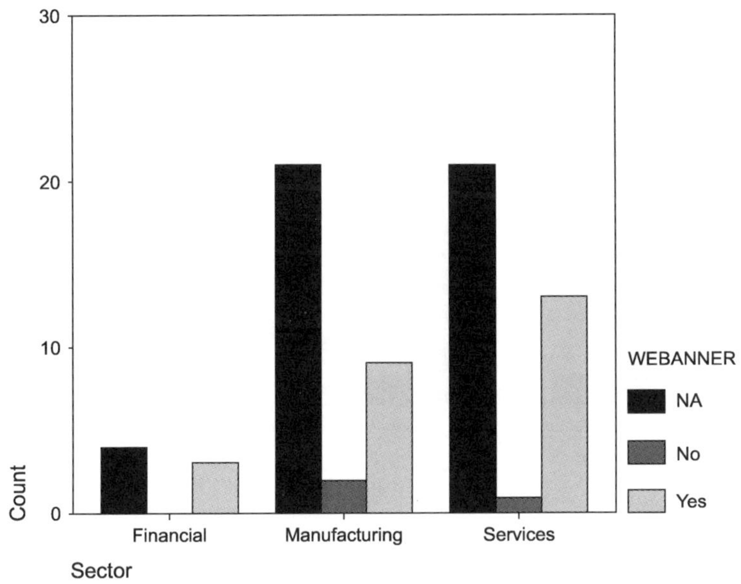

Fig. 3.27. Trends in the use of web banners.

going online, are organizations creating a new face in terms of branding concept, slogan, logo and name?

Certain technologies for online advertising like web seminar, pop up windows, e-zines are being used almost exclusively by the services sector. Web banners are used most heavily by the financial sector (50.0%) compared to manufacturing (27.3%) and services (35.3%), respectively (Figs. 3.27 and 3.28).

50% of the organizations surveyed in the financial and services sector use advertisements or links on other sites to drive traffic to their site, while only 18.2% of the manufacturing organizations surveyed, do so. Around 24.0% of the organizations in the manufacturing sector use incentives in printed material to drive customers to their website, as compared to finance (12.5%) and services (20.6%) (Fig. 3.29).

The survey instrument also contained a question on online advertising budgets. However, due to the few responses that were obtained for this question, data has not been reported here.

Among the organizations that currently have websites, only a few have changed their identity while going online in terms of logo, slogan, name or the branding concept. Among these, the branding concept (25.7%) and the slogan (23.0%) have been changed most often, while the name (12.2%) has been changed least.

Among the sectors, the manufacturing sector organizations have changed their slogan, branding concept and name most often (Fig. 3.30).

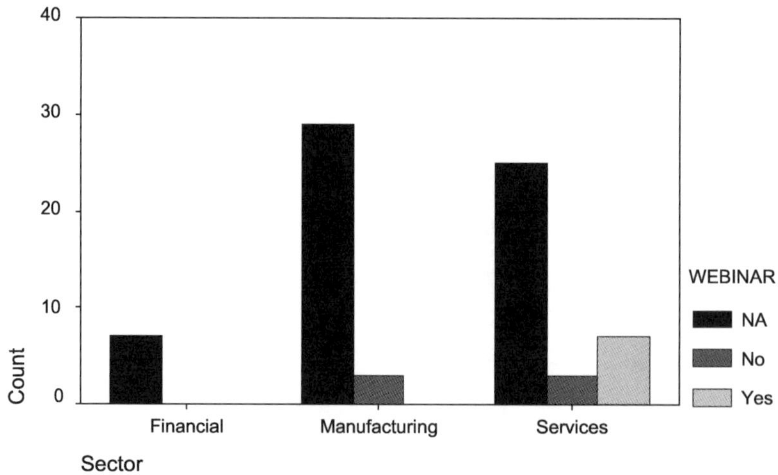

Fig. 3.28. Trends in the use of web seminars.

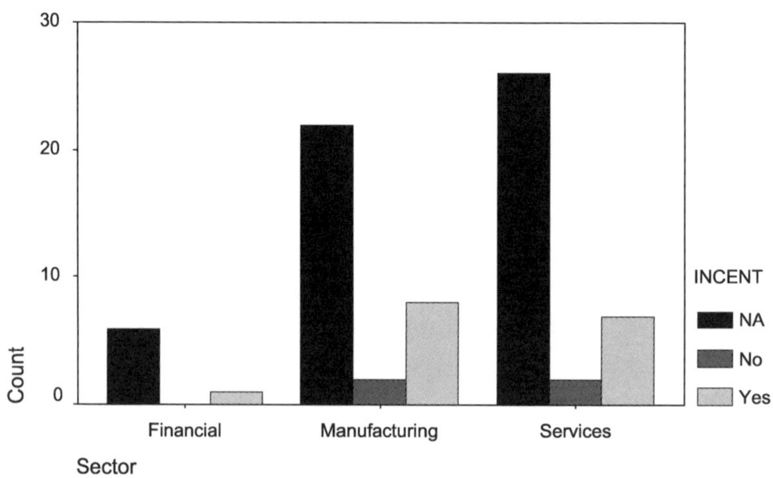

Fig. 3.29. The use of incentives to drive traffic to website.

Question 11 — For which functions is CRM becoming automated?

Order tracking and fulfilment is the most automated CRM function at 55.4% (Fig. 3.31). Other automated CRM functions include, customer complaint management (50%), help desk management (48.6%), integration with ERP and SCM (45.9%), content management (41.9%), and order placement (48.7%). CRM functions that have been automated the least include sales calls automation (28.4%).

57.0% of the financial and service sector organizations have automated (fully/partially) their help desk functions as compared to manufacturing (37.6%) (Fig. 3.32).

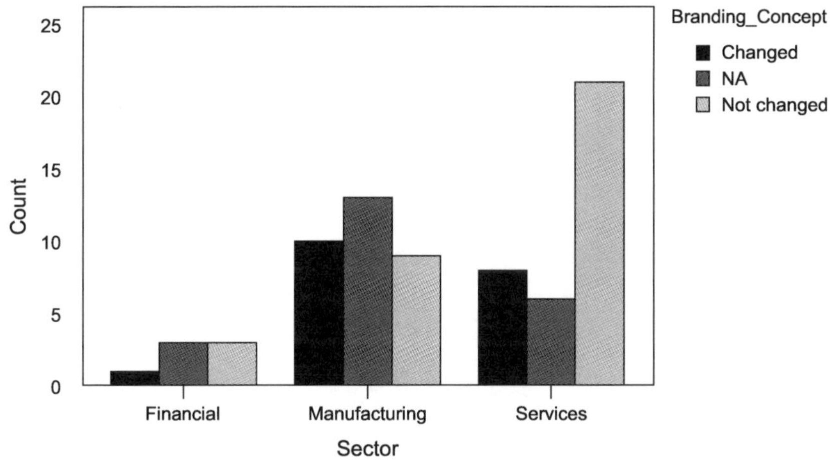

Fig. 3.30. Changing branding concept for online.

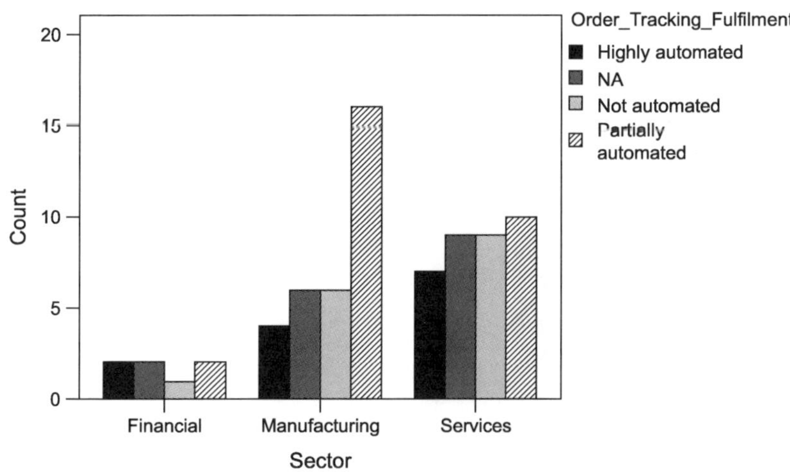

Fig. 3.31. Trends in automation of order tracking and fulfilment.

Furthermore, maximum integration with ERP and SCM solutions has been achieved by manufacturing organizations (59.4%) vis-à-vis financial sector (42.9%) and service sector organizations (34.3%).

The marketing function is the most highly automated in service sector organizations (48.6%), followed by the financial sector (43.2%) and manufacturing (25.0%).

Questions 13 — Is the number of organizations selling products and services online increasing? How is online business different from traditional business?

Less than half (43.2%) of the organizations use traditional as well as online channels to offer their products and services, while 54.1% use only traditional stores. Almost 86%

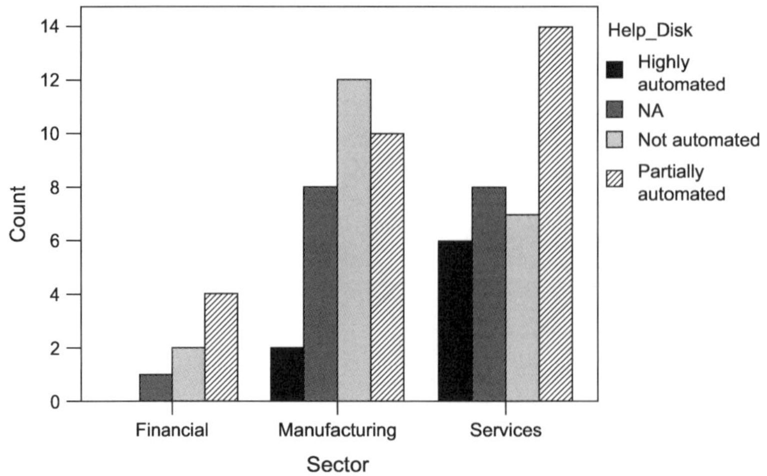

Fig. 3.32. Trends in help desk automation.

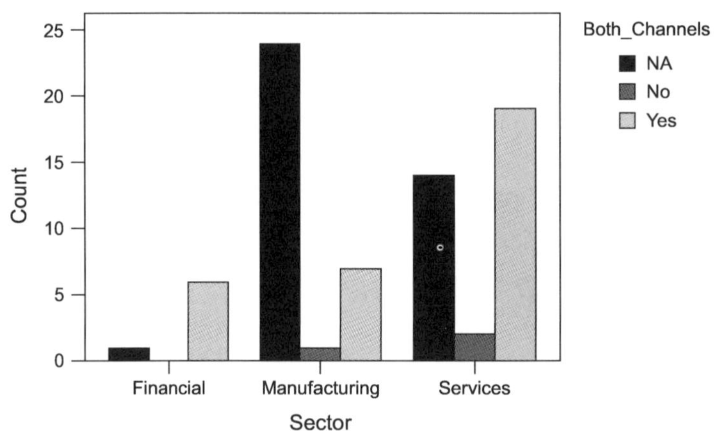

Fig. 3.33. Usage of online and traditional channels.

of the financial sector organizations use both channels as compared to manufacturing (21.9%) and services (54.3%) (Fig. 3.33).

Online business was found to be different from traditional business in terms of cost of products, pricing, operating margins, revenue, data collected and customers performing self-service tasks. The somewhat lower and significantly lower responses have been combined in the category lower and similarly for higher (Figs. 3.34 and 3.35).

The cost of products is lower for online for about one-fifth (17.6%) of the organizations, pricing is lower for almost 10% of the organizations, while the sales volumes are lower for almost 16.2% of the organizations. Data collected and the number of

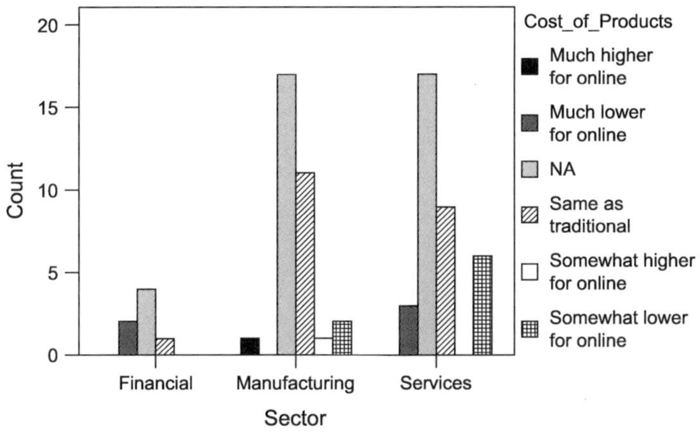

Fig. 3.34. Costs of products for online and traditional channels.

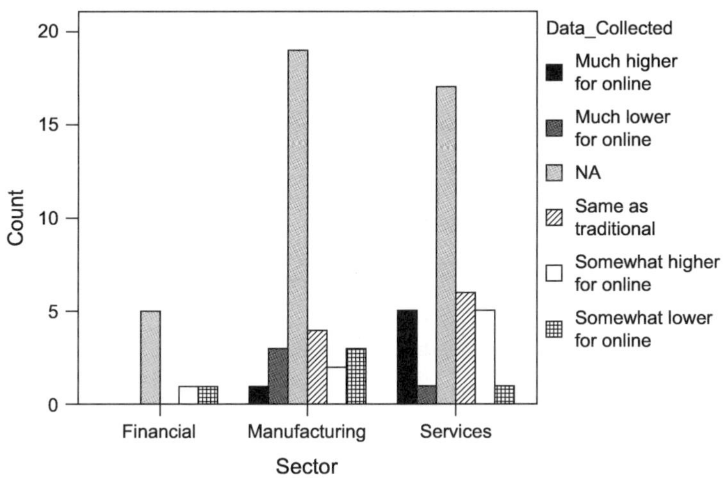

Fig. 3.35. Trends in data collection for online and traditional channels.

self-service tasks performed by customers are higher for online for 18.9 and 20.3% of the organizations, respectively.

Furthermore, customer self-service and operating margins were found to be highest in the services sector (25.3%) compared to financial sector (14.3%) and manufacturing (15.6%). Again, data collected was highest for services (28.6%) vis-à-vis financial sector (14.3%) and manufacturing (9.4%) (Fig. 3.36).

3.7. Trading Partnerships

Question 14 — What technologies are organizations using for communicating with their trading partners?

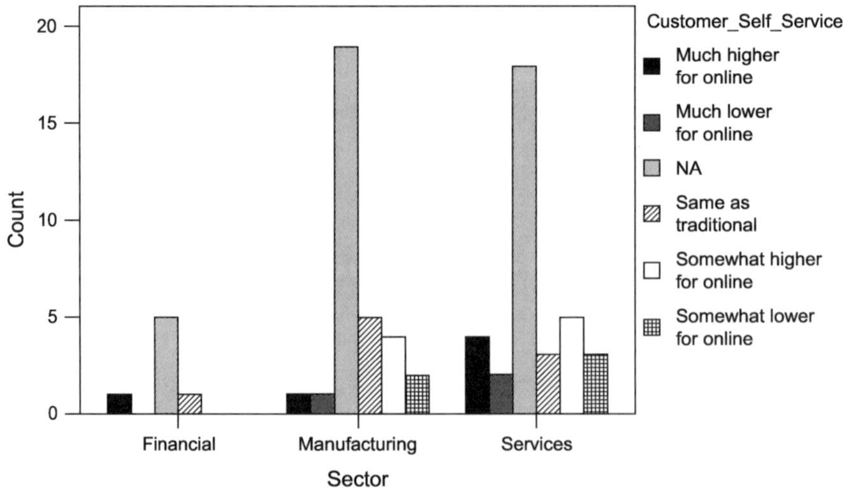

Fig. 3.36. Trends in customer self-service for online and traditional channels.

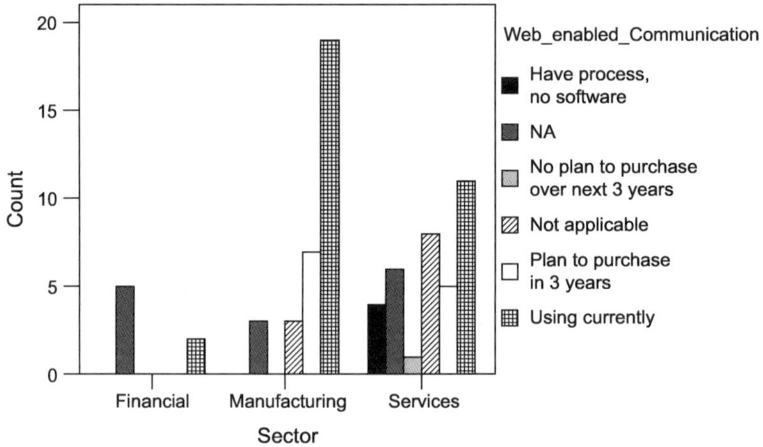

Fig. 3.37. Trends in usage of web-enabled communication.

Web-enabled communication (59.4% either have or plan to have in the next three years) and e-procurement (44.6% either have or plan to have) are the most popular technologies used for communicating with their trading partners (Fig. 3.37).

More than a quarter of the organizations (27.0%) plan to purchase an e-payment solution in the near future, followed by collaborative forecasting (23.0%) and collaborative planning (23.0%) (Fig. 3.38).

Over a fifth of the organizations have the process for partner relationship management (21.6%) and 12.2% intend to buy the product in the next three years (Fig. 3.39).

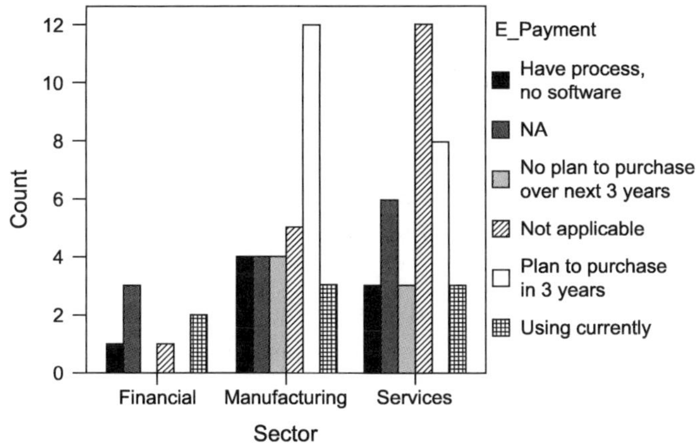

Fig. 3.38. Trends in usage of e-payment.

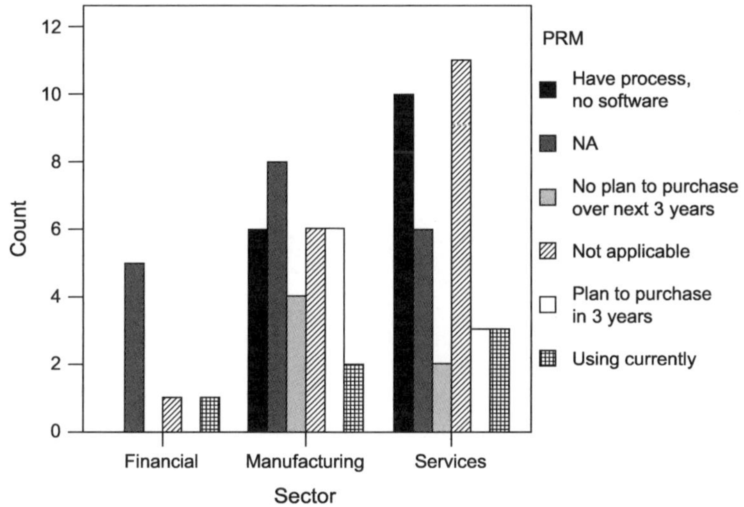

Fig. 3.39. Trends in usage of partner relationship management.

Only 2.7% of the organizations currently use e-compliance and around 13.5% do not intend to include it in short-term purchase.

XML-based communication is the most widely used in the financial sector, while EDI and web-enabled communication find most application in the manufacturing sector organizations. Almost one-third of the organizations in the manufacturing sector (31.3%) use demand planning and replenishment vis-à-vis financial (14.3%) and services (16.2%). E-payment is included in the short-term budget of almost 37.5% of the manufacturing organizations and 22.9% of the service sector organizations.

Question 15 — What IT-based channels and B2B mechanisms are organizations using for purchasing?

Direct purchasing (67.6%), long-term purchasing contracts (52.7%) and catalogues (36.5%) are the most used B2B mechanisms for purchasing, followed by flexible, short-term contracting (35.1%) (Fig. 3.40). Sell-side hubs (4.1%), e-exchanges (5.4%), aggregators (8.1%) and buy-side hubs (9.5%) are, respectively, the least used mechanisms.

Almost all the B2B mechanisms used for purchasing are most dominant in the manufacturing sector organizations in comparison with the financial and service sectors, respectively (Fig. 3.41).

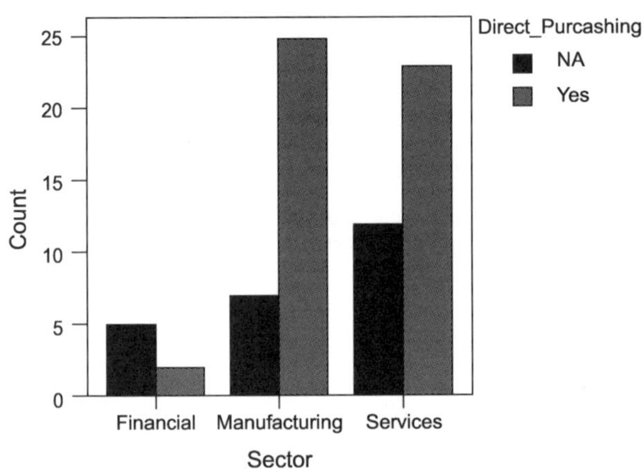

Fig. 3.40. Trends in use of direct purchasing.

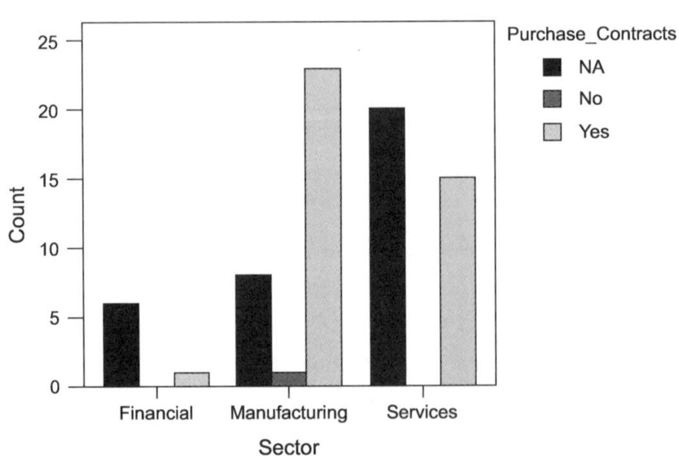

Fig. 3.41. Trends in use of purchase contracts.

3.8. Business Results

Questions 16 & *17* — What economic and operational business results are being impacted by technologies? What strategic areas are being impacted by information technologies?

The technology is indeed having a deep impact on the economic and operational business results. While comparing online business with traditional business, it was found to differ significantly with respect to R & D costs, production costs, service tasks performed by customers, technology costs and human resource costs, as shown.

More than half of the organizations (56.8%) report a decline in production costs, followed by 50% reporting a decrease in service costs and 46% in HR costs (Fig. 3.42).

44.6% of the organizations reported an increase in the number of new products and 43.3% reported an increase in the expenditure in technology. While manufacturing organizations have saved the most in internal communication costs (87.5%), production costs (68.7%), new products' time to market (59.4%) and HR costs (50%), service sector organizations have saved the most in customer service costs (60%) (Fig. 3.43), production costs (51.5%) and market research costs (45.7%).

An overwhelming 60.8% reported an increase in profits vis-à-vis 59.5% reported an increase in revenues, while 51.4% reported a higher market share (Fig. 3.44). The costs have also decreased for consultancy and collaboration (33.8%) and internal communication (75.6%). Almost half of the organizations (46%) reported a reduction in the new products' time to market and 35.1% reduction in new products' failure rate.

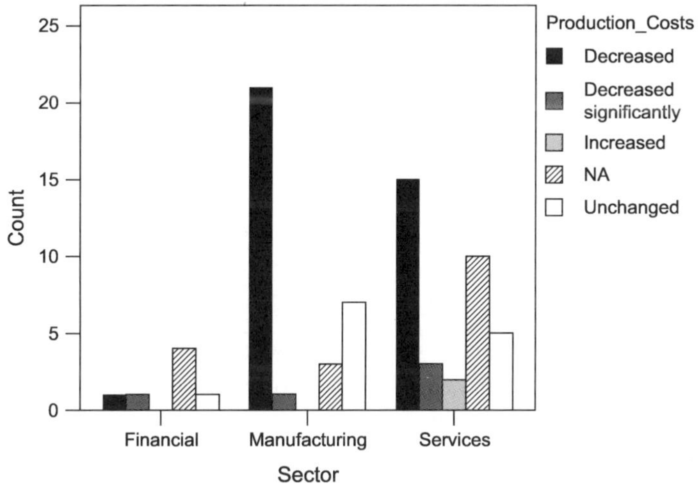

Fig. 3.42. Trends in production costs.

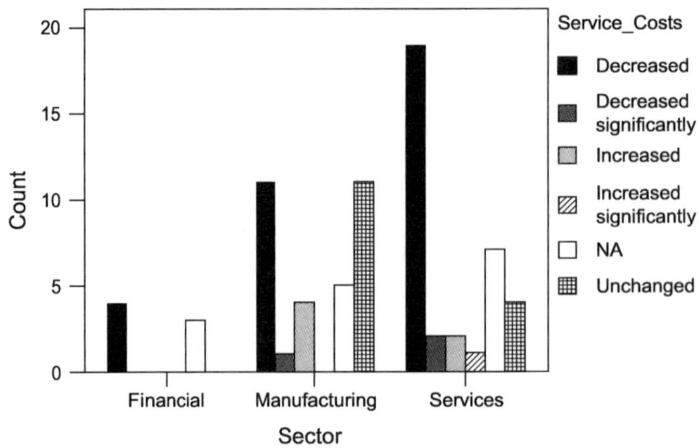

Fig. 3.43. Trends in customer service costs.

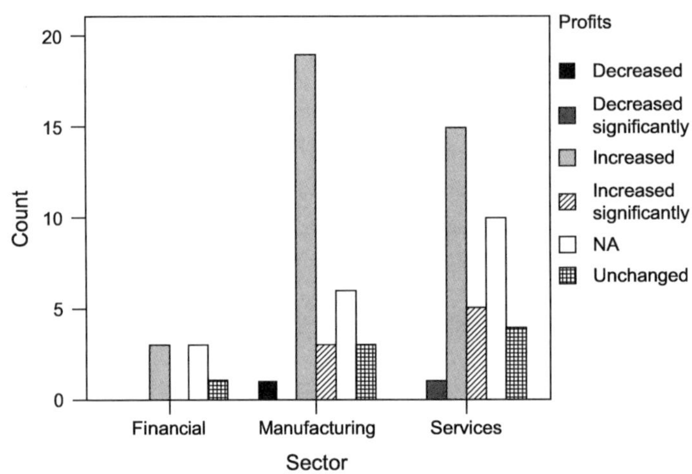

Fig. 3.44. Trends in profits.

The technology has significantly impacted certain strategic areas in the organizations. The understanding of customer satisfaction for current products and services (67.6%) and knowledge of competitor's products and services (64.9%), the understanding of customer buying behavior (63.6%) and future product expectations (62.2%) have improved due to technology (Fig. 3.45).

Across sectors, the technology has helped to increase the understanding of customer satisfaction for current products and services by 74.3% in services, 62.5% in manufacturing and 57.2% in financial sector organizations. Service sector organizations

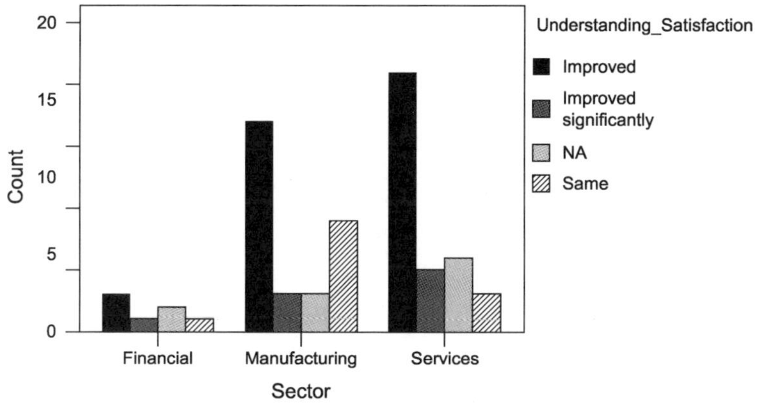

Fig. 3.45. Impact of technology on understanding satisfaction.

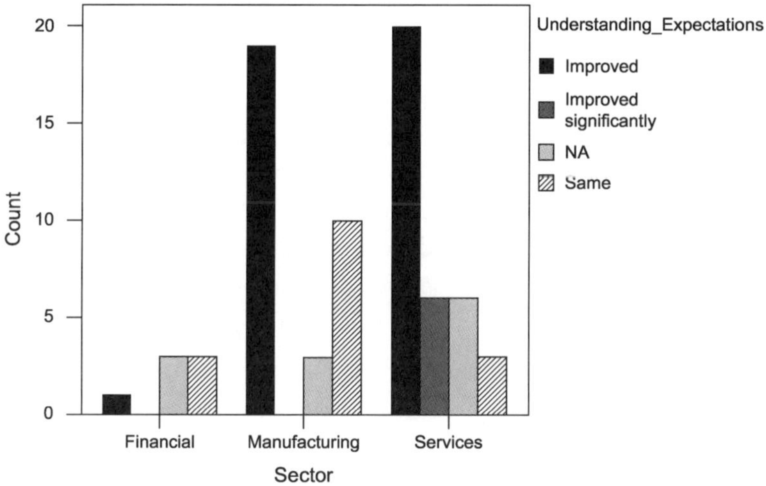

Fig. 3.46. Impact of technology on understanding expectations.

have benefited maximum in understanding customer expectations through technology (74.2%) as compared to manufacturing (59.4%) and financial (14.3%) sector organizations (Fig. 3.46).

3.9. Globalization

Questions 18 & 19 — Are organizations becoming more global? Is the geographic reach of organizations increasing?

Organizations are expanding their geographic reach with over two-thirds (70.2%) indicating an increase in trade in other countries, distributors/branches around the

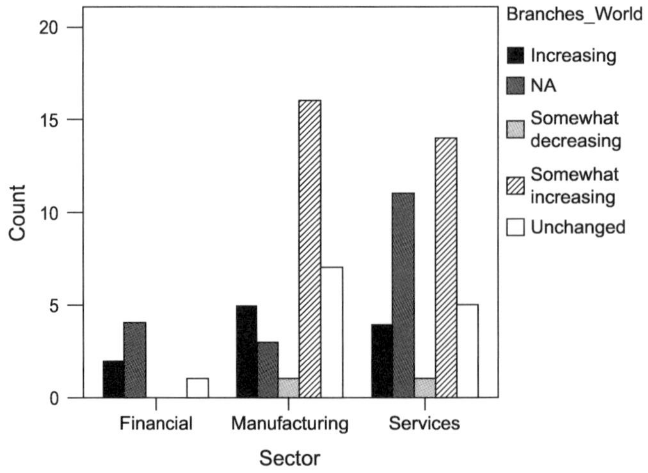

Fig. 3.47. Trends in number of distributions/branches around the world.

world (55.4%) and number of production/service bases (50%) (Fig. 3.47). The number of countries in supplier base, average distance to suppliers/vendors and the number of languages on the website are also increasing.

The trade in other countries has increased most significantly in manufacturing sector organizations (84.4%), as compared to financial sector (42.9%) and service sector (62.8%). The same trend holds good for distributors/branches across the world with manufacturing (65.6%) vis-à-vis financial sector (28.6%) and services (51.4%) (Fig. 3.48).

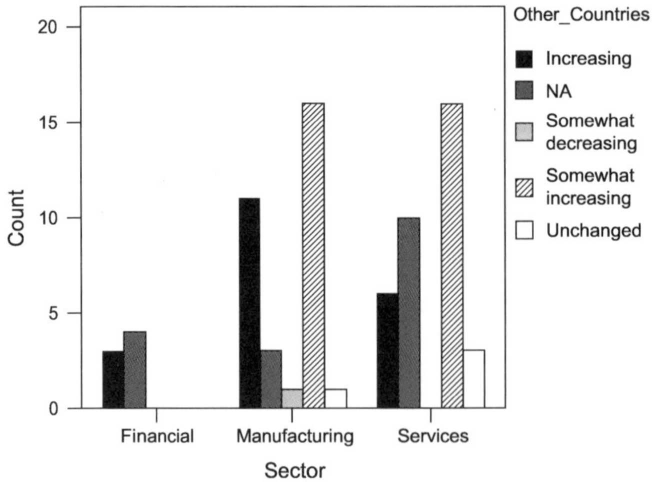

Fig. 3.48. Trends in trading in other countries.

With respect to globalization, over half of the organizations, either already have operations or plan to enter in the near future into USA (54.1%), South Asia (52.7%), Western Europe (51.3%) and Middle East (51.3%). Around one-third have/plan to have operations in Africa (35.1%), East Asia (35.1%) and Central and Eastern Europe (31.1%); about a quarter have/plan to operate in Canada and Mexico (29.7%) and Latin America (24.3%) (Fig. 3.14).

Across the three sectors, most number of service firms currently have operations in the USA (48.6%), while 28.6% of the financial sector organizations plan to operate

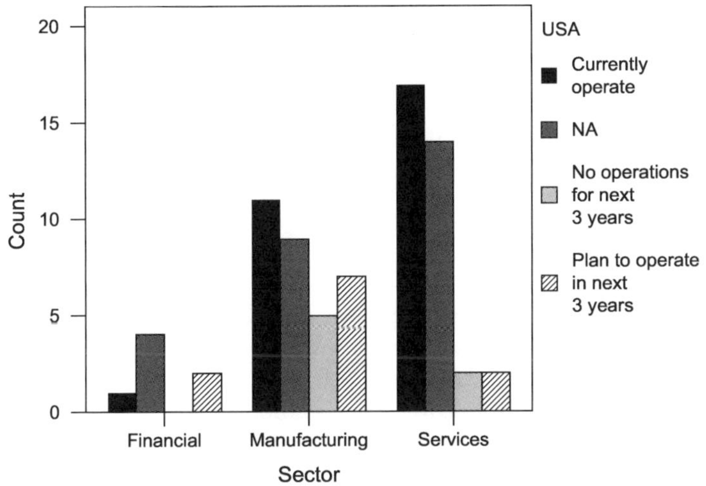

Fig. 3.49. Trends in organizations' US operations.

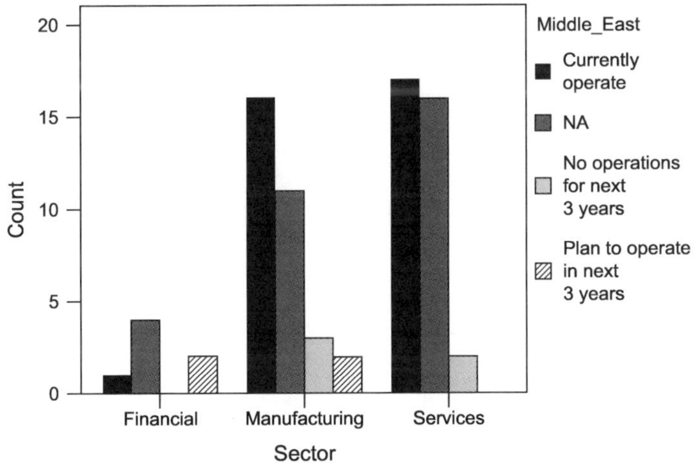

Fig. 3.50. Trends in organizations' Middle East operations.

there in the next three years (Fig. 3.49) . The same trend holds good for Canada and Mexico, while manufacturing sector dominates in the Western European region with 46.9% of the organizations currently operating as compared to financial sector (14.3%) and services (45.7%). 50% of the manufacturing organizations operate in the Middle East compared to 14.3% in the financial sector and 48.6% in the services sector (Fig. 3.50).

Bibliography

1. Karmarkar, US and V Mangal, The Business and Information Technologies (BIT) Survey, Annual Report 2003–2004.
2. www.worldinternetproject.org.
3. www.nasscom.org.
4. "WITSA Study: World IT Spending Rebounds Thanks Largely to Developing World". Available at http: //witsa.org/press/11-22-04DP-US 5.doc. Accessed on December 17, 2004.

Appendix A: Survey Methodology

The baseline BIT study was conducted as a survey through questionnaire mailed to target organizations in multiple industry sectors. Each subject in the study was an independent organizational entity that controlled its own information technology and information policy, and had a chief information officer (CIO) or similar management position within it. It is likely that since the subject organizations are able to make their own technology decisions (and investments), they also have profit and loss responsibility, although this is certainly not necessarily always the case. The surveys were addressed to the CIO (or similar position) as the person most likely to be knowledgeable about the subject.

The major issues of interest were developed, which were then used to generate survey questions. The survey instrument was mailed to a database of over 700 individuals across all industry sectors in India. The CIOs (and related positions) were requested to complete the survey by mail.

The survey instrument (questionnaire) has seven major sections:

1. *Technology adoption/infrastructure and budget trends* — technologies adopted and budget trend.
2. *Internal organization* — changes in the internal organization's workforce, structure and in BPO due to technologies.
3. *Customer facing interactions* — changes in advertising, image, relationship management and other customer facing interactions due to technologies.
4. *Trading partner relationships* — changes in partner communications and purchasing mechanisms used due to technology relationships.
5. *Business results* — operational and economic business results and strategic areas impacted by technologies.
6. *Globalization* — globalization of the organization due to technologies.
7. *Organizational profile* — the basic "demographics" of the organization.

Appendix B: Sample Profile

74 valid responses were received. The profile of the sample is as follows.

Sector wise break up
Financial Services: 8
Manufacturing: 32
Services: 34

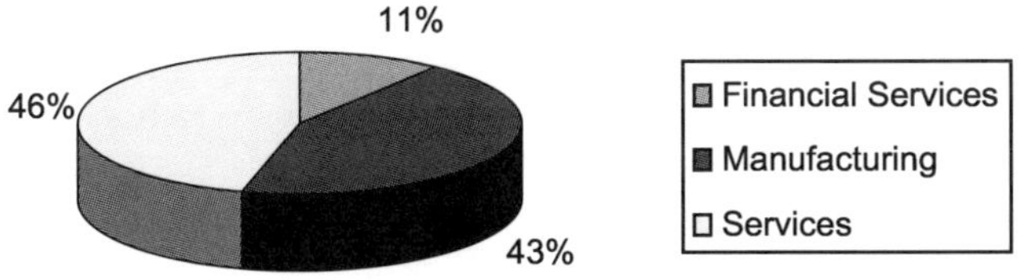

Size of organization in terms of annual revenues (%)

Up to 100 crores	24.32
100 crores to 500 crores	21.62
501 crores to 1000 crores	14.86
Over 1000 crores	20.27
No response or not applicable	18.92

Sectors of organizations (%)

Chemical	4.05
Insurance	1.35
Bank	6.76
Mutual Fund	2.70
Cement	2.70
FMCG	6.76
Engineering	20.27
Information Technology	16.22
Textile	4.05
Pharmaceuticals	4.05
Consultancy	10.81
Telecom	2.70
Publication	1.35
Retail	4.05
Marketing	2.70
Education	4.05
Media	2.70
Infrastructure	1.35
Other	1.35

CHAPTER 4

THE KOREA BUSINESS AND INFORMATION TECHNOLOGIES (BIT) SURVEY

HOSUN RHIM, KWANGTAE PARK and HONG-IL KIM

Summary

The Korean economy has been transformed to an information economy gradually. According to the GNP study conducted by our team, the primary information sector which produces information goods and services as a final product explains 46.1% of year 2000 GNP. The proportion of information economy used to be 40.4% in 1990. In spite of the importance of the information economy, research on the business and information technologies has been limited.

The Business and Information Technologies (BIT) project was initiated by the Center for Management of the Information Economy (CMIE) of UCLA in 2003. This project is to understand the impact of new information and communication technologies (ICT) on business practices over an extended time horizon. The BIT project consists of three parts: first, the annual survey of firms to collect data on how firms are using new technologies, and how firms, industries and economies are changing as a consequence; second, tracking the evolution of economies through analysis of national accounting data and GNP figures; third, in-depth study of industry segments.

- The Service and Logistics Research Center at Korea University has taken part in the project since 2004. This report presents the results of the survey which was conducted in Korea in 2004–2005. Some of the key results of the survey were as follows.
- The technologies used most frequently by organizations are websites/e-commerce, groupware/productivity tools, enterprise resource planning (ERP). In spite of its popularity, radio frequency identification are the least adopted technologies by organizations.
- Even though the lists of most/least adopted technologies are similar, the adoption rates between Korea and US show big difference.
- Since new decision-making tools and online technologies become increasingly available, workforces need to retrain constantly to keep up with changing technologies.
- IT function is most frequently outsourced by organizations, while finance, accounting, payroll are the least outsourced business functions.
- Order placement, Order tracking/fulfillment, integration with ERP/SCM, and customer complaints management have been automated by over one-third of

the organizations. However, content management of web sites and sales calls automation are the least-automated CRM functions.

- Direct purchasing, long-term purchasing contracts, and catalogues are most frequently used purchasing mechanisms.
- In business performance, production costs, commercial costs, and customer service costs have been reduced seriously. However, technology costs, internal communication, and R&D costs have increased. The revenues and profits have increased due to the technology.
- Trade in other countries, number of production/service bases, and number of countries in supplier base have increased as globalization progressed.

4.1. The Survey

The survey instrument was developed by research partners in US, Italy, and India in 2003. For self-completeness of this report, the major issues and summary of survey questions are provided as below.

4.1.1. *Technology adoption/infrastructure and budget trends*

Question 1 — What technology products do organizations currently have or plan to purchase in the next three years? What technology products do not organizations have and plan to purchase in the next three years?

Question 2 — What technologies have organizations invested in (and not invested in) over the last three years?

4.1.2. *Internal organization*

Question 3 — How are organizations changing internally in terms of their workforce and the workplace in the past year?

Question 4 — How are organizations changing internally in terms of their structure?

Question 5 — What business process are organizations currently outsourcing? Is business process outsourcing (BPO) more popular for certain functions in the organization such as accounting, marketing, IT, and finance?

Questions 6 & 7 — What is the outsourcing budget in organizations for IT and nonIT functions? What is the percentage of the total outsourced business that is offshore?

4.1.3. *Customer facing interactions*

Question 8 — Are relationships with customers developed and maintained using multiple touch points? What are the most popular touch points?

Questions 9 & 14 — How are customer views integrated into the organization using certain technologies? What mechanisms are used by organizations to perform customer segmentation?

Questions 10, 11 & 12 — Which online advertising methods have been used by organizations? Have organizations changed their logo, slogan, name (e.g. .com), and branding concept in going online? Are advertising budgets shifting towards online channels?

Question 13 — Which customer relationship management (CRM) functions have been automated?

Questions 15 & 16 — To sell products and services, which of the mechanisms do organizations use? How is online business different from traditional business?

4.1.4. *Trading partner relationships*

Question 17 — What application technologies are organizations using for communicating with their trading partners?

Question 18 — What IT-based channels and B2B mechanisms are organizations using for purchasing?

4.1.5. *Business results*

Questions 19 & 20 — What economic and operational business results and strategic areas are being impacted by technologies?

4.1.6. *Globalization*

Questions 21 & 22 — Are organizations becoming more global? Is the geographic reach of organizations increasing?

4.2. Results

The survey was sent by fax or delivered by interviewers depending on the location of the respondent. The collection process was managed by a reliable market research company. More than 50% of the respondents were at managerial level. About 260 responses were collected. The sample details are provided in Appendix A. The results are summarized as below.

4.2.1. *Technology adoption/infrastructure and budget trends*

- The technologies used most frequently by organizations are websites/e-commerce, groupware/productivity tools, enterprise resource planning (ERP).

- Business process modeling (BPM), biometrics, digital receipts, and radio frequency identification (RFID) are the least adopted technologies.
- Budgets for OS & networking, storage hardware, applications software, security hardware, and security software have increased. Budgets for on demand computing and offshore outsourcing have not increased significantly.

4.2.2. *Internal organizations: workforce trends*

- Workers need to retrain constantly to keep up with changing technologies, and the proportion of employees facing a screen has increased significantly.
- Neither teleconferencing nor telecommuting is widely used by the organizations.
- Organizations do not agree with the idea that outsourcing and automation of functions lead to workforce reductions.

4.2.3. *Internal organizational structure trends*

- The increasing availability of new decision-making tools and online technologies is the most significant trend.
- The span of control for most of the managers is widening, and organizations are becoming flatter due to technologies.
- Monitoring of customer-facing interactions and automated monitoring of workforce productivity are constantly increasing. Organizations provide incentives to employees based on their productivity.
- Some organizations become more geographically dispersed with the help of technologies.

4.2.4. *Internal organization — BPO*

- IT network management, IT programming, and IT data center operations are most frequently outsourced by organizations. Finance, accounting, payroll, and RFP, bids and contract management are the least outsourced business functions.

4.2.5. *Customer touch points*

- Face-to-face, e-mail, phone, company website (brochureware), and regular mail are the most frequently used by organizations. The least-used touch points are automated interactive voice response (IVR) and screen pop.

4.2.6. *Customer view integration and customer segmentation*

- Customer profiling, statistical data mining, and data marts/data warehouse are used for customer view integration. The least-used technologies to integrate the views into the organizations include data mining with neural networks and text mining.

4.2.7. *Online advertising and selling*

- For online advertising, organizations use web banners, and incentive in printed material to drive customers to company website. Advertisement or links on other websites to drive traffic to company website, and pop up windows are used by the organizations for online advertising.
- Fewer organizations have changed their logo, slogan, name, and branding concept in going online.

4.2.8. *CRM function automation*

- Order placement, order tracking/fulfillment, integration with ERP/SCM, and customer complaints management have been automated by over one-third of the organizations.
- The least-automated CRM functions include content management of web sites and sales calls automation.

4.2.9. *Traditional versus online selling*

- Cost of products, pricing, sales volume are lower for online than for traditional business. Self-service tasks performed by customers and data collected are higher for online than for traditional business.

4.2.10. *Trading partners relationships*

- Electronic data interchange (EDI), web-enabled communications, and e-procurement are somewhat used by the organizations.
- Sourcing/procurement management, partner relationship management (PRM), and e-compliance are the applications that organizations do not have and do not plan to have in the near future.

4.2.11. *Purchasing mechanisms*

- Direct purchasing, long-term purchasing contracts and catalogues are most frequently used. Sell-side exchange/hub, exchange/e-exchange, and joint venture and projects are the least used by the organizations.

4.2.12. *Business results*

- Production costs, commercial costs, and customer service costs have been reduced seriously. Technology costs, internal communication, and R&D costs have increased. Revenues and profits have increased due to the technology.

4.2.13. *Globalization*

- Organizations have expanded and are planning to expand their business operations in South East Asia, East Asia, and USA in the next three years. However, organizations do not plan to have business operations in Africa (34.7%), Middle East (30.9%), Latin America (29.8%), Canada & Mexico (28.6%), and South Asia (27.9%) in the next three years.
- Trade in other countries, number of production/service bases, and number of countries in supplier base have increased.

4.3. Details

4.3.1. *Technology adoption/infrastructure and budget trends*

Question 1 — What technology products do organizations currently have or plan to purchase in the next three years? What technology products do not organizations have and plan to purchase in the next three years?

More than half of the organizations (56.9%) currently have or plan to purchase websites and e-commerce technology products in the next three years, almost half of the organizations (49.3%) have/plan to have groupware and productivity tools. About half of the organizations (46.5 %) have/plan to purchase enterprise resource planning (ERP), 39.4% of the organizations have/plan to have collaboration and portal tools such as document management and portal. Over one-third of the organizations (38.2%) have/plan to purchase wireless technologies; 36.7% of the organizations have/plan to have Linux as operation system; over a third of the organizations (35.1%) have/plan to purchase storage area network (SAN) and network attached storage (NAS). However, these acceptance rates are much lower than those of US 2003–2004 data. For example, more than 90% of US organizations either already have or plan to have websites and e-commerce technologies within the next three years. These technology trends are shown in Fig. 4.1.

The technology products that fewer organizations plan to purchase in the near future are RFID technology (14.9% have/plan to have, while 8.8% do not plan to have), digital receipts (20.3% have/plan to purchase, while 6.9% do not plan to purchase), biometrics (20.6% have/plan to have, while 2.3% do not plan to have), and BPM (20.6% have/plan to purchase, while 13.4% do not have plan to purchase).

These trends are shown in Fig. 4.2.

Question 2 — What technologies have organizations invested in (and not invested in) over the last three years?

The technologies that the organizations have invested in most over the last three years are operating systems and networking software (increased or increased significantly in 71%

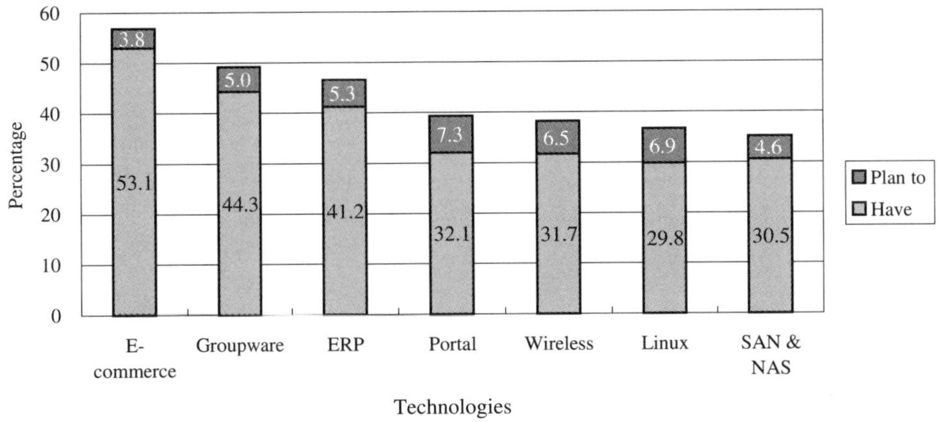

Fig. 4.1. Technology trends.

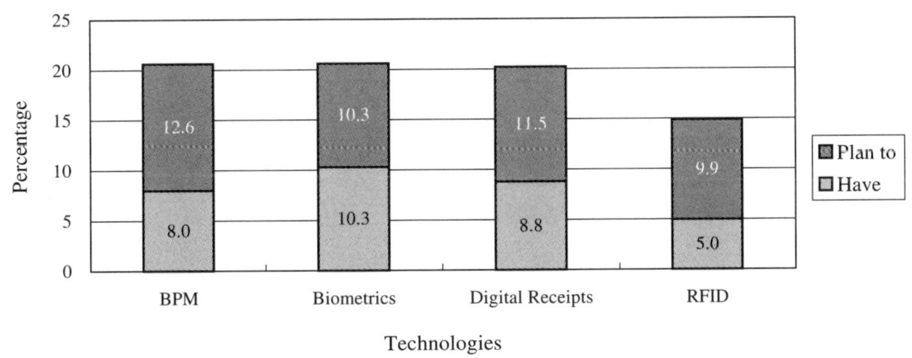

Fig. 4.2. Technology trends.

of the organizations), storage hardware (increased or increased significantly in 69.5% of organizations), and applications software (increased or increased significantly in 69.5% of organizations). Budgets for security hardware (increased or increased significantly in 67.9% of organizations) and security software (increased or increased significantly in 67.6% of organizations) have also been increased over the last three years.

The least-increased budgets are offshore outsourcing (6.1%) and on-demand computing (13%) in the last three years.

These budget trends are shown in Fig. 4.3.

4.3.2. *Internal organization*

Question 3 — How are organizations changing internally in terms of their workforce and the workplace in the past year?

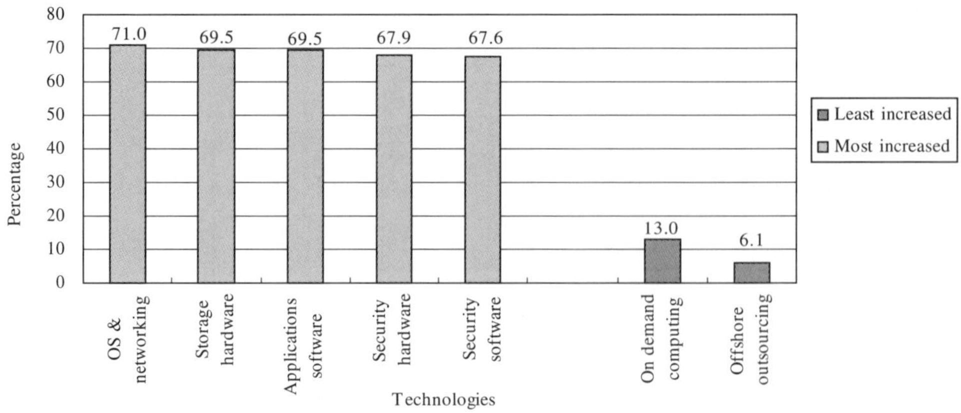

Fig. 4.3. Budget trends.

As shown in Fig. 4.4, workers need to retrain constantly to keep up with changing technologies (68.3%) and the proportion of employees facing a screen are significantly increasing (66.8%). The need for IT skills at lower levels is increasing (60.7%). The demand for intelligence in information at executive levels is also increasing (52.7%). The collaboration between workers from the use of internet-based collaboration tools is constantly increasing (52.3%).

The use of teleconferencingteleconferencing in the organizations is not on the rise (26.7% agree, while 37% disagree); telecommuting is also not widely used by the organizations (13.4% agree, while 50.8% disagree).

Organizations do not agree with the idea that outsourcing and automation of functions are leading to workforce reductions.

Codes for these trends are as follows:

1. The proportion of employees facing a screen is increasing
2. Workforces need to retrain constantly to keep up with changing technologies

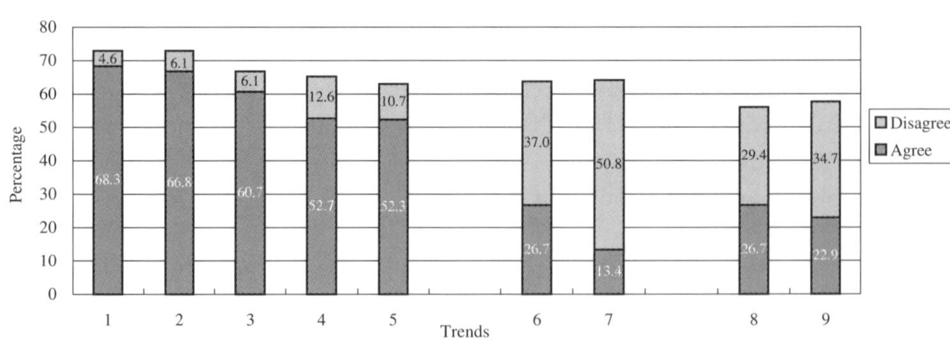

Fig. 4.4. Internal organization workforce.

3. The need for IT skills at lower levels is going up
4. The demand for intelligence in information at executive levels is increasing
5. The collaboration between workers from the use of internet-based collaboration tools
6. The use of teleconferencingteleconferencing is on the rise
7. More employees are telecommuting
8. The outsourcing is leading to workforce reductions
9. Automation of functions is leading to workforce reductions

Question 4 — How are organizations changing internally in terms of their structure?

More than half of the organizations (58%) answered that the increasing availability of new decision-making tools and online technologies is the most significant trend.

The span of control for most of the managers is widening (48.5%), and organizations become flatter (39.3%) due to technologies.

Almost half of the organizations (49.6%) answered that monitoring of customer-facing interactions is increasing significantly and automated monitoring of workforce productivity is constantly increasing (37%). The results have showed that over a third of the organizations (32.8%) provide incentives to employees based on their productivity.

Some organizations become more geographically dispersed (29%) with the help of technologies.

These trends are shown in Fig. 4.5.

Codes for the trends are as follows:

1. The span of control for most of the managers is widening
2. The organization is becoming flatter
3. Monitoring of customer-facing interactions is increasing

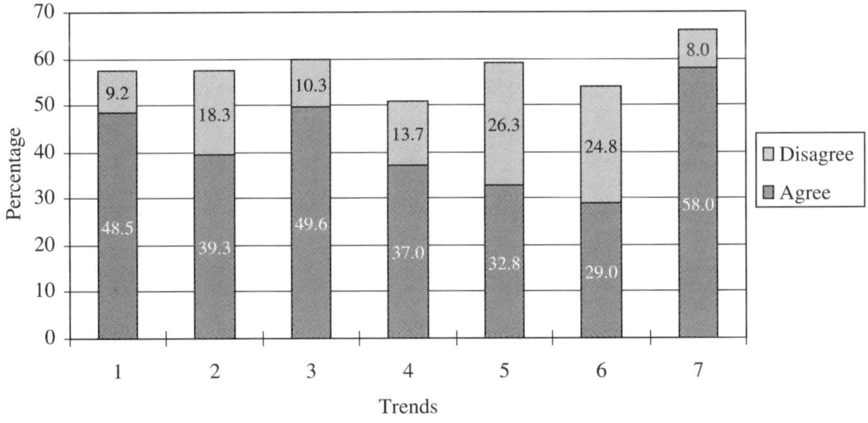

Fig. 4.5. Internal organization structure.

4. Automated monitoring of workforce productivity is increasing
5. Incentive are based on monitoring of productivity
6. The organization is becoming more geographically dispersed
7. New decision-making tools and online technologies are increasingly becoming available

Question 5 — What business process are organizations currently outsourcing? Is BPO more popular for certain functions in the organization such as accounting, marketing, IT, and finance?

IT network management, IT programming, and IT data center operations are most frequently outsourced by organizations (Fig. 4.6). IT network management is outsourced (partially or significantly or planned) by about half of the organizations (45.8%). About the same proportion of the organizations (45.4%) outsource IT programming; IT network management is outsourced by 33.6% of the organizations.

On the other hand, business process functions which are least often outsourced by organizations are finance (53.8%), accounting (50.4%), payroll (49.6%) and RFP, bids and contract management (48.9%). Positive answers (partially, significantly or planned to outsource) for these functions are 9.9, 14.1, 16, and 4.96%, respectively.

Questions 6 & 7 — What is the outsourcing budget in organizations for IT and nonIT functions? What is the percentage of the total outsourced business that is offshore?

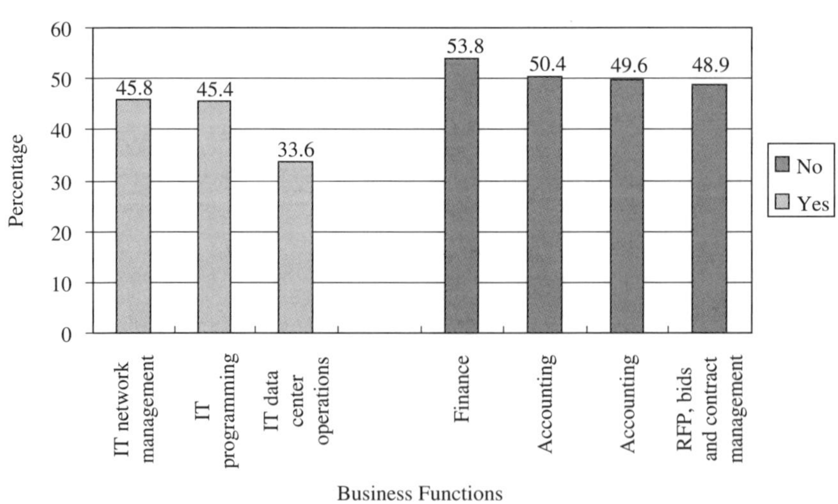

Fig. 4.6. Internal organization BPO.

Even though many businesses functions are outsourced by a large number of the organizations, many respondents (80.5% for IT/90.8% for nonIT) avoided to answer what the total budgets for outsourcing as a percentage of sales revenue are (Fig. 4.7).

Only 6.5% of the organizations answered that business processes are outsourced in other countries. The reason for low response rate is that data is confidential. These offshore outsourcing trends are shown in Fig. 4.8.

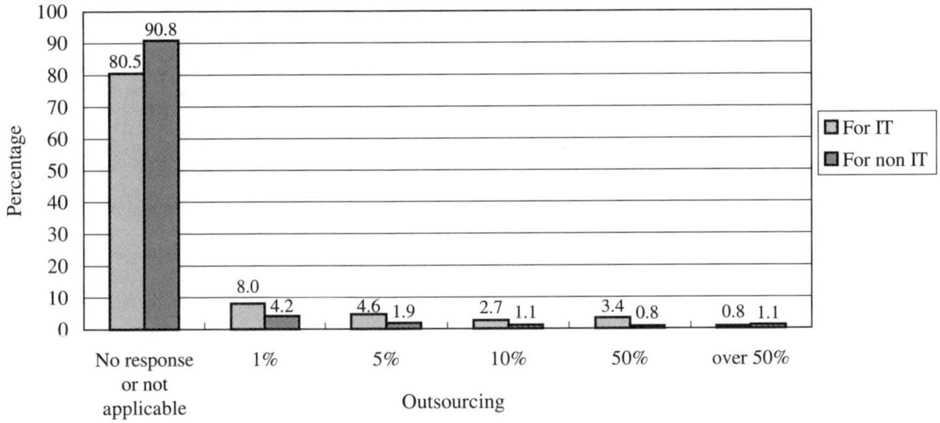

Fig. 4.7. Outsourcing as a percentage of sales revenue.

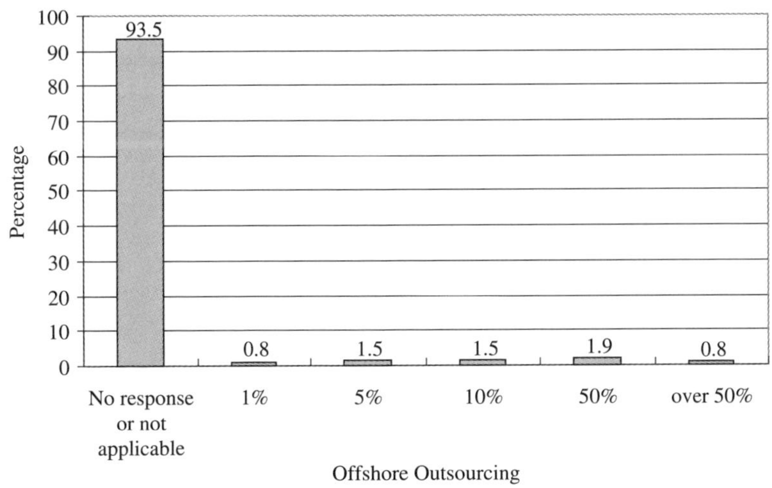

Fig. 4.8. Percentage of the total offshore outsourcing.

4.3.3. *Customer facing interactions*

Question 8 — Are relationships with customers developed and maintained using multiple touch points? What are the most popular touch points?

To interact with customers, organizations use multiple touch points. Face-to-face (14.4%), e-mail (14.3%), phone (13.0%), company website — brochureware (10.3%), and regular mail (10.2%) are most frequently used by organizations. The least-used touch points are automated interactive voice response (2.2%) and screen pop (1.2%).

Following the UCLA annual report, we group touch points into four categories: online technologies, other technologies, people touch points, and other touch points. Online technologies are e-mail, company website (brochureware), company website (transactional), screen pops, and online intermediaries. Other technologies include fax, phone, phone text messaging, phone (IVR — interactive voice response) and phone (CTI — computer telephony interaction). People touch points are fact-to-face interactions and referrals; other touch points include regular mail and any touch points that may not be in the list.

To interact with customers, over one-third (34.5%) of the organizations use online technologies as touch points, almost half of the organizations (44.1%) use other technologies. People touch points are used by one-fifth of the organizations (20.7%); other touch points are used by only 0.7% of the organizations. The frequency of the customer touch points is shown in Fig. 4.9.

Questions 9 & 14 — How are customer views integrated into the organization using certain technologies? What mechanisms are used by organizations to perform customer segmentation?

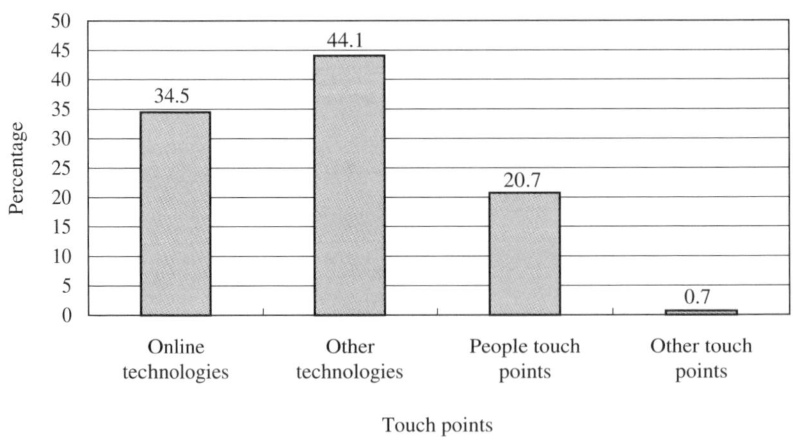

Fig. 4.9. Customer touch points.

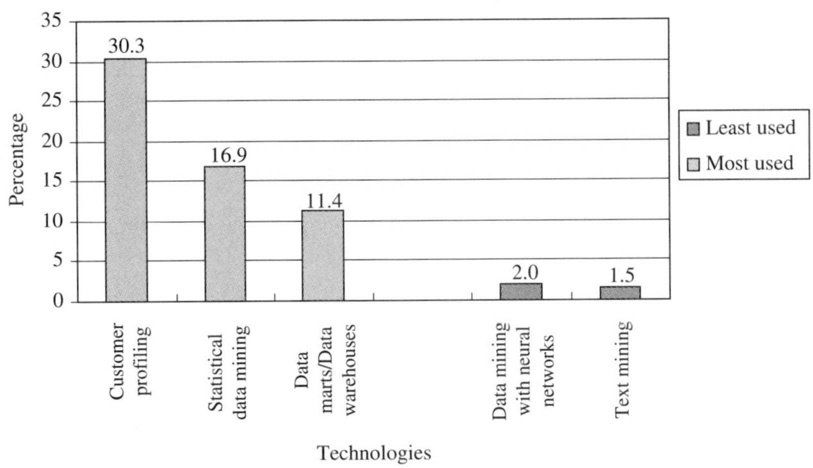

Fig. 4.10. Technologies for customer data analysis.

As shown in Fig. 4.10, customer views are integrated into the organizations using various technologies. For customer view integration, one-third of the organizations (30.3%) use customer profiling; almost a fifth (16.9%) of the organizations use statistical data mining. Data marts/data warehouse is used by 11.4% of the organizations. The least used technologies to integrate the views into the organizations include data mining with neural networks (2%) and text mining (1.5%).

To segment customers, portals are used by 17.4% of the organizations. 17.1% of the organizations segment customers by geography; dynamic/customized pricing is used for customer segmentation by 14.1% of the organizations. Personalize website by customers (6.3%) and automated cross-selling (2.6%) are the least frequently used methods for customer segmentation. These trends are shown in Fig. 4.11.

Questions 10, 11 & 12 — Which online advertising methods have been used by organizations? Have organizations changed their logo, slogan, name (e.g. com), and branding concept in going online? Are advertising budgets shifting towards online channels?

Various channels are used for online advertising. Almost one-fifth of the organizations (19.6%) use web banners for online advertising. 16.5% of the organizations use incentive in printed material to drive customers to company website; advertisement or links on other websites to drive traffic to company website is used by 13.7% of the organizations. 12.7% of the organizations use pop up windows for online advertising. These trends of the online advertising methods are provided in Fig. 4.12.

Fewer than 20% of the organizations have changed their logo, slogan, name, and branding concept in going online. Slogan (15.3%), branding concept (14.9%), logo (13%), and name (9.9%) have been changed by the organizations.

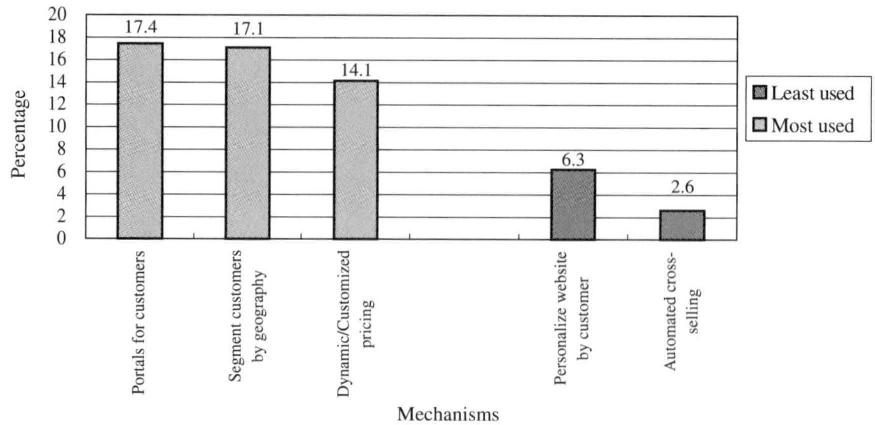

Fig. 4.11. Customer segmentation methods.

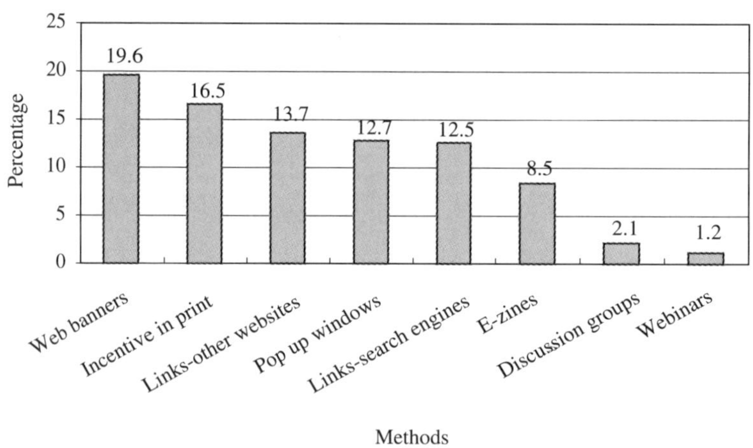

Fig. 4.12. Online advertising methods.

Since the survey question about online advertising budgets (question 11) was answered by fewer than 10% of the organizations, the results are not reported here.

Question 13 — Which CRM functions have been automated?

In CRM functions, help desk, order placement and order tracking/fulfillment have been automated (partially or highly automated). Over 35.5% of the organizations have automated order placement; 34.4% have automated order tracking/fulfillment; 32.4% have automated integration with ERP/SCM. Customer complaints management has been automated by 32.4% of the organizations. On the other hand, the least automated CRM functions include content management of web sites (23.7%) and sales calls automation automation (14.9%) (Fig. 4.13).

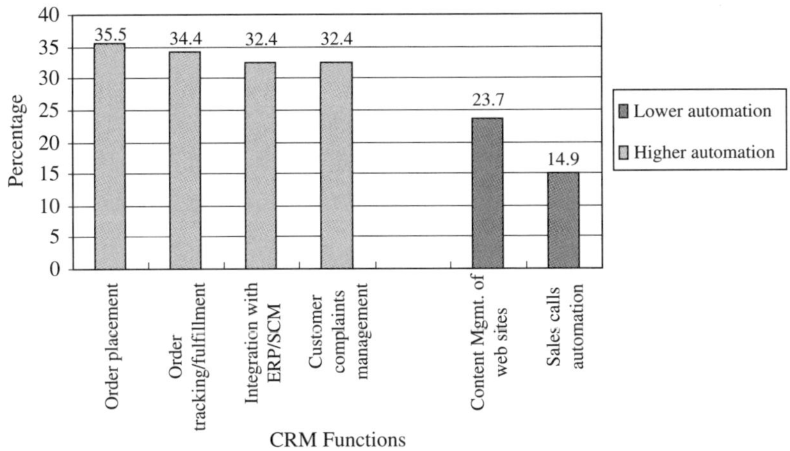

Fig. 4.13. Automation of CRM functions.

Questions 15 & 16 — To sell products and services, which of the mechanisms do organizations use? How is online business different from traditional business?

Almost half of the organizations (48.85%) offer traditional as well as online business mechanisms to sell products and services. 15.27% of the organizations have traditional stores but only 2.67% of the organizations have online stores.

As shown in Fig. 4.14, online business uses several factors: cost of products, pricing, sales volume, self-service tasks performed by customers, and data collected. These are different factors from traditional business. In online business, cost of products (lower and significantly lower in 22.1% of the organizations), pricing (lower and significantly lower in 23.3% of the organizations), and sales volume (lower

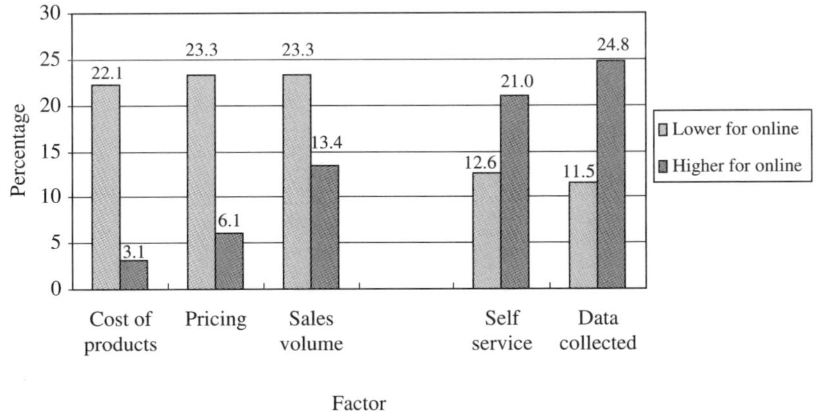

Fig. 4.14. Online versus traditional.

and significantly lower in 23.3% of the organizations) are lower than traditional business.

Self-service tasks performed by customers customers (somewhat higher and much higher in 21.0% of the organizations) and data collected (somewhat higher and much higher in 24.8% of the organizations) are higher than traditional business.

4.3.4. *Trading partner relationships*

Question 17 — What application technologies are organizations using for communicating with their trading partners?

For communicating with trading partners, EDI (17.6% of the organizations have or plan to purchase), web-enabled communications (15.6% of the organizations have or plan to have), and e-procurement (15.6% of the organizations have or plan to purchase) are somewhat used by the organizations. XML-based communications (6.1% of the organizations have, 7.3% of the organizations plan to have), and web-enabled communications (10.6% of the organization have, 5% of the organizations plan to purchase) are the next frequent applications that organizations have or plan to purchase in the next three years.

On the other hand, sourcing/procurement management (10.3%), partner relationship management (10.3%) and e-compliance (9.2%) are the applications that organizations do not have and do not plan to have in the near future. These trends are shown in Fig. 4.15.

Question 18 — What IT-based channels and B2B mechanisms are organizations using for purchasing?

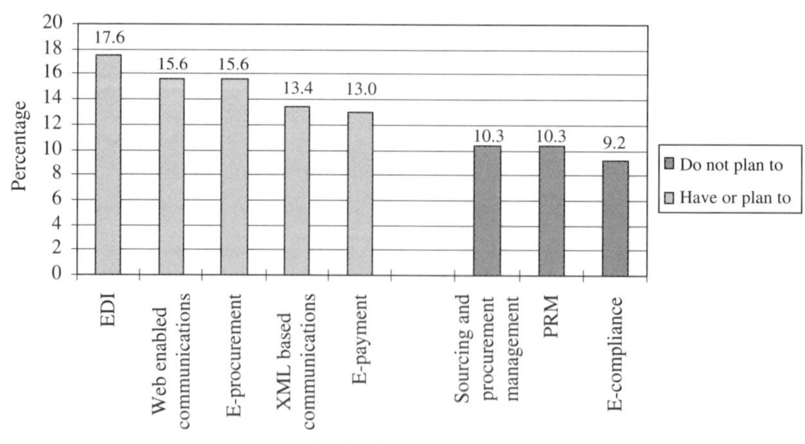

Fig. 4.15. Communication with trading partners.

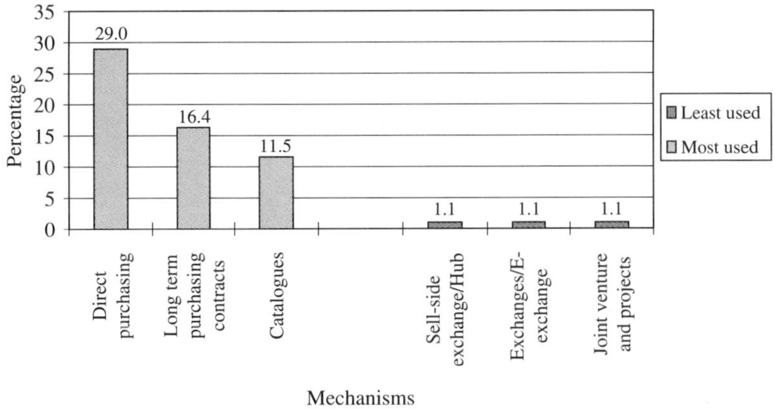

Fig. 4.16. Purchasing mechanisms.

For purchasing, direct purchasing, long-term purchasing contracts and catalogue are used by 29, 16.4, and 11.5% of the organizations. Sell-side exchange/hub, exchange/e-exchange, and joint venture and projects are the least-used by the organizations. These are shown in Fig. 4.16.

4.3.5. *Business results*

Questions 19 & 20 — What economic and operational business results and strategic areas are being impacted by technologies?

The technology has impacts on various economic and operational business results. The most outstanding cost reductions are production costs (19.1% of the organizations decreased and decreased significantly), commercial costs (17.2% of the organizations decreased and decreased significantly), and customer service costs (16% of the organizations, 16.4% of the organizations decreased and decreased significantly). The costs for market research (16% of the organizations decreased and decreased significantly) and human resources decreased and decreased significantly) have also decreased.

On the other hand, the costs for technology (31.3% of the organizations increased or increased significantly) have rather increased. Internal communication (22.9% of the organizations increased or increased significantly) and R&D costs (22.5% of the organizations increased or increased significantly) have also increased.

Revenues (22.1%) and profits (20.6%) have increased due to the technology. These business results are shown in Fig. 4.17.

The strategic areas of organizations have also been impacted by technology. As shown in Fig. 4.18, four strategic areas: knowledge of competitor's products/services (35.9%), understanding of customer satisfaction for current products/services (34.7%), understanding of customer buying behavior (33.2%), and understanding of customer expectations on future products (32.8%) have improved due to technology.

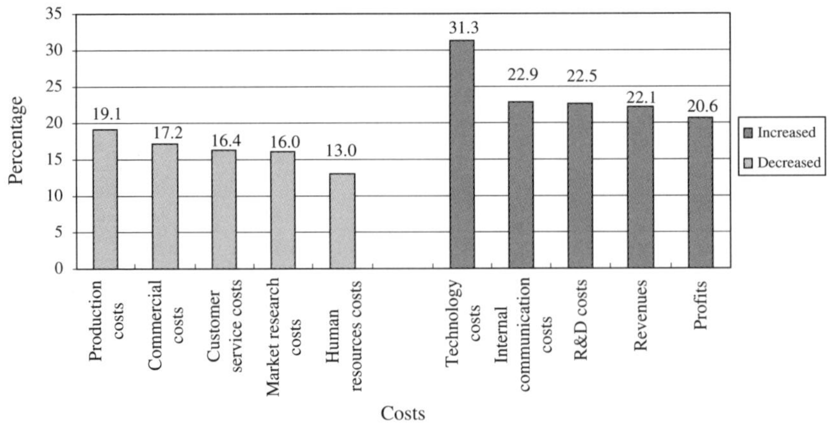

Fig. 4.17. Business results.

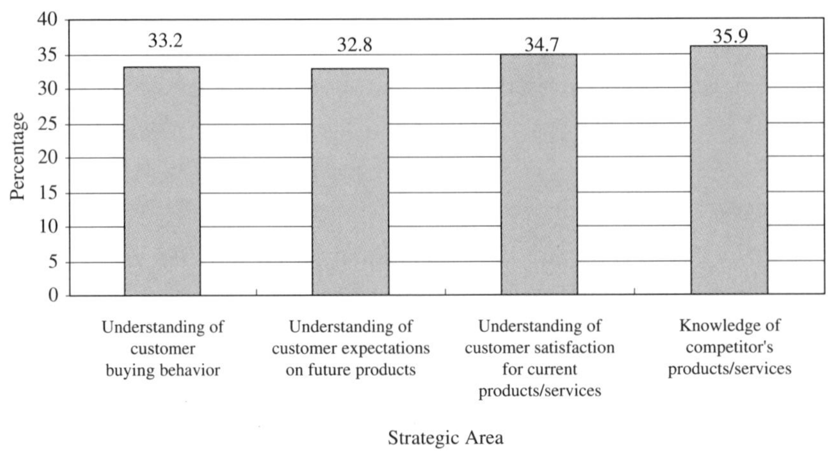

Fig. 4.18. Strategic areas impacted by technology.

4.3.6. *Globalization*

Questions 21 & 22 — Are organizations becoming more global? Is the geographic reach of organizations increasing?

As shown in Fig. 4.19, organizations have expanded and are planning to expand their business operations globally. 29.8% of the organizations currently have and plan to have business operations in South East Asia in the next three years. Organizations have and plan to have business operations in East Asia (24%) and USA (24%) in the near future.

On the other side, organizations do not plan to have business operations in Africa (34.7%), Middle East (30.9%), Latin America (29.8%), Canada & Mexico (28.6%), and South Asia (27.9%).

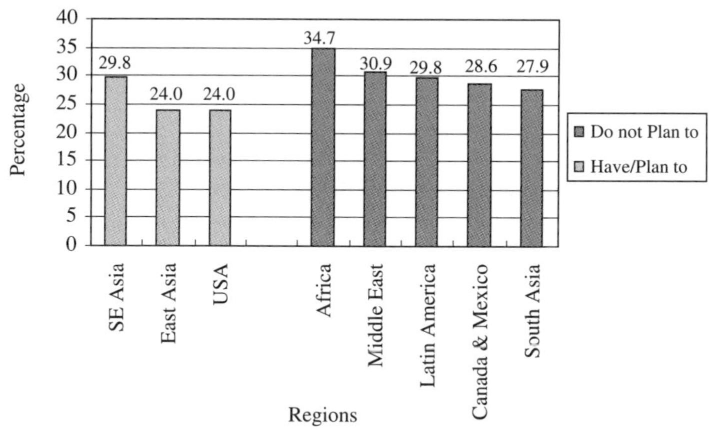

Fig. 4.19. Globalization regions.

These trends are shown in Fig. 4.19.

Almost a quarter of the organizations (24% of the organizations increased or increased significantly) are increasing their trade in other countries. The number of production/service bases and the number of countries in supplier base have been increased by 23.3 and 17.2% of the organizations (increased or increased significantly). The branches/distribution centers globally (16.4% of the organizations), the number of languages on website (16.4% of the organizations), and the average distance to suppliers (13.4% of the organizations) have also been increased. These are shown in Fig. 4.20.

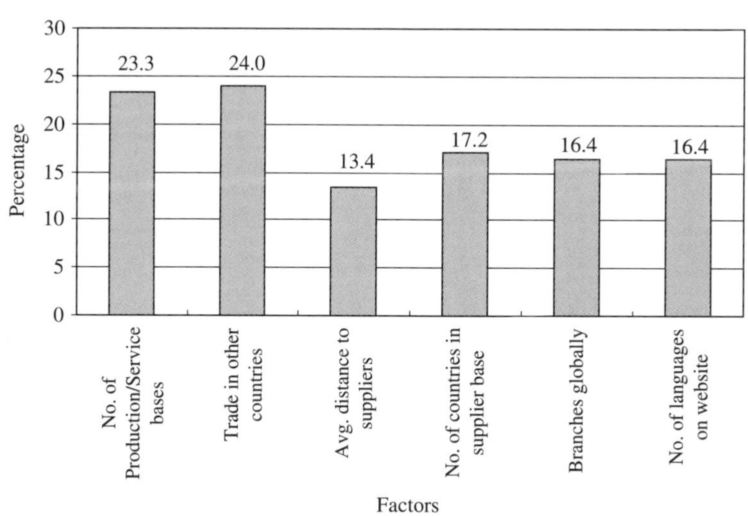

Fig. 4.20. Globalization trends.

Acknowledgment

This research was supported by Service and Logistics Research Center of Korea University Business School.

Appendix A: Survey Respondent Sample Characteristics

A total of 262 received. The following were the sample characteristics.

Titles of respondents were as follows	
CIO and other C level executives (%)	1.53
Directors (%)	6.87
Manager (%)	57.25
Staffs (%)	15.65
No response (%)	18.70
The size of organization in terms of	
Annual revenues %	
Up to 1 billion won	17.18
1 billion to 20 billon won	26.33
Over 1billion won	36.26
No response or not applicable	20.23
Number of employees (%)	
Up to 200 employees	42.37
200 to 1000 employees	30.92
Over 1000 employees	25.57
No response or not applicable	1.14
IT characteristics of IT organization in terms of	
IT budget as a percentage of annual revenue (%)	
Up to 1%	12.97
1% to 5%	17.56
Over 5%	18.32
No response or not applicable	51.15
Number of IT employees (%)	
Up to 10 IT employees	48.09
10 to 50 IT employees	22.52
Over 50 IT employees	24.05
No response or not applicable	5.34
Sectors of organizations (%)	
Professional, Scientific & Technical Services	21.76
Wholesale & Retail Trade	19.85
Manufacturing	19.85
Finance and Insurance	13.74
Government agency	10.69
Construction	6.11
Transportation	4.20
Other Services	2.29
Educational Services	0.76
Utilities	0.75

CHAPTER 5

ICT AS AN AGENT OF CHANGE IN SPANISH COMPANIES: CURRENT SITUATION AND FUTURE TRENDS

JOSEP VALOR, SANDRA SIEBER, MARISOL PÉREZ
and EULÁLIA SANZ

Summary

This study, carried out by the e-business Center PwC&IESE, is the Spanish Chapter of the Business and Information Technologies (BIT) Project, being spearheaded by the UCLA Anderson School of Management. The main objective of the project is to analyze the impact of the new information and communication technologies (ICT) on business practices.

The study has been conducted by a survey addressed to the chief information officers of Spanish organizations belonging to a wide range of industries. All the companies make independent decisions on issues related to their information systems. To allow for crosscountry comparisons, the Spanish Chapter has followed the guidelines set forth for all countries. As a consequence, this summary reports the main findings for Spain, comparing them with previous US results.

The results indicate that ICTs have a positive impact on business activities of Spanish companies, mainly by the reduction of (1) production costs, (2) internal information costs, (3) the creation of new work habits, and (4) the implementation of user-oriented strategies. Nonetheless, no significant changes can be observed neither in operating margins nor revenues, and the use of ICTs does not seem to have contributed to simplify organizational structures.

Comparing the results obtained in the Spanish survey with those of the United States, the main difference between the implementation of ICT in both countries lies in the organization of the workforce. While Spanish companies have experienced only small or even inexistent changes of their organizational structures, US companies have introduced more flexible structures, which increase the geographic dispersion of workers.

5.1. Introduction

Till date, information and communication technologies (ICT) have experienced a spectacular growth rate. According to IDC, global investment in ICT in the past 40 years has risen from 2000 million dollars to 900,500 million dollars.

Lately, this growth rate has slowed down. For example, Forrester estimates that this year in the United States, investment in ICT — which encompasses personnel; external services; telecommunications equipment, PCs, servers and storage; and software, both licenses and maintenance — will rise at a modest rate of 7%. Nevertheless, markets such as external services will continue to experience two-digit growth rates of up to 27%.

What is clear, however, is that nowadays, ICT has a massive presence in companies, backed by information systems to increase their efficiency and productivity. For many companies, technology has become a tool for achieving their strategies. In fact, a recent study from the US pointed out that more than 60% of the companies in that country define their technological infrastructure as a factor that differentiates them from their rivals.

In Spain, the situation is somewhat different. According to the market analyst Penteo, the importance of ICT in companies is on the wane. This firm claims that only 27% of the companies in Spain regard technology as a key. Despite this, almost half of the Spanish companies define information systems as being necessary.

Thus, information systems have become a key factor in company competitiveness. As a result, it is important to understand what executives look at when investing in IT. With the purpose of shedding light on the status of technology in Spanish companies, we have undertaken a study that analyzes six basic dimensions in the ICT — company strategy relationship, technology adoption/infrastructure, forward (customer) facing, trading partners, business results, and internal organization (management and work-place issues, and business process outsourcing). Analyzing these factors has enabled us to devise an X-ray of the situation of ICT on the Spanish business scene in an attempt to gain further insight into Spanish executives' behavior with regard to IT expenditures.

However, this research has also provided us with the opportunity to compare the behavior of IT decision maker in Spain with their US counterparts. Our study is in fact the Spanish chapter of a worldwide research project being spearheaded by the University of California at Los Angeles (UCLA). The project, which analyses the impact of the new ICT on business practices, is known as the Business Information Technologies (BIT) project. IESE Business School — Universidad de Navarra is the management school chosen to carry out this study in Spain, a project that has arisen from the desire to promote continuity and with the collaboration of prominent business schools all over the world. The study is also being conducted in Chile in conjunction with the Pontificia Universidad Católica de Chile, in France through the Theseus Institute, in Germany along with the European Institute for the Media; in India in association with IIT Mumbai, in Italy via SDA Bocconi, in Korea under the leadership of the Korea University Business School, and in Sweden through the World Internet break Institute.

The objective of the first edition of the BIT, sponsored by the e-business Center PwC & IESE, is to obtain an indicator that enables us to describe the changes that companies and industrial sectors all over the world have experienced in recent years with the introduction of new technologies, as well as to predict the future evolution of these chronologies.

5.2. Methodology

The BIT study has been conducted by a survey addressed to different organizations belonging to a wide range of sectors in industry. All of the companies make independent decisions on issues related to information technology systems, and each of these companies has a chief information officer (CIO) or a person in a similar position. Given the fact that these individuals make the decisions on investment in new technologies within the company, it is highly likely that they also have a certain degree of responsibility in terms of the organization's profits and losses (although this does not always hold true). The surveys were addressed to the CIOs.

One of the reasons why a survey was used (instead of interviews, case studies or direct data gathering) was the possibility of encompassing a greater number of sectors within the industry. Studying the impact of the new technologies in a larger swath of sectors leads to a greater understanding of the phenomenon. Of course, the impact of information technology is closely related to the nature of each industry, and the survey is being supplemented with studies on a sector-by-sector basis.

The survey was sent to 5567 companies from different industrial sectors in Spain. Between June and September 2004, a first wave of surveys was sent to the 250 leading Spanish companies in terms of turnover. Between October 2004 and April 2005, a second wave consisting of 5317 surveys was sent to Spanish companies of all sizes.

The data were gathered from 95 Spanish companies. The CIOs were asked to fill out the survey by e-mail, fax or through an online form.

The questionnaire used in the Spanish chapter of the BIT is based on the questions developed by UCLA, with the appropriate adaptations to the situation in Spain. The questions were generated after identifying the issues that were regarded as the most interesting and important to research. These issues were framed within specific hypotheses that could be confirmed or refuted through the responses to the study. The companies profile is presented in Table 5.1.

5.3. The Situation of ICT in Spanish Companies

5.3.1. *Technology adoption/infrastructure and budget trends*

5.3.1.1. *Adoption of technology and infrastructures*

Currently, the main technologies that Spanish companies make use are websites and e-commerce, groupware/productivity tools (such as Lotus Notes), and enterprise resource planning (ERP) systems.

Table 5.1. Companies profile.

Annual revenue	**Percentage**
Less than 10 million euros	13
Between 10 and 100 million euros	10
Between 100 and 300 million euros	7
Between 300 million and 1,000 million euros	8
More than 1,000 million euros	16
No answer	45
Percentage of revenue spent on ICT	**Percentage**
Less than 1%	21
Between 1% and 5%	33
Between 5% and 10%	5
Between 10% and 40%	11
More than 40%	2
No answer	28
Number of employees	**Percentage**
Fewer than 200	25
Between 200 and 600	13
Between 600 and 1,000	4
Between 1,000 and 5,000	24
Between 5,000 and 30,000	8
More than de 30,000	6
No answer	19
Number of ICT employees	**Percentage**
Fewer than 20	42
Between 20 and 50	18
Between 50 and 100	9
Between 100 and 250	6
More than 250	3
No answer	21
Sectors to which the companies belong (multiple choice)	**Percentage**
Manufacturing	27
Services	58
Physical products	17
Information products	14
Consumer	8
Corporate	23

Although digital receipts and business process modelling tools are currently not very widespread in Spanish companies — only 28% use them — within the next three years another 28% of the companies plan to acquire technology for digital receipts, and 29% claim that they are to implement business process modelling tools.

Specifically, as shown in Fig. 5.1, 89% of the companies use websites and e-commerce, while 85% have groupware/productivity tools, 79% of the Spanish companies make use of ERP systems.

On the other hand, only 9% of the companies surveyed use radio frequency identification (RFID), although 32% state that they plan to do so within the next three

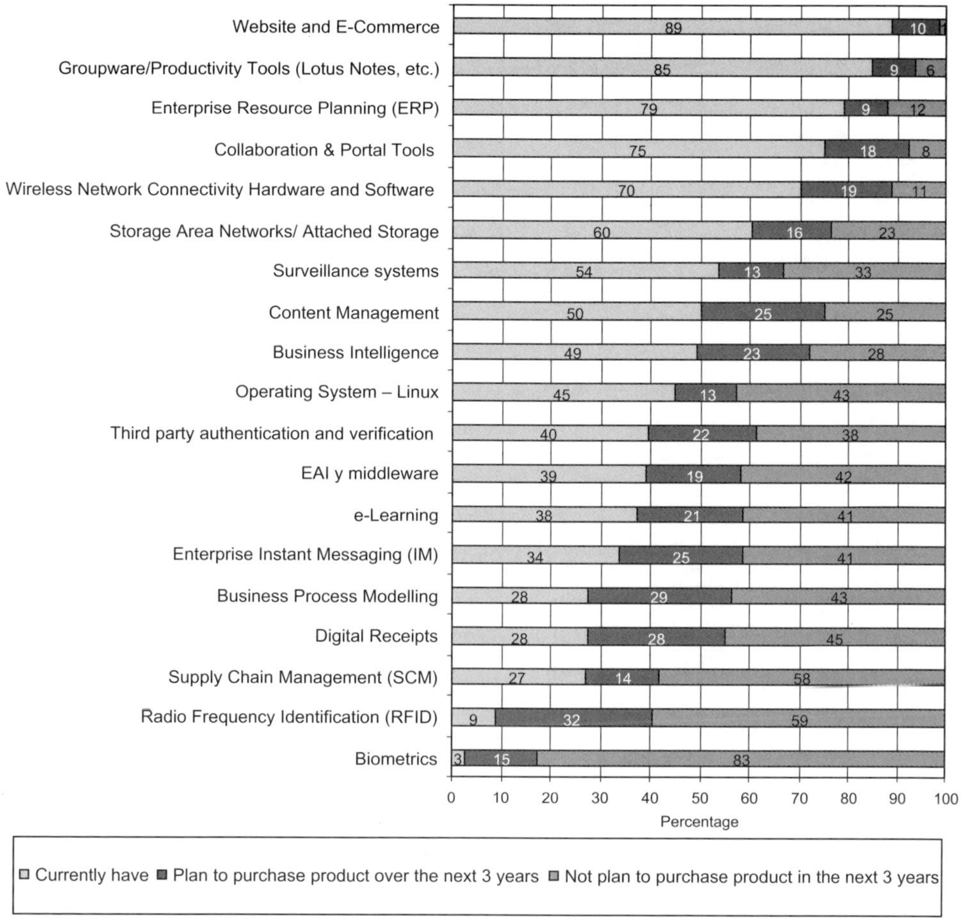

Fig. 5.1. Technology adoption/infrastructure.

years. The technology that has been adopted the least among Spanish executives is biometrics[a]: only 3% of the companies use it, and 15% plan to purchase this technology in the near future. 82% of the companies currently lack this technology and have no plans to purchase it.

If we compare the situation of technology in Spanish companies in 2004 with the situation forecast by the same executives for 2007 [see Figs. 5.2(a) and 5.2(b)], it becomes clear that websites and e-commerce will continue to be the most popular technologies, followed by productivity and group work tools. However, ERP systems

[a]Biometric technology involves using a personal characteristic as a password, that is, it entails identifying individuals through some physical feature (digital fingerprint, the iris, voice).

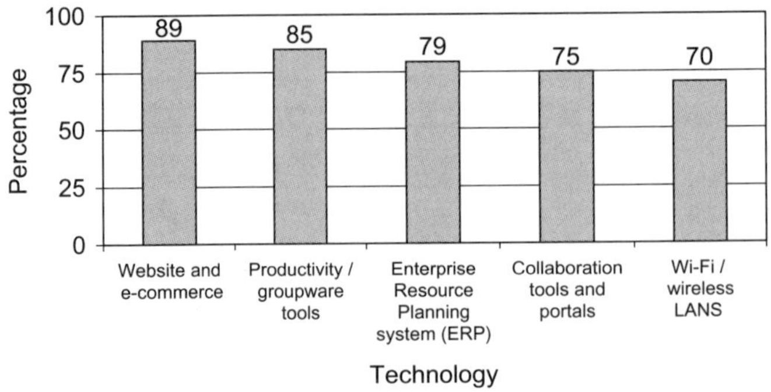

Fig. 5.2(a). Technology/Infrastructure: 2004.

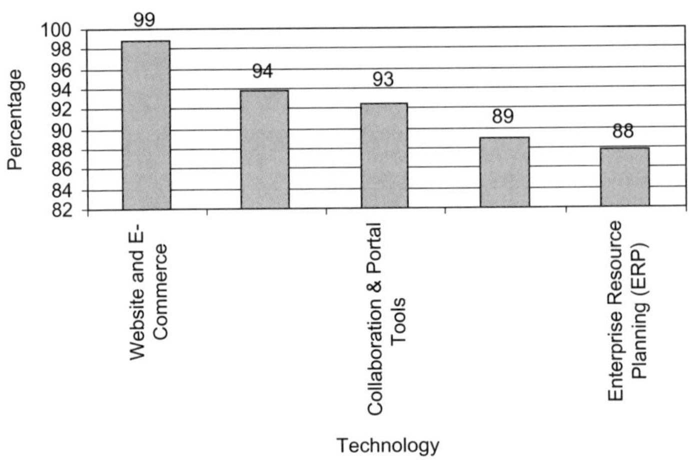

Fig. 5.2(b). Technology/Infrastructure: 2007.

will fall from third to fifth place in the list of most widely adopted technologies. Thus, the use of this technology is currently so widespread that it is already reaching its ceiling.

ERP is the tool that the companies have been using for the longest time; on an average, the Spanish companies have had this technology for seven years. Thus, it is logical that it is reaching its maximum penetration point.

Finally, the use of collaboration tools and portals is expected to increase until they are implemented in more than 90% of the companies. The same holds true with wireless network connectivity hardware and software, which will experience a 23% increase. This growth is considerable, if we bear in mind that the Spanish companies have had these technologies for a relatively short time: an average of three and two years, respectively.

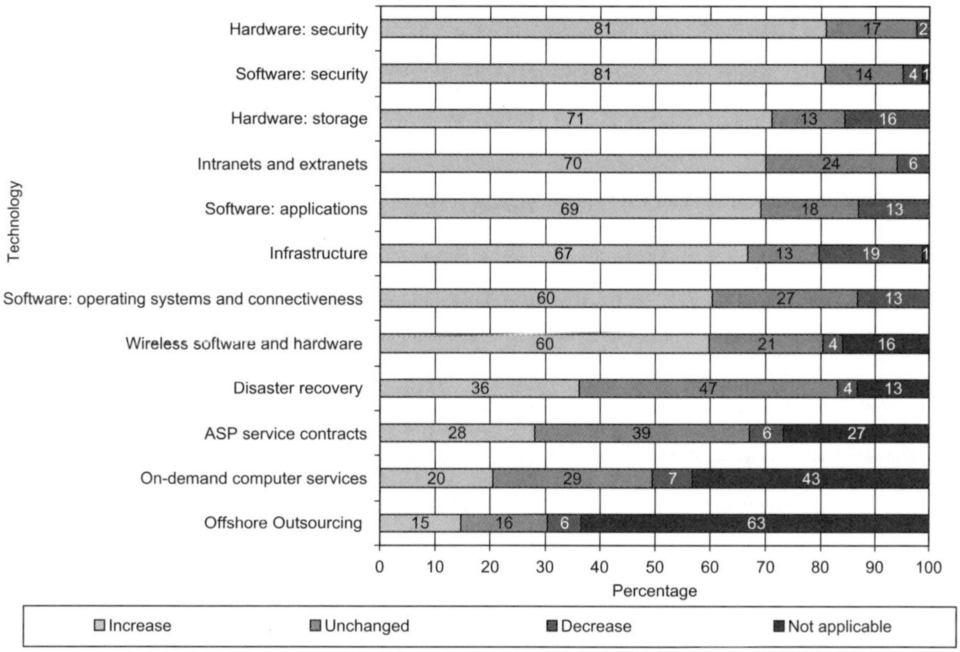

Fig. 5.3. Budget trends (past three years).

5.3.1.2. *Budget trends*

The IT budget item that has risen the most in the past three years is hardware and software security: more than 80% of the companies responding to the survey confirmed the growth in expenditures earmarked for both types of technology (see Fig. 5.3). In contrast, the most static factor is disaster recovery, and almost half the companies (47%) have not changed their investments allocated for this.

Likewise, investments in infrastructure are the line items that have experienced the greatest cuts in the past three years: almost 20% of the Spanish companies have lowered their spending on this, while hardware storage costs have also gone down by 16% in the companies surveyed.

Finally, the budget earmarked for outsourcing services to third countries (offshoring) and on-demand computer services are the ones that have increased the least in the past three years.

5.3.2. *Internal organization*

The issue of the impact of ICT on the internal organization of companies is broached from two perspectives: the standpoint of work and management and the standpoint of outsourcing processes.

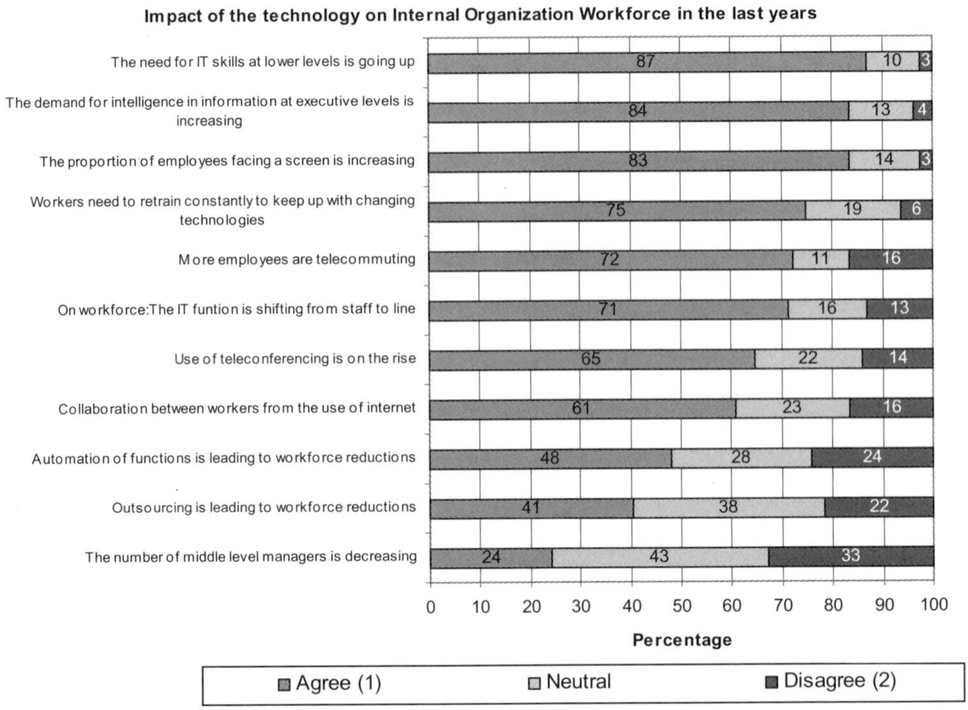

(1) Under this category, the answers "agree" and "very much agree" are grouped together.
(2) Under this category, the answers "disagree" and "very much disagree" are grouped together.

Fig. 5.4. Impact of the technology on internal organization workforce in the last years.

5.3.2.1. *Issues related to work and management*

In terms of the impact of technology on work and management (see Fig. 5.4), almost 90% of the companies agree (27% strongly agree and 60% agree) with the need to increase IT skills at the lower levels in the organization. No less important for 84% of the companies is the impact of IT on the demand for intelligent access to information at an executive level.

A full 83% of the companies surveyed claim that the proportion of employees working in front of a computer has risen, while 75% believe that ICT has generated the need to retrain workers, and 72% believe that the number of telecommuters has increased.

These results corroborate the fact that implementing ICT in the workplace is transforming the structures themselves have not been significantly affected, in that the organization is not more horizontal than before. In fact, only 24% of the companies responded that ICT has generated a reduction in middle-management positions, compared to 33% that have not noticed such a reduction. Likewise, 22 and 24% of the business people do not agree that subcontracting and automation, respectively, have translated into smaller staffs.

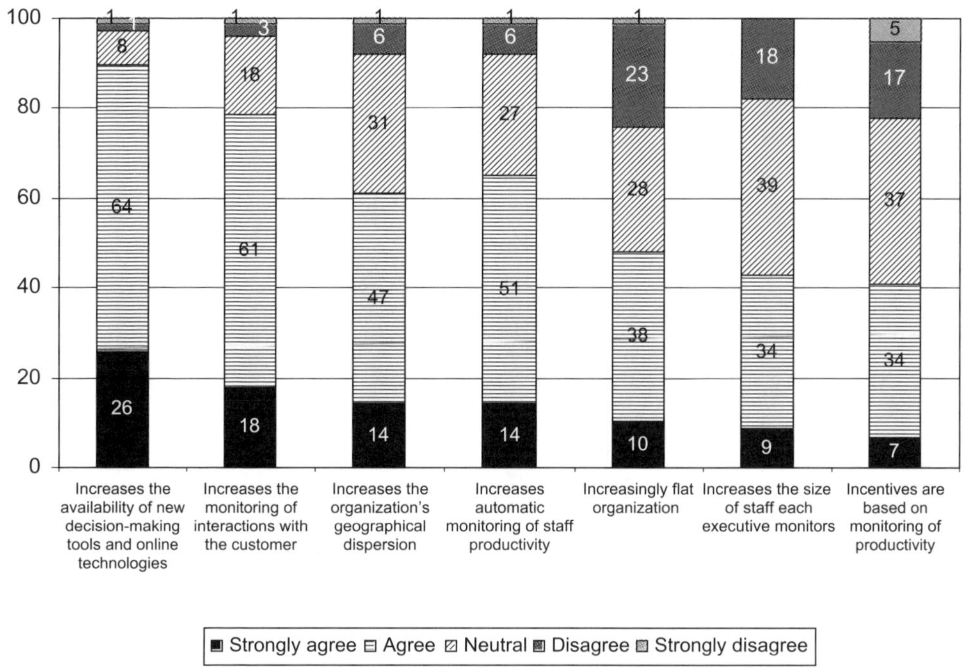

Fig. 5.5. Impact of technology on structure.

The results of the impact of technology on company structure (see Fig. 5.5) also indicate that the number of staff members supervised by a single executive has increased. Forty-three per cent of the respondents agreed with that statement, and 24% of the companies expressed their disagreement with the claim that ICT have led to a more horizontal organization.

However, in terms of the impact on company structure, 90% of the respondents believe that ICT has increased the availability of new tools for decision-making and online technology, while 78% claim that the monitoring of interaction with customers is enhanced. Thirty-seven per cent of the companies responding claimed neutrality on the idea that incentives are based on monitoring the productivity.

5.3.2.2. *Issues related to outsourcing processes*

Outsourcing business processes is yet another factor that has influenced companies' internal organization. Among the processes related to ICT, programming (85%) and network management (58%) are currently the processes that are most often outsourced.

Data management, on t he other hand, is the ICT process that is outsourced least often, but it seems to have reached its ceiling: 63% of the companies have not yet outsourced it, and none plan to do so within the next three years.

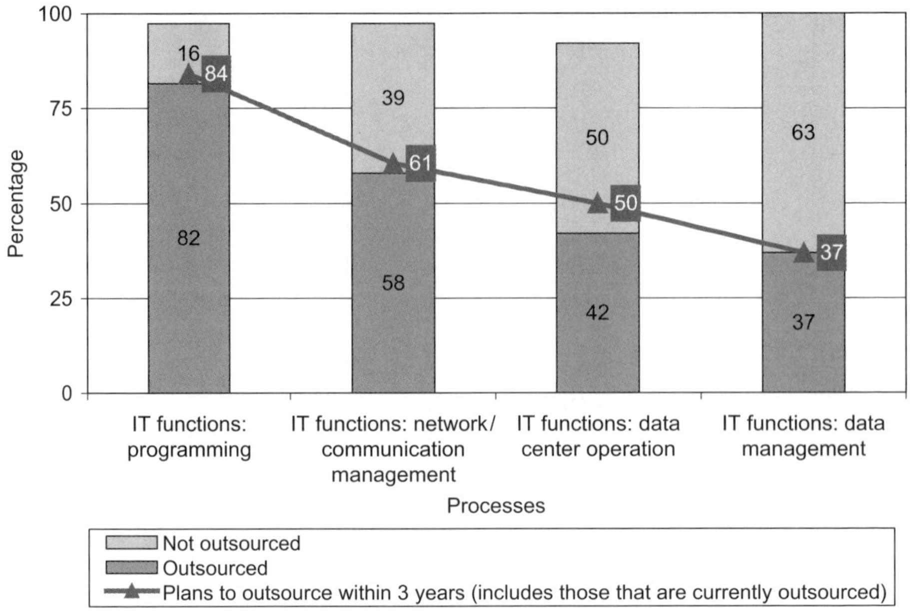

Fig. 5.6. Outsourcing of processes related to ICT.

In the next few years (see Fig. 5.6), programming will continue to be the most widely outsourced process in companies, with a rate of 84% predicted for 2007, followed by network management in 61% of the companies.

In terms of processes not directly related to ICT, customer contact and market research are the processes that are most frequently outsourced. Although accounting and finances are currently the areas that are least often outsourced (8%), the study stresses the fact that by 2007, 13% of the companies plan to outsource these services, which would mean a 67% increase over the 2004 rate.

The least often outsourced process not related to ICT is requests for proposals (RFP): 89% of the companies handle this internally. Thus, as a whole, processes related to ICT are more frequently outsourced than processes not related to technology.

In general, the sums earmarked for outsourcing ICT processes are quite low (see Fig. 5.8). Sixty per cent of the companies surveyed allocate a minuscule percentage to this area, namely less than 1% of their sales revenues, and only 4% spend more than 20% of their revenue.

As for processes not related to ICT (Fig. 5.7), the results are different, and companies tend to earmark a higher proportion of revenue to outsourcing this type of processes. To wit, 11% of the companies surveyed earmark more than 20% of their sales revenues to outsourcing processes not related to ICT, a percentage that is quite high compared to 4% of the companies that do so for ICT processes.

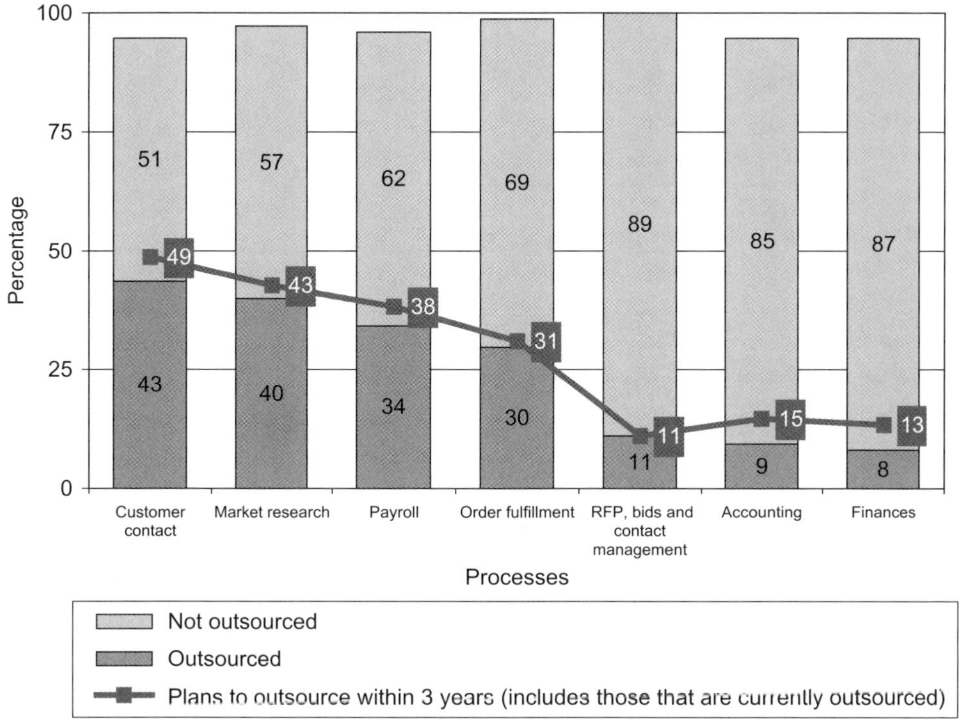

Fig. 5.7. Outsourcing of processes not related to ICT.

The amount budgeted to outsourcing in countries with lower costs (offshoring) is quite low, in that 71% of the companies earmark less than 1% of their sales revenues for this [Fig. 5.8(c)].

5.3.3. *Interaction with customers*

The customer contact point most commonly used by companies continues to be the telephone (90%). In second place is e-mail, used in 84% of the companies surveyed. Despite this, the companies continue to use direct contact with their customers. Indeed,

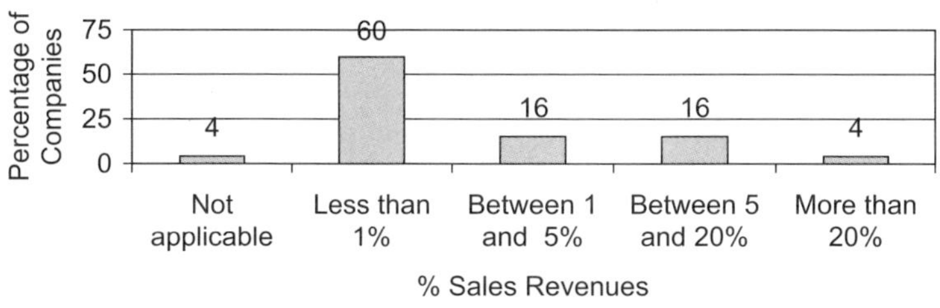

Fig. 5.8(a). Budget earmarked for outsourcing related to IT.

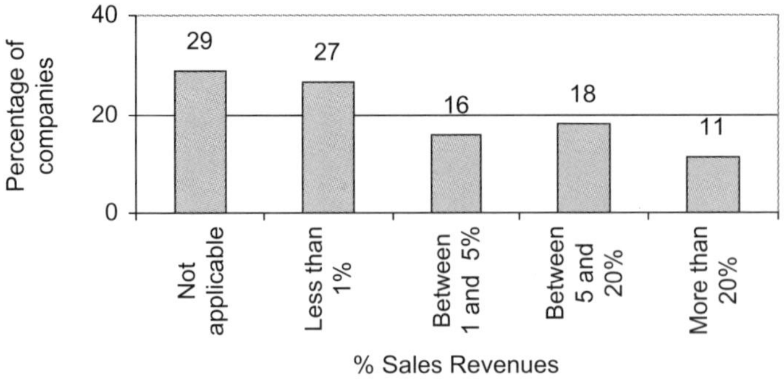

Fig. 5.8(b). Budget earmarked for outsourcing not related to IT.

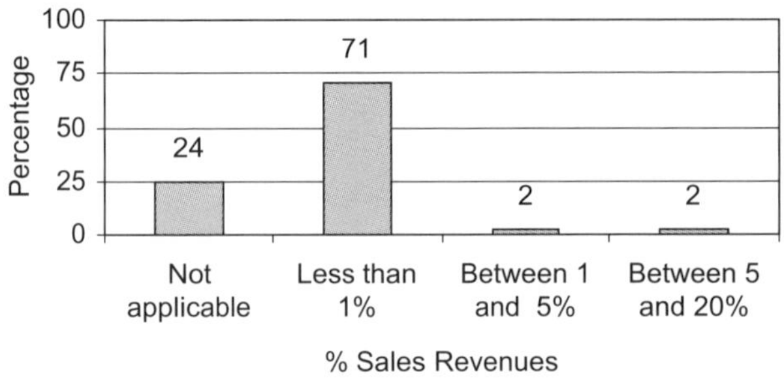

Fig. 5.8(c). Budget earmarked for outsourcing to countries with lower costs.

84% of the companies still use face-to-face contact often (see Fig. 5.9). The least popular technologies are telephone text messaging (12%), automated interactive voice response (12%), and screen pops (6%).

By grouping the customer contact points into four categories, we can more clearly see whether or not the companies use the new technologies to contact their customers. These groups are: online technologies, other technologies, direct points of contact, and other points of contact. Online technologies encompass e-mail, online catalogues, online transactions, online intermediaries or third parties, and screen pop-ups. Other technologies include telephone, fax, automated interactive voice response, computer telephony integration and phone text messaging. The direct points of contact refer to face-to-face contact and referrals. Finally, other points of contact are the traditional mails.

Following these groupings, online technology is the most widely used (36%), while the regular mail is least widespread in the companies surveyed (13%) (see Fig. 5.10).

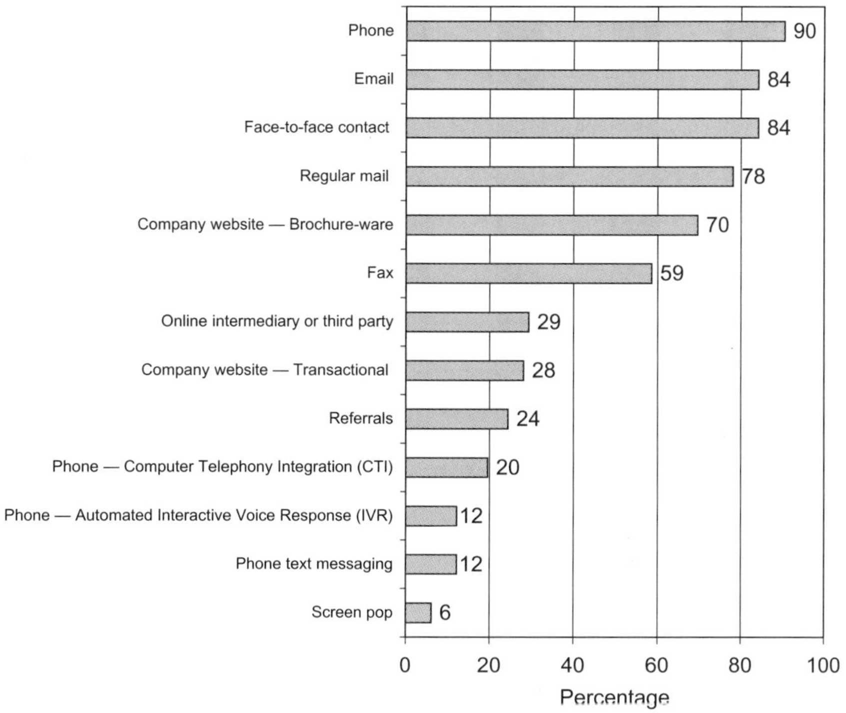

Fig. 5.9. Customer contact points.

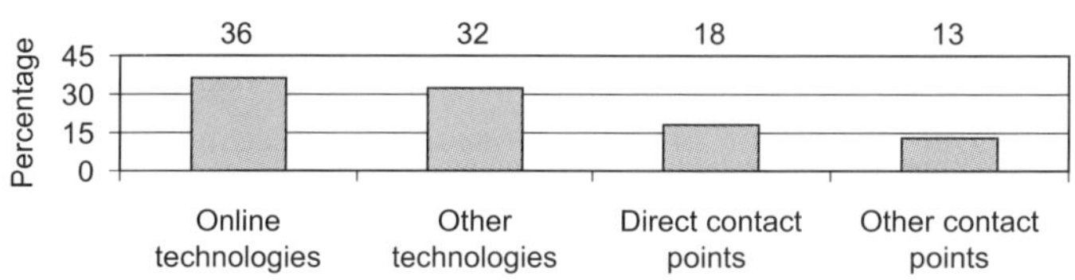

Fig. 5.10. Customer contact points.

5.3.3.1. *Customer relationship management (CRM)*

The most frequently automated process of CRM in Spanish companies is order tracking and fulfillment: 68% have this function systematized (30% have it highly automated and 38% partially). This is followed by placing orders in 66% of the companies (34% have this function highly automated and 32% partially systematized) (see Fig. 5.11).

The functions that are most often carried out manually are sales phone calls and marketing: 53% of the companies have not automated their sales phone calls, and 34% for marketing functions.

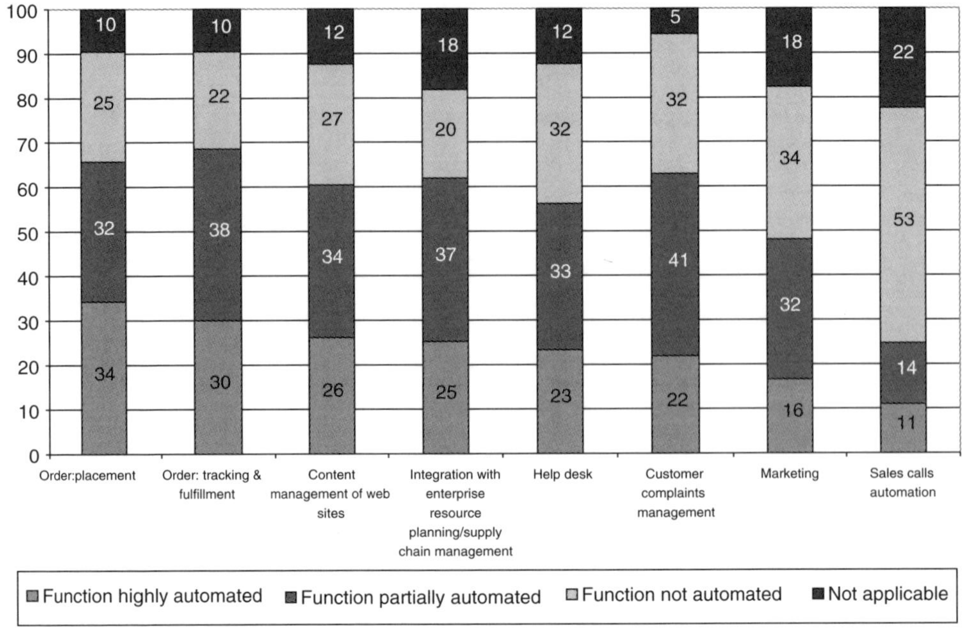

Fig. 5.11. Automation of CRM function.

5.3.3.2. *Mechanisms for customer segmentation and data analysis*

The majority of Spanish companies segment their markets by geographical areas and prices, two highly traditional formulas. Along these lines, the executives claim to rarely use customer portals, personalization of websites and segmentation according to access to online technology. Thus, it could be claimed that ICT has not yet become a popular tool for market segmentation (see Fig. 5.12).

As shown in Fig. 5.13, the technologies most often used to analyze customer data are customer profiles (65%), data marts and data warehousing (55%) and data mining, statistics (54%), and demand forecasting (52%). The least popular technologies in customer data analysis are fraud detection and data mining; and neural networks.

5.3.3.3. *Product sales channels*

The Spanish companies surveyed used both the traditional product sales channels as well as online sales. Twenty-two per cent of the companies continue to sell only via the traditional channel, while 75% use both traditional and online sales (see Fig. 5.14). Nevertheless, none of the companies in the sample sell solely online, and only 4% of the companies sell some of their products and services online.

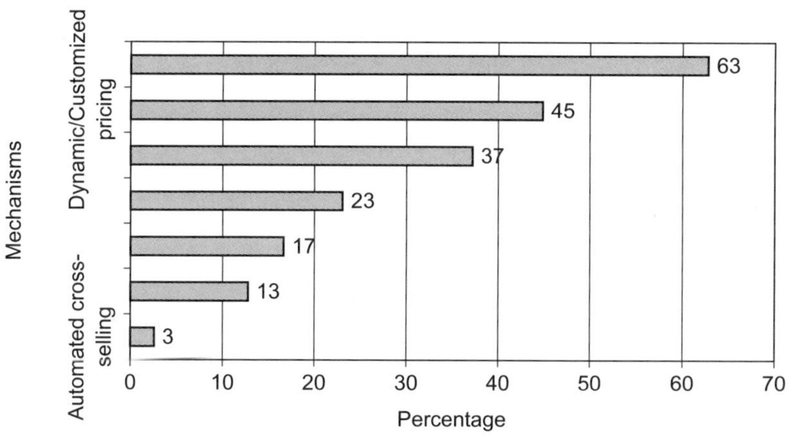

Fig. 5.12. Mechanisms for customer segmentation.

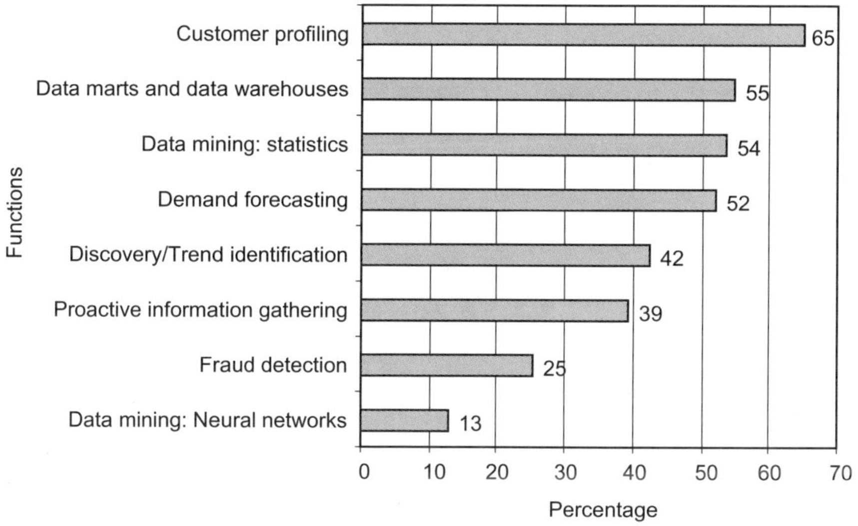

Fig. 5.13. Customer data analysis.

5.3.3.4. *Online advertising*

Most of the online advertising methods are wile used in Spanish companies. Pop-ups do not seem to be very popular among Spanish companies, with only 24% of the survey respondents using them to advertise. Web seminars (Webinars) are the method least often used (16%) (see Fig. 5.15).

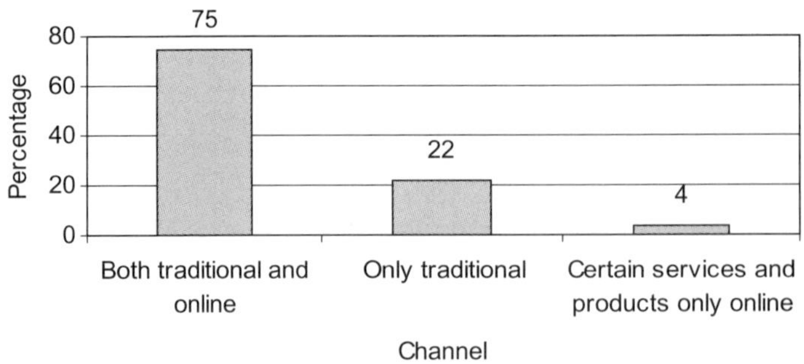

Fig. 5.14. Product sales channels.

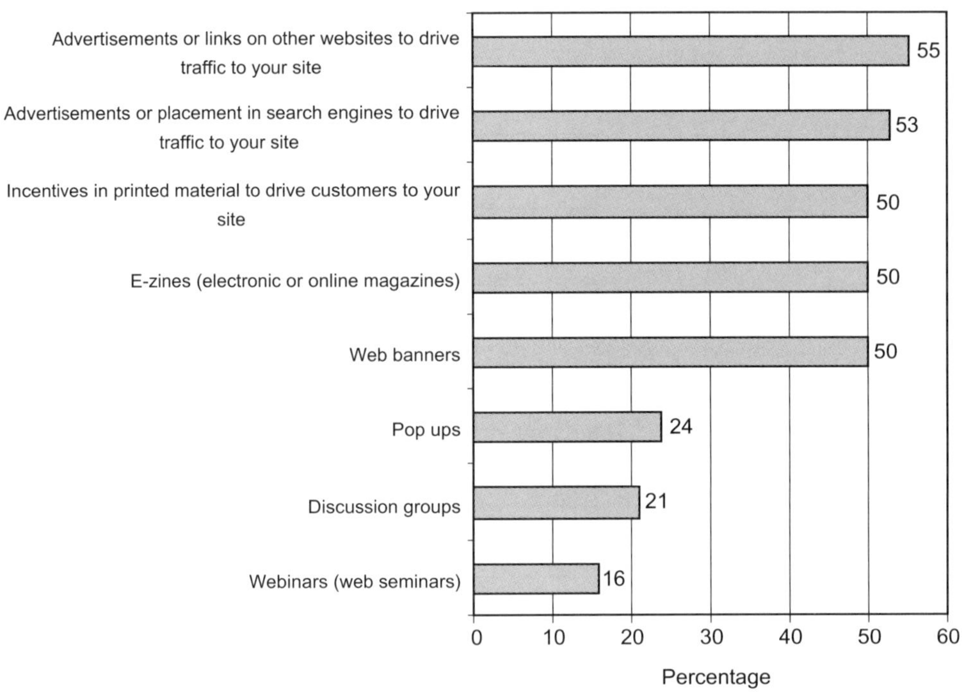

Fig. 5.15. Online advertising methods (multiple choice).

5.3.3.5. *Online versus traditional business*

The implementation of ICT in companies has not led to significant changes in their corporate images: 91% of the companies surveyed have kept the same brand concept in the online and offline environments, 89% have not modified their logo and 86% have not modified either their slogan or their name, as shown in Fig. 5.16.

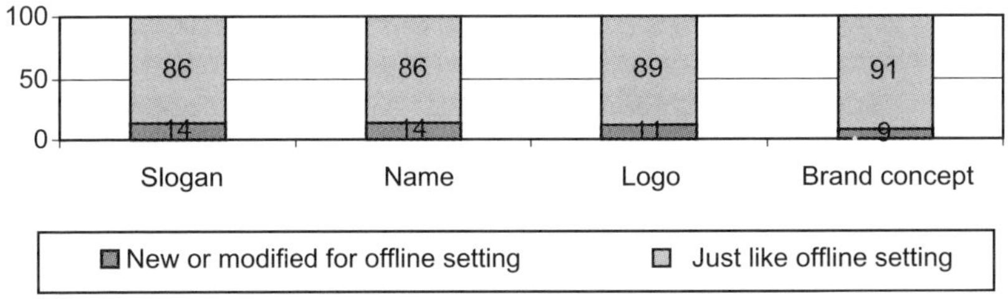

Fig. 5.16. Corporate image.

When comparing the online and traditional settings, the companies believe that both tasks by users and data collection have increased in the former, although the volume of online sales is still lower (see Fig. 5.17).

However, the results of online and traditional businesses seem to be quite similar, in that for 74% of the companies, prices and production costs are the same for both types of businesses. Thus, operating margins and income in both types of businesses do not differ substantially: for 68% of the companies, these margins are identical.

5.3.3.6. *Trading partners*

Most of the companies use some type of software to communicate with their suppliers, such as EDI (65%), web-enabled communication (58%), and demand planning and replenishment (55%) (see Fig. 5.18).

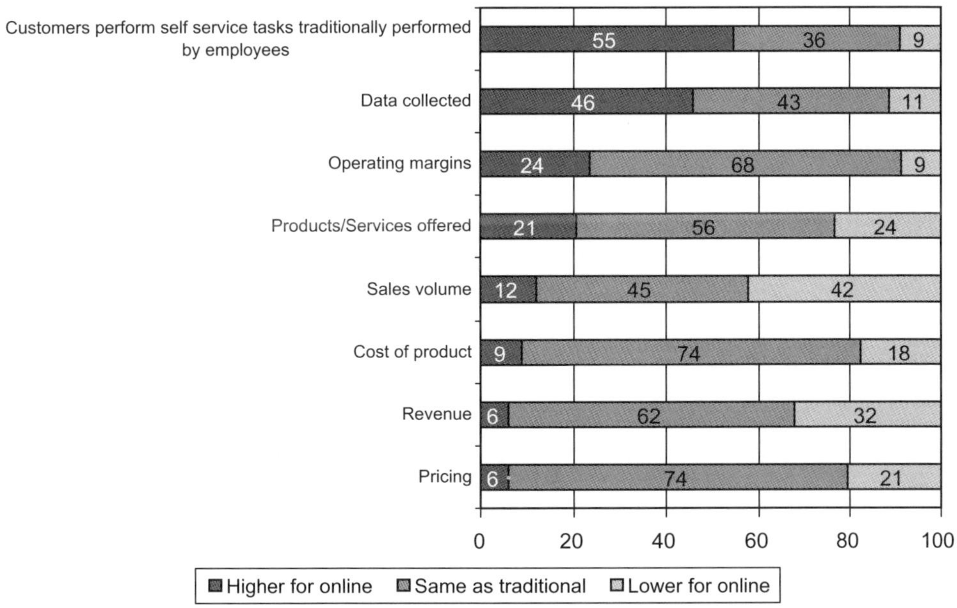

Fig. 5.17. Business results online vs. traditional.

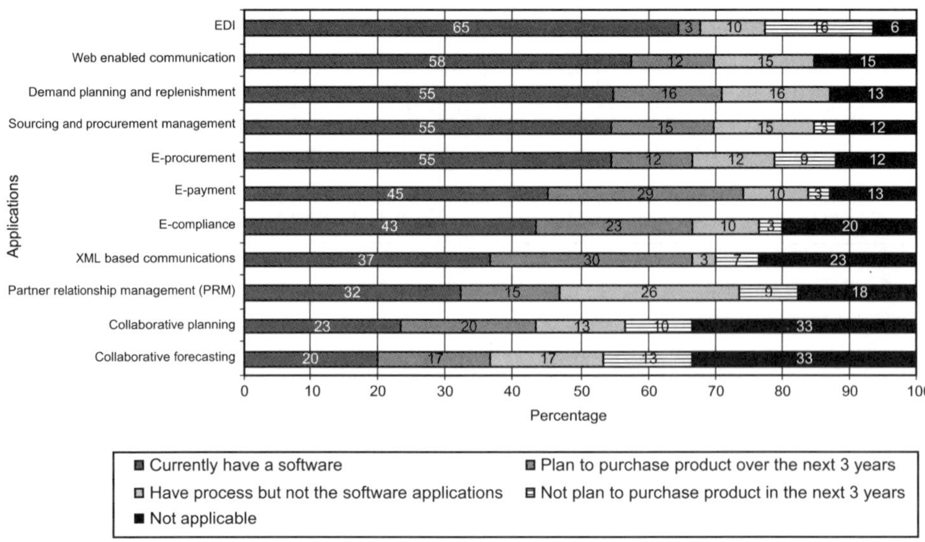

Fig. 5.18. Communication with trading partners.

The 26% claimed not to use any software to manage supplier relationships, and 17% lack solutions for collaborative forecasting.

By analyzing the forecasts for 2007, it can be seen that 74% of the companies plan to systematize electronic payment, a tool that is extremely underused at this time (see Fig. 5.19).

EDI will fall from being the leading application to fifth place in 2007, while electronic payment will shift from being used in 45% of the companies to 74%. The fall in EDI is due to the relatively high percentage of companies (16%) that do not plan to purchase this application within the next three years.

Likewise, electronic procurement will cease to be among the top applications, although it will experience 22% growth. The application that will experience the steepest growth between now and 2007 is collaborative planning, although it will remain toward the bottom of the list.

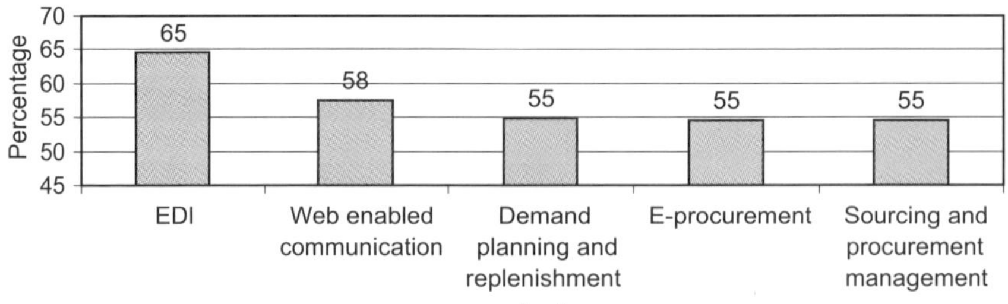

Fig. 5.19(a). Applications of software used in 2004.

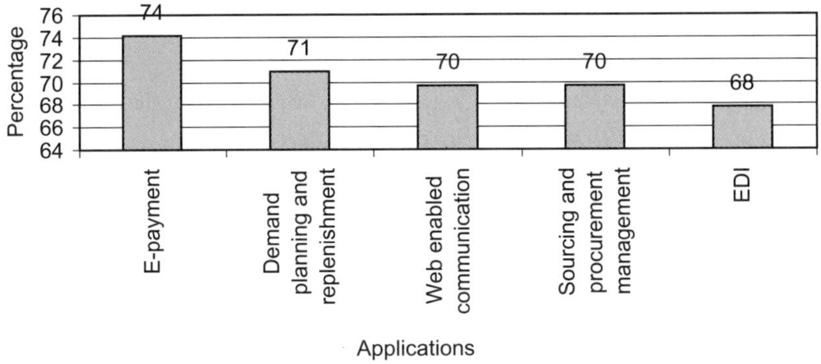

Fig. 5.19(b). Applications of software used in 2007.

5.3.3.7. *B2B mechanisms*

The main procurement mechanism is direct purchasing, used by 73% of the companies. More than half of the companies surveyed (55%) use catalogues as a B2B mechanism in the purchasing process. This is followed by long-term purchasing contracts and the electronic supplier market (49%). These data shed light on the fact that the companies are implementing ICT in their relationships with suppliers. The least widespread mechanisms are aggregators and exchange markets (Fig. 5.20).

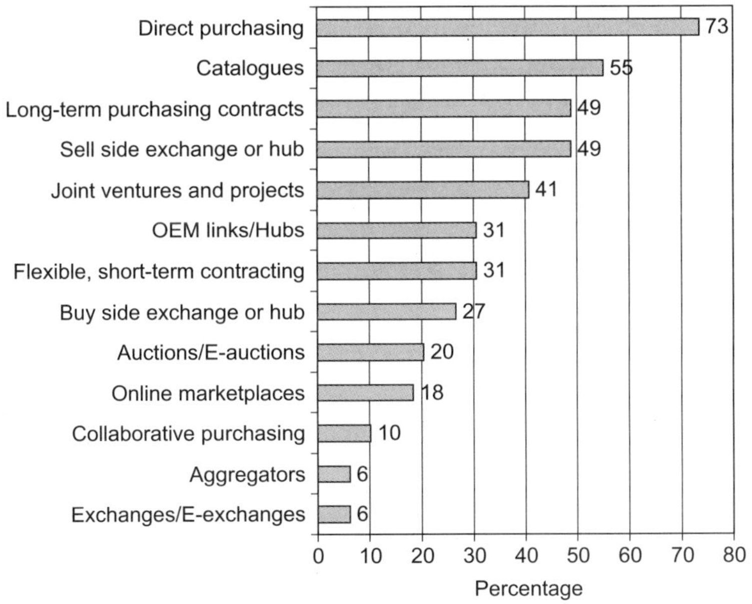

Fig. 5.20. B2B mechanisms.

5.3.3.8. *Impact of technology by business results*

ICT has positively affected business results. 64% of the companies surveyed claimed to have reduced their cost of production, 55% their internal communication costs, and 42% their human resources costs. In contrast, technology has not contributed to lowering investments in research and development (23%) and consultancy and collaboration services (18%).

None of the companies surveyed believes that the new technologies have lowered their market share; the majority (74%) believes that it has remained steady, and 26% think it has increased. However, almost half (49%) of the companies interviewed have noticed an increase in the technology costs. Only 5% of the respondents declared that the implementation of ICT in their businesses has increased the risk of new product failure.

Consequently with the results obtained in terms of comparisons of online and traditional business, few companies believe that the margins, profits and revenues have fallen with the introduction of ICT (see Fig. 5.21).

5.3.3.9. *Strategic areas affected by ICT*

Given the impact that the new technologies have been shown to have on businesses, companies have adjusted their business strategies to adapt to the new market circumstances. Thus, companies have increased their interest in learning about the competition's products and services and finding out users' satisfaction with current services. However, the majority of companies have not changed their strategies for getting to know about users' expectations for future products.

Additionally, the companies claim that none of their strategic areas has become less important after the implementation of ICT in their organizations (see Fig. 5.22).

5.4. The Situation in Spain Compared to the United States

The technological trends in Spain and the United States are quite similar. In both countries, the most widespread technological tools are websites and e-commerce. Nonetheless, despite the fact that these technologies stand as the most widely used in US businesses, they are used less there than in Spain (see Fig. 5.23).

Hardware and software for wireless network connectivity is the second most widely used technology in the United States, while in Spain this technology came in fifth place in 2004 and fourth place in the forecasts for 2007.

In the United States, ERP systems are not among the most widespread technologies, whereas in Spain they are currently in third place.

In terms of the least frequently used technologies (see Fig. 5.24), biometrics and RFID both stand out. Nevertheless, in the United States biometrics is more widespread

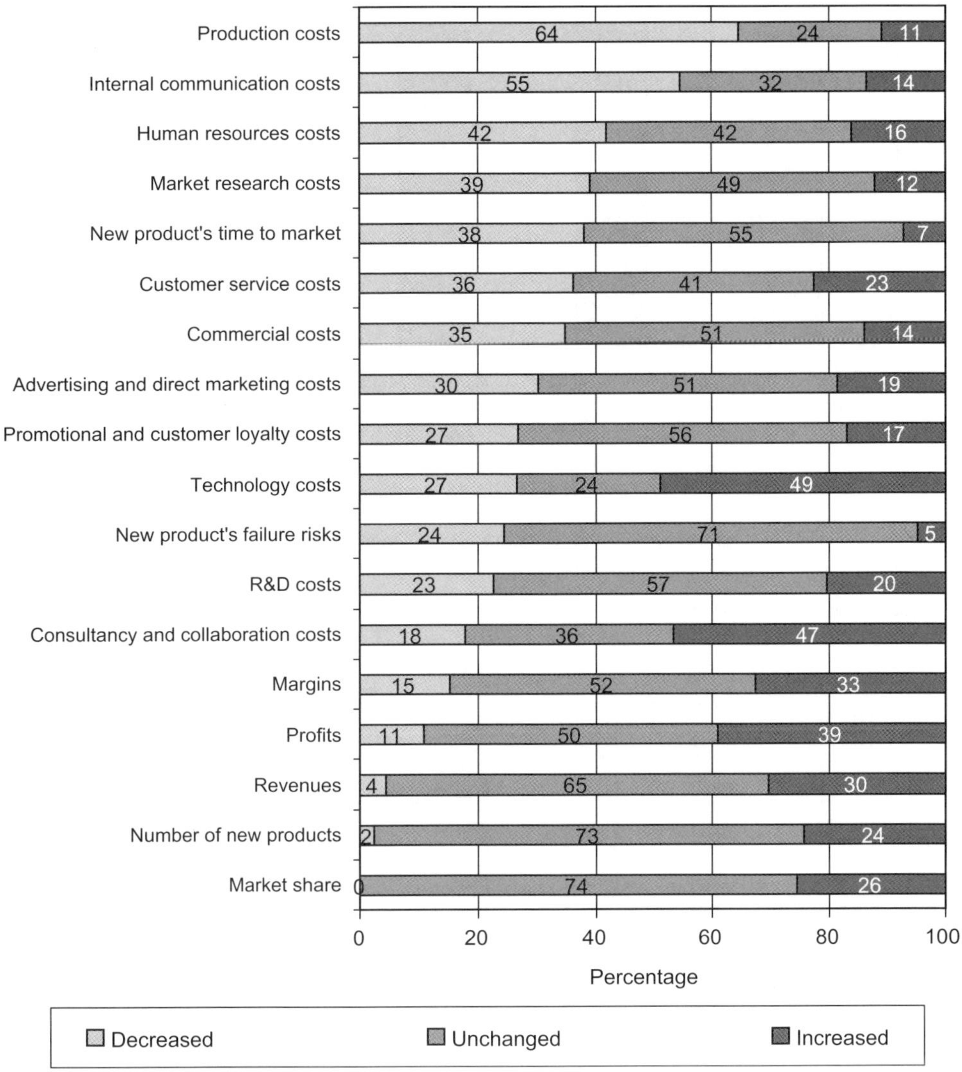

Fig. 5.21. Impact of technology in the business results.

than in Spain, where only 3% of the companies use it compared to 8% of the US companies. The forecasts for 2007 indicate that the same situation will prevail.

Spanish companies seem to be more willing to implement the use of RFID than US companies. Thirty-two per cent of the companies in Spain claim that they plan to adopt these technologies by 2007, compared to only 21% in the US. Furthermore, this technology is currently used less in the US than in Spain.

Budget trends in Spain show a greater inclination towards the adoption of hardware and software for security (see Fig. 5.25).

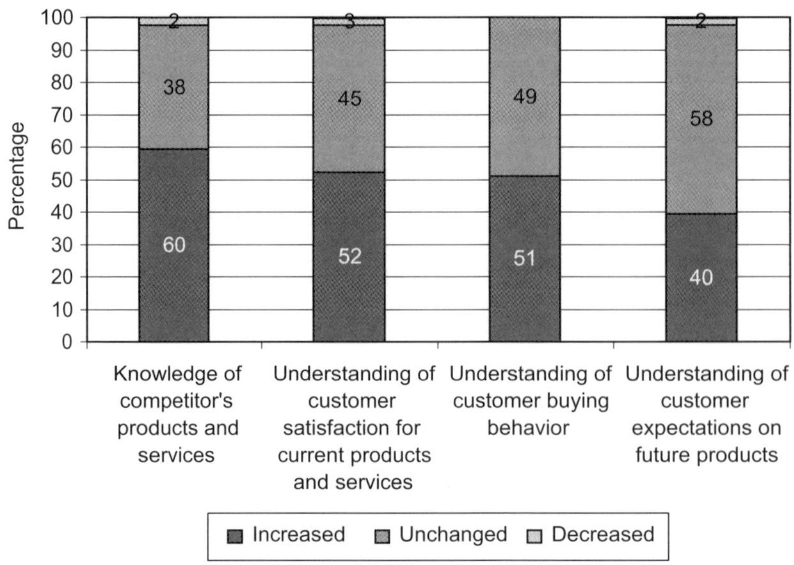

Fig. 5.22. Strategic areas impacted by technology.

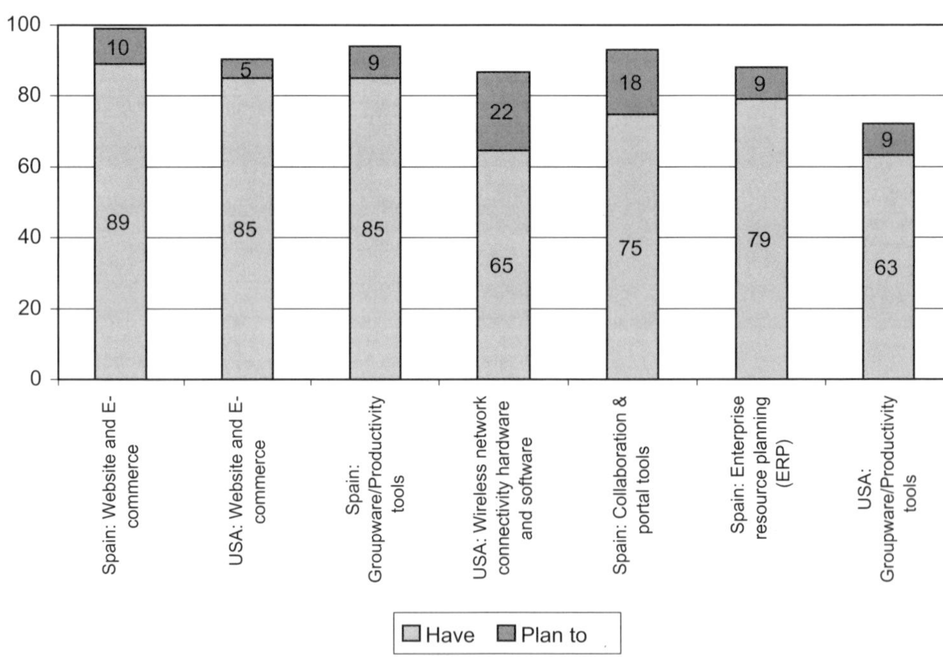

Fig. 5.23. Most used technologies Spain–USA.

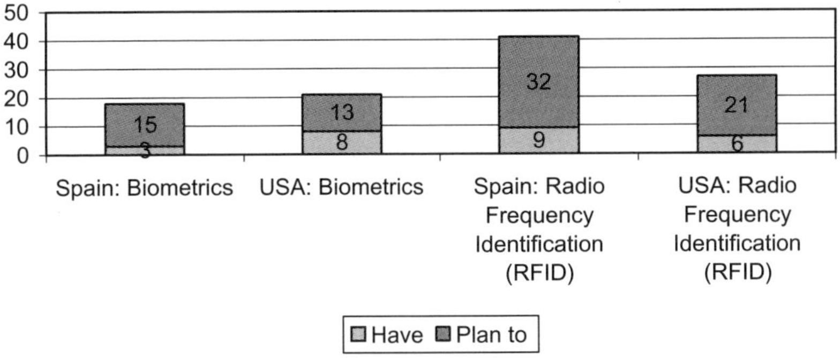

Fig. 5.24. Less used technologies Spain–USA.

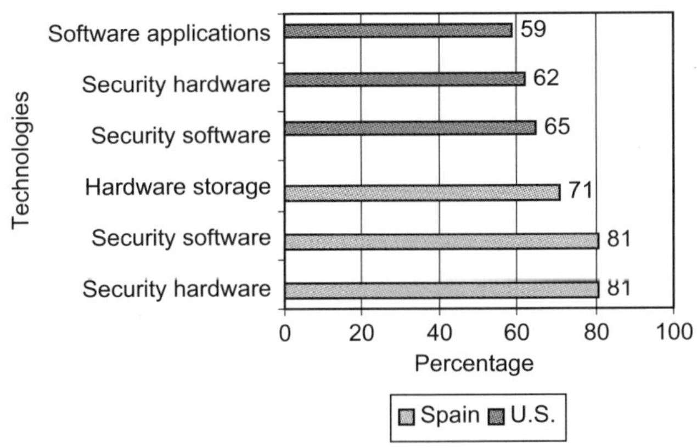

Fig. 5.25. Budget trends Spain–US.

However, for both countries, the items that have risen the least are those earmarked for on-demand computer services and outsourcing to third countries. In the case of Spain, the budget allocated for on-demand services has grown in only 20% of the companies, while this rate in the US is even lower (15%). Another 15% of the Spanish companies have increased their budget for outsourcing to third countries, a rate that in the US barely exceeds 10%.

In terms of the changes that have taken place in companies' internal organization [see Figs. 5.26(a) and 5.26(b)], both countries also converge in claiming that there have not been major changes in the number of middle-management positions or in the staff as a whole. What has undergone a significant transformation in both countries is the way of working after implementing ICT in companies. A high number of US companies responded that ICT has increased the intelligent demand for information at an executive level, the proportion of employees working at a computer and the need to improve skills at the lower echelons.

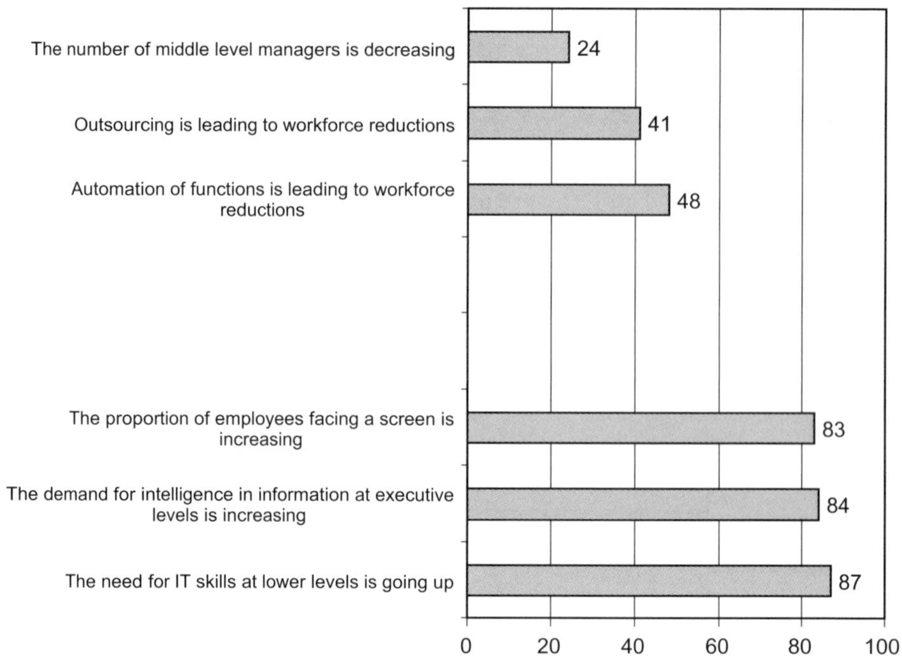

Fig. 5.26(a). Spain: internal organization workforce.

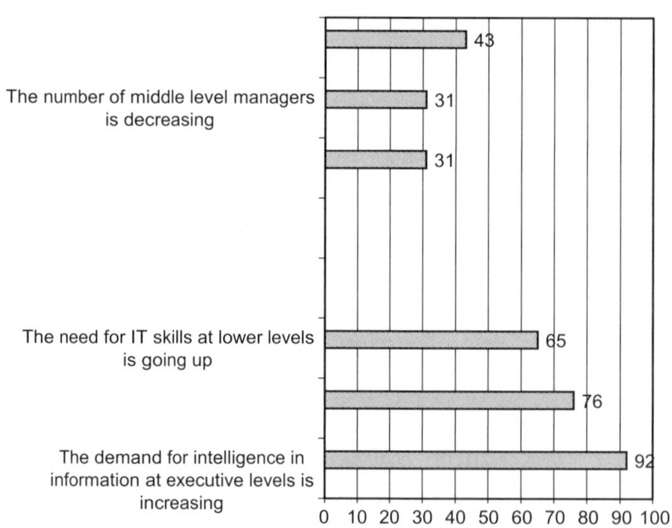

Fig. 5.26(b). USA: internal organization workforce.

When analyzing the responses from the US in terms of the impact of ICT on structure, the most significant trend identified in the Spanish companies was corroborated: the availability of decision-making tools and online technologies has increased.

However, unlike what has taken place in Spain, more than half of the American companies (54%) claim that their organizations are increasingly horizontal. In the US, geographical dispersion has also risen, which contributes to making companies' internal organization more flexible and horizontal. What is more, automated supervision of worker productivity has also increased, although the US responses resemble those of Spain in that the organizations do not provide employees with productivity-based incentives.

In the United States, the budget earmarked for outsourcing processes related to ICT is higher than that for unrelated processes. The same holds true in Spanish companies, despite the fact that in both countries the majority of companies allocate less than 1% of their sale revenues for this.

The way of contacting customers is quite similar in both countries. The Spanish and US companies mainly use online contact. This shows that — despite the fact that in both countries the telephone remains the main means of company–customer communication — the new technologies have gained substantial ground, especially in the case of e-mail and online catalogues (see Fig. 5.27).

In the United States, market segmentation is done by geographical zones, just as in Spain. The least widely used method is developing user communities (13% for Spain and 8.9% for the US) and automated crossselling (3% for Spain and 5.9% for the US).

The mechanism most often used in the US to analyze customer data are data mart and data warehousing applications, followed by statistics. For Spain, both mechanisms are also quite widely used, although customer profiles come in first place. Both US and Spanish companies do not make much use of neural networks.

In both countries, the prime methods of online advertising are advertisements on other websites, advertisements on browsers and incentives on printed matter. However,

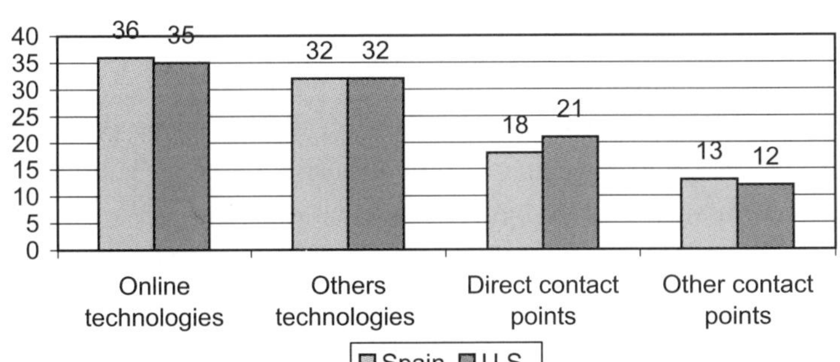

Fig. 5.27. Customer contact points Spain–U.S.

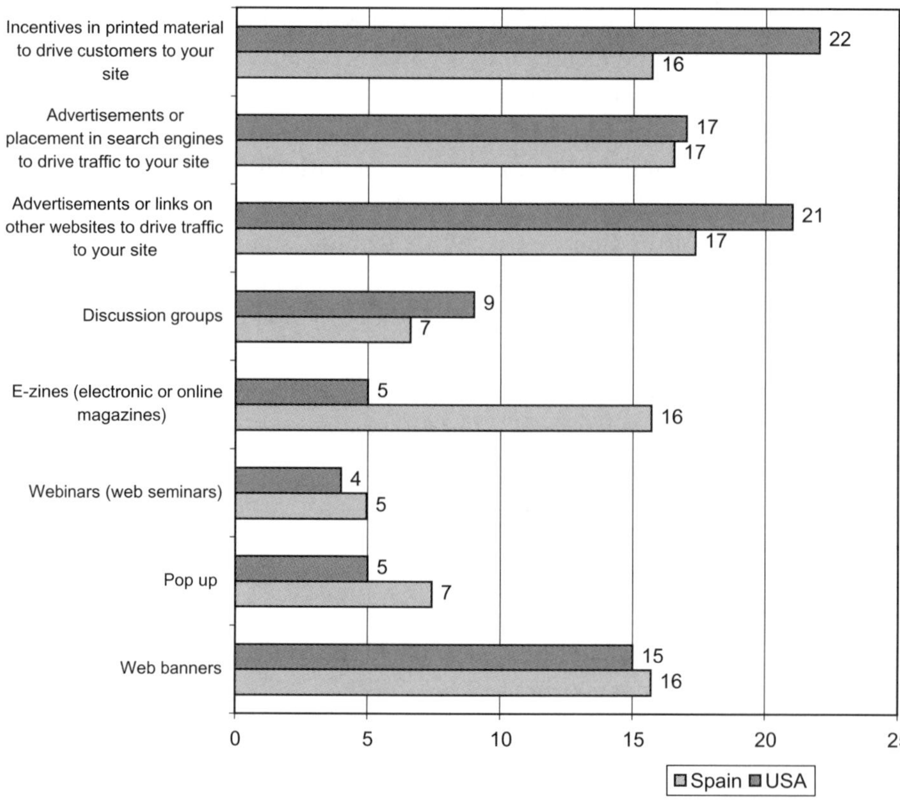

Fig. 5.28. Online advertising methods.

in the US the proportion of companies that use these advertising methods is higher (see Fig. 5.28). The Spanish companies prefer advertising in online magazines. Webinars, pop-ups and discussion groups come in last place in both countries.

The American companies express a greater willingness to change their corporate image as they join the online world. Indeed, while in Spain the majority of companies have not changed their corporate image (logo, slogan, name, brand concept), 23% of the American companies have modified their brand concept and logo.

Comparing online and traditional business results, we can see that fewer US companies believe that their sales volume are higher in online business (7.6%) compared to the 12% of the Spanish companies that do believe that their online sales are higher.

For both countries, the main difference between online and traditional settings is that the number of actions by users is higher in online business than in traditional business. The same holds true for data gathering.

In both countries, the most popular way of communicating with suppliers is EDI, although it seems to be more widely used in Spain: 65% of the Spanish companies make use of this technology compared to 45% of the US companies.

The communication based on XML technologies is more frequent in the US than in Spain. In Spain, only 37% of the companies use XML compared to 43% in the United States, making it the second most popular application in the US.

The least popular applications in both countries are supplier relationship management and collaborative planning and forecasting.

The technology affects an array of economic and operational results. The highest cost reductions in the US have taken place in internal communication (a reduction or significant reduction in 40.7% of the companies) and production (a reduction or significant reduction in 34.3% of the organizations) (see Fig. 5.29).

In both Spain and the US, the costs of customer services, human resources and market research have also gone down, as has the time to market for new products.

However, the costs of technology and consultancy and collaboration have risen for a significant number of companies: 53.2% in the US and 49% in Spain. Specifically, the costs of consultancy have risen to 29.8% in US organizations and 48% in Spanish organizations.

In both countries, the technology has also influenced companies' strategic areas. 51% of the US companies and 60% of the Spanish companies give greater importance to the customer satisfaction strategy for products and services, while 45.9% in the US and 52% in Spain are more interested in learning about the competition's products and services (see Fig. 5.30).

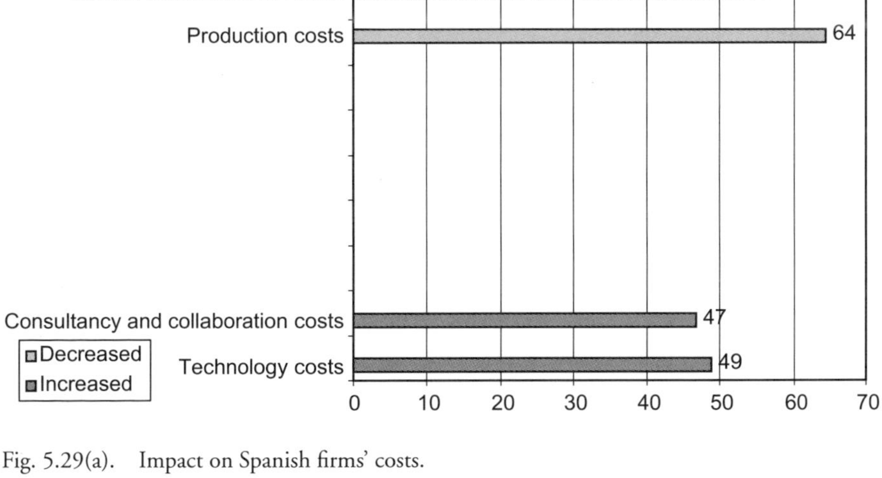

Fig. 5.29(a). Impact on Spanish firms' costs.

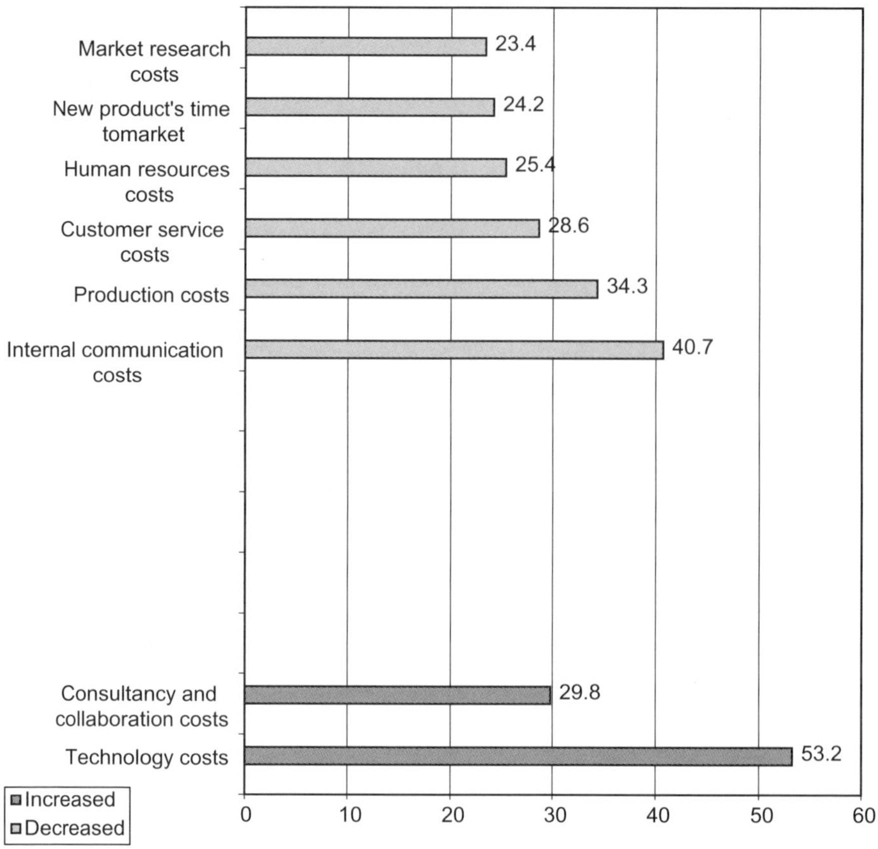

Fig. 5.29(b). Impact on USA firms' costs.

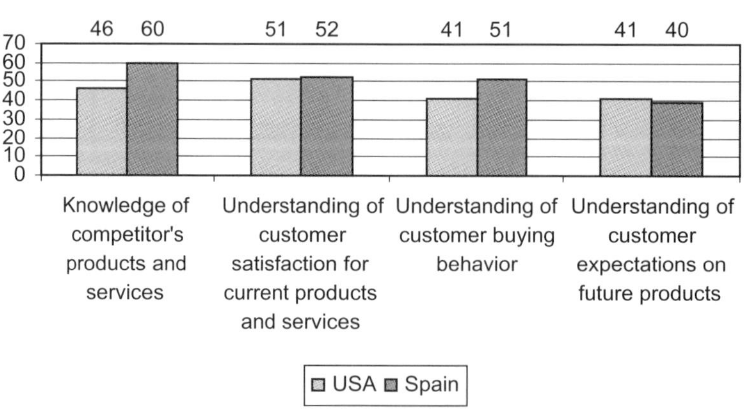

Fig. 5.30. Strategic areas impacted by technology Spain–USA.

5.5. Conclusions

The inclusion of ICT in businesses has made cost-cutting possible mainly in the areas of production and internal information flows. This is the overall impression of Spanish executives, who, nonetheless, believe that there have not yet been significant changes in operating margins and revenues.

Spanish companies believe that ICT is especially important for their internal organization, not only in terms of communication but especially in the creation of new work habits. Although the majority of companies have not noticed a significant drop in the number of middle managers, many claim, for instance, that the number of employees working in front of a computer has risen considerably.

In terms of customer relations, few Spanish organizations have specific technologies such as online transactions and online intermediaries. However, the majority do use e-mail and websites to communicate with their customers.

It is also clear that technology has contributed to making Spanish companies' strategies more user-oriented: a high percentage of companies expressed acute interest in user satisfaction with their product range. The interest in finding out about competitors' products is also on the rise, which indicates that the implementation of ICT in companies somehow generates stiffer competition between companies.

In general, the structure of the ICT budget in Spanish companies is highly similar to that in US companies. Both have noticeably stepped up their investments in hardware and software, especially for security purposes.

Furthermore, executives in Spain tend to outsource fewer services, in both ICT and other areas, than their US counterparts.

The main difference between the implementation of ICT in the United States and Spain lies in the organization of the work force. While ICT has not significantly contributed to simplifying structures in Spanish companies, more than half of the companies in the United States believe that their organizations are now more horizontal, while the geographical dispersion of workers has also increased.

ICT has already had a significant impact on most of the business world; however, executives are still waiting for many of the expectations aroused by technology in the past few years to come true.

Some detailed results are discussed below.

5.5.1. *Technological infrastructure*

Most of the Spanish companies (89%) have websites and carry out e-commerce transactions. However, the adoption of highly specific technologies is not yet widespread in Spain. Biometrics, for example, is only present in 35% of the companies in Spain.

In contrast, Spanish companies seem to be more likely to use RFID than US companies. 32% of the companies in Spain claim that they plan to adopt this technology by 2007, compared to 21% in the United States, this technology is less widely used in the United States than in Spain.

Prime among the top concerns of Spanish executives and their US counterparts is security. A full 81% of the companies in Spain and 65% in the United States invest in security hardware and software. On the other hand, both countries have reined in their investments in on-demand computer services and outsourcing to third countries. In Spain, the budget earmarked for on-demand services has risen in barely 20% of the companies, while the proportion in the United States is even lower (15%).

5.5.2. *Changes in the way of working*

In Spain, the impact of ICT on companies' internal organization is especially interesting, since although companies have undergone profound changes in the way of working, the impact of ICT on their organizational structures is rather scant, unlike in US companies.

Spanish companies have experienced a significant transformation in employees' working patterns: 87% of the companies acknowledge the importance of workers' ICT skills. However, the impact on organizational structure is more diluted, and strong hierarchies remain prevalent.

In the United States, on the other hand, ICT seems to have contributed to achieving more horizontal organizations. More than half of the US companies (54%) claim that their organizations are increasingly flat, while geographic dispersion is on the rise, contributing to making companies' internal organization more flexible.

5.5.3. *Greater customer orientation*

The interactions with customers have also been affected by ICT. 36% of the Spanish companies and 35% of the US companies use online technologies to keep in contact with customers. These percentages are higher than those registered for direct (including face-to-face) contact, which is used by 18% of the companies in Spain and 21% in the United States.

The most automated process within CRM in Spanish companies is order tracking and delivery: 68% have systematized this function, while orders can be placed automatically in 66% of the companies.

When contrasting the differences between online and traditional business, it is clear that ICT has contributed to increasing the actions undertaken by users during the purchasing process; indeed, 55% of the Spanish companies claim this to be so. 74% of the companies charge similar prices for products sold through both online and traditional channels, which indicates that ICT has not contributed to price cuts.

The communication with suppliers mainly takes place via EDI, although this software is more widely used in Spain (65%) than in the United States (45%). However, communicating via XML is still more popular in US than in Spanish companies (43% vs. 37%).

5.5.4. *Scant impact on business margins*

There is a widespread expectation that implementing ICT in businesses provides economic benefits; however, the results from the study indicate that the impact of ICT on revenues and margins has not been very significant. In the vast majority of companies, introducing the use of ICT has not led to significant changes in their results, which would indicate that these profits are often generated in the middle term. What is more, almost half of the Spanish companies have been forced to increase their investments in technology and in consultancy and collaboration services.

Overall, 64% of the companies claim to have reduced their production costs, while 55% have lowered their investment in internal communication.

Finally, ICT has served to open up channels of communication with customers, which in turn enables competitors in a given sector to study each other more keenly.

In conclusion, although we can discern the significant impact of ICT on both Spanish and US companies, our study leads us to believe that executives in both countries expect even greater results from the money they have been investing in technology in recent years.

Acknowledgment

The research was sponsored by e-business Center PwC&IESE.

Bibliography

1. Bartels, A, T Pohlmann and N Lambert (2005). North American IT spending in 2005. *Forrester Research.*
2. CIO Magazine Tech Poll April 2005 Reporte de CIO magazine, 2 de mayo de 2005.
3. Economic Research, Department of Economics, University of California.
4. El uso de la TIC por las empresas, Publicado por la Fundación AUNA, 2004.
5. Ghosh, A (2004). *Information and Communication Technology in India and its Impact on Business Sectors: A Pilot Study.* IIT Bombay: Shailesh J Mehta School of Management.
6. Hall, B and B Khan (2003). Adoption of New Technology, Institute of Business and INE Encuesta sobre equipamiento y uso de Tecnologías de Información y Communicación en las empresas. INE Inventario de indicadores para la evaluación comparada de Europa 2005, 2005.
7. Karmarkar, U and M Vandana (2004). Business and Information Technologies Annual Report, UCLA Anderson School of Management.

8. La microempresa española en la sociedad de la información, publicado en Red.es, 2004.
9. Las TIC y las transformaciones de la empresa catalana, publicado en Universitat Oberta de Catalunya, 2003.
10. Mandelli, A, A Biffi, C Dematté and YC Parolini (2003). First results form the Italian WIP-BIT study. Los Angeles: UCLA Anderson School of Management.
11. Markus, ML and YD Robey (1988). Information technology and organizational change: causal structure in theory and research. *Management Science*, 34(5), 583–598.
12. Markus, ML, B Manville and CE Agres (2000). What makes a virtual organization work?. *Sloan Management Review*, 42(3), 13–26.
13. Miralles, F, S Siebery and J Valor (2004). CIO herds and user gangs in the adoption of open source software. Proceedings of the 13th European Conference on Information Systems, Regensbury, Germany, May 26–28, 2005.
14. Orlikowski, W and J Baroudi (1991). Studying information technology in organizations: research approaches and assumptions. *Information Systems Research*, 2(1), 1–29.
15. Productividad, crecimiento económico y TIC, Gaptel, Red.es, 2004.
16. Restrepo, G (1999). Las Tecnologías de la Información y las Comunicaciones en la Empresa.
17. Valor, J and S Siebery (2005). Criterios de adopción de las tecnologías de información y comunicación e-business Center PwC&IESE.

PART II

RELATED STUDIES

CHAPTER 6

TECHNOLOGY INDUCED CHANGE IN FILM/TELEVISION DISTRIBUTION*

JON CHANG, KAI-WEI CHANG, JASON CHU, YUNCHONG LEE and YAN ZHAO

Summary

This research paper is an overview of technology-induced change in the entertainment-media industry value chain focusing on film and television distribution. Specifically, which key emerging distribution technologies are disruptive' enough to induce change is explored. The impacts of emerging technologies such as digital cinema, video on demand (VOD), personal video recorders (PVR), high definition television (HDTV) and video over wireless devices (VOWD) are studied.

6.1. Introduction

This research paper is an overview of technology-induced change in film/television distribution. Specifically, this analysis has to do with "end-chain" distribution technologies that are most tangible to consumers. There are two key perspectives that have been taken. They are as follows:

(1) The primary technologies examined are those that involve the delivery of motion pictures and related content to consumers across the film/television distribution chain; and
(2) The research focus is on determining whether the adoption of emerging technologies will be significantly disruptive to induce change, and if so, what changes can be predicted to occur.

The entertainment industry is a diverse and large landscape that encompasses many products and services. Although entertainment includes areas such as music, video games, and radio, this research is focused on the distribution of motion pictures and related content as a starting point because Hollywood "Studio" releases touch across a broad chain of incumbent and emerging industry participants. It provides us with a

*This paper was written as part of the Applied Management Research requirement for the junior authors, at the UCLA Anderson School of Management. The research was supervised by Prof. Uday S. Karmarkar who also participated in the study, and was part of the Business and Information Technologies (BIT) project being conducted at the Center for Management in the Information Economy (CMIE).

framework in which the emerging digital distribution methods can be analyzed by their value to consumers at different stages of consumption. The film/television industry is anchored by a small group of companies that are the gatekeepers to consumer demand. This research hopes to clarify how technology will change that relationship between content providers, industry carriers and consumers.

6.2. Scope of Analysis

The scope of this research project is to identify whether key emerging distribution technologies are disruptive enough to induce change. The core technologies that are the catalysts to change-compression, processing power, bandwidth, mobility and storage, have been packaged to deliver new products and services. Their influence is seen in the following emerging technologies:

(1) Digital Cinema;
(2) Video on demand (VOD);
(3) Personal video recorders (PVR);
(4) High definition television (HDTV); and
(5) Video over wireless devices (VOWD).

Quite simply, the research can be seen as a view of how entertainment distribution has evolved from the largest form factor (theatres) to the smallest (wireless devices).

This paper is organized as follows:

(1) Background of the film/television industry including key industry dynamics and current value chain structure;
(2) Explanation of the core technologies that are the catalysts for change;
(3) Analysis of Digital Cinema and high definition (HD) infrastructure in the Exhibitor/Studio value chain;
(4) Role of VOD in the industry rivalry between cable and satellite providers;
(5) The impending rise of HDTV;
(6) Feasibility of VOWD to bring content to the newest and smallest form factor; and
(7) Summary and conclusion of key research findings on the impact of technology induced change on the industry value chain.

6.3. Research Methodology

The methodology followed in this study was:

- *Identify major issues.* Collaboratively developed by advisor and team. Secondary research and initial interviews with industry participants will be used to determine what technology drivers are most significant to disruptive change in film/television distribution. From these technology drivers, the specific products and services that will serve as the basis for research were derived.

- *Form hypotheses around major issues.* Collaboratively developed by advisor and team. Once the specific products and services were identified as the scope of this study, major hypotheses were formulated. The goal of the project was to support or refute these hypotheses through primary research.
- *Test hypotheses.* Performed through primary and secondary research. Primary research was performed through in-depth interviews with industry participants using customized questionnaires developed by the Team.

6.4. Motion Picture Industry

6.4.1. *Industry structure*

In 2002, the US motion picture industry box office grossed more than $9.5 billion. The Top 20 films comprised 40% of the US box office gross with 78% of the total revenues generated by the six dominant "Studios": Warner, Disney, Sony, 20th Century Fox, Universal, and Paramount. Although annual market shares tend to fluctuate, the aggregate picture remains roughly the same with these six firms as the industry leaders. The motion picture industry is an oligopoly where the six major Studios and two smaller (but still significant) players account for almost 90% of the total market share in 2002.

Studios produce, finance or acquire the rights to motion pictures. It is important to understand that "Studios" are the licensors of original content and act as the gatekeepers of content throughout the industry chain. More importantly, the entertainment industry has strong vertical integration across media outlets to ensure that content can be distributed across the chain. For example, Viacom, the parent company of Paramount, owns the CBS network and pay/nonpay cable channels; Disney owns the ABC network and cable channels; Time Warner owns the WB network and a pay cable channel, News Corporation, the parent company of 20th Century Fox Film, owns the FOX network, and Vivendi, the parent company of Universal Pictures, owns a pay cable channel.

The dominance of a small set of firms reflects the strong barriers to entry for new entertainment distribution companies to emerge. On an average, 60–70% of the major theatrical film releases are unprofitable in theatres. The high economic uncertainties in this business and the enormous costs to market and distribute content make it difficult for any new entrants.

The basic Studio business model can be divided into two stages; production and window release. These are discussed further in the next subsection.

6.4.2. *Production*

Production costs are incurred in three stages; preproduction, principal photography, and postproduction. Economies of scale are hard to obtain because production procedures vary significantly for each film. Production costs have increased continuously over the past 20 years even though technology advances have created many production efficiencies.

Sharp increases in production and marketing costs have all but eliminated profit margins to studios from theatrical releases. However, this profit erosion is balanced by the Studios' ability to re-release content on multiple distribution formats embodied in the "window" release distribution structure.

6.4.3. *Window release distribution*

Once a film completes production, Studios develop a market strategy that covers the window release schedule. Every aspect of release is developed and formalized prior to the theatrical first-run and includes the following:

- Determination of the total number of film prints to be produced and which Exhibitors will receive them;
- Schedule for DVD/VHS replication and release; and
- Licensing for pay and nonpay television broadcasts.

The sequential release schedule is chosen based on marginal-revenue contributions that maximize total revenues. The order is as follows:

(1) Theatre release;
(2) Home video and video rentals;
(3) Current VOD;
(4) Network television (includes cable, satellite and terrestrial delivery); and
(5) Local channel syndication.

Roughly speaking, home video, video rental and current VOD begins three months after theatre exhibition. Network television generally premieres 9–12 months after theatre exhibition, and local channel syndication receives content two or more years after theatre exhibition. A brief summary of each release method follows. Detailed descriptions of these distribution channels are discussed further in the following subsections.

6.4.3.1. *Theatrical exhibition*

As new technology in production and distribution evolves, new windows for film release have been created and films are moving faster from one window to the next, thus threatening traditional theatrical exhibitors (Exhibitors). The proportion of total revenues from theatrical release has been getting smaller. The top five exhibitor firms account for 45% of the screens in the United States. These operators are Regal Cinemas, AMC theaters, Loews Cineplex, Cinemark theaters, and Carmike Cinemas.

6.4.3.2. *Home video distribution*

The US box office, especially the first weekend, is a critical indicator of the overall demand that Studios can expect from each major release. First weekend revenues not only represent the first line of revenues, but they also dictate revenue expectations for second and ancillary markets. Since the widespread adoption of VCRs, Studios have generated most of their revenues from the home video market. However beginning in the late 1990s, DVD sales and rentals have taken off. In 2002, DVD unit rentals and sell-through revenues exceeded that of VHS for the first time ($11.6 billion versus $8.7 billion, respectively). The home video industry has become a critical cash sources for Studios to recover their production costs. Consequently, this "cash cow" discourages Studios from creating (or experimenting) with products and services that may disrupt this business model.

6.4.3.3. *Cable/satellite distribution*

The "third leg" of content distribution comes from the monthly pay-TV content providers—cable and satellite. The majority of US households subscribe to either of these services. The cable industry earns roughly 80% of the revenue from subscription and 20% from advertising. To meet the quality needs of paying subscribers, it is critical that these subscription providers offer quality content whether that may be motion pictures, sports or specialty content. Given the prolific demand for pay-TV programming and broadband internet, satellite and cable providers have made huge investment in network infrastructure and product offerings to attract and keep customers. Satellite services have been an important entrant into this market space and have been the catalyst for significant competition between cable and satellite products and services. The top seven operators are shown in the table below with their respective market share in revenues and subscribers (Table 6.1).

6.4.3.4. *Terrestrial broadcast distribution*

Five national broadcast networks (CBS, UPN, ABC, FOX, and WB) out of six are owned by the parent companies of Studios. Furthermore, there has been tremendous consolidation among major networks, studios, and cable companies. These transactions have cemented the Studios' strategy to ensure that they possess total control of the different distribution channels to customers. Given the rising costs to develop content, Studios have generally taken the position that maintaining strong channel ownership is the best method to reach consumers.

Table 6.1. 2002 Cable/statellite shares.

	Revenue ($ in million)	Market share (% of revenue)	Market share (% of subscribers)
DirecTV	9176	14.41	12.5
Echostar	4821	7.57	9.1
Sum of Satellite	13,997	21.98	21.60
Comcast	21,112	33.16	24.3
Warner Cable	9244	14.52	10.3
Cox	5039	7.91	7.0
Charter	4566	7.17	7.5
Cablevision	4003	6.29	3.3
Sum of cable	43,964	69.05	52.40
Sum of top 7 operators	57,961	91.03	74.00
Others	19,707	30.95	47.6
Total market	63,671	100.00	100.0

Source: Morgan Stanley, C.

6.5. The Value Chain

Figure 6.1 illustrates how content goes from production to the end consumer.

The financial success of the US film/television industry is rooted in Hollywood's ability to adapt products and services to technological change, such as the emergence of television or the VCR. What is ironic about this adaptability has been the fact that the industry has traditionally fought technological innovation. The legality of recordable VCRs was originally challenged in court. The transition to color television was only possible due to a common ownership of NBC and RCA electronics (the primary inventor of color TV). In the past few years, another disruptive time period has come about with the advent of five key technologies. These technologies form the backbone of potential industry change that should ultimately benefit the end consumer.

6.6. Technology Drivers in Changing the Consumer Entertainment Experience

Technology advances change both business practices and consumer lives dramatically. In video-based entertainment distribution, technology not only provides more alternatives as to how content is processed, received and consumed, but it also drastically reduces the delivery costs to consumers. As a result, consumers enjoy more freedom as to when, where and how premium video content is enjoyed. However, technology creates new threats and opportunities for incumbent firms in the industry. Incumbents must compete more vigorously to: (i) deliver higher quality products and services; and (ii) continuously build core competitive advantages with technological innovation.

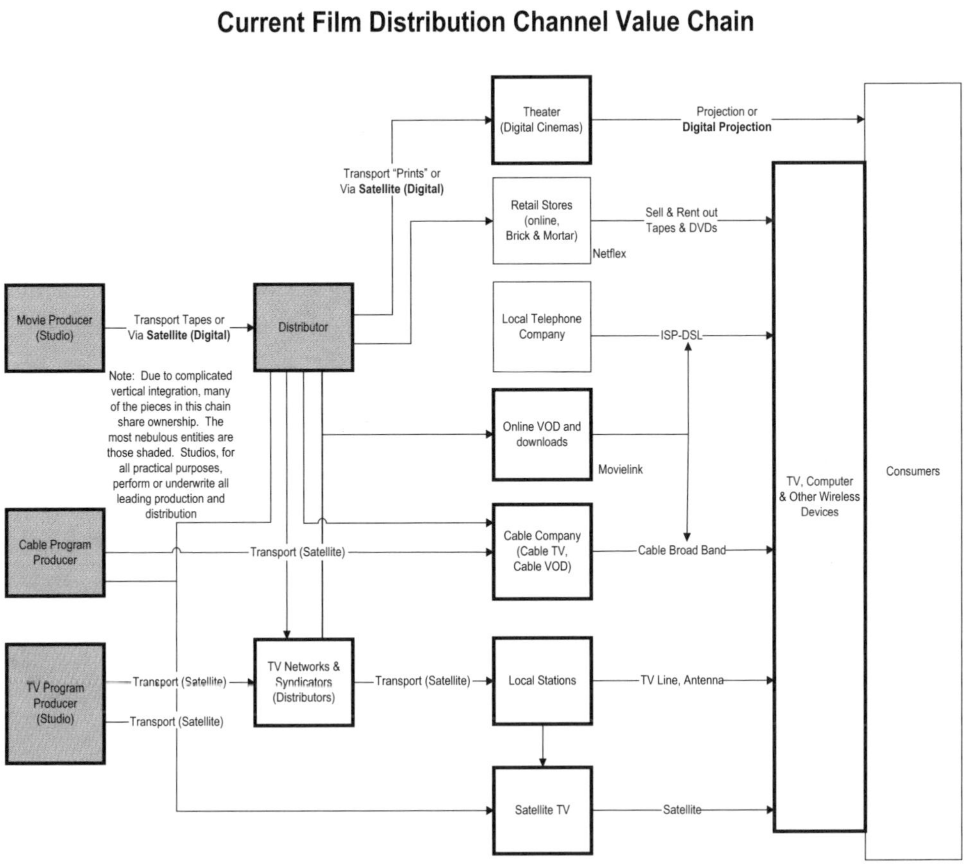

Fig. 6.1. Industry structure.

In this section, a brief look at those fundamental technological drivers is provided to build a link to the core technology topics examined in this research. They are bandwidth, mobility, compression, processing power, and storage.

6.6.1. *Bandwidth — faster delivery and more choices*

The internet boom has made the availability of mass broadband a reality whether as DSL, cable modems or Wi-Fi networks. With higher bandwidth, video on-demand can be delivered through current Telco[a] networks. Cable operators have also upgraded their cable systems to provide unprecedented high speed, two-way, data streams. Consumers have benefited from this oversupply of bandwidth that has not only caused price drops but has also given them more freedom in choosing how content may be consumed.

[a]Defined as a telecommunication service provider, such as the "Baby Bells".

6.6.2. *Mobility — wireless broadband*

Wireless broadband is an emerging reality. Although 3G services have not met with success in either Asia or Europe, the US market we will soon have 100 to 300 kbps data access rates on portable devices. Besides 3G, there are other wireless connection alternatives that also deliver new capacity to wireless devices. These alternatives include IrDA, Wi-Fi, and UWB.

The emergence of wireless broadband creates the opportunity for new channels of entertainment distribution and further frees consumers from location constraints. It will lead to new content providers that will better utilize the mobility created by wireless channels.

6.6.3. *Video compression*

The advancement of compression technology has greatly facilitated the dissemination of video content on multiple devices. Compression technology uses various bit rates to deliver content of all kinds on different screens and frame rates. It allows image quality to be delivered at levels not possible with analog technology and gives content providers a method to "centrally source" content that can be transformed to different entertainment platforms. Coupled with broadband technology, compression permits a new level of on-demand video-watching experience.

6.6.4. *Processing power*

In 1965, Gordon Moore observed that the logic density of silicon integrated circuits closely followed the curve (bits per square inch) $= 2(t - 1962)$. From late 1970s, the doubling period slowed to 18 months. This phenomenon is commonly known as "Moore's Law". The exponential growth of IC density described by Moore's Law has given more and more processing power to all kinds of devices both large and small. The processing power forms the basis of digital creation, processing, transportation and display of video content.

6.6.5. *Storage*

Since the hard disk drive was invented in 1952, technological advancement has led to astonishing improvements in storage capacity, speed, reliability and price/performance ratios. In the 1990s, the storage density of magnetic disks increased 75% per year, outpacing even Moore's Law. The result has been significant price reductions so that from 1992 to 2002, the cost of storage per Gigabyte fell by a factor of 400.[b]

[b] Based on data by Berghell Associates, Newport Beach, CA.

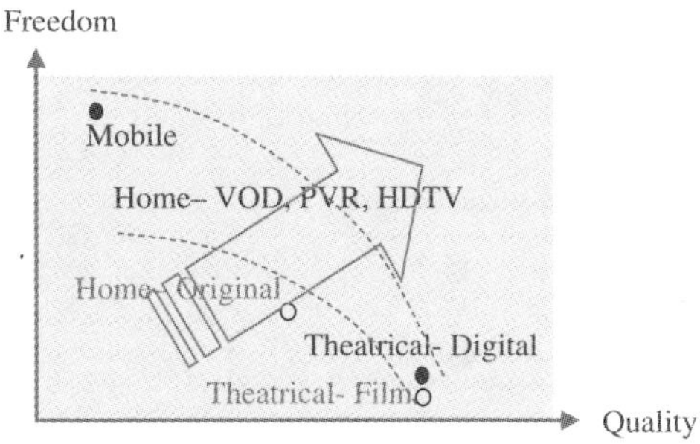

Fig. 6.2. Evolution plot of commercial video.

Similar to the trends in processing power, increasing density in storage media at lower costs has enabled affordable local storage on all kinds of devices. This facilitates the storage and dissemination of video on distribution devices far beyond what anyone might have imagined many decades ago.

6.6.6. *Applying technology drivers to consumer benefits*

The advances in key technologies have led to a birth of innovative products and services that may fundamentally change how consumers source and view film/television content. From the industry value chain, one can map the "consumer experience" by mobility and quality. This framework can serve as the research roadmap to identify the end products and services that may induce industry change. This framework is shown below with the commensurate "technology disruptors" that have been identified in this research study (Fig. 6.2).

For the purpose of our study, we divide the consumer experience of watching commercial video programs into three "experience" categories: theatrical, home entertainment, and mobile. The above figure shows the trends in the industry and the disruptive technologies that we have identified. We believe that these specific technology advancements will push the frontier of consumer experience forward in terms of both quality and freedom (time and place film/TV are watched).

Without a doubt, the technology disruptors are all derived from the root technology innovations described earlier. The chart below maps this relationship.

What follows are detailed analyses of the disruptive technologies and their impact on the value chain (Table 6.2).

6.7. The Emergence of Digital Cinema in Theatre Exhibition

As discussed earlier, Exhibition is the first stage of release for a major motion picture. Therefore, it is a natural starting point to examine how digital technologies have been (or will be) a driving force in changing this distribution channel. At the heart of

Table 6.2. Breakdown of technology disruptors.

	Theatrical experience	Home entertainment experience		Mobile experience
	Digital Cinema	VOD	PVR	Video on wireless
Bandwidth	□	●	○	●
Mobility	○	○	○	●
Video compression	●	●	●	●
Processing power	●	□	□	□
Storage	●	□	●	□

Note: ● very relevant; □ relevant; ○ irrelevant.

Exhibition is the 35 mm film format to master, distribute and view movies. 35 mm film is an incumbent technology that is not only a global standard, but it is also the preferred recording format for other entertainment content (e.g., television shows, documentaries, etc.). Although the entertainment industry has found ways to capture, edit and enhance 35 mm film with digital tools, there are inherent limitations to this medium. Digital technology has finally reached the stage where the entertainment industry now has a preview of the future platform for Exhibition. That platform is loosely known as "Digital Cinema".

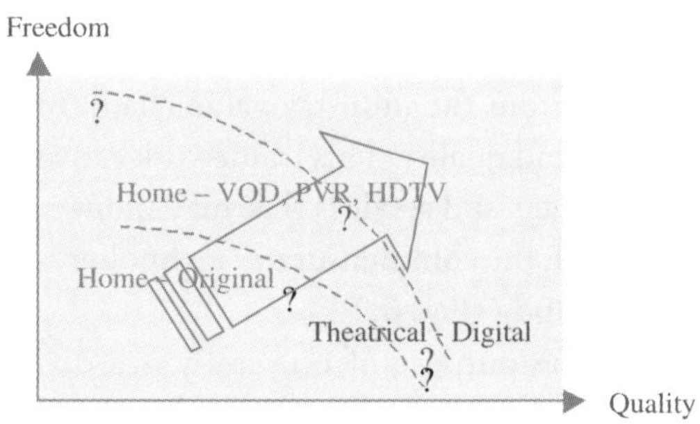

Described in more detail throughout this section, Digital Cinema encompasses the move to deliver Exhibition content in full digital format without the use of film reels. Digital Cinema can be summarized as a technological solution that allows Exhibitors to receive content as a compressed and encrypted digital file, decode it via a hardware system and project it on to a screen. Although many motion pictures will continue to be shot in film for the foreseeable future, Digital Cinema will allow studios to distribute movies under a whole new film-free architecture. More importantly, Digital Cinema has the potential to change the Exhibition business model by providing readily available access to "alternative content". This latter possibility is closely tied to the industry shift to new HD video formats that provide the level of quality necessary for the "big screen". In short, Digital Cinema is a distribution technology that is highly aligned with changes taking place at the production level. Rationalizing the move to Digital Cinemas, and its potential, is the topic of this section.

Our framework to analyze Digital Cinema is as follows:

(1) A brief description of the current economic climate in Exhibition;
(2) Background of 35 mm film technology;
(3) Technology and the value proposition of Digital Cinema;
(4) Value creation and value destruction in the Exhibitor value chain; and
(5) Necessary conditions and recommendations for a successful change platform.

6.7.1. *Film exhibition*

The scope of film exhibition can be measured by screen count. In the United States, there are roughly 35,000 screens owned by 6000 theatres. Worldwide, there are approximately 114,000 screens. Exhibitors primarily earn revenues from two key sources — movie ticket sales and concessions. The dominant licensing model between Exhibitors and Studios is a rather complicated revenue sharing model based on a percentage of box office receipts.

Historically, Exhibitors have earned 50% of the total box office receipts over the course of an engagement. However, they are required to pay licensing fees on a sliding scale basis such that most of the box office receipts in the first two weeks are paid to the licensor. In recent years, Studios have been more aggressive in taking a larger percentage of box office receipts. It is not uncommon for Exhibitors to receive only 10% of the box office receipts for the first week of a major release. Exhibitors are at a high risk for engagement losses if a motion picture loses popularity quickly. Under the licensing arrangement, Exhibitors commit to an engagement far before the actual release date so that Studios can allocate physical prints. This constraint imposed by a finite set of prints is a limitation that Digital Cinema is poised to eliminate.

Since 1995, growth in Exhibition, as measured in box office receipts and by the number of admissions, has been fairly respectable. The industry as a whole, however, has been struggling. Numerous Exhibitors have recently entered, or plan to enter Chapter 11 bankruptcy to reorganize their property obligations. This financial distress is attributable to an overcapacity of new screen construction that took place between 1995 and 2000. The "megaplex" cinema model of 16+ screens per theatre, with stadium seating and larger overhead expenses, drove a surge of expansion. From 1995 to 2000, screen count increased by 34%, but admission revenues could not sustain these capital expenditures. Industry experts believe that overcapacity has not been sufficiently addressed and Exhibitors still need to shrink another 10–15% in screen count to reach the market equilibrium. Table 6.3 highlights key trends in Exhibition from 1995 to 2000.

It is interesting to note that the number of films released has fallen since 1995. This trend is partially due to the growing costs needed to market and produce a major release. In 2002, the MPAA estimated that it costs roughly $90 million to produce and market a leading release. With higher screen capacity, motion pictures are going

Table 6.3. Exhibition screen trends.

Year	US Trend Data			
	Box office gross ($US MM)	Admissions (Billions)	Screen count	Films released
1995	5494	1263	27,805	511
1996	5912	1339	29,731	471
1997	6366	1388	31,865	510
1998	6949	1481	34,186	509
1999	7448	1465	37,185	461
2000	7661	1421	37,396	478
2001	8413	1487	36,764	482
2002	9520	1639	35,280	467
1995–2000 Absolute growth		12.53%	34.49%	

Source: www.MPAA.org

into wider release on more screens and consequently "burn" faster. Both digital piracy and the home video market have also facilitated the burn rate by giving consumer more options to watch releases outside of theatres. Furthermore, box office gross is disproportionately reliant on a fraction of releases. Roughly, 80% of the box office gross comes from half of the titles released. In short, the economics of the Exhibition business have gotten much riskier over the past five years. Exhibitors are unwilling to pursue risky projects that drain cash unless there is a financial benefit that can be legitimately realized in a reasonable time frame.

This review of the current economic climate of the Exhibition industry highlights key issues related to the potential adoption of Digital Cinema:

(1) Exhibitors are not focused on new massive capital investments having just updated their facilities.
(2) Exhibitors are open to alternative revenue models that improve bottom line results so long as those revenues are not highly risky. This can be seen in the growing number of advertisements for the use of theatres for large-scale corporate presentations and/or training.
(3) Exhibitors want to maintain their core business of showing feature releases and selling concessions (which can account for over 50% of an Exhibitor's profits) at peak hours. The average utilization of a theatre screen is 10–15%, highlighting the fact that core Exhibition profits come from a narrow window of peak business hours.

At its most basic as a value proposition to Exhibitors, an investment in Digital Cinema must be a mechanism that can: (i) increase (or help maintain) revenue dollars per admission; (ii) increase total admission; (iii) increase screen utilization; or (iv) decrease operating costs. One of these core value propositions must be realized if the industry is to assume the burden of adopting a new technology platform. Whether the Exhibition industry might be partially (or fully) subsidized in adopting Digital Cinema is a key issue addressed later in this analysis.

The sheer volume of screens also highlights a key infrastructure issue: network externalities related to the 35 mm film format. Across theatre screens worldwide, theatre projection systems are standardized to show 35 mm film stock. This allows content providers to manufacture a finite set of film prints that can be re-circulated to different regions. Although some leading motion pictures have same-day global release on a limited basis, the majority of US theatrical content is still released regionally to accommodate the logistics of managing physical film prints.

To fully appreciate the 35 mm incumbent technology that Digital Cinema seeks to replace, a discussion of this platform is discussed below.

6.7.2. *The 35 mm film format*

6.7.2.1. *Physical format*

The celluloid film has been in existence for over 100 years. The longevity of this platform can be exemplified by the fact that a film print produced 50 years ago can still be played on today's projection systems. Stored and used properly, film has an exceptionally long shelf life. Traditionally, motion pictures and leading television content are originally shot on film. It remains the standard in recording visual content because its resolution and color/contrast retention are superior to those of any existing digital video formats. The Film's inherent resolution equivalent to roughly 4000 horizontal lines is particularly important to Exhibitors because a high resolution is necessary for large screen display.

It is important to separate the use of film to shoot content versus the use of film as a distribution platform. Live action content is first shot or acquired on film. It is then digitized using a tele-cine film scanner in the postproduction phase where content can be edited, visual effects can be added and other color correcting process can be performed. Once a feature is completely edited, the digitized feature is transferred to a color negative original. This color negative original serves as the basis for the film duplication process. Roughly, 2000–3000 physical prints are produced for each major release at a cost of approximately $1500–$2000 per print. This cost is fully borne by studios. Total Exhibition print costs are roughly $4 million per feature, or $2 billion annually excluding shipping and handling costs. A diagram of the complete process is shown below:

When proponents discuss the marginal cost savings of Digital Cinema, they are focusing on annual print costs. The ideal Digital Cinema solution would receive content electronically so that physical media would no longer be necessary. All the steps shown after the Color Negative Original would be eliminated. Although capturing original content in digital form has made incredible strides in quality in the past few years, it is a separate topic from Digital Cinema and the move to a new distribution model

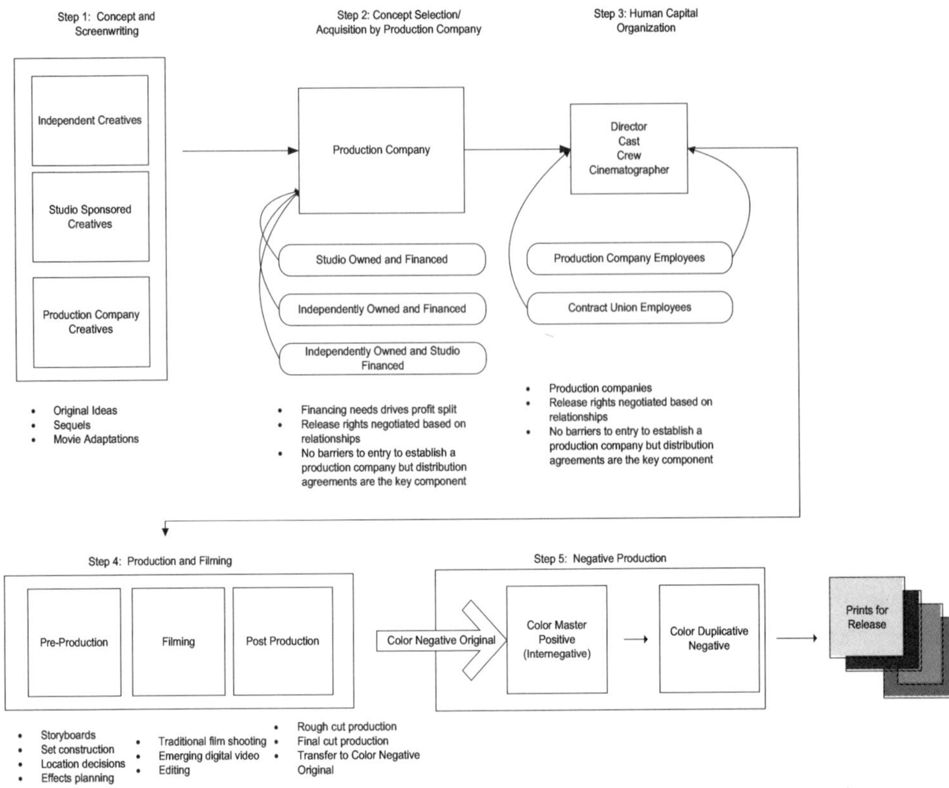

Fig. 6.3. Production process for exhibition prints.

for Exhibition. For major motion pictures, it is simply not a significant issue as to whether content is originally captured on film; those costs are secondary compared to the costs to acquire talent, create effects and market a release. Many leading directors and cinematographers have a professional and emotional attachment to shooting film such that it will remain a viable platform for many years. However, today's younger cinematographers who use digital film technologies will be influential in the adoption of more digital film technologies, going forward originally captured on film; those costs are secondary compared to the costs to acquire talent, create effects and market a release (Fig. 6.3).

6.7.2.2. *Exhibition distribution*

As previously stated, film prints are leased to Exhibitors who then mount the prints on projectors for screening. These projectors cost roughly \$30,000–\$40,000 and have a lifecycle that can last 20 years. Under ideal situations with well-mastered, scratch-free print stock and fully optimized projectors, content can be shown at a high quality resolution that exceeds that of current Digital Cinema technologies. However, this ideal situation is generally not met over the course of a released engagement. Film prints routinely get scratched, dirtied and mishandled. Older projection systems may have minor playback inconsistencies. Consequently, many Exhibition releases are shown at a lower quality than theoretically possible. For releases that stay in circulation for a long time (for example, over six weeks), degradation can be significant. However, it is important to note that lower quality does not correlate to fewer admissions. Box office trends have been historically positive in the last 20 years. Given that the underlying film technology has remained fairly stable, consumers value the theatre experience tremendously. It remains a service that at current levels, it does not appear to be immediately challenged by another entertainment substitute in the way that television originally challenged theatres in the 1950s. The consumers' willingness to pay for current theatrical content suggests that the market is satisfied with current playback systems and that other factors (e.g., admission prices, Exhibition location, facility amenities) are more important to gain consumer wallet-share.

6.7.2.3. *Incumbent technology summary*

From a technological perspective, it is very clear why 35 mm film is the dominant platform for theatrical content. Despite its limitations, its advantages are that:

- It is compatible for global Exhibition since projectors are standardized worldwide.
- Film distribution offers sufficient quality to the marketplace even with inherent degradation.
- The infrastructure and labor associated with handling film is cost-effective and stable.
- There are no substitute products that offer superior value to Exhibitors.

It is this last point that makes the value proposition of Digital Cinema a challenging issue. One of the core issues related to any new technology adoption has to do with expected benefits commensurate with investments. It is necessary for the Digital Cinema technology to define real value to Exhibitors. Understanding the technology and its value proposition is critical for the determination of what factors are needed to take place for this new platform to be embraced.

6.7.3. *Digital cinema technology*

6.7.3.1. *Introduction*

The simplest way to understand the concept of Digital Cinema is to examine the nature of the alternative digital distribution system. This is a theoretical model of a Digital Cinema distribution system with alternative methods for content transmission.[c] In this model, content must first be sourced from the content provider. There are two hypothetical sources: (i) a post production facility (e.g., a facility where motion picture

[c]A diagram can be found at http://www.evs-cinema.com.

content is digitally mastered); or (ii) a live event that is being captured in HD video. Content would first be transmitted to a "Network Operational Center" or some other telecommunications intermediary that would compress and encrypt the content. This data would then be relayed to Exhibitors in one of the three ways: (i) physical media (e.g., DVDs, portable hard drives, etc.); (ii) satellite transmission; or (iii) Internet Protocol ("IP") transmission.

Once an Exhibitor has received the content file, the Exhibitor would then transmit the encrypted data to specific screen projectors through its own Local Area Network. The screen projectors would decrypt the content for projection onto a screen. Thus conceptually, the architecture of a Digital Cinema system is rather simple. There are numerous benefits that come from this arrangement. The most discussed are:

(1) Consistent high quality content projection with none of the degradation of film;
(2) Cost savings to Studios from eliminating multiple prints for distribution;
(3) Cost savings to Studios from eliminating ground shipping and transportation logistics for print distribution;
(4) Central server capability to change, manage and organize content by Exhibitors;
(5) The ability to show real-time, live-action content at a high quality; and
(6) The ability to perform same-day global releases for motion pictures on a much wider scale.

These benefits are described in more detail below.

6.7.3.2. *Costs and quality*

Digital files do not degrade. Therefore, Exhibitors and consumers are assured that content quality will be the same from the first to the last showcase. Studios greatly benefit in cost savings, since the duplication costs for Digital Cinema content are (for all practical purposes) negligible; the industry could save roughly $1 billion per year in print costs. Furthermore, shipping and transmission costs could be negligible compared to the logistics necessary to ship cumbersome film reels, each of which weighs roughly 40 lbs. However, those cost savings may not be realized under many conditions and warrant further examination (to be discussed later).

6.7.3.3. *Content optimization and release*

Theoretically, a fully networked Digital Cinema megaplex would have the ability to change screen content easily because the Exhibitor would not be limited to the physical number of prints leased under contract. An Exhibitor could add screens for a particular release by simply serving another digital file for public showing. Furthermore, major releases could be released globally rather than regionally. This latter option is increasingly seen as a method to counter piracy, since consumers in other regions would not have to wait for high-demand releases.

In addition, proponents of Digital Cinema cite the ability to generate additional Exhibitor revenues from "alternative content" such as concerts, live-action sports and other entertainment events. However, current projectors are not designed to capture direct-feed content such as terrestrial broadcasts or other satellite-transmitted feeds. More importantly, there is an issue related to capturing content at a significant resolution appropriate for a theatre screen. For example, it would be impossible to show traditional US television content on a theatre screen because current broadcast quality is insufficient. Any live broadcasts would need to be captured and transmitted at the appropriate quality commensurating with Digital Cinema.

Conceptually, Digital Cinema offers a range of benefits to both Exhibitors and studios. However, as of early 2003, there were only 154 Digital cinemas worldwide. Furthermore, there were only 60 feature films released in Digital Cinema format, since the technology was introduced in 1999 with the premiere of Star Wars Episode 1 on four digital cinemas. Exhibitors have stopped any significant investments in further adoption until fundamental issues of standards, quality and cost are resolved.

The stagnation in Digital Cinema adoption warrants a deeper analysis of the technology's value proposition. There is a significant question about the return on investment that Exhibitors expect, and whether the current business dynamics are short-term transients, or permanent structural impediments to Digital Cinema's adoption. These questions are analyzed in detail below.

6.7.4. *Digital cinema value analysis*

6.7.4.1. *Increasing consumer willingness to pay*

The primary consumer value proposition of Digital Cinema is consistent high quality content exhibition that is comparable to first-run release. Unfortunately, there is no tangible evidence to suggest that Exhibitors can generate significant incremental revenues for this consistent quality by charging an admissions premium.* few movies make it past six weeks of release where degradation can become significant. Since movies go through lifecycles faster in today's economy, film degradation is not perceived to be a serious threat to consumer satisfaction. This suggests that the consumer willingness to pay cannot be the driver to have Digital Cinema replace traditional film projectors.

6.7.4.2. *Technology adoption costs*

The costs are the first barrier to any potential technology adoption. The current Digital Cinema projection systems cost \$100,000–\$150,000. In addition, there may be other ancillary technology costs associated with network and infrastructure costs that can

Estimation 1. Digital cinema adoption break even analysis.

Initial investment cost per screen	$200,000
Film duplication dollars saved per screen	$2000
Total print copies saved to break even	100
Average number of weeks for a release	6
Total releases per screen (52 weeks)	8.7
Years to break-even	11.5

raise the total costs to over $200,000 per screen. This is roughly 500% more costlier than film projectors. It is not difficult to do a simplified break-even analysis to identify how many digital movie releases would be necessary to recover the costs of the initial system, if we assume transmission and other support costs to be negligible *and assuming that the studios were willing to subsidize the full conversion cost.*

This rough analysis provides important insights about the cost barriers related to technology adoption. First, currently, no studios subsidize Exhibition equipment costs. Because the revenue benefits of Digital Cinemas to Exhibitors are so unclear; there is no way to calculate a reasonable break-even analysis using Exhibitors as the technology investor. As an alternative, using content providers as the technology investor helps clarify how current technology costs are prohibitively expensive even if we assume that the primary beneficiaries of the transition were willing to provide financial assistance.

Although the break-even analysis shows that a return does not happen for many years, it would suggest that a slow but steady adoption of Digital Cinemas could be a plausible strategy, since there is a clear payoff. However, the real issue is not the initial investment costs; it is the fact that nobody can reliably estimate the lifecycle and operation costs of these systems. There is a fundamental lack of Digital Cinema standards with the result that no system in place can be assured a long lifecycle. Already, many Digital Cinema systems in operation are out of date; new projection systems with roughly double the resolution are almost ready for sale. It is this additional uncertainty in infrastructure costs that makes it unattractive for studios and Exhibitors to pursue business models that can finance Digital Cinema procurement.

6.7.4.3. *Technology transmission and content organization*

As previously discussed, there are three alternative methods to distribute a digital film: (i) physical media; (ii) satellite; or (iii) IP. Physical media involves the use of special DVD's or portable hard drives to physically store and transport digital movies. Fixed media has a significant cost advantage over the other two methods. Digital Cinema content requires more data storage than normal DVD's so that 15–20 disks are needed for each release. However, today's systems are not fully designed for rapid content exchange. In the case of current DVD-based systems, it can take hours to install content and troubleshoot a system. This is a significant cost to Exhibitors considering that

Exhibitors can quickly change content with current film projection systems. One of the Digital Cinemas' potential and eventual benefits is the ability to change content quickly. But, this is simply not the case in the near term where digital content loading and manipulation is slow compared to having labourers physically move film reels.

IP transmission involves the use of the TCP/IP protocol to deliver content. Because of the open network landscape, one must assume that this transmission method will only be adopted once an acceptable level of encryption is developed. The costs of high speed access have fallen dramatically in the past few years such that high-capacity broadband is relatively affordable. However, a high-speed broadband line is not available to all locations. In addition, the average 2 h Digital Cinema movie file is 100 GB in size. This would require hours of continuous streaming to send one movie.

The most ambitious model to transmit Digital Cinema content is the use of satellites. The satellite transmission rates are 45 Mbps. It is also the best method for the content to be delivered globally. However, costs are the problem with satellite transmissions. First, transmission infrastructure must be rented or constructed to transmit content to the satellite. Second, satellite transponder (e.g., access) time must be purchased. The current market costs for one full-time satellite transmission channel at 45 Mbps is $2 million per year. Finally, Exhibitors would also need to invest in base stations that can receive the satellite relay. In other words, satellite transmission would be cost-effective only if a substantial number of screens are converted to Digital Cinemas at once so that fixed transmission costs could be spread across many Exhibitors 2.[d] This "big bang" technology adoption requirement across independent businesses is simply not congruent with the traditional technology adoption curve.

The characteristics of each transmission method highlight the fact that today no single platform has a clear advantage. Although fixed media is the most primitive method, it requires no significant capital investment by the Exhibitor for receiving content. In 2002, there were 474 megaplexes (16+ screens) in the United States and 1437 multiplexes (8–15 screens). These large venues would be most suitable for full Digital Cinema networks that use satellite delivery. However, large-scale venues are still a minority of theatre facilities; most of the theatres have less than eight screens. Smaller theatres may not substantially benefit from a satellite delivery system. Research suggests that more than anything else, Exhibitors priorities are that content should be delivered reliably and affordably and that the delivery method is not a significant priority.

6.7.4.4. *Alternative content*

Because the transition to Digital Cinema has significant cost savings for content providers but zero (and in fact negative) cost savings for Exhibitors, the industry must be provided with the incentives to adopt this new technology. The most common

---

[d]Conceptually, the costs would be spread if we assume that many Exhibitors are equipped to receive satellite transmissions. That way, when one movie title is transmitted, many base stations can receive the content at one time.

revenue model championed to Exhibitors is the alternative content such as sports, concerts and other live-events.

Historically, Exhibitor content and television broadcast content have been largely mutually exclusive. The US television standard resolution, NTSC, is inferior and is fundamentally different. It is simply not technologically possible for broadcast events to be fed to theatre screens with NTSC signals. However, that barrier is disappearing with the emergence of better HD video equipment and HDTV.

Since HDTV will be covered later in this paper, its attributes will not be discussed here. But what is important about HDTV is the following: although, HDTV transmissions are not fully appropriate for Digital Cinemas, greater proliferation of HD production hardware encourages more HD content to be shot and potentially delivered to Digital Cinemas. The fundamental difference that separates an HDTV signal from a Digital Cinema signal is the data compression rate, a measure of image quality. An HDTV data compression rate of 19.2 Mbps is over 50% lesser than the generally accepted data rates for quality Digital Cinema content. Fortunately, the HD content can be mastered at the high data rates acceptable to Digital Cinema and can be down-converted to HDTV or DVD quality resolutions. By having a standardized HD infrastructure, alternative content becomes a greater reality of whether it is the live-events that are delivered via satellite or the HD recorded content that is physically delivered to an Exhibitor. Boeing Digital Cinemas, a technology solutions provider, has already demonstrated the satellite's ability to: (i) perform HD live-stream content; and (ii) transmit content to global sites. Quite simply, the bottleneck of having to master filmed content for current projectors is gone with a Digital Cinema system. The critical question lies in identifying what type of HD content is an acceptable value proposition to Exhibitors.

When technology revolutionizes products and services, it is often difficult to identify unarticulated consumer demand. Exhibitors are challenged to do so if they hope to earn incremental revenues from alternative content. Certain content, such as high-profile sports events, would be ideal for Digital Cinemas. However, it is hard to imagine that current licensees of sports content (e.g., major US networks) would ever allow licensors to contract with Exhibitors given the networks' enormous bargaining power in signing exclusive contracts. The content acquisition could thus be a serious barrier.

More important, there is an enormous inertia among incumbents that discourages leading Exhibitors from exploring alternative content business models. It is hypothesized that certain venue changes (e.g., alcohol sales, different seating arrangements, etc.) may be needed to attract consumers to watch alternative content. Risking change is inconsistent with theatre Exhibition. Most leading Exhibitors can be considered "pragmatists" in the adoption technology curve. They have expertise and are comfortable with the proven incumbent business model. As previously stated, Exhibition peak hours are a narrow time interval. It cannot be expected that Exhibitors are willing to risk these business hours to explore unproven content models. The Exhibition industry is still trying to contract and conserve cash due to prior over-expansion. They are not in a position to explore strategies that involve risky cash flows. Although it is not difficult for large Exhibitors to invest modestly in Digital Cinema systems, yet it is costly to invest marketing, research and management resources to this initiative. For example, although Regal Cinemas has a proprietary network digital projection system, this system is used to display advertisements and not releases. This exemplifies pragmatism in technology adoption. We believe that this incumbent inertia is vastly underestimated in the debate about alternative content on Digital Cinemas.

6.7.4.5. *Value summary*

It is quite clear that a deeper analysis of the industry and technology forces shows how difficult the landscape will be for Digital Cinemas to be pervasive. People continue to predict the adoption rates of Digital Cinema systems, but these predictions are fundamentally flawed because there are structural business incentive issues that have not been resolved. Without a doubt, costs are a critical factor. However, arguing that costs alone are the driving factor vastly oversimplifies the issues. A framework for technological change is necessary to add clarity to how this new distribution chain can come about.

6.7.5. *Necessary conditions to induce change*

6.7.5.1. *Standards setting*

In content-delivered technologies, network externalities are critical to mass adoption. Some technologies become de facto standards, while others become established through industry/government approval. Since 2002, no official standards exist for Digital Cinema systems. This has been an important barrier that discourages investments. For example, the first Digital Cinema systems were 1280 pixels ("1K") in horizontal resolution. This was deemed deficient by many cinematographers and film producers. New 1920/2048 pixel systems ("2K") are much more acceptable in quality and better match the resolution of most digital movie effects. The old and new systems are not easily upgraded that early adoption was clearly risky. For content providers, the lack of standards has also made content delivery overly complex and costly. Studios had to master different Digital Cinema files for different Digital Cinema systems. More importantly, a universal encryption standard is lacking. Security is a crucial element in digital technology, and a consensus encryption standard need to be developed for any significant content to be progressively released.

Fortunately, the standards issue is expected to be resolved fairly soon. Studios, seeking to define acceptable guidelines, have established the Digital Cinema Initiative (DCI). DCI is a consortium effort that was formed in early 2002. DCI is expected to deliver technology guidelines (e.g., minimum resolution, compression methods, encryption needs, etc.) that can be translated into real industry policies. The goal is to develop a standard that is significantly open in architecture such that multiple vendors can compete with global interoperability. An ideal goal would be the completion of an industry standard by 2003–2004 such that technology providers can have some confidence about how to proceed with product development. Therefore, the first barrier to potential adoption, that of standards, appears to be addressed. However, the rate at which a Digital Cinema standard can be completed and embraced is still highly unclear.

6.7.5.2. *Cost considerations*

Earlier, a hypothetical break-even analysis was performed as a measure of cost magnitude. As previously stated, there are no outstanding initiatives by the Studios to subsidize equipment costs to Exhibitors, even though there are clear cost benefits. There are three reasons why a subsidy is highly unlikely:

(1) The "Paramount" antitrust decree makes it illegal for studios to require Exhibitors to meet content quotas/must-carry requirements. Studios cannot subsidize Digital Cinema systems in exchange for some degree of content control.
(2) Studios are not technology companies and they do not want to be engaged in funding Digital Cinema developments.
(3) Subsidizing Digital Cinema effectively means that Exhibitors can use these systems for alternative content. This latter scenario currently provides no value to Studios.

The only viable business model is for Digital Cinema systems to be independently funded and operated by Exhibitors such that Exhibitors maintain full control of content management.

Under the latter proposition, there is only one procurement model that is reasonable for Exhibitors. That model is a leasing arrangement whereby Exhibitors minimize the risks of technology obsolescence and service costs. The leaseholder would have to be the technology provider or a business intermediary that has competencies in leasing contracts and would be willing to assume the risks of product service and upgrades. A leasing model effectively translates one-time projection system costs into a stream of operating costs to Exhibitors. Using this idea, one can perform a rough calculation of how far costs must fall before Digital Cinema systems are financially attractive to leading Exhibitors.

The analysis is performed as follows. Three leading publicly-held Exhibitors who reported positive operating income were chosen. The operating income is defined as revenues that have less operating expenses excluding interest and nonoperating income/expenses. Each company's operating margin (operating income/revenues) is calculated. It was then assumed that the maximum annual expense burden from a

Estimation 2. Viable digital cinema system costs.

	AMC Entertainment		Cinemark Theatres		Regal Cinemas	
FYE	3/28/2002		12/31/2002		12/26/2002	
Screen count	2899			3031	4164	
Revenues	$1,341,506,000		$939,265,000		$1,544,400,000	
Operating costs	$1,289,947,000		$810,371,000		$1,311,600,000	
Operating profit	$51,559,000	3.8%	$128,894,000	13.7%	$232,800,000	15.1%
Ceiling cost from adopting Digital Cinema systems	$13,415,060	1%	$9,392,650	1%	$15,444,000	1%
Ceiling cost per screen	4627		3099		3709	
System costs at 5% cost of capital	$92,550		$61,977		$74,179	
System costs at 10% cost of capital	$46,275		$30,989		$37,089	
System costs at 15% cost of capital	$30,850		$20,659		$24,726	

Digital Cinema operating lease would be 1% of sales.[e] This expense was then divided by the number of screens per Exhibitor to determine the maximum acceptable incremental costs per screen. This cost can be considered as a perpetuity to a leaseholder. The principal system value is then the incremental cost divided by a cost of capital (three different rates are used so as to develop a range of system costs). This is the requisite price range that makes Digital Cinema adoption financially realistic.

The analysis above suggests that total Digital Cinema system prices must be similar to current film projection system prices if the Exhibition business model stays substantially static. That requires the system prices to fall some 75% for major Exhibitors to consider widespread adoption. The above analysis excludes any additional transmission and/or distribution costs such as satellite or IP. Such costs only compound the adoption burden, suggesting that physical media may be the best method at the early adoption phase. Therefore, technology companies should be most focused on building products that can facilitate rapid exchange of content and not necessarily on the most sophisticated infrastructure network capabilities.

6.7.5.3. *Change dynamics*

It becomes quite apparent that Digital Cinema technology companies are left with a "chicken and egg" problem. New technology becomes more affordable through

[e] 1% of sales was chosen as the ceiling point at which an Exhibitor would be willing to take on additional Digital Cinema operating costs assuming revenues are constant. Anything more is considered as a material financial impact that would not be acceptable without clear revenue benefits.

incremental adoption and R&D learning. However, leading Exhibitors are the wrong market segment to pursue in the initial stage because they do not perceive sufficient value in such investments costs.

This research takes the position that Digital Cinema's value is tied to the availability of HD content. Consequently, it may be more appropriate to target entrepreneurs that operate small specialized/boutique theatres as the first potential customers of Digital Cinema systems. Madstone Films, an independent company that finances and showcases its own movies on Digital Cinema systems, is an example of an appropriate early adopter. The company produces and displays in digital format that does not compete with leading Studio releases. Although there are many HD recording formats, yet it is the "24p"[f] format that is most important to Digital Cinema's future.

24p, the digital HD shooting format that offers the closest quality to film, has made significant advancements in the past two to three years. Industry experts expect it to be a leading method to shoot content in the near future. Star Wars Episode II is the most well-known release that was shot on 24p video. The International Telecommunications Union, a prominent standardization body, has already certified this format as a global production standard for movies and television shows. The global standardization to 24p is a key development for Digital Cinema's adoption. It will make it cost-effective for more HD contents to be produced worldwide as 24p technology costs fall. Already, 24p production can reduce production budgets by as much as 50% compared to film. The proliferation of 24p recording will encourage more HD contents to be produced. This content diversity will help drive entrepreneurs to identify content that has niche market demand. In turn, this will be the source for value in the first Digital Cinema systems.

Having examined Digital Cinemas, the first window release, it is logical to examine how technology will impact motion picture distribution at the next level. That level is the pay-TV industry and specifically, the emergence of VOD. VOD is the product that cable operators have used in their battle with satellite operators to be the leaders in subscription television.

6.8. VOD and the Cable/Satellite Industry Battle

In our research, VOD is defined by two platforms: cable VOD and Internet Protocol (IP) VOD. They are contrasted below:

- Cable VOD. MPEG-2 streaming video is delivered over broadband digital cable architecture to a digital set-up box and is viewed on a television.

[f] 24p is the short form for HD video captured in progressive-scan resolution at 24 frames per second. The traditional film is shot at 24 frames per second. This recording format is most aligned with film since frames per second is a key standardization attribute.

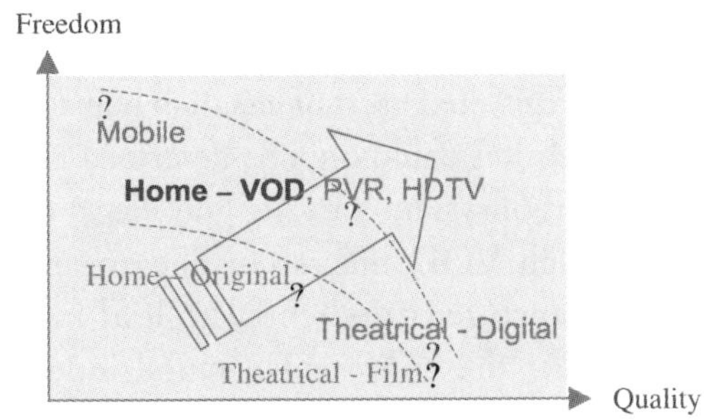

Cable VOD is analogous to renting a video without actually renting a DVD or VCR cassette. VOD subscribers will select the content from an on-screen library menu and cable operators will then stream the video from servers to a subscriber's set-top box connected to a television. VOD technology also gives consumers the ability to pause, rewind and fast-forward content just like a VCR. When the rental period expires, the movie is erased from the subscriber's set-top box. Consumers pay for each VOD title request. Besides cable VOD, cable operators also provide subscription VOD (SVOD), which is VOD offered at a monthly flat rate. This flat rate billing provides viewers with unlimited access to a digital library of content. Currently, most of the VOD are movies, TV series and sports. Movies are far away from the key anchor services for VOD, attracting large diverse audiences and revenue streams. However, some VOD programming companies are also actively marketing special-interest VOD services, targeting genres such as hobbies, recreational activities, fitness, self-improvement and education. The goal is greater market segmentation of what, when and where entertainment content can be enjoyed.

At the end of 2002, there were over 7 million VOD-ready households in the United States. This number could easily double, if not triple, by the end of 2003.[g] Currently, almost all of the major cable operators are market-testing VOD. Charter, Insight, Adelphia, Cablevision, Comcast, Cox, Insight, Mediacom and Time Warner Cable are all testing or actively deploying VOD services.

- IP VOD: Internet streaming video delivered to a personal computer

In IP VOD, subscribers browse authorized website, view trailers of available titles, pay for a movie rental with a credit card and download content. After downloading the film, subscribers generally have 30 days to begin viewing the film unless specified otherwise at the time of rental. Once a film is started, consumers generally have 24 h to watch it. Subscribers can watch films any number of times during this 24-h period with VCR functionality, including pause, rewind, and fast-forward. The download time depends on the size of the movie file, connection speed, and the amount of traffic on the internet. Normally, it takes 40 mins to an hour with an average DSL/Cable broadband connection. After the rental period, the file becomes inaccessible.

---

[g]Source: Company reports, industry reports, Williams Capital.

Currently, IP VOD is relatively insignificant in the market. The major IP VOD providers include Movielink, Intertainer, and CinemaNow. Combined, these providers have total registered users of less than half a million. Most of the movie content available at these websites could only be described as "B" movies because they are low-risk titles in the event of system hacking and illegal content dissemination.

Although VOD may seem like an ancillary product within the current release window structure, its potential to lead industry change is massive. In theory, VOD could render the entire video rental industry obsolete. This scenario is unlikely in the near term because incumbents have serious investments in the current business model. However, the VOD issue is most relevant in the high stakes battle between cable providers and dish satellite networks. The massive investments to deploy VOD are important to the future structure of the subscription television industry. In the following, VOD is examined as follows:

(1) A technical overview of VOD infrastructure;
(2) Factors in VOD adoption and the emergence of satellite networks;
(3) Availability of VOD content; and
(4) VOD forecasts and expected industry change dynamics.

6.8.1. *VOD infrastructure*

A typical VOD system is broken into several major categories as depicted below.

These components are described in further detail:

- Set-top box. A set-top box allows subscribers to select video from a TV menu screen. It will then decode the request and send the message across the access network to an application server located in a service provider's network. The set-top box then receives digital video streams from the video server and displays the video on screen with full VCR functionality.
- Application server. The application server is the head-end or hub that is the counterpart to the set-top box. The application server authenticates users, checks subscription details, organizes billing and delivers film selections. There can be many application servers in a network dedicated to different applications or segments, such as movies on demand, sports on demand, etc. (Fig. 6.4).
- Content storage. Digital asset management software has to be in place to manage the content, content groups and content information for each asset in the system.
- Video server. The core hardware to deliver video streams. The keys to the success of these servers are their scalability and fault tolerance. For VOD to reach critical mass, the service provider's video server architecture must be sufficiently robust to offer thousands of titles over a dozen different subscription packages. For example, where there are two million subscribers, accessing 2000 films using 10 different

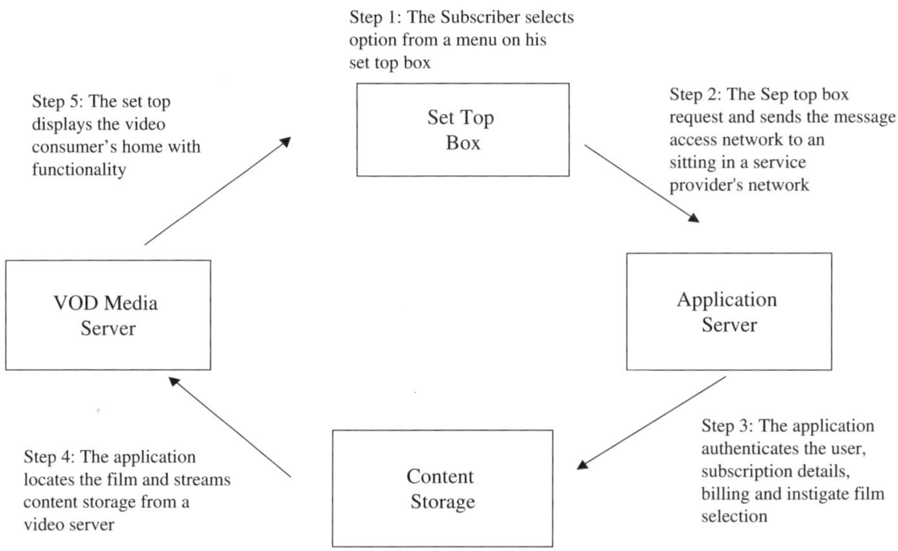

Fig. 6.4. VOD delivery system.

subscription packages and five different interactive applications, the complexity is exponentially huge ($2,000 * 10 * 5 = 100,000$ variations). There have been significant improvements in video server technology in the last five years. Video servers that used to cost thousands of dollars per stream are now around $300 per stream.

Without a doubt, the infrastructure for change can be implemented, but the question is whether widespread adoption will take place such that VOD has the opportunity to induce significant industry change. Whether VOD will be widely adopted depends mostly on the following two factors: (i) cable operator's willingness to deploy VOD; and (ii) the rivalry of cable and satellite providers. These issues are examined in further detail.

6.8.2. *Factors affecting VOD deployment*

Cable operators face high capital expenditure costs and low profit margins in deploying VOD. Therefore, it is critical to perform a break-even analysis to determine whether there are realistic profits to cable operators from investing in VOD.

6.8.2.1. *Infrastructure costs and product margins for VOD*

One of the most important value propositions of VOD is its ability to provide impulse buyers with instantaneous service. Hence, "denial of service" to a cable VOD subscriber is inexcusable; one disappointed subscriber could disrupt the potential lifetime customer value. To avoid denial-of-service problems, cable operators must purchase servers, maintain storage and allocate bandwidth for enough simultaneous VOD services during peak viewing times — typically weekends. This bandwidth and infrastructure is largely idle during nonpeak hours. VOD subscribers' nonlinear demand pattern significantly increases the cost of VOD deployment. However, based on Seachange International data, it is estimated that cable operators need to spend only $107 per subscriber to upgrade digital cable systems to VOD.

This estimate does not consider the opportunity costs of bandwidth reserved and consumed by VOD. The opportunity costs are not easily available and industry participants have apparently not tried to calculate them. Although cable operators invested $70 billion to upgrade their systems to digital infrastructure,yet no information is available on how much capital expenditures should be appropriated to VOD. Therefore, the $107 VOD capital expenditure per digital cable household is most probably an underestimate.

Cable VOD competes with other entertainment alternatives — mainly the local video rental store. Hence, the pricing of VOD must at least be comparable to that of video rental stores to be competitive. The maximum price that cable operators can charge for new content (approximately 30 days after DVD release to the rental market) is around $4. Around 50% of the subscription fees go to Studios (the licensor). Therefore, cable operators only get $2 for each new-title subscription. Considering other marketing and operating costs for each movie title, it is estimated that cable operators get less than $1 per hour of net revenue. Nevertheless, estimates show that VOD provides significant marginal revenues to cable operators that makes it a profitable venture. As a result, VOD is being deployed at a rapid pace and it is the fastest growing sector of the cable TV industry. In the past two years, the household penetration of VOD that surpassed the initial penetration rate of home computers, was at double the penetration rate of VCRs, and triple the initial penetration rate of both basic cable and the Internet.[h] However, the profitability of VOD has been overestimated because cable operators have excluded the opportunity costs of the bandwidth reserved for VOD services. Moreover, although VOD has decent revenue potential, it alone does not seem to explain the cable operators' enthusiasm for providing this service. Upon deeper examination and research, it appears that the VOD deployment is directly tied to the fierce competition with the satellite industry. This industry battle has been significant, and competition has bred product and service innovation as evidenced by VOD growth.

6.8.3. *Satellite competition*

Since 1994 (the inception of DirecTV), the number of satellite subscribers has jumped from 4 million to over 20 million users, with a CAGR of 23%. In contrast, the cable

[h]Deutsche Banc Alex Brown, US cable industry outlook, 6 September 2001.

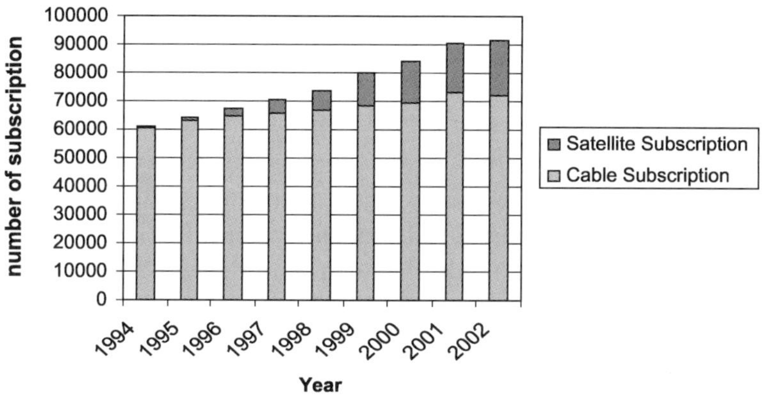

Fig. 6.5. Cable growth versus satellite growth.
Source: National Cable & Telecommunication Association.

industry's CAGR was 2% during this time period. Nine years after its debut, DirecTV has surpassed all but two cable operators in the number of subscribers, making it the third largest multichannel video provider in the US Meanwhile, EchoStar is ranked fourth among the multichannel video providers. Not only has satellite demand grown at a much faster rate than cable, its growth has come from stealing cable's most profitable consumers (Fig. 6.5).

Not surprisingly, satellite and cable subscribers are similar in nearly every way. They have comparable incomes, education levels, and online shopping habits. However, one key exception exists — satellite subscribers on an average buy more services. According to Forrester Research, although satellite subscription prices are competitive with cable, satellite subscribers pay an average of $42 a month, $8 more than the average cable household. Roughly, 50% of the satellite subscribers purchase premium channels and a third of them rent pay-per-view programs. In contrast, only a third of the cable customers subscribe to premium channels and less than a third of them rent pay-per-view programs.[i]

Further examination of data from the same source reveals the severity of cable customer defections to satellite. 48% of the cable defectors bought premium cable channels and 36% rented cable pay-per-view. In comparison, only 35% of the existing cable customers have premium channels and 26% of them rent pay-per-view. Most interesting, roughly 22% of the cable defectors used to have digital cable, the best cable product to fight satellite defection. This data shows that digital cable may not be as attractive as cable operators had initially hoped.

However, cable operators have found VOD to be an effective agent to reduce defection — the percentage of subscribers dropping digital cable service in a given

[i]Forrester Research, How cable TV can beat satellite, April 2002.

month drops from 6% to 4% in VOD-enabled regions. Moreover, the costs of deploying VOD are reducing. Recognizing this trend, the first priority of major cable operators has been to deploy VOD to fight customer defection. Although cable operators would prefer making profits from VOD, yet they are content to break-even (or even incur minor losses) just to prevent subscribers from switching to satellite services.

Satellites, restricted by their capacity, cannot serve individual VOD streams to millions of subscribers nationwide. Consequently, satellite companies compete with VOD using pay-per-view movies on multiple channels, starting every 15 min. This value proposition is inferior to that offered by cable VOD. First, cable operators can provide a digital library of hundreds of movies to subscribers, who can choose whatever titles whenever desired. Satellite subscribers can access only a narrow collection of titles at any given time. Moreover, since most of the satellite subscribers still do not have Personal Video Recording (discussed later), they cannot enjoy the rewind, stop and fast-forward features enjoyed by cable VOD subscribers.

6.8.4. *VOD content acquisition*

As discussed above, VOD is an important strategic tool in the industry battle between cable and satellite companies. However, one critical question remains as to whether VOD will proliferate. That question is whether Studios will provide VOD content. Our research has shown that Studios are not excited about VOD. However, Studios will provide VOD content to cable operators under two premises: (i) profits from the current release window are maintained; and (ii) piracy is kept at bay.

6.8.4.1. *Continuation of the existing release window*

As discussed earlier, Studios use a time-lapse distribution release method to maximize revenues. This model has worked well in the past and hence Studios strive to maintain the status quo. Consequently, Studios will support VOD if and only if VOD increases revenues while keeping the existing release window structure intact. That is why current VOD is available 30–60 days after DVD/VHS release and not before it. Although the VOD release window may move closer to 30 days after DVD/VHS release, yet it is highly unlikely to move any closer. The chart below shows how Studios prioritize distribution methods to maximize profits (Table 6.4).

6.8.4.2. *Mitigating piracy*

Generally speaking, Studios have different attitudes toward cable and IP-based VOD. Studios are comfortable with cable VOD because it is a “closed-system” that is difficult to hack. Therefore, four of the seven major studios, Sony, Fox, Universal Studio and Time Warner actively promote VOD on their websites. MGM and DreamWorks are

Table 6.4. Comparison of VOD, DVD/VHS sell-through and rental.

	Revenue model	Importance	Margin
VOD	Revenue sharing: movie studio share VOD rental revenue with cable operators	Insignificant	Approximately 50% of VOD sales
DVD/VHS sell-through	Mass distribution: movie studios distribute their DVD/VHS product through major merchandisers such as Wal-Mart	Most significant	Highest Approximately 80–85% of the DVD/VHS sales
DVD/VHS rental	Video rental store purchase DVD/VHS from studios and obtain authorization to rent them out. No revenue sharing	Significant	Lowest, less than 40% of the DVD/VHS rental revenue

also providing new releases to cable VOD. Disney plans to provide VOD content once the company is satisfied with certain piracy security issues. It is safe to conclude that Studios will base their decision regarding cable VOD on its revenue potential rather than piracy concerns unless any significant piracy technologies emerge in the cable market.

On the other hand, IP-based VOD exposes Studios to a higher risk of piracy. Given the popularity of P2P networking and current antipiracy technology, Studios have refused to put premium releases on IP VOD. Some research agencies argue that Studios are optimistic about IP-based VOD and have shown their support by creating Movielink, a joint venture established by MGM, Paramount, Sony, Universal Studio and Time Warner. However, Movielink does not necessarily indicate optimism. Rather, Movielink was probably created because Studios are unclear about IP-based VOD and sought a "beta" service for testing.

6.8.5. *Projected VOD platform winner*

Because of the aggressive infrastructure upgrades of cable operators and endorsement from Studios, cable VOD is now well-positioned to reach mass adoption in the next three to five years. On the other hand, IP-based VOD may have a much harder time to take off. The cable will be the dominant carrier of VOD for the following reasons.

- Consumer viewing habits. Cable VOD has a clear competitive advantage over IP-based VOD. Apparently, most of the people prefer watching video on a TV rather than on a PC screen. A survey by Forrester shows that only 18% of the internet users regularly watch streaming video, and only 7% say that they would pay for movies online.[j] High-tech companies such as Motorola and Cisco do manufacture DSL-based set-top boxes that bridge from PC-based broadband connections to TV. However,

[j]The first figure, regarding streaming video usage, comes from an online survey of 11,000 North American Internet users conducted in the fall of 2000. The second, on willingness to pay, comes from an online survey of 5644 American consumers, which Forrester conducted in conjunction with Greenfield Online in October 2000.

this solution may cost more than $300 to consumers, an expensive proposition for a small consumer segment.
- Support from studios. Our research with Studios confirms satisfaction with potential cable VOD revenues. But, piracy clouds any enthusiasm for IP-based VOD. Most of the Studios are hesitant to provide new content to IP VOD, a sentiment that does not appear to be likely to change any time soon. Lacking compelling content, IP-based VOD will have a hard time drawing subscription revenues.
- Strong customer relationship. At the end of 2002, there were over 7 million VOD-ready households. VOD-ready households are on track to reach 36 million in 2005[k] representing 75% of the digital cable TV market. Given the existing billing relationship and familiarity between cable households and cable operators, the latter will enjoy a huge competitive advantage in marketing their VOD services over IP-based VOD providers.

From 2000 to 2002, digital cable households grew quickly from 6 million to 19.2 million subscribers with a CAGR of 50%. This growth is similar to that of satellite in its early years. It is believed that digital cable had a higher potential growth rate because of its huge existing customer base; satellite operators needed to start from scratch. After the initial growth of digital cable, growth is expected to slow to that of satellites. Assuming CAGR for digital cable subscription to be 18%, 37 million households should be converted to VOD by 2006. This large subscriber base should yield roughly $4 billion in annual revenues to cable operators, an attractive and powerful value proposition.

6.8.6. *VOD summary*

The expected emergence of cable VOD provides consumers with a new channel for entertainment distribution that complements current consumption options. It is an option that has the general endorsement of Studios because it provides them with a potential method to increase revenues. However, the underlying technologies that have allowed Digital Cinema and VOD to be born have also led to the emergence of Personal Video Recorder (PVR) technology, a technology that is coupled with HDTV, gives consumers an unprecedented ability to enjoy television content via a method unexpected by Studios. This technology is the third stage of the "experience chain" that has potentially significant impact on the entertainment industry.

6.9. PVR as a Disruptive Device

PVR is analogous to VCR, except that the storage medum is now a digital hard drive or even possibly DVD disks. Like a VCR, PVR allows users to fast-forward, rewind,

[k]Yankee Group, June 2001.

and pause video content. What distinguishes PVR from VCR most strikingly is the ability to automatically search and record content at very high capacities and without degradation in repeated playback quality. The technology in service format can even recommend content based on a user's past viewing habits. Many PVR devices come with multiple tuners to allow consumers to record different channels simultaneously. Most controversially, certain PVR devices have a 30-second skipping mechanism aimed to bypass commercials, effectively killing the normal business model of broadcast TV advertisements. Unlike the VCR in which the users need to painstakingly rewind or fast-forward, PVR gives users instant access to any part of the recorded content. It is a technology that severely aggravates the current consumption model of television content. Although its adoption has been slow, its potential for change is significant enough to warrant a review of how the technology could be adopted to build trilateral benefits to consumers, PVR manufacturers, and broadcast content providers.

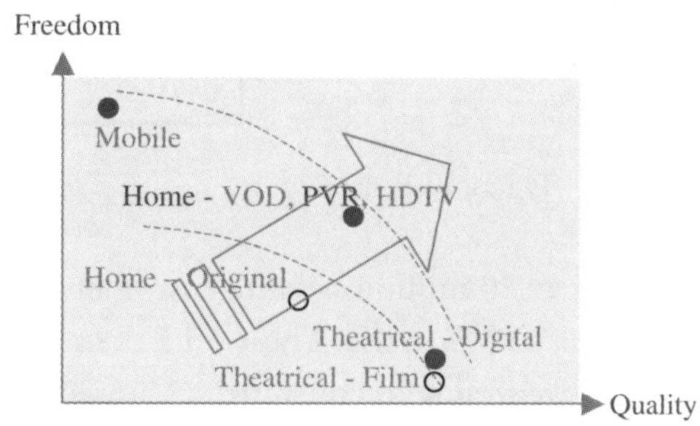

6.9.1. *PVR technology*

PVR works by converting a standard analog TV signal to a digital signal that is stored on a hard drive and then converted back to analog during playback. However, there are two exceptions to this conversion. First, incoming digital signals such as digital cable and satellite are recorded straight from the source without analog–digital conversion. Second, there is no re-conversion on digital HDTV. Figure 6.6[1] shows how a typical PVR system works. When there is no digital to analog conversion, there is simply no degradation, giving the user extremely high quality content.

6.9.2. *Economics*

PVR led to new market entry with the debut of TiVo in 1999. The barrier to entry in this market is low, since core PVR technology device is simply a hard disk and a CPU with enough processing power to perform audio/video compression. Currently, there are many different PVR-type devices in the market, but their adoption has been slow. Most of the research has attributed this to poor consumer awareness and confusion. Furthermore, consumers view standalone PVRs as a luxury good given their relatively high prices. There are 624,000 TiVo users and roughly 1.5 million satellite PVR users

[1]TiVo case, Kellogg School of Management.

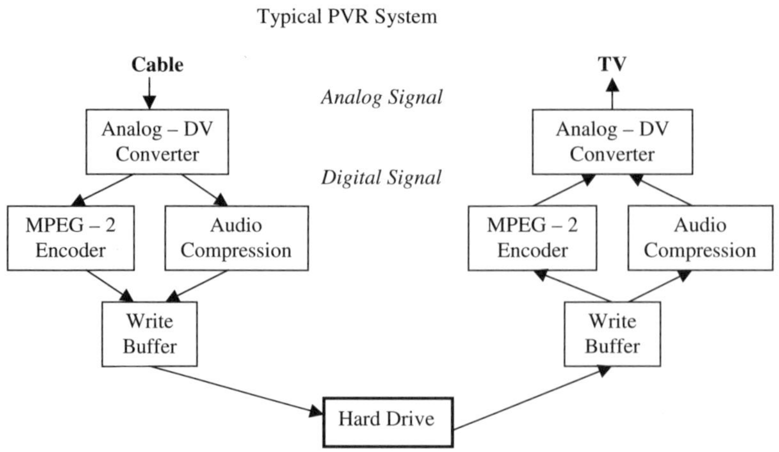

Fig. 6.6. Typical PVR system.

out of over 20 million satellite customers. Only about one out of 20 US consumers has even seen a PVR in use. These statistics suggest that PVR suffers from a serious shortage of perceived value to consumers. Consequently, it appears that something is needed to encourage wider adoption. Identifying this driver first requires an examination of: (i) what PVR devices are available; and (ii) how they are sold.

6.9.3. *PVR providers and business models*

Most of the PVR technologies today are widely available to consumers through a standalone PVR box, cable and satellite set-top boxes, PCs and soon as DVD/RW recorders. The underlying technology for all these devices is the same. However, the key technology and revenue model differences are summarized below with further details available for each specific device category (Table 6.5).

6.9.3.1. *Standalone box*

Different providers of standalone boxes have adopted different revenue models to penetrate the market. TiVo is the leader in this product class. TiVo s revenue model consists of selling PVR devices and collecting subscription fees (monthly or one-time lifetime price) for an advanced programming guide delivered via telephone line transmission. It also charges advertisers and paid programmers to be showcased on TiVo menu screens. In effect TiVo has taken on a network operator role, by having an exclusive "private network" of its users. Theoretically, TiVo can utilize its database of viewer preferences to perform targeted advertising as well. However, with its small user base of 624,000 users (<1% of the US market), the TiVo business model has not been effective and the company's net loss in 2002 was $55 million. Consequently, the company has tried

Table 6.5. PVR products.

	Standalone box	Cable & satelite set-top box	PC PVR	DVD/R/RW
Major players	TiVo Replay TV	Panasonic (Moxie DVR Systems) Satelite-DirecTV(TiVo) Statelite-EchoStar (own PVR)	Internal add-ons (Hauppauge's WinTV. ATI's all-in-wonder radeon) External add-ons (ATI's TV wonder. Show Shifter with DivX) Maccintosh (EyeTV by El Gato) WindowXP Home Ent.	Toshiba (Expected)
Price range	$249 & up	$800 & up EchoStar-addl. $150 DishPVR	Add-ons: $50 & up PC - $1500 ~ $2000	
Programming guide: Fee	TiVo-$299 Life or $12.95/month Replay TV - $250 Life or $9.95/month	DirecTV-$4.99/month -free if premimum package EchoStar-Free	Free	No programming guide
Method	TiVo-Phone Line ReplayTV-Broadband	Cable–broadband Satellite–phone line	Phone line or broadband	
Storage capacity	Up to 320 GB (160 hrs)	Store on DVDs	Depends on PC harddrive	
Network ability	Home Network with other PCs and stand-alone boxes USB expansion slots	None set top boxes	Home network only	
Other revenues	TiVo-License to others (upfront software fee, upgrade software fee, & per-box royalty fee) -Advertising fee on its home page & show case			
# Users/ subscribers	TiVo-624,000	EchoStar DishPVR> 600,000 Just under 1,500,000	N/A	N/A

to move its business model towards technology services. Licensing TiVo technology to hardware manufacturers and pay-TV operators has become a core strategy. These licensing deals provide TiVo with a steady income source: an upfront payment for its software technology; additional funds when the software is updated; and a per-box payment royalty when the product is sold. Current licensees are Sony, Philips, and Toshiba. Pay-TV licensees, such as DirecTV, also charge customers an additional monthly service fee for PVR using TiVo technology.

It appears that the standalone business model has not proven sustainable because its performance does not create a "must have" proposition to customers given current prices. Even though the device has high consumer satisfaction, only 5% of all potential customers have seen TiVo in action, making it difficult for "word of mouth" diffusion to be effective. Furthermore, in retail stores, commission–based salesmen have little incentive to promote TiVo, since it takes an average of 15 min to sell a TiVo versus 1 or 2 min to sell other similar-priced electronic products. This makes it unlikely for standalone PVR devices to be the industry threat to broadcast advertisers as many have believed.

6.9.3.2. *DVD/R/RW PVR*

Major hardware manufacturers have already introduced DVD recorders for television use. One important feature is that these players record videos straight to DVD and not to a hard drive. Hence, they do not use PVR technology yet. In a way, these players are not much different from traditional VCRs, except in providing superior digital quality. The most important feature these players lack is an interactive channel guide. The users have to rely on their own TV programming guide to set the exact time for recording. Currently, DVD recorders cost over $800. However, these device makers do have a very strong value proposition for their customers. Consumers that utilize the functionality of a DVD/R/RW are most probably consumers who will enjoy PVR functionality. Therefore, DVD recorders with PVR technology will come to market soon. Toshiba's next generation of DVD recorders (due by year end 2003) have full PVR functionality via a built-in hard drive. A hard drive combined with a DVD recorder allows consumers superior flexibility in archiving content. However, costs will be a significant barrier to adoption for the next few years; current DVD recorders and DVD media are still priced too high to attract the mass market. Therefore, DVD/R/RW PVR hybrids will remain in the technology savvy consumer segment for the near term.

6.9.3.3. *PC PVR*

PC PVR can be categorized into three types: internal add-ons, external add-ons, and complete PC PVR packages. All the three choices give users the same PVR experience but unlike standalone PVRs, users must watch the content on a computer screen rather than on a television. Add-on products provide the programming guide service free of charge in the hope of winning over customers. Some add-on cards cost as little as $50 suggesting that pricing is competitive with other PC accessories.

In building a complete PC PVR package, Microsoft collaborated with several computer manufacturers and chipmakers to develop the Windows XP Media Center Edition PC, rolled out in 2002 and priced from $1500 to $2000. Microsoft has long been experimenting in the home entertainment area, first with WebTV, the TV-enabled internet service, a TV-PVR set-top box, and now the Windows XP Media Center Edition. Although its previous attempts were unsuccessful, Microsoft is counting on the adoption of its newest entertainment center to be fueled by price drops in PC components and the increasing trend of using PCs for entertainment.

Although PVR PC costs are very competitive, the PC home entertainment market will remain a niche market for the computer savvy user because most of the consumers differentiate PC use from TV leisure entertainment. For regular viewing of TV and movies, consumers prefer simple devices over complicated PCs that face operating reliability, crashes, obsolescence and virus-related problems. Therefore, PVR PC will probably not be a factor in wide PVR adoption.

6.9.3.4. *Cable and satellite set-top box*

Incapable of providing true VOD, satellite operators have rolled out set-top boxes with PVR to counter cable VOD. They hope to use this technology to keep growing market share. In comparison, cable operators have been slow to add PVR functionality to set-top boxes. First, cable operators can provide more lucrative VOD services. Second, cable operators have just spent billions upgrading their networks to digital cable. Another round of set-top box upgrades would be too costly and serves no strategic aims. Charter Communications is the only cable operator pursuing the PVR system. In contrast, satellite operators offer PVR products. DirecTV charges an additional $200 for a PVR set-top box and adds a monthly fee of $4.99. EchoStar only charges for the PVR set-top box at $150 and has no monthly fee. As a result, DirecTV consumers have been switching to Dish Networks for free PVR monthly service. Aggressively pursuing the PVR market, EchoStar has rolled out their latest product (DishPVR) in 2003 with HDTV decoding and up to 250 h of standard program recording or up to 40 h of HDTV recording.

Unlike standalone PVR and PVR PC products, satellite companies have a real opportunity to help PVR "cross the chasm" given their significant user base. Satellite operators have aggressively incorporated PVR technology in set-top boxes for survivability and perceive this technology as a compatible time-shifting solution that enhances their core services. Satellite PVR is the primary feature to counter cable VOD.

However, the current PVR pricing for satellite subscribers, is not in alignment with its adoption potential. There are over 20 million satellite subscribers, but only

Estimation 3. PVR break-even investment by statellite companies.

Cost		
	Satellite bears PVR costs	\$200
X	(Customer base)	18.5 million + N
Benefit		
	Life time value of a satellite customer	\$3,300
X	New customers from cable	N
Solving for cost < benefits imples that $N >$ 1.2 million new customers are required to break-even.		

1.5 million of them (roughly 7%) have PVR set-top boxes. The current PVR prices of \$200 (plus \$4.99 monthly fee) from DirecTV and \$150 from EchoStar may have to be eliminated and satellite operators might consider giving away the technology for free to build loyalty in existing customers and to win over cable subscribers. Although this may appear to be too costly and risky for satellite operators, there is significant merit to this strategy if examined critically. Below is a break-even analysis of the satellite PVR giveaway hypothesis.

Assumptions:

- DirecTV will drop its additional \$4.99 monthly fee to compete with EchoStar. Therefore, satellite operators will bear the PVR cost of \$200 per device.
- As satellite providers announce the free giveaway of PVRs, all current satellite non PVR subscribers (18.5 million) will demand a free PVR.
- A number of new customer (N) previously using cable services will sign up to satellite service due to free PVR devices.
- Life time value (LTV) of a cable/satellite customer is \$3,300.[m]

From the above analysis, it appears that satellite operators can still be profitable after giving away PVR products, assuming there is no change in the customer lifetime value. Furthermore, this strategy is more attractive when one considers the gains in more subscription fees from a larger customer base. One significant risk is whether satellite operators can indeed win and maintain an appropriate customer base. However, the calculations appear to be reasonable: gaining at least 1.2 million new satellite customers out of 71 million total cable customers is only a 1.7% defection rate. This rate is much lower than the current 4% digital cable defection rate to satellite. This analysis suggests that a free satellite PVR proposition can be defended from a business perspective.

Under this business strategy, at least 22 million households will have PVR, which would be a 21% market penetration. With proven high satisfaction among most of the current PVR owners, this penetration rate should only go up through customer

[m] Industry estimate.

referrals and as hardware prices continue to fall. Cable operators may also jump on the PVR bandwagon and TV manufacturers could begin embedding this technology into televisions.

6.9.4. *Summary of PVR adoption dynamics*

Given the low historical adoption rate of PVR (2% in four years), PVR cannot reach mass adoption unless an aggressive adoption model is promoted. As a standalone product, PVR lacks significant consumer value and is overly complex to market. As a DVD product or PC product, it is a niche consumer good to technology savvy customers. Therefore, PVR will only be adopted through aggressive price subsidies in a manner that is attractive to a wide set of consumers. Satellite operators are best poised to provide these subsidies because their survival is in jeopardy as they compete with digital cable services.

If PVR can reach mass adoption, then the disruption it creates for broadcast advertising may become a serious issue. In this section 6.12, potential business practice changes are outlined if widespread PVR adoption can occur. Currently, PVR is a luxury consumer electronics product that is still trying to seed initial market penetration. This is in contrast to HDTV, a product whose adoption seems all but assured. A brief discussion of HDTV follows because it is an important part of the changes taking place in how consumer experience video entertainment at home.

6.10. HDTV

Unlike the other technologies examined in this research, HDTV will only be discussed briefly because HDTV:

(1) has both government and private interests aligned to push adoption;
(2) is not significantly disruptive to the Studio window release revenue model; and
(3) needs only falling prices, to keep adoption progress going.

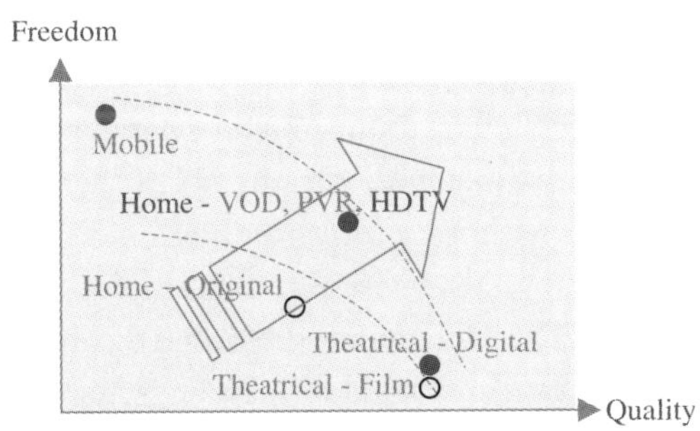

However, the presentation of HDTV is important because the adoption of more HD infrastructure has relevance to Digital Cinema. Furthermore, HDTV is another product that seems likely to help cable companies battle satellite companies for market share. After years of stagnation, HDTV appears poised to replace traditional NTSC television standards. Its adoption is no longer in doubt because the government has

Table 6.6. Digital compression formats.

Vertical lines	Pixels	Aspect ratio	Picture rate
1800	1920	16.9	60I, 30P, 24P
720	1280	16.9	60P, 30P, 24P
480	704	16:9 and 4:3	60P, 60I, 30P, 24P
480	640	4:3	60P, 60I, 30P, 24P

Notes:
1. P Progressive scanning.
2. I Interlaced scanning.
3. Picture rate: fields per second. For interlaced scanning, 60I = 25 frame per second.

legally mandated that terrestrial networks transmit HDTV signals. Furthermore, cable and satellite companies have adopted policies to increase HDTV content to consumers. We will only summarize HDTV as follows:

- Introduction to HDTV and the HDTV standard, and
- Apparent impact on the value chain.

6.10.1. *Technology attributes*

The current traditional TVs (NTSC)[n] deliver pictures with a resolution of upto 200,000 pixels. HDTV's have up to 2 million pixels. It is those extra pixels that create a picture that is ten times sharper than traditional TV. HDTV also has a screen that is significantly wider than it is tall (16:9 aspect ratio) and promises improved sound quality that is comparable to CD s or digital surround sound.

The current standard that the Federal Communications Commission (FCC) has adopted is a broadcasting standard developed by the Advanced Television Systems Committee. The current standard mandates HDTV signals transmitted over a single 6 MHz channel, which is the current terrestrial broadcasting mode. This system requires a compression of about 19 Mbps data to fit a 6 MHz channel. Consequently, this signal is incompatible with current NTSC service and cannot be received by standard TV receivers without a converter box.

The digital television system employs MPEG-2 video compression to encode video. In the ATSC document, there are 18 compression formats listed as follows (Table 6.6):

The first six digital formats are generally regarded as HDTV formats, the third line of the table lists SDTV formats (Standard Definition TV, a digital television system with quality slightly better than NTSC), and the last four formats are lower quality formats not meant for television broadcasting. It should be noted that the ATSC formats

[n]NTSC stands for National Television Standards Committee and is the color television standard in use in the United States today.

Table 6.7. Digital TV formats.

Networks/Cable	Formats
CBS	1080i
ABC	1080i
NBC	1080i

are not FCC mandated formats, but rather a "code of conduct" agreed upon by ATSC members.[o] Although the FCC has approved a digital HDTV standard, it does not have jurisdiction over channel allocation in cable and satellite networks. Cable companies can freely choose whether or not to adopt HDTV broadcasting, and what standards they will use.

6.10.2. *HDTV standards*

Because the HDTV standard does not mandate performance standards, it is not a true single standard. Broadcasters are free to choose their video compression format. The following table shows the format choice of the "Big Four" networks and one major US cable company (Table 6.7):

HDTV decoders will be compatible with all digital formats.[p] Therefore, consumers should not care which HDTV sets they buy because the intention is full compatibility with the multiformats. Though the ATSC standard may seem confusing, it should not be an obstacle towards mass consumer adoption. Most of the HDTV tuners are designed to be compatible with multiformats so that consumers can choose the receiver they like without worrying about the compatibility.

6.10.3. *Evolution of HDTV*

The FCC mandated that network-affiliated stations of ABC, CBS, Fox, and NBC in the top 30 markets build digital transmitting facilities by 1 November, 1999. All other commercial stations must construct DTV broadcast facilities by 1 May, 2002. As a result of this mandate, most of the stations and TV networks are trying to meet this goal even though many small-market broadcasters have balked at HDTV conversion. This suggests that the standards set will ultimately stratify the market into the "HDTV" and the "noHDTV" providers. Although the rollout has been slower than anticipated, it has been progressing.

Unlike NTSC, HDTV is an "all or nothing" transmission. This means that the cable and satellite industries are best poised to deliver digital content. However, the absence of an FCC must-carry policy by cable and satellite has been the decisive impediment to

[o] ATSC members include all leading television industry manufacturers and service providers.

[p] DTV Guide, April 2002, Consumer Electronics Association.

delivering HDTV content in the service chain given that current cable and satellite subscribers constitute more than 70% of the US homes. These companies have been slow to adopt HDTV because it consumes massive bandwidth resources. Therefore, it is the lack of content that has largely stranded HDTV till date. However, competition between cable and satellite companies has gotten fierce and this competition has helped to drive HDTV content. HDTV technology is now the standard in most of the large screen televisions (over 40") sold today. Therefore, its evolution may be slow but it is assured.

6.10.4. *HDTV value chain impact*

As previously stated, HDTV should not have a large impact on the Studio release window model because it simply enhances the consumer's enjoyment of movies and television. In fact, Studios can probably generate additional revenues with HDTV by producing HDTV DVDs. The current DVDs lack HDTV quality; therefore, there may be an opportunity to segment the DVD market.[q] However, this opportunity will probably be on hold until new DVD technology can increase the capacity of DVD disks to accommodate HDTV content on one disk. As discussed earlier, the underlying technology used to produce Digital Cinema content is the same as that used to produce HDTV content. So long as HD content is recorded appropriately, there is an opportunity to produce downstream derivative products.

The competition between cable and satellite providers is highly tilted in favor of the cable industry. Cable operators are in a better position to offer more HDTV content than satellite networks. Most of the terrestrial broadcasters in the leading markets have HDTV transmission equipment in place. Therefore, the HDTV infrastructure changes will not be a bottleneck to consumer adoption. In short, there is a significant clarity regarding HDTV because there is a unifying front growing to push adoption. Unlike PVR, HDTVs are easy for consumers to understand once they walk into an electronics store and see HDTV. This is a powerful tool in pushing technological innovation.

6.10.5. *Summary of video distribution to theatres and homes*

To this point, we have covered video distribution technologies from the theatre to the home. Studios have been flexible in adapting content from one incumbent platform (theatres) to others (VCRs, VOD, DVD, etc.). However, there is another important delivery channel to explore, and that is wireless delivery. The combination of data compression technology and wireless communication creates the potential for a new distribution channel for VOWD. In the following section, the opportunities and obstacles for video distribution on wireless mobile devices through 2.5G and 3G networks

[q]For the curious, the difference in a regular DVD and HDTV is the number of progressive-scan resolution lines (480 versus 720).

are explored. Unlike the previous technology discussions, VOWD is the most immature product that is still addressing key technology issues. Understanding these issues and how they affect the viability of VOWD concludes the last technology disruptor covered in our analysis.

6.11. Emerging Mobility

6.11.1. *Technology overview*

In order for streamed video to be delivered through a wireless platform, content needs to be first encoded properly and then stored in a server. Carriers need to then provide sufficient bandwidth to deliver the content at certain frame rates and resolution. Finally, device manufacturers need to provide cell phones/PDAs that can receive and play the video content. On the hardware side, color screens are then compulsory. On the software side, the operating system needs to support the video compression format. This process is illustrated on the right diagram, highlighting the technical competencies needed to make VOWD a legitimate possibility. Specific details about these competencies then follow (Fig. 6.7).

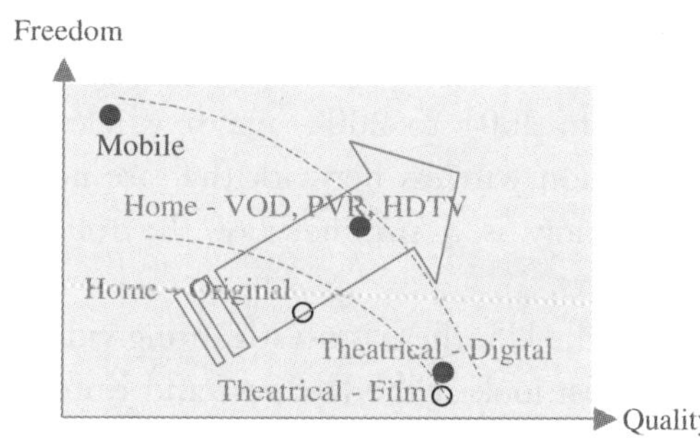

6.11.1.1. *Video compression*

When content is created, it needs to be compressed using compressor/de-compressor (CODEC) software to be stored and transported. The media format needs to comply with 3GPP.[r] There are several competing CODECs including various forms of MPEG-4, Real Networks, and Microsoft Media Technologies. There is no dominant standard

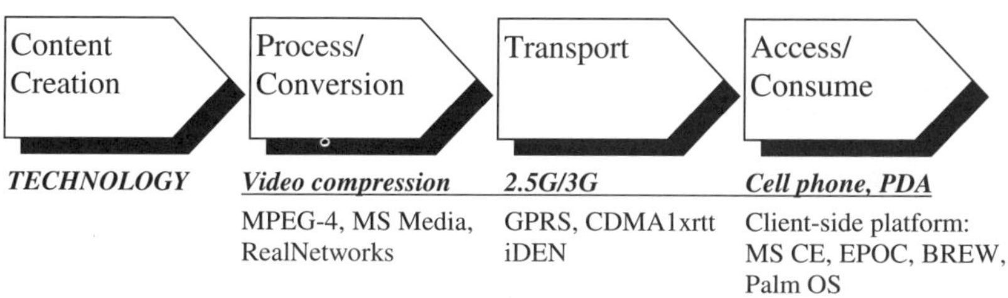

Fig. 6.7. Wireless delivery.

[r]The 3rd Generation Partnership Project is a collaboration agreement established in December 1998.

till date. MPEG-4 video compression enables wireless media at variable bit rates (down to 9.6 kbps) and has been selected as the multimedia standard for 3G networks by 3GPP. In comparison, Thin Multimedia has a proprietary wavelet codec called Thin Client Media 3(TCM-3), a different codec from MPEG-4, but with an upgrade path to MPEG-4. This technology has been used by Korea's SK Telecom. Alternatively, Microsoft and Real Networks, the compression technologies competing on the PC platform, each claim more than 125 million registered copies of their CODECs by 2001.[s] There is little opportunity for all the three standards to emerge intact in the future. The winning standard will depend on their partnership with device manufacturers and content owners. This standards battle is the first stage in making VOWD a reality.

6.11.1.2. *Wireless network: 2.5G and 3G*

Below is a summary of the potential 3G networks and their data speed ratings.[t]

From 2001 to 2002, major wireless carriers in the US began to roll out next generation wireless network that are necessary if VOWD is to be brought to market. Below is a summary of the rollout upgrades by major US cellular service providers.

In the US, there is no streaming video service provided on cell phones. Therefore, one must look at the Japanese and Korean markets to see what may be viable on the different technology platforms. The data below summarizes NTT DoCoMo's FOMA[u] i-Motion service (Fig. 6.8 and Table 6.8).

According to this specification, a streamed video clip requires 47–52 kbps to deliver acceptable performance. This screen size is actually below the resolution specified by QCIF[v] (144 by 176 pixels). NTT DoCoMo's better V-Live streaming video service

	Wireless Networks	Peak Speed (Kbps)	Expected actual speed (Kbps)
IS-41 Core Network	GPRS (2.5G)	115	20-40
	Edge	384	80-110
	W-CDMA	384	200-300
GSM Map Core Network	CDMA 2000 1x	153	60-80
	CDMA 2000 1x EV-DO	2400	200-300
	CDMA 2000 1x EV-DV	4800	200-300

Fig. 6.8. Wireless evolution.

[s]Gartner: Streaming Video Over GPRS: Hype or Reality, 4 May 2001.

[t]The migration paths from 2G to 3G is available on International Telecommunication Union's web site at http://www.itu.int.

[u]Freedom of Mobile Multimedia Access: NTT DoCoMo's 3G service based on W-CDMA technology, supporting up to 384 kbps.

[v]QCIF: Quarter Common Interface Format, standard for streaming video for mobile application specified by 3GPP.

Table 6.8. US 2.5G technology.

	Technology	Peak speed (kbit/s)	Advertised data Rate (kbit/s)	Initial rollout
Verizon Communications	CDMA2000 1XRITT	144	60 to 80	Jan-02
Ongular Wireless	GSM/GPRS& 155	20 to 40	Jun-02	
AT&T Wireless Services Inc.	GSM/GPRS	115	20 to 40	Jun-01
Sprint PCS Group	CDMA2000 1XRTT[a]	144	50 to 70	Summer 2002
Nextel Communications Inc.	Enhanced iDEN[b]	NA	30 to 50	Jan-03

Notes:
[a]The first generation of CDMA2000 calls for speeds up to 144 k bit/s, but vendors claim typical speeds of 50 k to 80 k bit/s.
[b]Short form for Integrated Digital Enhanced Network.

Table 6.9. FOMA platform.

Video processing	Encoding formats	MPEGA4 simple Profile Level 0 and MPEG4 simple Profile Level 1 with 3GPP restriction
	Screen size	subQCIF (128 X 96 dots)
	Frame rate	15 fps maximum
	Bit rate	Approximately 40 bps
Audio processing	Encoding formats	AMR
	Bitrate	12.2 kps, 6.7 kps
	Sampling rate	8 kHz

(MPEG4 format on 3GPP-compliant FOMA phones) requires at least 64 kbps bandwidth (Table 6.9). In Korea, the largest carrier (SK Telecom) adopted Thin Multimedia's TCM-3 technology, which claims to be capable of providing video-on-demand service on both CDMA1x and GPRS[w] 1 network. However, bandwidth will fluctuate according to the number of users within a particular cell. Video streaming requires low bit rate errors and high-density cell sites. Coupled with spectrum constraint, this makes a commercialized video service (which would require minimum of 56–64 kbps at 15 fps) difficult under current GPRS network although Thin Multimedia's technology has slightly lower bandwidth requirement. For CDMA technology, it is uncertain that the 1xrtt technology can deliver satisfactory streaming video in a stable and consistent manner. Nevertheless, by 2004, all major US carriers will upgrade to GPRS or CDMA1xrtt (with the exception of Nextel which uses enhanced iDEN).

[w]Cellcom, Israel's #1 operator, will use Thin Multimedia's solution to provide video services on its GSM network.

6.11.1.3. *Devices and client-side platforms*

Currently in the US market, some cell phones and PDAs have video players but only a few can play streaming video (e.g. Nokia 3650 with RealOne player). For downloaded video, the video length is usually limited to 100 kB, unless the device supports external memory expansion. For video applications, a color screen is very important. The current color-screen cell phones/PDAs are available in US, but remain too expensive for many consumers. Battery life is also a serious concern for both 3G and video applications as these technologies consume more electricity. Clearly, there are technology constraints that impede service quality.

In order to display streaming video, a device needs to have either a hardware player, or a software player. For video player companies, it is critical to partner with mobile chip manufacturers or device companies to build their technology standard into devices. Similarly, there is a battle to be the dominant cellular device operating system. The dominant operating system will dictate how OWD will evolve. The current leading operating system specially designed for 2.5G and 3G cell phone is Symbian's EPOC, backed by major cell phone manufacturers like Nokia[x] Symbian OS phones were available in the first half of 2001. Both Emblaze and Packet Video, leaders in the emerging video over wireless space, have optimized their video software for Symbian. On the other side, Microsoft has continued their partnership with Intel to the wireless platform in hopes of being the leading cellular OS provider. The company has already finished developing "Smartphone 2002" OS supporting both GSM and CDMA technology.

Qualcomm, the largest CDMA chip manufacturer, has developed the proprietary BREW[y] system. In the US, Verizon and ALLTEL have adopted the BREW platform for their data services. Interestingly, Palm has been a slow mover, and currently has not allied with any streaming video software providers (Emblaze, PacketVideo or Virage). They are adopting a wait-and-see approach. Even Linux is emerging as an operating system on handheld devices.

6.11.1.4. *Conclusion of technology review*

From the analysis of video technologies and client-end platform on cell phone platform, it is clear that VOWD is still in the introductory stage of the product life cycle. The market is waiting for a dominant design to emerge. One of the critical differences

---

[x] Symbian is collectively owned by Ericsson, Nokia, Panasonic, Motorola, Psion, Samsung Electronics, Siemens and Sony Ericsson. It licenses software for data-enabled 2.5G and 3G mobile phones.

[y] Binary Runtime Environment for Wireless: a thin application execution environment that provides an open, standard platform for wireless devices.

between mobile data services in the US and in Japan is that NTT DoCoMo[z] can take the lead in setting a single standard for content providers and cell phone manufacturers. The US carrier market is much more fragmented compared to that in Japan. One reason for the success of DoCoMo's low-bandwidth data service is that a dominant design — i-mode — has fostered subscription growth to 30 million in less than three years. In comparison, the largest US carrier, Verizon Wireless, only holds a 23% market share. This is not strong enough to predict a dominant design for VOWD. Therefore, the existence of many variations of compression standards and client-end platforms create difficulty for the adoption of video on cell phone /PDA for the following reasons:

- Video software companies have to form partnerships with various operating system providers.
- Device manufacturers have to support multiple platforms.
- Wireless carriers have to decide on which type of system and format they will base their data content.
- Video content providers need to choose CODECs and may have to support multi formats.

The growth stage of video on cell phone/PDA will start with the emergence of a dominant design. However, significant growth is more dependent on business considerations — partnerships, complementary assets, and motivations — than on compression technology. Most importantly, it is dependent on whether the appropriate content will be provided. Similar to other entertainment media, content is often the driver for mass adoption to stir.

6.11.2. *Content — value proposition and costs*

6.11.2.1. *Cell phone data content in general*

Currently, the most successful cell phone data service is NTT DoCoMo's i-mode. Launched in February 1999, the data rate was 9.6 kbps until upgrades to 28.8 kbps took place last May (NTT DoCoMo's FOMA was launched in selected area in October 2001). By May 2002, data subscribers (32,988,000) accounted for 80% of the NTT DoCoMo's cellular base[aa] Despite low data rates, entertainment services accounted for more than half of the NTT DoCoMo's cellular data traffic. Entertainment services include games, character downloads, ring tones, wall papers, horoscope, fortune telling, Karaoke information, hit songs, FM radio information, club event information, etc. 46% of the NTT DoCoMo's content is games, entertainment, melodies and images.[bb]

[z] Has 60% of cell phone subscriber market.
[aa] Gartner Research, NTT DoCoMo: i-mode Wireless Internet Services, 26 July 2002.
[bb] Gartner Research, NTT DoCoMo: i-mode Wireless Internet Services, 26 July 2002.

Since DoCoMo introduced the next generation FOMA, only 112,300 people in eight months have subscribed. This is disappointing considering that i-mode signed up 5 million people during the first year.

In South Korea, ring tones and picture downloads are dominant wireless applications, but information content has not been popular. The largest Korean wireless carrier SK Telecom has 8.4 million wireless internet users[cc] (service coded NATE) on its 2.5G network by March 2003. However, since SK Telecom launched its EV-DO service in January 2002, it only attracted some 230,000 subscribers for its EV-DO service out of its 17 million subscriber base by January 2003. In the US, ring tones take almost 80% of the wireless internet market according to Moviso, with pictures or games as distant followers. Two preliminary conclusions can be drawn from these findings: (i) entertainment applications are popular on cell phone platforms; (ii) low bandwidth data service has already been successful in some markets in Asia; and (iii) bandwidth is less critical than content availability in terms of data usage.

6.11.2.2. *Video on cell phone*

Unlike the content we see in traditional distribution channels, content on handheld mobile devices has unique characteristics and consumption patterns. Because the goal of this research is to explore the opportunity for cell phone /PDA as a new distribution channel for video products, the focus is on commercial video content rather than user-created content.

In general, handheld devices have a small screen size (low resolution), short battery life in high bandwidth networks, and high portability. The current QCIF[dd] video standard has 15 frame rates per second (compared with 24 fps for film and 30 fps for NTSC TV). That rate serves as a basis for the type of video that may emerge. Commercial video content on handheld devices can therefore be categorized into entertainment products and information products.

Entertainment products

Traditional video entertainment includes movies, TV programs, and video games. Due to the short viewing times and lower display quality, long content is not appropriate for wireless handhelds. Traditional entertainment content focuses on high quality audio/video to deliver a pleasant experience to viewers who sit and enjoy entertainment. However, for wireless handheld devices, the experience is totally different. A few consumers will set aside time beforehand to access entertainment on a portable device.

[cc]User is defined as a person who uses wireless internet services more than once per month via a handset, PDA, and VMT, etc.

[dd]The format specified by 3GPP.

Therefore, mainstream entertainment content from Studios and TV networks cannot be easily moved to the mobile platform.

Till date, successful entertainment content on cell phones have been device personalization (ring tones, wall paper, etc.) and simple games. Currently, some major Studios (Sony Picture Entertainment, Universal Studios, and 20th Century Fox) are forming partnership with carriers, cell phone manufacturers, and game publishers to bring their content onto wireless platform for film-based games, ring tones, and pictures. However, it is still not clear whether it is appropriate to bring mainstream video entertainment content to wireless devices. Globally, Korean telecom carriers are the pioneers in delivering commercialized video content on 3G networks. SK Telecom's 3G mobile multimedia service "June" provides customers with movies, TV programs, MTV's on cell phone. Since last November, Korea's SK Telecom has launched four wireless films including Project X", "Egg and Gangster", "My good Partner" and a new love story for its new CDMA2000 1X EV-DO network. The typical length of each episode is about 2–2.5 min. The budget for the new release is about $500,000. These movies have been produced by independent studios specifically for the mobile platform. As a result of SK Telecom's heavy marketing efforts, its EV-DO subscribers grew 73% in January 2003. Although this growth may not be directly related to just these short movies, yet they have certainly added to the appeal of high-bandwidth mobile access.

Besides entertainment, VOWD has the potential to be a significant platform for advertising. For example, Viacom's MTV had a wireless promotional campaign for its Video Music Awards on AT&T and Sprint. MTV also reached an agreement with Motorola on a three-year $75 million joint marketing agreement.[ee] Because cell phone advertising has the potential to target specific audiences better, it must be used carefully to prevent consumer backlash from excessive advertising spam. Based on current events, video promotion clips on mobile devices seem likely to be more popular going forward.[ff]

Information products

The traditional information content includes news, sports, weather, etc. In the PC world, on-demand news video has not been very successful. Although all four major networks have video streaming from their websites, yet demand has been weak. It is still unclear whether people will pay for general information video on-demand.

The basic economic theory argues that given many substitutes and low switching costs, charging premium prices will be difficult. Therefore, the information content that is significantly differentiated and targeted at niche markets may have a better

[ee] MTV content will appear on Motorola cell phones' menu.

[ff] In February 2002, NTT DoCoMo, Dentsu Inc. and ActiveSky conducted a three-week trial of streaming mobile advertising in greater Tokyo.

prospect than general video information services. In addition, people tend to access information on cell phones on an ad hoc basis and are usually clear about what they seek. As a result, time sensitive, information video content may be most viable on mobile devices where users are focused on results and not on passive entertainment.

Because the current video content is not well-suited for wireless devices, new content must emerge for VOWD to be popular. The device interface, time, location and video-watching needs are different from the products of traditional content providers such as Studios. There will be a need to differentiate video content over wireless devices to provide a compelling value proposition to consumers. Among others, interactive entertainment and live broadcasts of activity-based or location-based information contents are examples of new content necessary to create real demand for video over wireless devices.

6.11.2.3. *Cost to consumers*

Like all emerging technologies, consumer costs must be examined to add analysis depth and realism. The following chart shows data charges on 2.5G networks by selected US carriers (Table 6.10).

For streamed video at a 56 kbps data rate, one-minute of video would have a file size of 420 kB. At 0.6 cents per KB (the lower bound pricing rate), one-minute of video would cost consumers $2.52 in airtime alone. Therefore, flat rate charging is more appropriate for streamed video applications.

The data charge by kB seems appropriate under slow network speeds, but under high network speeds of 2.5G and 3G, the cost to consumers for heavy bandwidth applications such as video streaming would be too high. The following table shows a comparison of monthly average revenue per user (ARPU) of US carriers and NTT DoCoMo (Table 6.11).

In 2002, the data contribution to monthly ARPU for NTT DoCoMo is about $13. At 78.8% i-mode penetration, average data spending per i-mode customers is

Table 6.10. Current wireless data services pricing.

	Charge by data volume	Unlimited access
AT&T mMode	$2.99 to $19.99 per month with 0 to 8M data included, over quota rate is 2 cents to 0.6 cents per k byte	No
Verizon Express Network	$35 with 10M(0.8 cent after) $55 with 20M(0.6 cent after)	$79.99 per month
Sprint PCS Vision	Additional 1 cent per K byte on voice only plan	$10 in additional to voice plan
Cingular	$19.99 (100 K incl., $0.2 per K after)	$59.99 per month

Source: Company websites.

Table 6.11. ARPU statistics.

	U.S	NTT DoCoMo
Voice ARPU$	52.34	53
Data ARPU$	0.89	13
Total ARPU$	53.23	66

Sources: Morgan Stanley, Gartner Research.

roughly $17. It is interesting to note that the United States and Japan have similar voice ARPU. Considering the fact that the Japanese are more likely to access the internet through cell phones, one can assume that the monthly spending on data services in the US should be roughly $20 if data services are to reach mass adoption. For video streaming to become a popular activity on cell phones then, this $20 should be a flat monthly charge for data.

6.11.3. *Incentives and economics across the wireless value chain*

In this section, each participant in the wireless value chain is examined to determine the economic dynamics and motivations for VOWD. The focus is on identifying the VOWD obstacles in the value chain, who may lead content aggregation, and what kind of business model can best facilitate video streaming services. To determine the motivation and incentives of each participant, the following forces are deemed most relevant:

- Strategic priorities;
- Competitive pressures; and
- Risk and return.

The following chart shows major participants in the value chain (Fig. 6.9):

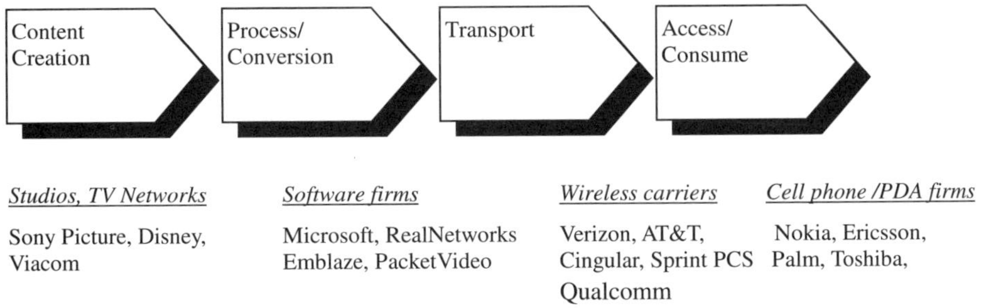

Fig. 6.9. Wireless industry participants.

6.11.3.1. *Video content owners*

Studios have already begun moving some derivative content onto the mobile platform. The following chart shows various partnerships of Studios and TV networks on the cellular platform. The current partnerships relate to games, ring tones, and pictures. No video content is currently licensed.

Currently, mobile data services are of low priority for Studios and TV networks who are more concerned about Digital Cinema and traditional home entertainment distribution markets. As previously stated, mainstream Studio content is simply inappropriate for mobile viewing, and the market is still too immature for these companies to devote significant resources to the wireless initiative. It is possible that wireless video advertising for mainstream Studio content may be pursued, but only after VOWD has taken off. The current leading content owners — Studios and TV networks — do not have the incentives and/or pressure to push content on the wireless platform. The one exception is Sony Pictures. Expanding content to mobile devices is a part of Sony's core strategy to build a huge connected platform for AV, PC, and mobile devices. In early 2003, Sony announced its new strategy theme, "A World About U" (Table 6.12).

As discussed earlier, new entrants must appear to provide content that is better customized for mobile devices and its unique consumption pattern. Innovation must come from outside the current content leaders. Similar to the events in Korea, independent studios must catalyze and originate short films on mobile devices. New entrants will also emerge as information providers begin tailoring services specifically for mobile usage (see analysis in Content section). In short, content for VOWD must come from new thinkers that are not the current leaders in video entertainment.

6.11.3.2. *Video processing companies*

The competition is getting fierce for companies pushing their proprietary solution as the dominant standard. Microsoft's strategic focus is the handheld operating system and delivering Windows powered devices and media players. In contrast, companies

Table 6.12. Partnership agreements.

Partners	Examples
Cell phone manufactures	Nokia's Starcut with Universal Studios, Motorola with MTV
Technology solution providers	Qualcomm with various studios, Emblaze with ESPN PacketVideo with SPE, 20th Century Fox, Warner Bros
Wireless carries	Major carriers with Sony Pictures, Sprint PCS with Disney ESPN and ABC
Wireless marketing companies	SkyGo with ESPN
Game publishers	THQ Wireless with 20th Century Fox

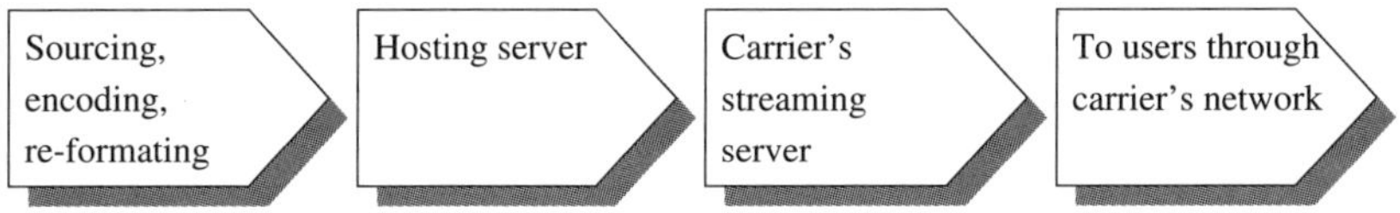

Fig. 6.10. Example of roaming eyes solution.

Table 6.13. Major carrier ranking.

Ranking	Company	Subcribers (000s)	Market share (%)
1	Verizon Wireless	32,491	23.0
2	Cingular	21,925	15.5
3	AT&T Wireless	20,859	14.8
4	Sprint PCS	14,760	10.4
5	Nextel	10,612	7.5
6	T-Mobile	9,913	7.0
Industry total		141,349	

Source: Company filing.

such as RealNetworks, Emblaze and PacketVideo are focusing on the audio/video delivery technology in pushing media solutions in mobile devices. These companies are aggressively forming partnerships with device companies, chip manufacturers, and content partners. RealNetworks already has access to much content and a partnership with Nokia to build their technology into Nokia's cell phones. Emblaze has established Roaming Eyes as its content syndicator and has recruited partners including Cnet, ESPN, Reuters, NY1, and Tomorrow TV. PacketVideo has over 30 partners including 20th Century Fox, Sony Picture Digital Entertainment, and Warner Bros. All of these companies believe that first mover advantages are critical to tipping VOWD to their technologies and ultimately, their own survival (Fig. 6.10).

6.11.3.3. *Wireless carriers*

By the end of 2002, the US had 141 million wireless subscribers; this is 48% of the US population.[gg] Table 6.13 shows the market share data for the major US carriers.

For data services, no US carrier has been successful in generating strong demand. AT&T has 300,000 m-mode subscribers till date (1.4% of their total users). Verizon has 150,000 – 200,000 users on their Express Network (0.6% of their total subscribers). Sprint has 630,000 Vision subscribers (4.3% of the total users). Clearly, 2.5G penetration is still very low with the weighted average of the above three carriers to be 1.66%. Only Sprint PCS is pricing aggressively to attract more users to their 2.5G services.

[gg]US population estimated to be 291 million, courtesy of the US Bureau of the Census.

This low penetration suggests that carriers may not be bullish on selling data services if they may conflict with voice service resources. This is examined in further detail next.

Profitability of voice and data

The following calculation shows revenue per kB for voice signals (Table 6.14). In addition, Table 6.15 shows revenue per kB for data signals (excluding unlimited plans):

From the above comparison, current data plans offer more revenue per kB transmitted. However, nonflat fee data rate plans are designed for low-bandwidth data services. Earlier, we suggested that flat rate monthly charges were deemed most appropriate for commercial video applications. For a flat rate plan then, assuming voice revenue is at the maximum of 0.17 cent per kB, the following chart (Fig. 6.11) shows the maximum data download before data services generates less revenue for the given spectrum resources than voice services.

Assuming that the consumer data spending (for airtime alone) at mass adoption levels will be $20 per month, the monthly data download that would make carriers indifferent to voice or data services is only 28 mins of video. This capacity is too small. Moreover, video applications are more likely to be consumed during the day (there is little need at home or at night) when voice traffic is high. This actually suggests that carriers may not have an incentive to push video applications if there are resources and capacity trade-offs between data and voice services.

Previous calculations have shown that current data charges by data volume generate more revenue per unit of resources than that from voice. Furthermore, the success of

Table 6.14. Voice profits.

Voice	
Voice data rate (kps)	8 kps*
Voice data rate (kps)	1 kB/s
Per minute charge	<$0.1
$ per kB	$0.0017

Assuming analog voice signal is translated to digital signal by vocoder at 8 kbps.

Table 6.15. Data prices.

	Plans Charging by MB	$ per kB
AT&TmMode	$2.99 to $19.99 per month with 0 to 8 M data included, over quota rate is 2 cents to 0.6 cents per K byte.	$ 0.0025 to 0.02
Verizon Express Network	$35 with 10M, $55 with 20M	0.00275 to 0.0035
Sprint PCS Vision	Additional 1 cent per K byte on voice only plan	0.01
Cingular	$19.99(100 K incl.)	0.2

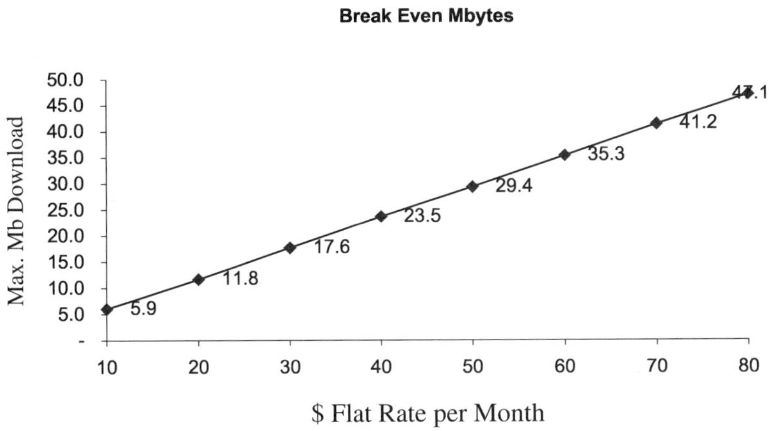

Fig. 6.11. Wireless data pricing analysis — Breakeven megabytes.

data applications in Asia has demonstrated that low-bandwidth data services (particularly SMS) can generate significant revenue if a compelling business model is set in place. There is no guarantee that high-bandwidth data services will generate higher revenue per unit of resources.

Another important problem for carriers in providing high-bandwidth data services is spectrum resource. Under current carrier networks, spectrum capacity is already tight in some markets. Video applications are especially capacity-consuming. Currently, over 98% of the ARPU is contributed by voice. Carriers do not want to disturb voice service with unproven demand for video applications. From a carrier's resource perspective, VOWD may cannibalize voice services. This issue is a clear problem in building industry enthusiasm for VOWD.

The viability of 3G upgrades

From the technology analysis, video streaming seems most appropriate on 3G networks, specifically EDGE/W-CDMA and CDMA1xEV-DO, although current CDMA1xrtt may also be able to deliver the service. Every carrier will need more spectrum capacity as wireless usage expands. To upgrade from 2.5G to 3G, carriers need to acquire additional spectrum. It is expected that FCC will auction an additional 175 MHz of spectrum to support 3G around 2005/2006. The total new investment in this spectrum may exceed $10 billion; this may postpone the adoption of 3G until 2005–2007. A significant difference between US carriers and that NTT DoCoMo is that NTT DoCoMo does not pay for its spectrum.

There are ways to increase the capacity on existing spectrum such as: (i) building more base station radios to cell sites; (ii) adding new cell sites; and (iii) upgrading vocoder technology, which basically means upgrading to 3G. Most of these measures require significant capital outlays and new cell phones to consumers. In the US, carriers often subsidize cell phone purchase. From 2001 to 2002, wireless carriers' cell phone subsidies in the US rose 18%, from $3.8 billion to $4.5 billion.[hh] The rollout of 3G may potentially require large capital expenditure on cell phones given the US marketing model. This is a significantly different business environment than that of NTT DoCoMo.

In addition, the capital expenditures for upgrades from 1xrtt to 1xEV-DO and GPRS to EDGE/W-CDMA are much higher than the previous upgrades. The 3G upgrade is estimated to be roughly $50 billion dollars for the top six US carriers.[ii] High-bandwidth products such as video are not likely to generate more dollars per unit of resources consumed. Furthermore, low-bandwidth products have been proven to be profitable in other markets. This makes it difficult to believe that carriers will simply "build" 3G believing that content, services and customers will follow. This is aggravated by the tight financial position of the telecommunications industry. Stock prices of leading wireless carriers have dropped from 80 to 90% in the past three years (AWE, PCS, and NXTL). In the bond market, Sprint PCS and Nextel have bond rating below investment grade. AT&T Wireless has a BBB rating. The debt to total capitalization (market value) for AT&T Wireless, Sprint PCS and Nextel was 41.7, 82.6 and 51.0%, respectively, by the end of 2002.[jj]

From the above analysis, it appears that the demand for high-bandwidth data services are not strong enough to promote carriers to further upgrade their networks to 3G. However, they may upgrade because of the need for more voice capacity. Voice traffic is unquestionably the dominant traffic on cell phone networks and will remain so for at least five years. However, current GPRS upgrades do not improve voice efficiency, whereas 1xrtt almost doubles voice efficiency. GSM network carriers may want to upgrade to EDGE or even W-CDMA to improve voice capacity, especially in places where capacity constraints are acute. Among the four largest nonCDMA carriers, AT&T has the most spectrum resources among all wireless carriers in the US, and thus AT&T may not upgrade immediately. Nextel plans to acquire additional spectrum from the FCC. This leaves Cingular and T-Mobile with the most incentive to upgrade. They are two of the top three debt-rating wireless carriers. Since 1xEV-DO only improves data capacity, CDMA carriers may be more cautious to upgrade unless there is sufficient demand. 3G services are expected in some US cities by 2004,[kk] but

[hh] Estimates by wireless consultancy InCode Telecom in La Jolla, CA.

[ii] A simple estimate for upgrade cost from 2G to 3G. Average cost of 3G base station $750,000 * 86000 base stations in US + $10 billion spectrum cost = $75 billion. The top six carriers have 78% of the base stations, which translates to $58.5 billion cost. 2.5G upgrade will cost $8.5 billion for the top six carriers. The remaining expenditure will be roughly $50 billion for the top six carriers (Source: US Bankcorp Piper Jaffray, SG Cowen).

[jj] Company filings.

[kk] NTT DoCoMo's investment in AT&T Wireless requires AT&T to launch W-CDMA technology in certain areas of Dallas, San Diego, San Francisco, and Seattle, or agreed upon alternate cities by 31 December 2004, covering approximately 8 million POPS. Verizon is also capable of providing 3G in San Diego and Washington DC.

the conversion process will be slow and may extend over the five-year horizon. The commercial video applications have not been a reason for carriers to upgrade their network, but if carriers do choose to upgrade, it is very likely to be one of the 3G applications.

Competitive pressure and content partners

With the cell phone penetration of about 50%, the subscriber growth rate is expected to slow. In the top 20 US markets, the penetration rate is closer to 60%. When a market reaches saturation, the growth of one carrier will have to be at the others' expense. Carriers will then have to differentiate their services to avoid price competition and win new customers. In the voice service, service is difficult to be differentiated. Therefore, the decline of voice ARPU is simply inevitable.

Facing pressure in lost voice ARPU, carriers will be motivated to provide satisfactory data services to boost total ARPU and keep attrition rates low. Currently, major carriers like Verizon and Nextel are still focused on selling data services to business customers who tend to have higher ARPU. Consumer data applications are of lower priority along with commercial video streaming. A change in strategic focus is necessary for US carriers if consumers are expected to adopt handheld data services.

6.11.3.4. *Device manufacturers*

Currently none of the top six US wireless carriers sell cell phones supporting streamed video. Only AT&T and T-Mobile support the Nokia 3650 which has a video player. However, most of the carriers support the Pocket PC/PDA standard and major cell phone companies have already begun partnering with technology firms to build streaming video capabilities into these devices. However, storage is a significant issue in video streaming on handheld devices. Streaming video requires enough cache to function smoothly (i-motion capable cell phones can only play 100 kB video now). To meet the requirement of streaming video, the device must have more in-built memory or support memory expansion cards.

Device manufacturers have an incentive to push new video-capable phones because if they become popular, they will benefit substantially. Nokia established a company named Starcut in early 2000 as its mobile movie entertainment aggregator. Starcut takes care of content design and implementation to facilitate the fusion of mobile media and entertainment. It has a licensing agreement with Universal Studios. Sony Ericsson is another company that has the motivation to push video applications on cell phones. Clearly, the device technology companies are more interested in trying to stimulate video services for the handheld market because it is a method to increase hardware sales.

6.11.3.5. *Independent content aggregator*

In addition to the players in the value chain, companies acting solely as content aggregators for mobile platforms are beginning to emerge. The most prominent example is Moviso, which was acquired by Vivendi Universal Net USA in 2002. Partnering with key mobile carriers, mobile service providers, and media/ entertainment /consumer brands, Moviso provides ring tones and picture downloads for mobile phones. Moviso claims about 70% market share in this category. For ring tones and pictures, Moviso's value-added activities are content recreation, format conversion, and multiplatform supporting (supports four media types and seven major handset protocols). For video applications, Moviso may still provide value in porting data to different hardware but compared with content processing companies, Moviso's value-added services to both carriers and content producers are somewhat limited.

6.11.3.6. *Conclusions on the wireless value chain*

The following table summarizes our analysis of various participants in the wireless value chain, and our estimates of the future trend. We believe that, unless every party in the value chain has economic benefits and incentives in place, video on wireless distribution cannot become a mass market business even with sufficient consumer demand. First, carriers lack the expertise and incentives to assist content producers develop the market. Second, there are significant variations in hardware and formats due to the lack of VOWD standards. Regarding the potential content aggregators, early aggregators are expected to be technology solution providers (Table 6.16).

6.11.4. *Ways to the future — recommendations*

6.11.4.1. *Clearing obstacles*

From this analysis of technology, content demand, and service provider incentives, some of the obstacles in the wide adoption of VOWD have been identified. On the technology side, there is no dominant standard for video compression on handheld devices. This uncertainty makes investments risky for service providers who need to pick a hardware platform. On the device side, there are no carrier-supported cell phones capable of streaming video even though the technology is available. The problem is that manufacturers need to choose a technology that has the right content partners; otherwise they must support multiple formats, a costly proposition. However, the key problem is that carriers need to expand network speed and capacity by upgrading to EDGE/W-CDMA or 1xEV-DO. This upgrade process will be very slow and take over five years based on current conditions in the telecommunications industry.

It is clear that early video content providers will be traditional content owners, but they have little incentive to push this line of business. To solve the incentives issue, new

Table 6.16. Value chain summary.

	Motivation	Potential to be content aggregator	Early movers
Video content owners	Medium • Outside strategic focus (excl. Sony) since traditional contents may not be appropriate • Can leverage current products by producing derivatives • Studios/TV networks with successful Internet contents may have more incentive	Low • Customers do not like to tie-in with single content owner • Conflict of interest	• Sony Pictures, ESPN • New entrants who provide non traditional contents
Content processing companies	High • Core business • Competing for standard • New firms striving for survival	Medium to high (early) • Standard war requires content support • All major players have already started to build content	RealNetworks, Emblaze, PacketVideo, etc.
Wireless carriers	Medium to low • Need 3G investment and subsidize new 3G video-capable phones • Spectrum/ capacity constraint • Less profitable than low bandwidth applications • Firms first upgrade to 3G may have incentive to differentiate their service (in a matured market)	High (late) • More control over content quality • Avoid tie-in one processing technology (compared with current Verizon model)	Cingular, T-Mobile upgrade to EDGE

Table 6.16. *(Continued)*

	Motivation	Potential to be content aggregator	Early movers
Device manufacturers	Medium to high • Selling more devices • Just one function of the device and demand is still not proven	Medium to low (early) • Create demand for new devices • Move from product to service (build-in menu) • Sourcing content is not strategic focus • Lack production capacity	Sony, Nokia
Independent content aggregators	Medium to high • Leveraging established relationships with carriers, and media companies	Medium to low • (Unlike ring tone and pictures,) Key value-adding activity is absent for video applications	Moviso, etc.

entrants need to enter the value chain and provide more and new varieties of content suitable for mobile devices. This can only happen after carriers make clear moves to enable and push VOWD. The critical part of the chain is still the wireless carrier. Actions that need to be taken on the carrier's part before the wide adoption of VOWD must include the following:

- Upgrade to 3G to increase speed and capacity of network.
- Although current 1xrtt is capable of transmitting video streams, yet the lack of economic incentives will stop its adoption.
- Carriers need to have sufficient capacity to provide high bandwidth data and not have to face tradeoffs between various products.
- Make content partnership a more formalized process and create clear and attractive revenue sharing plans.
- Set content standards and interface specifications.
- Carriers should support multiple video formats.
- For nonflat rate plans carriers should adopt flexible and intuitive airtime charge rates.
- Low bandwidth products may be charged on per piece or per mega byte basis.
- High bandwidth video products may be charged by the minute.

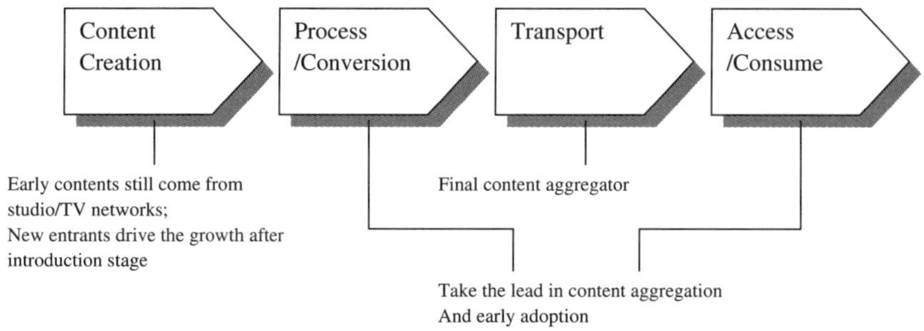

Fig. 6.12. Adoption process for VOWD.

6.11.4.2. *Adoption process*

The following chart summarizes the process of adoption in the early and growth stage of the product life cycle for VOWD (Fig. 6.12).

Video processing and device/chip manufacturers will take the lead in content aggregation in the introduction stage as evidenced by RealNetworks, Emblaze, PacketVideo, Nokia, and Qualcomm. Early content will still come from traditional content owners because this is low risk experimentation that is not overly costly. However, new content specifically designed for handheld devices will emerge to drive the growth of video on handheld devices after the very early stage. Hopefully by that time, carriers will already have infrastructure in place to stimulate demand. The final content aggregator will then be the wireless carrier after initial trials video services. These carriers will have the power to set up the process and interface standard. They may ultimately be the true beneficiaries of this new class of services, a markedly different structure compared to traditional video content where bargaining power lies with content licensors.

6.12. Final Research Conclusions across the Entertainment Value Chain

The easiest way to summarize the research findings is to update the diagram of the value chain for entertainment distribution with the key findings. For the most part, the chain will remain intact. However, there are certain changes that will take place, all of which are induced by the technology discussed in this analysis (Fig. 6.13).

6.12.1. *Digital cinema findings*

The entry of more content suppliers should increase Exhibitor bargaining power in acquiring alternative content. If enough small-scale entrepreneurs can prove the viability of alternative content, then leading Exhibitors would follow. In fact, Exhibitors would have an incentive to follow since greater content supply would drive their bargain power up in content acquisition. If Exhibitors can drive acquisition costs down for alternative content, then it may even be possible to show alternative content admission-free

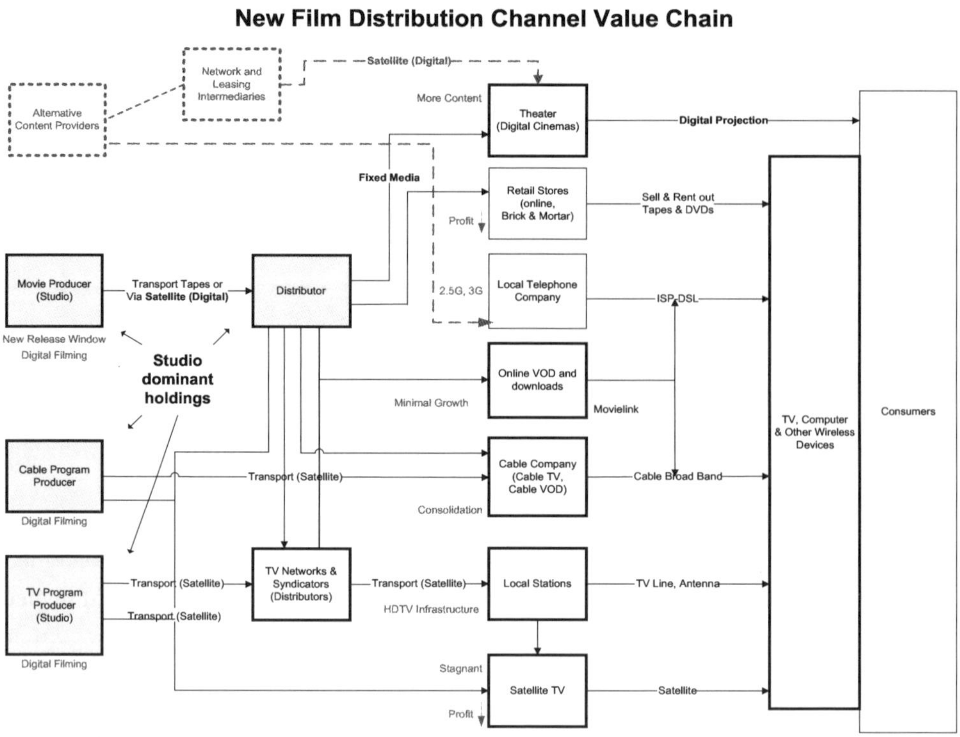

Fig. 6.13. Revised industry structure.

to consumers to generate additional concession sales. The impending move to HDTV will give consumers excellent viewing quality at home. The content that can be enjoyed at HDTV resolution (sports, live events, etc.) will be a significant value proposition to consumers. Therefore, Exhibitors should not pursue business models that seek to acquire content that will be associated with HDTV. The theatre content needs to be sufficiently differentiated such that the theatre experience remains unique. In short, change dynamics in the Digital Cinema space will not come from leading Exhibitors and Studios. It must come from new content providers and entrepreneurial Exhibitors that can build niche market demand. The companies that are engaged in building and promoting Digital Cinema technologies should focus on building this potential Exhibition market to help seed the foundations of Digital Cinema.

6.12.2. *Implications of VOD and the cable/satellite battle*

Four significant business implications have been identified with the impending release of VOD.

(1) *The existing Studio release window is under threat. VOD will move up to the same release window as sell-through and rental DVDs.*

Currently, studios maximize their profits from consumers by controlling the release window of movies. This window is timed and priced based on consumer willingness to pay. Research has identified the margin of DVD sell-through to be approximately 85% to Studios. Ideally, releasing sell-through DVDs before DVD rentals will maximize profits. However, this structure is not the case now due to market dynamics. Generally speaking, the earlier the release window, the more profitable it is to Studios.

Studios will face greater pressure from cable operators to place VOD early in the release schedule, preferably right after theatrical release. The current DVD sell-through and rental releases are at the same time as VOD — 30–60 days after theatre exhibition. Industry experts believe that demand should move VOD to as early as 30 days after DVD sell-through and rentals, but probably no earlier. This belief does not appear to be accurate. The existing release window now depends on two things: (i) the revenue streams of Studios; and (ii) the bargaining power of distribution channels. VOD changes these dynamics significantly.

Ideally for Studios, DVD sell-through should be released earlier than rentals. However, with revenue from rentals growing rapidly, rental businesses like Blockbuster substantially increased their bargaining powers, forcing Studio to compromise and move the rental window parallel with sell-through. Studios have refused to move VOD releases earlier to not jeopardize sell-through revenues. However, VOD provides studio with higher margin than video rentals. Therefore, if video rentals are released with sell-through, it is reasonable to expect VOD to move to the same release window. The only reason that has not happened yet is that VOD is still an insignificant revenue source. With the deployment of VOD infrastructure, VOD revenue will grow rapidly and replace a substantial percentage of the revenues from rentals. If that is the case, then the power balances among Studios, video rental companies and cable operator will shift. VOD will become a bigger revenue stream and Studios will probably acquiesce to cable operators and move VOD in parallel with video rentals.

(2) *Consolidation of cable operators*

Cable operators used to be entrepreneurial startups in specific geographic locations. Some of the operators are still run by the original owners but the number of small-scale operators is dwindling. The top five US cable operators serve 78% of the cable subscribers. These companies have increased in size primarily by acquisition. Today, there are only two major competitive technologies (cable and satellite) in delivering video entertainment, and the number of player in these competing technologies are relatively few (two in satellite and five to six significant players in cable). This will only get smaller. The number of firms in cable industry approximately depends on the following formula:

$$\text{Profit} = (\text{Total market revenue/number of firms})^{*}\text{gross margin} - \text{Fixed costs}$$

When fixed costs rise at a higher rate than either revenue growth or gross margin, the number of firms must fall equilibrium. The variables of this equation are described below.

Fixed costs

Traditionally, cable operators were regional monopolies that charged rates are under government regulation. In 1994, satellite operators emerged and took away significant cable subscribers. To compete with satellite operators, the cable industry started a never-before-seen multibillion infrastructures upgrade beginning in 1996 totaling over $70 billion.

Total market revenue

Multichannel subscription is nearing saturation. 87% of the US households subscribe to either cable or satellite services. Therefore, the competition of cable and satellite has reached the stage of zero-sum competition. Therefore, large growth in cable industry is not expected.

Gross margin

During a 39-month period from 1996 to 1999 — during which time cable rates were regulated and satellites were still relatively unknown to most of the US consumers, cable price increase average more than 7.6% annually.[ll] Since cable rates were de-regulated in 1999, cable price increases have moderated in the face of competition. From 1 April 1999 (the date of cable rate de-regulation) to 30 June 2002, annual cable price increases averaged only 5.15%. The gross margin is not expected to pick up in the foreseeable future.

Number of firms in the cable industry

With mounting fixed cost, stagnant industry growth and gross margin, the number of cable operators has to decrease to maintain reasonable profitability.

The cable industry consolidation can be rationalized given these factors. Many individual cable operators are unsure whether their capital expenditure can generate sufficient enough revenues. Uncertain about the future, they must either sell their business or postpone capital expenditures. Generally, cable operators slow to upgrade have higher defection rates to satellite. For example, AT&T Broadband has almost 20% of the cable subscribers. Assuming market shares are proportional to capital expenditures, AT&T Broadband must spend $14 billion in seven years to upgrade its infrastructure to digital. Although they are hesitant to make such a huge investment, in 2002, AT&T broadband lost 481,000 subscribers and their EBITDA margin dropped to an industry that was low. Charter, the fourth largest cable operators, also lost 357,000 subscribers

[ll]US Bureau of Labor Statistics.

last year. Not surprisingly, these two operators have the lowest percentage of upgraded infrastructure. Given this "do or die" situation, AT&T sold their business to Comcast. More cable operators will withdraw from the industry because they are unwilling, or unable, to upgrade systems.

(3) *Stagnant growth of satellite*

The satellite enjoyed much higher growth than cable operators due to its technological advantage — more channels and better picture and audio quality. However, with the cable industry upgrades to two-way broadband infrastructure, the cable industry is quickly moving from an inferior to superior technology — higher channel capacity, true VOD, more HDTV channels and high-speed internet. By 2002, over 80% of the US households were served by cable systems with 750 MHz of frequency bandwidth capacity, a much larger capacity than that of satellite. Cable operators can transmit around 1000 digital channels, while satellite can only transit about 200 digital channels. As HDTV channels take up four times as much bandwidth as regular digital channels, satellite operators have a huge disadvantage in providing HDTV. Therefore, cable will reverse its disadvantage in the previous battles and may end up winning the war.

(4) *Video rental stores will suffer a big blow*

Video rental stores will become the biggest victims of VOD. When VOD reaches 35–40 million households by 2006, it will bring in significant revenues and will force Studios to move VOD to the same release window as that of rental. Hence, video rental will lose almost all of its competitive advantage over VOD (Table 6.17).

6.12.3. *New business models upon wide adoption of PVR*

It is highly unlikely for PVR to reach mass adoption under standalone business models. However, satellite operators have a real incentive to drive this technology in their competition with cable. This channel is the best method to proliferate PVR. If accomplished, the technologically disruptive behaviors of PVR may be possible. In the world of widely adopted PVR, the traditional advertising-revenue based business model of the broadcasting industry must change. Some potential scenarios are outlined.

Table 6.17. Video rental versus VOD.

	Video rental	VOD
Price convenience	Equal	Equal advantage
Availability	Advantage (within driving distance in most areas)	Disadvantage (only available to 7 million households by the end of 2002)
Content	Advantage (first release window after theater)	Disadvantage (30–60 days after video rental)

6.12.3.1. *Targeted advertising*

Since user viewing histories can be potentially gathered, advertisers can buy usage data, analyze consumer viewing preference, and better target advertising. For example, if the data shows that most people that watch West Wing also watch certain sport channels, advertisers of sport equipment could advertise during West Wing and get better marketing results. Furthermore, advertisers can advertise selectively to targeted PVR users depending on specific viewer history. For example, an airline ad will only appear on the screen of the PVR user who recently watched the travel channel.

6.12.3.2. *Shorter, enticing parts of content*

Advertising may begin using shorter, high profile image ads that are viewable during digital fast-forwarding. Broadcasters could even make ads appear on the sides or top and bottom of the screen during the program or whole commercial segments so that viewers cannot avoid ads. The first and last spot in commercial slots will become most costly, since those are more likely to be watched.

6.12.3.3. *Embedded advertising in VOD and DVDs*

As regular TV advertising becomes less and less effective, advertisers will focus more on other means of advertising such as on magazines, internet, banners, VOD, and DVDs. New advertising schemes in VOD and DVDs take embedded ads one step further by preventing users from fast forwarding advertisements. Advertisers could pay content/VOD providers to have embedded commercials. With additional revenues, VOD and DVD providers could sell this content at a lower price. The natural question is whether or not there is a market for VOD or DVDs with embedded commercials at a fraction of the price of uninterrupted regular VOD or DVDs. Consumers sensitive to costs may prefer a $1 VOD titles with commercials over a $4 regular VOD title or choose a $5 DVD with commercials over a $20 regular DVD.

6.12.3.4. *Cheap broadcasting and advertising*

With the traditional peak/off peak TV program and advertising pricing model less important, the window for broadcasting and advertising could be expanded to 24 h a day. Networks and broadcasters will exploit these unused time slots and bandwidth.

The first change would be increasing number of TV programs shown at off peak hours. The cost difference between broadcasting and advertising at the peak and off peak hours may become much less. To reach an equivalent viewing audience size, program producers and advertisers can expand broadcasting content at non peak hours, since PVRs do not discriminate based on when programs are broadcast. Furthermore, niche programming may be more effective, since PVR technologies can identify consumer market segments.

6.12.3.5. *Better advertising and content*

About 70–80% of the PVR users regularly skip commercials. PVR users also spend about 75% of their time watching recorded programs and 25% on normal broadcasted programs. This means that the PVRs will not undermine all advertising, just poorly focused advertising. TiVo learned that the most popular commercials are still watched by most users.

Ineffective TV advertising may cause TV advertising costs to drop significantly. Broadcasters would have no choice but to improve the quality of TV programs to catch the 20–30% of PVR viewers that do not regularly skip commercials. There may be tremendous amount of incentive for content providers to produce high quality programs that benefit consumers.

6.12.3.6. *Exclusive broadcasting and advertising on PVR devices*

As consumers rely heavily on PVR devices as the "portal" for accessing content, the PVR interactive menu can easily become an "exclusive" network broadcaster. The interactive PVR portal can also support a new form of advertising. Just like internet portals Yahoo, PVR service providers can also advertise on programming guide pages analogous to internet banners with click-through. Currently, there is already pop-up prompt advertising software called Wink that can work with TV programming guide.

6.12.4. *VOWD conclusions*

VOWD is still not on the agenda of content owners and carriers at this stage. Neither streaming video services nor cell phones with streamed video capabilities are available in the US market. This technology topic, compared to the other topics in this research, is the most nebulous.

VOWD will be heavily dependent on carriers' upgrading to 3G networks, specifically from GPRS to EDGE (and beyond) and CDMA1xrtt to 1xEV-DO or 1xEV-DV. However, incentives to upgrade systems to 3G are unclear. Murky demand for high-bandwidth service, the existence of proven revenue models for low-bandwidth applications, the dominance of voice revenue, costs and carrier financial health are all barriers to 3G. On the other hand, the need for some carriers to improve voice efficiency, and competition among carriers puts pressure on service differentiation and may provide some inertia for 3G upgrades, specifically EDGE. Nevertheless, completion of a large-scale upgrade is beyond a five-year horizon.

With respect to commercial video content on VOWD, the impact to Studios and TV networks should be limited. It is unlikely for VOWD to become a significant channel for established content owners to deliver video entertainment. However, it may well be a business opportunity for new entertainment/informational content providers. News, sports and other time-sensitive information contents may first appear on handheld devices, but the ultimate driver for VOWD may need to come from new content creators. The growth and importance of emerging business will determine whether carriers will act as video content aggregators. The technology solution providers and device/hardware manufacturers are likely to be early content aggregators, but eventually, carriers will have to provide support for multi formats and devices and become the ultimate content aggregator. In addition, in latter stages of market development, current wireless content aggregators may enter in to the video content segment by providing multiplatform support. To facilitate this process, carriers need to have a formalized process for content partnership, a clear technical interface, and a motivating revenue share model that works. Although streamed video to handhelds is technologically feasible, there are too many uncertainties to predict its adoption, let alone its ability to induce disruptive change.

6.13. Closing Remarks

The research embodied in this report summarizes how new technologies are leading to products and services that may change how entertainment content is enjoyed by consumers. Some technologies, such as HDTV, are less disruptive to current business practices, while others such as VOD seem to have significant disruptive effects. The goal of this research has been to examine the effects of technology in disruption and evolution of video distribution channels. Of course, overall, the clear beneficiaries of new technology have been consumers. Their enjoyment of motion pictures and related entertainment is destined to be better than ever.

Acknowledgments

The authors of this research would like to thank Dr. Vandana Mangal (BIT project in CMIE), Gigi Johnson (The Entertainment and Media Center at UCLA Anderson School) and other members of the UCLA Anderson School of Management for assisting us in completing this research.

References

Research reports

1. 3G wireless: Where's the content. Gartner Research, April 2001.
2. An overview of GPRS wireless data applications. Gartner Research, 21 February 2003.

3. Asia/Pacific and Japan cellular markets: Weaving the wireless web. Gartner Research, 18 March 2001.
4. AT&T wireless. SG Cowen research report, 18 March 2003.
5. Cable & Telecommunication Industry overview 2002. National Cable & Telecommunication Association, 2002.
6. Confusion about client-side platforms to continue in 2002. Gartner Research, 24 January 2002.
7. Consumer perspectives of HDTV III. eBrain, April 2002.
8. Content convergence: Impacting everyone. Gartner Research, 21 November 2001.
9. Interactive TV: Crouching consumers, hidden opportunities. Gartner Research, 18 April 2001.
10. Motion Picture Association 2002 MPA market statistics. www.mpaa.org.
11. Nextel communications. SG Cowen research report, 18 March 2003.
12. NTT DoCoMo: i-mode wireless internet services. Gartner Research, 26 July 2002.
13. Premium VOD channels for digital cable television — technology backgrounder. Chaos Media Networks, 2002.
14. Screen digest report on the implications of digital technology for the film industry. Department for Culture, Median and Sport, September 2002.
15. Sprint PCS. SG Cowen research report, 18 March 2003.
16. Star wars: Episode II attack of the clones — A case study in digital cinema. SMPTE Seminar, 5 October 2002.
17. Streaming video over GPRS: Hype or reality. Gartner Research, 4 May 2001.
18. The AZ HD glossary of high definition TV. Doremi Technologies, 2002.
19. The transition to digital television. National Cable & Telecommunication Association, April 2002.
20. The wireless data report: Start here to activate. Morgan Stanley, 5 September 2002.
21. The wireless LAN report. US Bancorp Piper Jaffray, August 2002.
22. Thin multimedia and SK telecom: Streaming new revenue with wireless video and multimedia services. Aberdeen Group, Inc.
23. Video CODECs are key to microsoft's media strategy. Gartner Research, 1 April 2002.
24. Video on demand: Tapping deeper wells. Chaos Media Networks, January 2002.
25. Video over DSL: Enabling the telecommunication industry to deliver advanced video service: White paper. Contribution from Aliant, Analog Devices, Aware, iMagic TV, Inovia Telecoms, In-Star/MDR, Irdeto Access, Pace Micro Technology, Video Tele.com, May 2002.
26. White paper: What is 3G?. Generics, March 2003.
27. Wireless 2003. SG Cowen research report, March 2003.
28. Wireless services: Japan. Gartner Research, 18 June 2002.
29. Wireless technology: Cutting through the 3G hype. Gartner Research, 2 December 2002.
30. Bayus, B (1993). High definition television. Management Science.
31. Pank, B (2002). The Digital Fact Book.
32. Kasrel, B (2000). HDTV: High-demographic TV. Forrester Research.

33. Skvaria, C and B Dooley (2002). Mobile internet access services in the U.S.: Perspective. Gartner Research.
34. Perschon, C (2001). Digital Cinema.
35. O'Brien, DP, J Bernoff, J Parr and G Flemming (2002). Cultivate consumers with ITV ads. Forrester Research.
36. Scheirer, E (2001). Movie distribution's new era. The Forrester Report.
37. Gibboney H and V Rick, Digital cinema: Episode II. Credit Suisse Equity Research, 4 June 2002.
38. Clark, JA (2000). Practical digital cinema distribution in an evolving technology environment. Grass Valley Group.
39. Kolko, J, JL MacQuivey, A Denton, CS Golvin and C Li (2002). Devices & access North America. Forrester Research, September.
40. Kolko, J, JL McQuivey and A Denton (2002). PCs: Still stuck on hold. Forrester Research.
41. Kolko, J, JL McQuivey and J Gordon (2002). Privacy for sale: Just pennies per day. Forrester Research.
42. Nail, J, C Charron, J Bernoff, CS Golvin and J Kolko (2003). The year of consumer control. Forrester Research.
43. Farrell, J (1992). Standards setting in HDTV. Brookings Paper on Economic Activity, Microeconomics.
44. Bernoff, J (2001). HDTV broadcasting stalls. Forrester Research.
45. Bernoff, J (2002). How cable TV can beat satellite. Forrester Research.
46. Bernoff, J (2002). Some startling truth about on-demand TV. Forrester Research.
47. Bernoff, J and K Bruce (2001). AOL time warner should buy TiVo. Forrester Research.
48. Bernoff, J and K Bruce (2002). Moxi debuts the first true entertainment gateway. Forrester Research.
49. Bernoff, J and K Bruce (2002). Replay's cable rebirth accelerates smarter TV. Forrester Research.
50. Bernoff, J and K Bruce (2001). Sonicblue bids to control home entertainment. Forrester Research.
51. Bernoff, J and K Bruce (2001). Charlene Li, Joyce Tong, Meredith Gerson, Cable's on-demand salvation. Forrester Research.
52. Bernoff, J and CD Howe (2002). UltimateTV woes energize ITV competitors. Forrester Research.
53. Bernoff, J, C Li and C Howe (2002). Don't put a PC in my entertainment network. Forrester Research.
54. Bernoff, J, C Li, J Parr and G Flemming (2002). How cable TV can beat satellite. Forrester Research.
55. Bernoff, J, C Li, S Roshan and G Flemming (2002). Will ad-skipping kill television. Forrester Research.
56. Bernoff, J and C Carron (2003). News corp. will remake DirecTV a La BskeyB. Forrester Research.
57. Bernoff, J and C Charron (2002). Some startling truths about on-demand TV. Forrester Research.

58. Bernoff, J, GF Colony, J Sorley and M Dorsey (2000). Smarter television. Forrester Research.
59. Bernoff, J and J Nail (2003). Visible world makes TV ad targeting work. Forrester Research.
60. Bernoff, J, JL Butt, Aber, Jr. A. and Kertzer, S (1999). TV viewers take charge. Forrester Research.
61. Batchelder, R (2002). MPEG-4: Good enough for internet and desktop video. Gartner Research.
62. Ollmar, R and H Stephansen (2002) Tanberg television, White paper — The complete guide to TvoIP.
63. Warner, S and W Appiah (2003). U.S. equity research note. William Capital.
64. Hawley, SC (2002). Advanced media strategies. A brief introduction to interactive TV for telcos and broadband service provider.
65. Morley, S (1999). From studio to theatre: Delivering the movie electronically. Qualcomm.
66. Morley, S (1998). Making digital cinema actually happen. Qualcomm.
67. Grimsditch, T and F Pearce (2000). BskyB Kick-starts the UK PVR market. Forrester Research.
68. Grimsditch, T and F Pearce (2001). Pay TV pushes PVRs to the masses. Forrester Research.
69. White paper (2002). Creating the New TV services platform. AssetHouse Technology Limited.
70. Wireless semiconductors: Outlook on WLAN and 2.5G/3G semiconductor devices. WR Hambrecht+Co., 24 September 2002.

News

1. 20th Century Fox and THQ Wireless announce multi-year license for 'The Simpsons' content. 20th Century Fox press release, 19 March 2003.
2. AT&T Wireless to sponsor Fox's 'American idol'. Reuters, 16 January 2003.
3. Cinema concessions: an essential luxury: evaluating popcorn for the big screen (July 2002). *Screen Digest Magazine.*
4. Coming soon: More ads tailored to your tastes. (August 2001). *American Demographics.*
5. DIRECTV and TiVo to introduce new high-definition. http://www.variety.com [9 January 2003].
6. DoCoMo to test multimedia advertising (15 February 2002). *Nordic Wireless Watch.*
7. Mobile carriers scramble to improve networks (19 November 2001). *Digital Korea Herald.*
8. Nokia and RealNetworks to integrate RealNetworks digital media technology on Nokia's mobile phones. http://www.pc4d.com.
9. PBS Launches second campaign on TiVo showcases. http://www.variety.com [4 March 2003].
10. Reebok's "Official Linebacker" gets larger audience than action on the field, according to TiVo. http://www.variety.com [27 January 2003].
11. The road to plexual healing (9 October 2002). *Daily Variety.*
12. TiVo unveils new DVR design that supports HDTV. http://www.variety.com [9 January 2003].

13. TiVo, 20th century fox sign pact for promoting top films on TiVo service in 2003, http://www.variety.com [30 January 2003].
14. TiVo, best buy teamed to deliver short film by standard film trust directly to living rooms of TiVo households. http://www.variety.com [2 January 2003].
15. TiVo's new home media option(TM) transforms DVR into entertainment center. http://www.variety.com [9 January 2003].
16. Toshiba creates a new DVD domain with TiVo. http://www.variety.com [9 January 2003].
17. Universal Studios brings blockbuster movie content to Club Nokia. http://www.pc4d.com.
18. V-Live 3G live streaming video deal. http://www.3g.co.uk [30 April 2002].
19. Jezierski, A and S Krishnan (2003). 3G: How do we get there from here? *Business Communications Review.*
20. Morrissey, B (2003). MTV, Motorola Ink $75M marketing pact. http://www.internetnews.com.
21. Giardina, C and S Lehane (2001). Digital cinema — projecting a new market. *Film and Video Magazine.*
22. Saunders, C (2002). ITV firms boost ad products for VOD. Internetenws.com.
23. Luening, E (2001). MTV to launch wireless promotion. CNET News.com.
24. Joyce, E (2003). Cable's VOD coming on strong. Internetnews.com.
25. Joyce, E (2003). VOD, the first skirmish in the battle. Internetnews.com.
26. Fried, I and B Charny (2002). Microsoft's phone software ready to talk. *CNET News.*
27. Ozer, J (2002). MPEG-4 everyone — at a price. *Emedia Magazine.*
28. Sauer, J (2002). Mobile media the future is now. DTV Group.
29. Mann, J (2000). Economics push movie exhibitors towards uncertain end. The Kansas City Star.
30. Borland, J (2001). Mobile markets fall flat for many consumers. CNET News.com.
31. Deok-hyun, K (2003). Outlook gloomy for SK telecom. *Korea times.*
32. Berniker, M (2003). Verizon to roll out wireless broadband. http://www.internetnews.com.
33. Hamblen, M (2002). Service offerings 2.5G and 3G wireless packet data services. Computerworld.
34. Buday, M (2000). 24p primer. *Motion Picture Editors Guild Magazine.* May/June.
35. Finneran, M (2003). Navigating the two roads to 3G. *Business Communications Review.*
36. Hiltzik, M (2002). Digital cinema take 2. *Technology Review.*
37. Crockett, R (2003). Web phones take wing now. cell phones can deliver nifty net services fast, and Americans are signing up by the millions. *Business Week.*
38. Olsen, S (2001). Wireless advertising shows promise despite glitches. CNET News.com.
39. Cohen, S (2002). Digital distribution. *Editors Guild Magazine.*
40. Bohannon, WK (2001). The next picture show — NAB gets digita. eMedia Live.

Appendix A: Company Web Sites

http:// www.cbsnews.com
http://abcnews.go.com
http://foma.nttdocomo.co.jp

http://mirror.ati.com
http://onlinestore.cingular.com
http://www.accessdtv.com
http://www.activesky.com
http://www.attws.com
http://www.barco.com
http://www.broadcastpapers.com
http://www.carmike.com
http://www.charter.com
http://www.direcTV.com
http://www.dishnetwork.com
http://www.divxnetworks.com
http://www.elgato.com
http://www.emblaze.com
http://www.evs-cinema.com
http://www.foxnews.com
http://www.hauppauge.com
http://www.howstuffworks.com
http://www.kodak.com
http://www.loewscineplex.com
http://www.microsoft.com
http://www.moviso.com
http://www.mpaa.org
http://www.nbc.com
http://www.nextel.com
http://www.nttdocomo.com
http://www.packetvideo.com
http://www.panasonic.com
http://www.qualcomm.com
http://www.realnetworks.com
http://www.regalcinemas.com
http://www.roamingeyes.com
http://www.showshifter.com
http://www.sktelecom.com
http://www.skygo.com
http://www.sonicblue.com
http://www.sonypictures.com
http://www.sonystyle-imaging.com
http://www.starcut.com/
http://www.streambox.com

http://www.symbian.com
http://www.techtv.com
http://www.telemann.com/
http://www.tivo.com
http://www.t-mobile.com
http://www.toshiba.com
http://www.verizonwireless.com
http://www1.sprintpcs.com

Appendix B: Interviews

Following the guidelines of the University of California Office for the Protection of Research Subjects, all interviews performed for this research are confidential and are not available for public release.

CHAPTER 7

IMPACTS OF INFORMATION AND COMMUNICATION TECHNOLOGY ADOPTION ON BUSINESS PRACTICES AND PERFORMANCES: AN EXPLORATORY STUDY

HOSUN RHIM, KWANGTAE PARK and HONG-IL KIM

Summary

The emergence of information and communication technologies (ICTs) has changed the life style of consumers. However, literature on their influences on businesses is limited. In this paper, we explore the impacts of ICTs on business practices and resulting business performances. Customer relationship management, supply Chain Management, business process outsourcing and globalization are considered as business practices. Business performances include overall business performances and functional area costs. The data sets are collected as a part of The Business and Information Technologies (BIT) project. The results from path analysis models are compared using Korea and US data sets. In both countries, ICTs have a direct impact on overall business performance. However, Korea shows stronger indirect impacts on business performances through selected business practices.

7.1. Introduction

The emergence of the Internet has changed everyday life of an average person in Korea. People watch movies on computers, and pay bills with mobile phones. According to Nielsen NetRatings in 2001, South Korea was ranked first among the 10 Asian and European countries in the number of website page views per month at home (Cho, 2001). While consumers in Korea rapidly adopt new information and communication technologies (ICTs), business sectors show different attitudes on the new ICTs. Rhim *et al.* (2005) report that adoption rate of ICTs in business sectors in Korea is much lower than that in the US. Different adoption rates will result in different business performances. In this paper, we explore the impacts of ICTs on business performances in the two countries (Korea and US).

Technologies exist in embedded forms (Burgelman *et al.*, 1998). ICTs are not exceptional. They are embedded in business practices. Improvement of business performances are accomplished through the business practices. In this paper, we consider four business practices: customer relationship management (CRM), supply chain management (SCM), business process outsourcing (BPO), and globalization. Kopczak and Johnson (2003) explain implications of CRM, BPO, and globalization with SCM. They maintain that SCM has resulted in major shifts in business focus. Since supply chain is viewed as a series of processes, suppliers may be regarded as outsourced business processes. They also argue that by linking CRM, pricing and supply chain information, companies can create tailored sales opportunities that increase revenue, optimize the use of resources and maximize profits. Globalization is essential in this process. Lambert (2004) collects data from Global Supply Chain Forum and identifies the eight processes that need to be managed and integrated for successful supply chain management. CRM is one of the processes.

Four business practices (CRM, SCM, BPO, and globalization) will have impacts on business performances. Thus, adoption of ICTs may have direct and indirect impacts through these business practices (see Fig. 7.1). The direct impact of ICT adoption may be understood as a change of performances through other business practices, which are not included in the four business practices. As business performances, we consider overall business performances and functional area costs such as R&D, production, marketing, and human resource management (HRM) costs. Including costs of functional areas is essential, since technology adoption is not a sole responsibility of technology or R&D departments. Phaal *et al.* (2001) emphasize the importance of understanding, communicating, and integrating technology with marketing, financial, operations and human resource strategies. Thus, in this paper, we explore the impact of ICT adoption

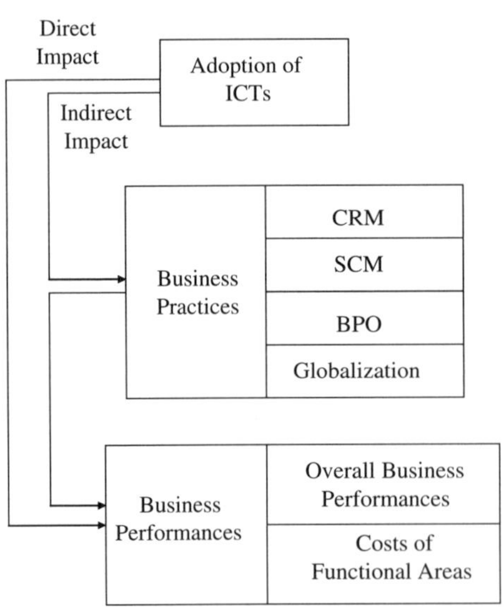

Fig. 7.1. Impacts of ICT adoption on business performances.

on the business practices and business performances of ICT adoption through the business practices.

Our study adds to the literature in several ways. First, we employ a unique and novel data set. The data set is collected by teams of The Business and Information Technologies (BIT) project. This project was initiated by the Center for Management of the Information Economy (CMIE) of UCLA in 2003. This project is to understand the impact of new ICT on business practices over an extended time horizon. Annual survey of firms is performed to collect data on how firms are using new technologies, and how firms, industries and economies are changing as a consequence. We select Korea and US data sets among available data sets and compare the results. Second, most of the researches are limited to partial analysis. For example, Chen and Ching (2004) examine the relationship between information technology intensity and CRM performance. Ranganathan *et al.* (2004) study the relationship between web technology and supply chain coordination. In this paper, we combine these analyses together and find significant path of ICT adoption to business performances.

The rest of this paper is organized as follows. Section 7.2 reviews literature and develops research hypotheses. Section 7.3 describes the data and method. Section 7.4 presents the results of path analysis model. Section 7.5 concludes the study.

7.2. Development of the Research Hypothesis

7.2.1. *ICTs and CRM*

Falk (2005) reports based on e-business watch data for EU-4 (Germany, France, Italy, and the UK) that CRM systems are significantly positively correlated to information technology intensity. Chen and Ching (2004) examine the relationship of information technology (IT) intensity and organizational absorptive capacity with CRM practices and performance. Their survey results suggest that CRM practices mediate the effect of IT intensity and organizational absorptive capacity on CRM performance. Among many aspects of CRM, we focus on CRM automation. That is, we explore the relationship between ICT adoption and CRM automation.

7.2.2. *ICTs and SCM*

Ranganathan *et al.* (2004) explore the use of web technologies for organizational SCM. They argue that web technology has made supply chain coordination a viable managerial and strategic option. Gunasekaran and Ngai (2004) classified the literature available on IT in SCM to develop a framework for studying the applications of IT in SCM. Fiala (2005) emphasizes the importance of information sharing among supply chain partners. We examine the relationship between ICTs and communication with trading partners in a supply chain.

7.2.3. *ICTs and BPO*

It is reported that computer service companies are jockeying to grab a share of the BPO market (*Wall Street Journal*, 24 September 2003). According to *BusinessWeek* (12 January 2004), BPO is the fastest growing IT service niche. That is, BPO cannot be implemented without ICTs. Rao (2004) reports the case wherein IT is used to speed up the BPO. Although a vast literature focuses on the IT outsourcing, we investigate the influence of ICTs on degree of BPO. The degree of BPO is measured by both number of outsourced functional areas and significance (partial or total).

7.2.4. *ICTs and globalization*

While globalization increases the geographic dispersion of IT services, evidence shows that ICTs promote globalization. D'Antoni (2005) reports that IT staffs are tasked to supporting globalization efforts. Prahalad *et al.* (2004) find that IT infrastructure for remote delivery is becoming a commonplace and that the search for new resources has never been more intense. Beaverstock (2004) maintains that ICT is a globalization driver of professional service business. Lovelock and Yip (1996) present a similar argument for general service businesses. The degree of globalization is measured by geographic reach in terms of operations of organizations.

On the basis of the previous literature, we have the following hypotheses:

H1a: Adoption of ICTs will increase CRM automation.
H1b: Adoption of ICTs will promote communication with trading partners in a supply chain.
H1c: Adoption of ICTs will increase the degree of BPO.
H1d: Adoption of ICTs will increase geographic reach of operations of organizations.

7.2.5. *ICTs and business performances*

Adoption of ICTs may affect business performances directly or indirectly. Indirect impacts are generated through business practices such as CRM, SCM, BPO, and globalization. Direct impacts are created through other activities which are not considered as business practices. The literature on these direct and indirect impacts is provided in Table 7.1. For business performances, we consider the overall business performance and four functional area costs: R&D, production, marketing, and HRM costs. The overall business performances include profits, revenues, and market share.

H2a: Adoption of ICTs will reduce functional area costs.
H2b: Adoption of ICTs will improve general financial performance.
H3a: CRM automation will reduce functional area costs.
H3b: CRM automation will improve general financial performance.

Table 7.1. Direct and indirect impacts of ICT adoption.

ICT adoption	Ranganathan *et al.* (2004), Hou (2004)
CRM	Starky and Woodcock (2002), Brown (2005), Ahearne *et al.* (2004)
SCM	Min and Mentzer (2004), Gimenez and Ventura (2005), Mehta (2004)
BPO	Sussan and Johnson (2003)
Globalization	Mehta (2004)

H4a: Communication with trading partners in a supply chain will reduce functional area costs.
H4b: Communication with trading partners in a supply chain will improve general financial performance.
H5a: BPO will reduce functional area costs.
H5b: BPO will improve general financial performance.
H6a: Increased geographic reach will reduce functional area costs.
H6b: Increased geographic reach will improve general financial performance.

7.3. Method

7.3.1. *Data*

While both Korean and US data sets are collected in 2004, collection methods are different. Survey questionnaires were mailed in US, while they were delivered by interviewers in Korea to increase the response rate. Out of 24,000 surveys 250 were returned in US, and 262 surveys were collected in Korea. Korean data set includes larger proportion of small-sized companies with respect to the number of employees than US data set (see Table 7.2). The proportions of industry sectors are also provided in the table.

7.3.2. *Measure and model*

ICT adoption and business practices are measured by multiple items. ICT adoption are measured by asking whether the responding organization currently have, do not currently have but plan to purchase in the next 3 years, or do not plan to purchase in the next 3 years 19 ICT products. The points are given 3 (currently have) to 1 (do not plan to purchase in the next 3 years) and summed up to generate the index of ICT adoption. 19 ICT products include ERP, Linux, RFID, wireless network connectivity,

Table 7.2. Sample characteristics.

		Korean data set	US data set
Collection period		2004	2004
Collection method		Delivered by interviewers	Mailing
Sample size		260	250
Size of organization (No. of employees)	Up to 200	42.37%	16.94%
	200 to 1000	30.92%	38.71%
	Over 1000	25.57%	39.11%
Sectors of organization	Professional, Scientific & Technical Services	21.76%	5.51%
	Wholesale & Retail Trade	19.85%	32.08%
	Manufacturing	19.85%	3.81%
	Finance & Insurance	13.74%	—
	Government Agency	10.69%	9.32%
	Construction	6.11%	3.81%
	Transportation	4.20%	1.27%
	Other Services	2.29%	2.12%
	Educational Services	0.76%	15.25%
	Utilities	0.75%	2.97%
	Healthcare & Social Assistance	—	7.63%
	Information	—	4.66%
	Others	—	4.24%

website/e-commerce, etc. For CRM automation, organizations are asked whether certain functions are from highly automated to not automated. The CRM functions include help desk, sales calls, order tracking, customer complaints management, etc. (8 items). The communication with trading partners in a supply chain is measured by partner relationship management, e-procurement, e-payment, collaborative planning, etc. (11 items). The functional areas of BPO when asked in organizations include IT functions, customer contact, payroll, market research, accounting, etc. (11 areas). The geographic reach of operations is measured by geographic areas where organizations currently have business operations, plan to have business operations in the next 3 years, or do not plan to have business operations in the next 3 years. For business performances, the overall business performance and marketing costs are measured by multiple items.

To test the reliability of multiitem variables, we check the value of Cronbach's coefficient alpha (see Table 7.3). Since the values are all greater than 80%, the constructed indices can be regarded as consistent.

To test the hypotheses, we use a path analysis model. The path analysis models start from the drawing of simple path diagrams. The path diagram for our hypothesis tests is shown in Fig. 7.2.

Table 7.3. Reliability of variables.

	Cronbach's coefficient alpha
IT adoption	0.929
BPO	0.783
CRM automation	0.875
Communication with partners	0.927
Globalization	0.952
Marketing costs	0.802

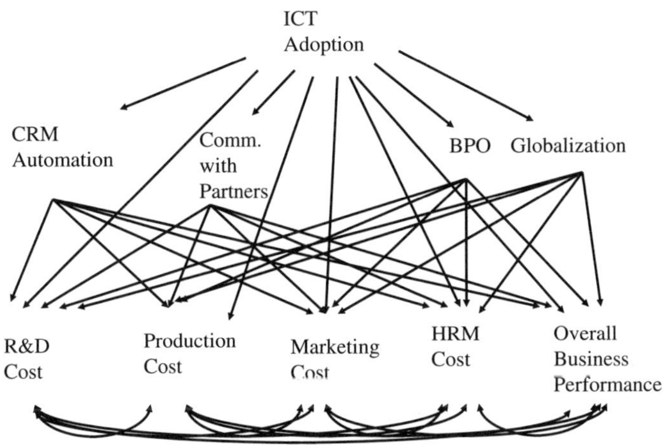

Fig. 7.2. Path diagram for hypothesis test.

7.4. Results

We use SAS CALIS procedure for analyzing the path model. The overall fit of the model is tested based on goodness-of-fit index (GFI), adjusted goodness-of-fit index (AGFI), and chi-square value. For both data sets, GFI and AGFI are greater than 0.9 and 0.8. Chi-square values are also greater than 0.1. Thus, fit values are in acceptable ranges (see Table 7.4). The significant paths are selected by t-value with 10% significance level. The significant coefficients in Korean and US path diagrams are shown in Figs. 7.3 and 7.4, respectively.

Table 7.4. Overall goodness of fit.

Korea	goodness-of-fit index (GFI)	0.96
	adjusted GFI (AGFI)	0.92
	Pr > chi-square	0.24
US	goodness-of-fit index (GFI)	0.94
	adjusted GFI (AGFI)	0.89
	Pr > chi-square	0.14

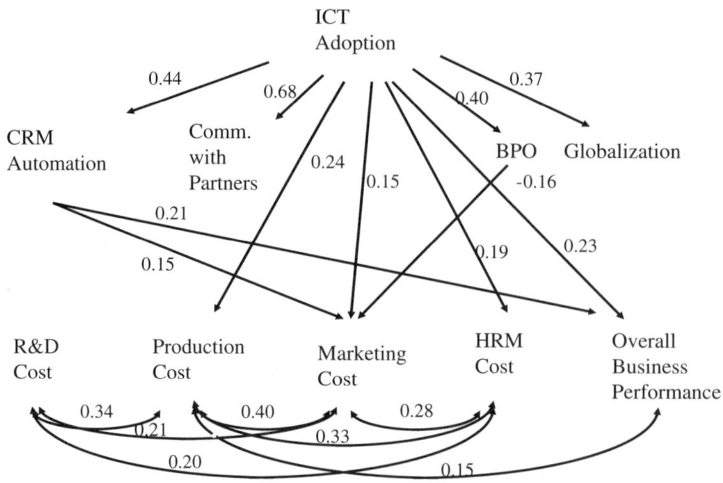

Fig. 7.3. Significant paths in Korea.

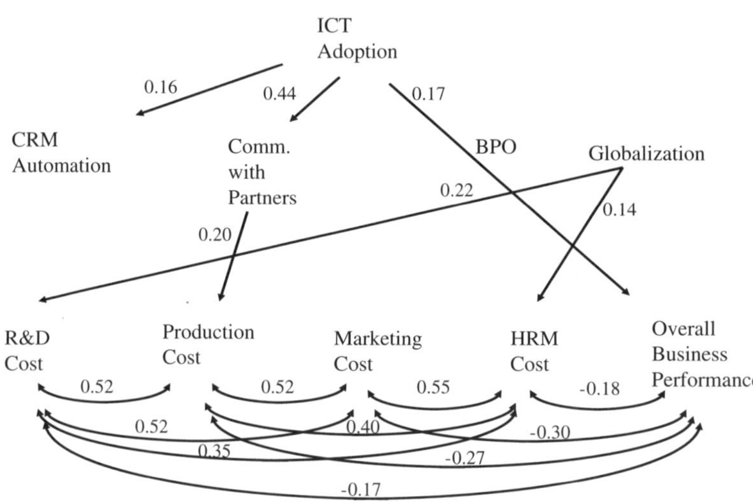

Fig. 7.4. Significant paths in US.

7.5. Discussion and Conclusion

In Korea, four business practices are all affected by ICT adoption. The most affected practices are communication with partners in a supply chain. However, this practice does not result in any significant improvement in business performances. This implies that performance improvement from SCM practices is hardly quantifiable even though ICTs have contributed to smooth communication in a supply chain. CRM automation and BPO have impacts on business performances. Especially, CRM automation has led to improvements in overall business performance. ICT adoption reveals its direct impact on business performances, except R&D cost. Actually, R&D cost is not affected by any business practices, either. This suggests that R&D is yet an isolated area from ICTs and from powerful business practices in Korea. Improvements in functional area costs are positively correlated to each other. Among various costs, only production cost shows significant correlation with improvement in overall business performance.

Relatively small number of paths is significant in US. ICT adoption has influences on CRM automation and communication with trading partners in a supply chain. The latter practice is directed to production cost reduction. However, the production cost is negatively correlated with the overall business performance. Our conjecture on this negative relationship is that there is time lag between improvements of functional area cost and overall business performance. In spite of this limited influence, ICT adoption has positive impact on the overall business performance as in Korea. Globalization, even though not influenced by ICT adoption, contributes to improvement in R&D and HRM costs.

In this paper, we study the impact of ICT adoption on business practices and performances in Korea and US. This study is an exploratory analysis based on a unique data set. Our future research is to elaborate the analysis. For example, we may include firm-size and industry-sector effects in the model. The collection of second year data set will provide a clue on the time lag issue, which are left to our future study.

Acknowledgments

This research was supported by Service and Logistics Research Center of Korea University Business School. The authors are very grateful to Dr. Uday Karmarkar and Dr. Vandana Mangal of the US BIT team who kindly allowed them to use the US data set.

Bibliography

1. Ahearne, M, N Srinivasan and L Weinstein (2004). Effect of technology on sales performance: Progressing from technology acceptance to technology usage and consequence. *The Journal of Personal Selling & Sales Management*, 24(4), 297.
2. Beaverstock, JV (2004). Managing across borders: Knowledge management and expatriation in professional service legal firms. *Journal of Economic Geography*, 4(2), 157.
3. Burgelman, RA, MA Maidique and SC Wheelwright (1998). *Strategic Management of Technology and Innovation*. Chicago: Irwin.
4. Brown, P (2005). When old is new again. *Optimaize*, 4(8), 15.
5. Chen, JS and RKH Ching (2004). An empirical study of the relationship of IT intensity and organizational absorptive capacity on CRM performance. *Journal of Global Information Management*, 12(1), 1–17.

6. Cho, NJ (2001). Structure and trends of electronic commerce in Korea. *Int Conf on Management Education for 21th Century*.
7. D'Antoni, H (2005). Behind the numbers: Companies that go global look at basic issues. *Information Week*, April 11, pp. 70.
8. Falk, M (2005). ICT-linked firm reorganization and productivity gains. *Technovation*, 25(11), 1229.
9. Fiala, P (2005). Information sharing in supply chains. *Omega*, 33(5), 419–423.
10. Gimenez, C and E Ventura (2005). Logistics-production, logistics-marketing and external integration: Their impact on performance, *International Journal of Operations & Production Management*, 25(1), 20–39.
11. Gunasekaran, A and EWT Ngai (2004). Information systems in supply chain integration and management. *European Journal of Operational Research*, 159(2), 269–295.
12. Hou, F (2004). A research on the relationship between internet usage and organization performance in south korea electronic commerce organizations. *International Journal of Services Technology and Management*, 5(4), 362.
13. Kopczak, LR and ME Johnson (2003). The supply-chain management effect. *MIT Sloan Management Review*, 44(3), 27–34.
14. Lambert, DM (2004). The eight essential supply chain management processes. *Supply Chain Management Review*, 8(6), 18–25.
15. Lovelock, CH and GS Yip (1996). Developing global strategies for service businesses. *California Management Review*, 38(2), 64–86.
16. Mehta, J (2004). Supply chain management in a global economy. *Total Quality Management & Business Excellence*, 15(5,6), 841.
17. Min, S and JT Mntzer (2004). Developing and measuring supply chain management concepts. *Journal of Business Logistics*, 25(1), 63–99.
18. Phaal, R, CJP Farrukh and DR Probert (2001). Technology management process assessment: A case study. *International Journal of Operations & Production Management*, 21(8), 1116–1122.
19. Prahalad, CK, MS Krishnan and A Donker (2004). The building blocks of global competitiveness. *Optimize*, September, 30–35.
20. Ranganathan, C, JS Dhaliwal and TSH Teo (2004). Assimilation and diffusion of web technologies in supply-chain management: An examination of key drivers and performance impacts. *International Journal of Electronic Commerce*, 9(1), 127–161.
21. Rao, NR (2004). BPO: Beyond information technology, *Businessline*, 1 March.
22. Rhim, H, K Park and H Kim (2005). The Business and Information Technologies (BIT) Survey in Korea. Working paper, Korea University Business School.
23. Starkey, M and N Woodcock (2002). CRM systems: Necessary, but not sufficient. REAP the benefits of customer management. *Journal of Database Management*, 9(3), 267–275.
24. Sussan, AP and WC Johnson (2003). Strategic capabilities of business process: Looking for competitive advantage. *Competitiveness Review*, 13(2), 46–52.

CHAPTER 8

THE IMPACT OF NEW INFORMATION TECHNOLOGY ON THE US MORTGAGE INDUSTRY

SUNIL CHAUDHARY, MICHELLE GREEN, RAMIN MAHMOUDI and VICKI TING

Summary
This paper identifies the technologies that will have significant impact on the United States consumer loan origination process in the next five years and what their impact will be on the major industry trends. Major industry trends considered include "the paperless mortgage," one-stop shop, automation and outsourcing, and the continuing role of brokers and agents. Enterprise software and extensible markup language, intelligent systems, electronic signatures, security, and document imaging are identified as the key technologies. The paper concludes that the technologies will affect the loan origination process, but the level of change with respect to the industry trends may not be significant. The paperless mortgage will not be commonplace and the role of brokers and agents will not be eliminated in the next five years. On the other hand, the adoption of the five technologies will increase the level of automation and the use of outsourcing and the creation of one-stop shop for both home buying needs as well as diversified financial needs in the next five years.

8.1. Introduction

The scope of this paper is to identify the technologies that will have significant impact on the United States consumer loan origination process in the next five years and what their impact will be on the major industry trends. While the mortgage industry encompasses residential properties as well as commercial real estate, this paper focuses on residential mortgages although some of the conclusions may have application to the commercial loan origination process as well.

For most of the residential homeowners, the dream of the perfect house also includes the reality of obtaining a mortgage. The common borrower complaints involve submitting a volume of financial paperwork to the lender, deciphering the information about the multitude of loan products available and trying to determine which loan product is appropriate, and signing a plethora of documents at closing with little time for review. Overhanging the entire process is the shadow of doubt that one is somehow paying too much in points, fees, and closing costs.

Over the years, many industry professionals have attempted to improve the process, both in terms of back office processing as well as the customer experience. Technology has had an important role in these changes. For example, the development and spread of the Internet has led to the "online mortgage" through which customers can complete their initial loan application and obtain a contingent approval for a loan. Although the Internet and other technologies are improving the mortgage process, much of the loan origination process and customer interaction with the lender remain cumbersome and involves the management of voluminous amounts of paper.

This paper analyzes the loan origination process and identifies major industry trends. It then identifies the five key technologies that are expected to significantly improve the process and address the industry trends in the next five years. The paper begins with an overview of the mortgage industry including the size of the market and key players. Next, the major industry trends of "the paperless mortgage", one-stop shop, automation and outsourcing, and the continuing role of brokers and agents are discussed. The description of the end-to-end information chain emphasizing the loan origination process follows. The five key technologies are then identified. They are: enterprise software and extensible markup language, intelligent systems, electronic signatures, security, and document imaging. The paper concludes that the technologies will affect the loan origination process, but the level of change with respect to the industry trends may not be significant. The paperless mortgage will not be commonplace and the role of brokers and agents will not be eliminated in the next five years. On the other hand, the adoption of the five technologies will increase the level of automation and the use of outsourcing and the creation of one-stop shops for both home buying needs as well as diversified financial needs in the next five years.

8.2. Industry Background

In 2003, the United States mortgage industry consisted of approximately $9 trillion in loans outstanding of which just under $7 trillion consisted of residential mortgages.[a] It is a highly competitive market which has developed through the growth and development of the housing industry. Approximately 80% of the new mortgage loans originated in 2003 are conforming loans[b] which are a commodity product. The government sponsored enterprises, Fannie Mae and Freddie Mac,[c] are the principal market makers for mortgage-backed securities (MBS) based on conforming loans. Their dominance in the

[a]Mortgage Bankers Association: Mortgage and Market Data as of 27 October 2003, www.mortgagebankers.org/marketdata/data/mortgage_loans_outstanding.html. Accessed 12 March 2004.

[b]Fannie Mae estimate from www.fanniemae.com/global/pdf/ir/resources/fanniemaeglance.pdf. Accessed 12 March 2004.

[c]Fannie Mae is chartered under the Federal National Mortgage Association Act and Freddie Mac is chartered under the Federal Home Loan Mortgage Corporation Act.

secondary market has made conforming loans the primary loan product for residential mortgages and has also made the product a commodity.

The number of new loans each year consists of new purchases and refinancings. With the decline of interest rates from 2002 to 2003, the mortgage industry experienced a boom in the number of new loans. The combined total volume of new purchases and refinancings reached an estimated total of $3.8 trillion in 2003 from just over $1 trillion in 2000.[d] The number of new loans is very cyclical and can be volatile due to its dependence on interest rates. It is unlikely that the recent high growth in the number of new purchases and refinancing will continue in the near future and management of expected interest rate increases will shape the reactions of the industry moving forward.

Among the most significant developments to transform the mortgage industry has been the increased specialization of various parts of the mortgage information chain. In the 1970s, integrated companies, such as savings and loans, used to generate, hold, and service loans. The savings and loan scandals in the early 1990s had a serious negative impact on the savings and loans and mortgage industry. In addition, increased industry competition and the development of secondary markets for mortgage backed securities have led to the gradual separation of the steps in the mortgage process. A specialized set of mortgage bankers may originate and fund loans but immediately bundle the loans into portfolios to sell as MBS in the secondary markets. Even the servicing rights may be sold separately to other institutions.

However, as the information chain may be separating into specialized segments and each segment undertaken by a different entity, the companies in the mortgage industry seem to be consolidating. The top 10 mortgage lenders in the industry are all large companies and have strong businesses in conforming loans. The industry has been traditionally fragmented but consolidation in the industry is increasing. In 1993, the top 10 mortgage banks accounted for 23% of the market compared to 67% in 2003.[e] Small mortgage lenders in the industry tend to focus on nonconforming loans for which the secondary market is not as well developed. This allows for more pricing flexibility and the opportunity for small lenders to find a profitable niche.

8.2.1. *The regulatory environment*

The mortgage industry is heavily regulated and most lenders are subject to three main types of regulation: real estate industry regulations, banking regulations, and privacy

[d] Mortgage Bankers Association of America, "MBA Long Term Economic Forecast," 22 January 2003, www.mortgagebankers.org/news/2004/MBALongTermForecast2004.pdf.

[e] Miller, Paul, Annett Franke and Steve Stelmach, "Mortgage Industry — Year 2004 Outlooks," Friedman Billings Ramsey, 9 January 2004.

regulations. Many of the mortgage lenders also own retail banks as a source of capital for their mortgages and to stabilize their year-to-year revenues. Through the retail banks, mortgage lenders become subject to the banking regulations. Mortgage lenders are subject to privacy regulations because of the type of personal data collected in loan origination and servicing. Because of the risk of fraud in real estate and banking, these industries are heavily regulated by both state and federal governments. The steps in the mortgage process and information chain are deeply influenced by the need to comply with government regulation and therefore, the use of technology in the mortgage process is also bound by the industry regulations.

8.2.2. *Current state of technology in the mortgage industry*

The use of technology has shortened the process time and has improved the efficiency of the mortgage process. More powerful computing, cheaper data storage, and the ability to transfer bigger data packages over networks have helped mortgage companies to decrease their operations costs and improve their profitability. In the past three decades, technology has reduced the costs of storage, transmission, and processing of information by 25–35% annually, a trend which is expected to continue.[f]

Some of the most influential of these technologies include:

- Electronic payment technologies which improve the speed and efficiency of mortgage payments.
- The Internet and wide area networks and local area networks which have become a powerful means of communication to provide new channels for finding new borrowers and improve information flow among the multiple parties involved in the mortgage process.
- Statistical programs for credit scoring as means to analyze and summarize the credit risk of borrowers.

As effective as technology adoption has been in the mortgage industry so far, the mortgage industry is not known as an early adopter. The choice of which technologies to develop and adopt are influenced by many factors including cost, ability to comply with industry regulations, attitudes of borrowers and industry professionals, and lack of standards among industry participants. However, increasing competition in the mortgage industry from the gradual standardization of loan products into commodities, consolidation of large mortgage banks, and interest rate pressures force mortgage lenders to search for methods to lower costs and maintain a competitive advantage.

---

[f] Guldimann, Till M., "Technology in Reshaping Finance and Risks," *Business Economics*, January 2000, 44–51.

8.3. Major Trends

Several trends have emerged from the research. These trends include a mix of long standing goals of the mortgage industry, such as the "paperless mortgage", and new trends that have developed with the introduction of new technologies.

8.3.1. *Paperless mortgage*

The paperless mortgage has been a goal of the mortgage industry for over a decade. Borrowers and lenders alike have recognized the problems of organizing, processing, and storing the paper documentation associated with a mortgage. A borrower file can consist of several hundred pages which can be bulky to transfer or store. If a borrower file can be reduced to an electronic file, it can be sent more easily between the lender and the borrower or between agents of the lender collecting the documentation for the mortgage. Also, the physical storage space for the file which must be archived after the loan is funded can be significantly reduced.

Despite the paperless mortgage being the "holy grail" of the mortgage industry, it has not yet happened. A truly paperless mortgage requires the integration and automation of the entire loan origination process on a single platform including the adoption of standards for the exchange of data and documents. In addition to the technology challenges, issues regarding government regulations, document integrity and fraud, and borrower acceptance must be addressed before the paperless mortgage can become a reality.

8.3.2. *One-stop shop*

The concept of a one-stop shop is that one company provides a variety of related products and services from different industries. A mortgage lender can be a one-stop shop for home buying needs, which may include homeowners insurance, home equity lines of credit (HELOC) as well as mortgages. Lenders can also be a one-stop shop for broader financial services and provide commercial banking products, brokerage services, and credit cards in addition to products related to home purchases.

The emergence of a one-stop shop for either home purchase or broader financial services depends on several economic factors. First, economies of scale need to be present such that larger companies can capture cost savings from higher volumes. This seems to be true in the commodity market for conforming loans and mortgage servicing. Because there is little or no product differentiation, lenders with large loan portfolio can negotiate better pricing in securitization from Fannie Mae and Freddie Mac. For servicing, the high fixed costs necessary to establish an internal servicing department favor lenders which can spread those fixed costs across a large loan portfolio. Economies of scope should also be present such that cost savings can result from one company operating in different but related industries. One possible area for economies of scope is crossselling financial products, such as credit cards or insurance, to existing mortgage borrowers.

The trends in the industry indicate that the largest companies in the mortgage industry are increasing their share of the market and dominate the commodity conforming loan market. Most of the small mortgage lenders tend to focus on niche markets for loans with less than perfect credit ratings which have higher risk and more flexibility in pricing.

8.3.3. *Automation and outsourcing*

Automation and outsourcing are means to reduce costs in a process. They are possible when a step in the process can be isolated and reduced to relatively simple tasks. Automation is one obvious area where new technologies can influence the information chain in the mortgage industry. Because human labor costs are relatively high and human error is a possibility, automation has the potential to reduce labor costs and significantly reduce errors in the process. Outsourcing is another way to reduce labor costs by shifting away from expensive, specialized labor to less expensive, low-skilled labor. Outsourcing often includes offshoring, sending the work outside of the United States. However, the ability to introduce either automation or outsourcing into a process often requires analysis of the process to separate and isolate individual steps.

8.3.4. *The continuing role of brokers and agents*

The reduction of human beings in a process can potentially reduce labor costs for a company. With the aid of technology, many tasks that used to be performed by service personnel have been increasingly replaced by self-service. For example, the number of bank tellers has been significantly reduced with the wide adoption of automated teller machines (ATMs). Mortgage industry professionals speculate whether advances in technology will eventually lead to the extinction of mortgage brokers and loan agents. Despite the potential cost savings and service improvements that may exist with automation and self-service, the need for human contact or the additional complex reasoning skills that a person can bring to a process often preclude the complete removal of people from a process.

8.4. The Mortgage Information Chain

8.4.1. *Overview of the information chain for the mortgage industry*

The information chain for the mortgage process consists of three main segments: loan origination, securitization of loan portfolios, and servicing (Fig. 8.1). Loan origination is the first step in the process and securitization and servicing follow and may take place in parallel. The following diagram illustrates the three main steps.

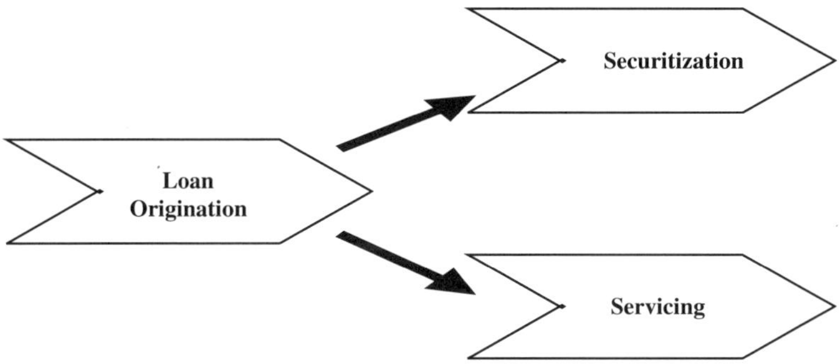

Fig. 8.1. Information chain for the mortgage process.

8.4.1.1. *Traditional loan origination*

Loan origination is the process through which the mortgage is created. It begins with borrower acquisition and ends when the loan is funded and final documents are signed. This paper focuses primarily on the loan origination portion of the information chain which is described in more detail in the next section.

8.4.1.2. *Securitization*

Since the first issuance of MBS in 1969, the development of a secondary market has increased the liquidity of mortgage instruments and helped to provide more consistency in pricing, loan terms, and underwriting guidelines. It has also helped to transform mortgages into commodity products. MBS were developed to create a market for the future stream of cash flows provided by mortgages. A package of loans can be bundled together and securities issued based on the loan package. The selling lender can realize a present cash flow from the sale of the loan package which can be used to make additional loans.

The price for a package of loans is determined by the performance of the loans relative to what is expected. For example, if a certain loan pool is expected to have a 3% loss, then it must have no more than a 3% loss. Generally, the loss comes from borrower default or prepayment of a loan. If the loan pool does not perform as well or better than expected, the lender may have difficulty in securitizing future pools of loans or obtaining a good price for them.

A lender is not limited to securitizing only loans that it has originated. It can also purchase loans from other banks which is referred to as "correspondent lending". Lenders can create more robust loan pools by combining loans which they have originated with loans purchased from other lenders. For large commercial banks in the mortgage industry, the correspondent channel is also used to obtain servicing rights.

8.4.1.3. *Servicing*

Servicing is the customer service that takes place after a loan has been funded. It consists of forwarding the monthly mortgage payments to the investor who purchased the loan pool to which the loan belongs, confirming borrower information, and answering questions the borrower may have about the loan.

Servicing is not always performed by the lender originating the loan. Because of the labor involved in responding to customer calls, the fixed costs of a servicing system is high. Often smaller mortgage companies will outsource the servicing at a per-loan servicing charge. If a mortgage company decides to service its loans directly, it can keep the servicing fees which are approximately 0.25–0.375% of the stated interest rate for the mortgage. For example, for a mortgage at an 8% interest rate, 0.25–0.375% goes to the servicer and 7.625–7.5% goes to the investor upon securitization. In addition, a loan originator can sell the servicing rights to another mortgage company with a servicing system at the same time it securitizes the mortgage.

Most of the internal servicing systems tend to be in large mortgage companies because the fixed costs of the servicing system can be spread across a larger portfolio of loans. In addition, large companies can get ancillary income from crossselling other financial products, such as credit cards, life insurance, or mutual funds, to its servicing customers. Finally, larger companies are better at refinancing their own portfolio and preventing refinancings with another lender, known as "run-off". They also have higher guaranteed fees with Fannie Mae and Freddie Mac for their loan pools and can negotiate volume discounts with vendors.

8.4.2. *Detailed information chain for loan origination*

The first step of the mortgage information chain is loan origination which can be described in more detail as a series of six steps. These six steps are illustrated in Fig. 8.2 below and are described in the following paragraphs.

8.4.2.1. *Borrower acquisition*

The first step in loan origination is to find the borrowers who are the customers of the mortgage lenders. Two main channels are used to contact borrowers. The first is the retail channel through which the lender has direct communication with the borrower. This communication can be in a branch office, through a call center, or more recently,

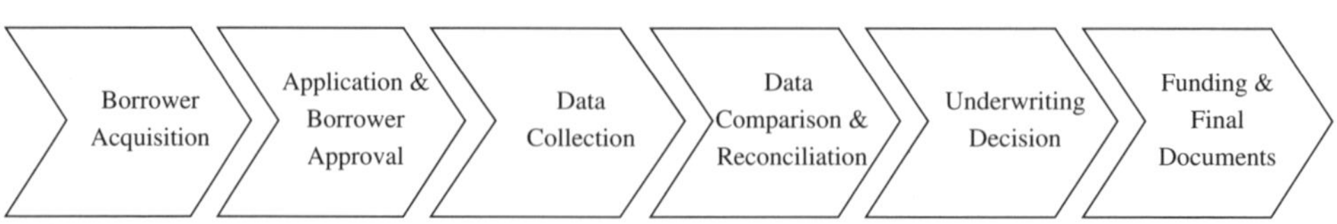

Fig. 8.2. Six steps in loan origination.

through the Internet. The second major channel is the wholesale channel through which a mortgage broker facilitates the loan origination process but the lender funds the loan. The lender maintains relationships with many mortgage brokers, but it is the brokers who have the direct relationship with the borrower.

8.4.2.2. *Application and borrower approval of loan product*

The loan application traditionally begins when a new homebuyer meets with a mortgage broker or representative of the lender to discuss financing the new home purchase. The mortgage brokers or lender representatives assist the buyer with completing a standard residential loan application called a Form 1003 and determining which loan products may be applicable. For the traditional loan origination process, the borrower must choose a loan product at the time of submission of the loan application. The customer is also inherently giving approval to the lender to proceed with the remaining steps in the loan origination process by providing financial documents to support the loan application and paying a nonrefundable application fee.

If the borrower is working with a mortgage broker, the broker then calls the rate lock desk at a lender and forwards the borrower information formatted on the Form 1003. This conversation is usually recorded. After receiving the information, the lender determines the appropriate interest rate either with a rate sheet or electronically, locks the interest rate, and then sends a confirmation of the rates to the broker. Afterwards, the buyer compiles his or her income, employment, and asset information to send to the lender with the completed Form 1003.

8.4.2.3. *Data collection from borrower and third parties*

Once the lender receives the Form 1003 loan application and supporting borrower documentation, the lender then begins the verification process. The verification process begins when the lender collects data from the borrower and third parties to assess the borrower's credit risk as well as the real property to be purchased. These third parties include the borrower's employer, banks or financial institutions where the borrower has accounts, credit reporting agencies, and the county recorder's office. Additional documentation may be requested by the lender during the verification process and when submitted, such documentation must be matched to the borrower's file. Waiting for documents and matching documents from the buyer or third parties to the file can take several weeks.

8.4.2.4. *Comparison and reconciliation of data*

In the second part of the verification process, data about the borrower and the property are collected by the lender and reviewed and verified against other sources of the same data. For example, the monthly salary reported by the borrower on the Form 1003 loan application must exactly match the monthly salary reported by the employer. If the borrower reports monthly income of $4000 but the employer report $3855, the lender must reconcile the information and decide which is more accurate for purposes of analyzing the credit risk. Almost all information provided by the borrower must be independently verified with third parties such as the employer, other banks, county recorder's office, appraisers, and property inspectors.

This process of comparing and reconciling is one of the primary means of protecting the lender from fraud. It also assures that the data used in making the underwriting decision and pricing the loan is as accurate as possible. Problems and inconsistencies which arise when reviewing the data often result in a request for additional documentation from the borrower or third parties. The two steps in the verification process of collecting data and then analyzing them may be repeated many times.

8.4.2.5. *Underwriting decision*

The end of the verification process results in a borrower file with data about the borrower and the property to be purchased with which the lender can make a decision about funding the loan. The decision to fund the loan and the terms on which it will be funded is known as the underwriting decision. The underwriter making the decision reviews the borrower file and determines the credit risk for the loan based on the verified data in the file. If necessary, adjustments are made to the terms of the loan or the interest rate.

8.4.2.6. *Funding and final documents*

Once the decision is made to underwrite the loan, the loan approval is communicated to the borrower with the final terms of the loan including interest rate. The lender prepares documents to reflect the terms of the loan which must be signed by the borrower. These documents include the promissory note evidencing the loan itself as well as documents granting a security interest in the property. Once the borrower signs and delivers the loan documents, the lender funds the loan.

8.5. Technologies Impacting Loan Origination

The immediate targets for the use of technology in the mortgage industry are the reduction in the time the process takes as well as the amount of paper and its movement in the process, the paperless mortgage trend referred to earlier. Although these two ideas are separate, there is a strong correlation between them in that a significant amount of time in the process is allocated to the movement of paper and therefore a reduction in paper movement will in turn lead to a reduction in time for the end to end process. The security and validity associated with an electronic environment is also a focal point for technological solutions.

The five technologies that will have the greatest impact on the mortgage industry over the next five years are:

- Enterprise systems and XML.
- Intelligent systems.
- E-signature.
- Security.
- Document imaging.

These five technologies directly address the business and regulatory issues that inhibit the reduction of paper and time in the process. Without the adoption of all five, the mortgage industry will not be able to move to a complete electronic system. In the subsequent sections, each of the technologies is discussed in more detail covering its definition, its effect on the information chain, and the issues in its adoption.

8.5.1. *Enterprise systems and extensible markup language (XML)*

Extensible markup language (XML) is a computer language used to set up standardized rules for defining content, formatting, and classifying documents that can be shared on the Internet. This allows for data exchange across platforms and applications. XML is one of the building blocks required to successfully implement enterprise software. Enterprise software is a class of software that enables different functions and processes to be integrated seamlessly to allow for a complete electronic flow of information without manual intervention. Some examples of enterprise software are enterprise resource planning (ERP), data warehousing, and customer relationship management.

8.5.1.1. *Enterprise systems and XML in the mortgage industry*

The major driver of use of XML currently is the need for application integration. Mortgage companies have begun to adopt this technology to achieve the goal of the paperless mortgage. However, many companies in the mortgage industry still lack a long-term strategic approach to XML adoption and have not assessed the long-term benefits of this technology. This has resulted in a patchwork use of XML by constituent parties and low penetration.

The mortgage industry is at the juncture where widespread use of an XML standard could pave the way for the creation of an enterprise software system for the mortgage industry. The Mortgage Industry Standards Maintenance Organization (MISMO) is a committee of industry professionals created to establish the XML standard for the mortgage industry. Because a standard has not been adopted across the industry, an effective enterprise software system to manage the end to end process of loan origination has not been developed.

8.5.1.2. *Impact of enterprise systems on the information chain*

An enterprise system impacts each stage of the information chain as it is the method of communication from one step in the process to the next. As a result of the specialization of different steps of the mortgage information chain, separate systems were developed for these different steps. For example, an enterprise system can take data gathered from a borrower using the mortgage broker's Internet interface to directly produce loan documents for the lender. Without the enterprise system, the borrower's data collected using the broker's interface would need to be re-entered into the lender's system because the two systems were developed independently. An enterprise system would coordinate the different systems in each step of the information chain and eliminate redundant steps and inefficiencies.

These enterprise systems are fully open source and web-based systems. Once deployed, they would run entirely on the Internet, support all major hardware and databases, and scale to virtually unlimited number of users and transactions. Their integration capabilities will allow real-time collaboration among market participants and with support systems and services.

8.5.1.3. *Adoption of enterprise systems*

In order for enterprise systems to be successful, players in the industry need to agree on standards. MISMO is attempting to accomplish this and is trying to encourage the adoption of MismoXML as a standard. The recently formed e-Mortgage alliance, an organization of software companies developing software for the mortgage industry, is encouraging the use of defined standards in the development of the enterprise software to eventually reach the goal of the paperless mortgage.

8.5.2. *Intelligent systems*

Intelligent systems are computer systems that "act appropriately in an uncertain environment, where appropriate action is that which increases the probability of success, and success is the achievement of behavioral subgoals that support the system's ultimate goal".[g] In other words, intelligent systems are computer systems that can learn and perform functions such as decision making, image recognition, and planning. Some technologies that perform these functions are expert or rule-based systems, fuzzy logic, and neural nets.

[g]Albus, J, "Outline for a theory of intelligence". *IEEE Transactions on Systems, Man, and Cybernetics*, May/June 1991, 21(3), 473–509.

8.5.2.1. *Intelligent systems in the mortgage industry*

Intelligent systems are currently being used for two purposes in the mortgage industry, automated underwriting and customer relationship management. The use of intelligent systems in automated underwriting is much more mature than its use in customer relationship management. Automated underwriting systems (AUS) are rule-based systems which are software with a set of binary rules that help in electronically reviewing a loan application. The AUS reads and evaluates the loan application based on the rules and comes up with an output to the broker or customer that includes interest rates for the loan product specifically requested and various prices and other loan products for which the borrower may be qualified. AUS's are used to evaluate the level of risk a particular loan represents and determines whether that loan would be a benefit to the current portfolio. As more and more loans are funded and tracked to see which ones go to term, refinance, or default, the additional information allows the rules to be modified so that better risk assessment decisions can be made. Fannie Mae and Freddie Mac have developed AUS's such that if the system reports that the loan qualifies, Fannie Mae and Freddie Mac commit to buying the loan subject to verification and validation of the information provided.

Intelligent systems are also in their nacient stage for use as customer relationship management tools. Customer relationship management allows companies to track and understand customer behavior on the aggregate as well as learn about the behaviors of individual customers. By evaluating such a behavior, mortgage companies can provide better service by having customer call history available to the operator receiving a call as soon as the customer is connected, as well as target product crossselling opportunities appropriately.

8.5.2.2. *Intelligent systems impact on the information chain*

Intelligent systems, specifically AUS's, have changed the order of the steps in the information chain. Prior to AUS's, an underwriting decision could not be made until after customer application data was verified. With an AUS, a contingent but binding, underwriting decision can be made within minutes of a customer submitting an application. For example, IndyMac Bank, a mortgage lender located in Pasadena, California, has developed an AUS called "electronic-mortgage information and transaction system" (e-MITS) that enables it to make an underwriting decision within three minutes of the submission of a loan application. This change in the information chain allows IndyMac to provide better customer service as potential borrowers receive a binding underwriting decision much earlier in the process. The AUS also streamlines IndyMac's processes. Prior to the adoption of e-MITS, IndyMac had underwritten approximately three loans for every one loan funded. After e-MITS, the company underwrote approximately 10 loans for every 8.5 loans funded. Also, a loan application can be submitted

24 h a day rather than just during business hours and metrics collected by IndyMac indicate that applications are submitted around-the-clock.

AUS's also provide better risk assessment as the system refines its underwriting decisions by storing more information about the existing outstanding loans. Improved risk evaluation allows the mortgage companies to compile better performing loan portfolios which in turn makes it easier to sell their new loans in the MBS market. The improved evaluation of risk and increasing sophistication of the intelligent systems over time will allow mortgage companies to provide increased customization of pricing that can lead to individual pricing of loans. Individual pricing results in better customer service as each potential borrower will obtain the best price for their particular circumstances.

Increasing use of customer relationship management systems will enhance customer acquisition capabilities. First, the systems will allow for more targeted marketing campaigns. Only individuals who qualify or meet certain criteria will be contacted about opportunities. Hopefully, the criteria will not only limit the target audience to those financially qualified, but will also limit the audience to those potentially interested in the offer. These offers could be for initial loans, but could also reflect crossselling opportunities. As the mortgage industry needs to manage the fluctuation in revenue streams based on interest rate changes by finding products that even out revenue, cross-selling products to customers becomes increasingly important. Customer relationship management systems will enable mortgage companies to use their marketing dollars efficiently to increase their customer acquisition statistics. In addition, new federal regulations regarding "do not call lists" and privacy require that solicitations be for specific product offers and only go to households with which companies have had a prior relationship. Customer relationship management systems allow companies to identify potential customers with whom they have existing relationships and to leverage the information to best crosssell products while complying with federal regulations. Also by effectively crossselling to customers, mortgage companies make progress toward becoming a "one-stop shop" for their customers.

8.5.2.3. *Intelligent system adoption*

Fannie Mae and Freddie Mac have influenced the adoption of intelligent systems within the mortgage industry. By requiring that applications be sent electronically through their proprietary AUS's, Fannie Mae and Freddie Mac have brought the industry to accept AUS's much sooner than would have otherwise occurred. However, this small victory does not mean that intelligent systems are prolific within the industry. Intelligent systems are time and resource consuming endeavors that require a lot of planning and capital to implement. As the mortgage industry is very competitive, these systems need to prove their value. AUS's have been proven cost effective far more than have customer relationship management systems. Therefore, companies for whom Fannie

Mae's and Freddie Mac's systems are not sufficient, namely, companies which have significant nonconforming loan businesses, have independently developed AUS's. These intelligent systems are critical to establishing a competitive advantage and enabling these companies focusing on nonconforming loans to succeed.

Customer relationship management systems have not been adopted as quickly. This may be because there are no requirements for companies to use them. Therefore, it is up to each individual company to adopt and implement a system. Before a company will invest the capital and resources into development, proof of value needs to be established. Till date, that proof has not surfaced. As other companies and other industries demonstrate the value of customer relationship management tools, mortgage companies will likely assign resources to their development, and intelligent systems will play a greater role in the industry.

8.5.3. *Electronic signatures*

Electronic signatures or "e-signatures", generally refers to any type of signature in electronic form attached to or associated with an electronic document or record. It is the electronic equivalent of a traditional pen-and-ink signature, also called a "wet signature". Whether involving basic imaging or sophisticated encryption, e-signatures typically represent certain basic assumptions also associated with wet signatures:

- the signatory can be identified by his or her signature;
- the signatory agrees to be bound by the contents of the signed document;
- the signed document will not be changed after it has been signed;
- a signature on one document will not be transferred to another document without the authorization of the original signatory.

E-signatures can vary from the attachment of an image of a wet signature to password protection to digital signatures. "Digital signatures" typically refer to authentication methods which rely on public key cryptography (PKC). PKC is a method that uses two mathematically related keys, one private and one public. The private key is kept by the individual and is used to sign the documents. The public key is given to the corresponding party who will need to authenticate the documents. When using PKC to sign a document, a one-way algorithm is used that transforms a string of characters into a shorter value of fixed-length referred to as a "hash", "hash result", or "message digest". The private key is used to encrypt the hash to produce the digital signature which is attached to the electronic document. The electronic document is sent and the recipient uses the public key to retrieve the hash and decrypt it. If the two hashes match, then the document and signature are authenticated. If the document has been modified the hashes will not match. Although many of the e-signature technologies involve document and signatory authentication and fraud prevention that is more secure than the traditional wet signature, general acceptance and adoption of e-signatures is slow.

8.5.3.1. *E-signatures in the mortgage industry*

In October 2000, the US Electronic Signatures in Global and National Commerce Act (e-SIGN) went into effect. This federal regulation was designed to remove some of the legal uncertainty surrounding the use of e-signatures and to encourage the use of e-signatures in government and commerce. Many state governments have also enacted regulations allowing the use of e-signatures and encouragement of e-signatures has been included in other federal laws such as the Government Paperwork Elimination Act. In general, most of the e-signature regulations remain technology neutral to allow government entities and businesses flexibility to adopt new technologies that best fit their needs.

8.5.3.2. *E-signatures impact on the information chain*

Because of the extensive paperwork involved in the loan origination process, e-signatures can be an important tool to reduce the amount of paper and streamline the process. Beginning from the completion of the standard Form 1003, almost all brokers and lenders currently require a wet signature on this form. Some brokers and lenders may even require that the form itself be completed in the customer's own handwriting. Because of this requirement, it is more likely that a borrower will need to meet with a broker or loan agent to obtain a copy of the form and complete it. This can make comparison shopping for loan products more difficult for customers because working with nonlocal or out-of-state brokers or lenders would involve higher transaction costs to physically transfer the signed loan application. With an e-signature, a borrower could potentially apply for a loan in any geographic location by downloading a copy of the standard Form 1003, completing it electronically, signing it electronically, and then submitting it over the Internet to a broker or lender. Currently, many brokers and lenders type in information from the physical Form 1003 into a computer as part of loan processing. E-signature can remove the extra data transfer step and allow lenders with competitive interest rates and fees to compete more effectively for buyers across the country and eventually even internationally.

E-signatures can also help to transform the verification process and it is likely that this may be the first place for initial adoption of this technology. The various pieces of financial information of the borrower must be verified and checked with third-parties such as employers, financial institutions, and the government. Traditionally, this verification process had been undertaken by specially trained underwriters. More recently, in order to lower costs and increase loan throughput, the process has been increasingly broken down into smaller steps. Each step is then evaluated for automation potential or completion by less-skilled labor, including outsourced labor. As each step of the process is completed, which is not a simultaneous event because information from third parties is received at different times or the borrower must be contacted to provide additional information, some type of indication or sign-off is needed. E-signatures can help with the internal sign-off during verification of each piece of borrower information. Moreover, innovative mortgage lenders can keep borrower files in entirely electronic form and transfer portions of the verification process to different physical locations to better allocate its labor pool. For example, if a mortgage lenders has regional offices in Los Angeles and Cleveland and the Los Angeles offices is suddenly swamped with new loan applications, some of the workload can be electronically transferred to the Cleveland office to process. Also, if the lender has worldwide offices, the differences in time zones can be used such that the processing work is continuous 24 h a day as the files are electronically transferred from one office to another. E-signatures help coordinate the sign-off for each portion of the verification process which can now be done by multiple individuals in different physical locations. If there are questions on particular portions of the verification process, the e-signature can trace the individual who performed the work regardless of his or her physical location.

Finally, e-signatures can improve the final stage of loan origination, the drawing of documents. Typically, borrowers must physically go to an escrow agent or have a thick stack of documents sent to them to sign to finalize the loan. These documents include notarized signatures for actual transfer of title and the promissory notes evidencing the mortgage to acknowledgments of receipt of required disclosure forms. Even if the loan and verification process involved documents in electronic form, currently, all final documents must be printed out and manually signed by the borrowers. E-signatures can keep all of these documents in electronic form and allow them to be easily transferred to the borrower for signing and then to the requisite institutions and agencies for eventual archiving. The electronic storage of real estate documents can save the lender money in terms of physical space necessary to store the loan documents for each loan of every borrower. The "paperless mortgage" has been a long standing goal for the mortgage industry yet still remains elusive. E-signature is an important step in that direction.

8.5.3.3. *E-signatures adoption*

If e-signature technology of various types already exists, has the potential to improve the efficiency and throughput of the loan origination process, can possibly improve the customer experience, and has been explicitly sanctioned by federal and state governments, it is difficult to understand why it has not been adopted. The primary reason for the delay in adoption cited by many mortgage industry professionals is the lack of a developed body of law specifically enforcing the use of electronic signatures. While governments have put regulations in place, there has been little litigation to develop the case law regarding specific circumstances of enforceability of e-signatures. Most lenders do not want to risk their billion dollar portfolios on an e-signature without a more developed body of law regarding enforceability, and simultaneously, no lender wants to be the test legal case. Moreover, attitudes and habits can be difficult and slow to change and real estate transactions are notorious for preserving ancient tradition. The widespread trust in e-signatures does not seem to exist yet and paradoxically, trust is difficult to develop without widespread use and widespread use is difficult to develop without trust.

8.5.4. *Security*

Security represents a number of different technologies and roles within a system. In this paper, security refers to document integrity, authentication, and authorization. Document integrity refers to methods that ensure that a document has not or cannot be modified. There are several technological implementations to ensure documents have not been tampered with: file creation and modification dates, read-only files, password protection, the checksum method, and PKC. The checksum method refers to the process of adding up the number of bytes in a document and verifying that the number has not changed. If a file changes, it is very hard to change it in such a way that the number of bytes remains the same. PKC, which can be used as a sophisticated e-signature technology, has the added benefit of ensuring document integrity. The creation and encryption of the hash with the private key and the subsequent decryption and comparison of the hash by the document recipient using the public key is a means of authenticating the document.

Authentication and authorization are security concepts that are usually addressed together. Authentication is the process by which a system verifies that the person trying to access the system is who he or she claims to be. Authorization is the process by which the system verifies that the person authenticated has permission to access the information. Another security concern related to authentication and authorization issues is the theft of information while it is being transferred through the network, known as "packet sniffing". User identifications (ID's) and passwords are used to accomplish both authentication and authorization. However, if someone is packet sniffing while user ID's and passwords are being transmitted, then the systems are compromised as authorized users can be impersonated. Therefore, encryption is a necessary tool for implementing a solid authentication and authorization system. Encryption of data and user ID's and passwords renders the data stolen useless as an unauthorized user will not be able to read the information obtained.

8.5.4.1. *Security in the mortgage industry*

Within the industry, there are security concerns at two major points, the storage of the data within the mortgage banking company databases and the delivery of the information from the borrower as well as third parties. The document integrity, authentication, and authorization for the data stored within many mortgage banking companies is handled through user ID's and passwords. Because the process is still largely paper based, many of the security functions in the application process are handled by people within the current process. Notaries validate that the borrower is who he or she claims to be. Underwriters validate the documents from third parties. Documents are mailed to specific people handling an application. Security is also handled by building trust between the parties. Although trust building is not a fool-proof method, the sense of security from this method is an entrenched factor within the industry. As the industry moves to a more electronic industry, the concerns for security grow as the human relationship built on trust no longer exists. More secure systems are required to replace the trust that existed in the old process. In addition, the number of privacy regulations enacted also raises the level of security that the mortgage industry needs to provide.

8.5.4.2. *Impact of security technologies on the information chain*

Designing security systems is a process of assessing the level of risk to the organization if the system is compromised and making a determination of how much investment in security should be made. The technological solution adopted should match the level of security required. With the privacy requirements imposed by federal regulations and the need to find a replacement for trust created by human interaction, the security systems in the mortgage industry must provide the highest level of security. The cost of a security system is not a use by use cost, so if the system requires building the most secure environment possible for a significant amount of the transactions, it might as well be used for all transactions. Using methods such as file creation and modification dates, read-only files, password protection, and the checksum method for document integrity would be insufficient to the high level of security required for some of the transactions in the origination process. These types of technologies are easily compromised. A skilled hacker can change the read-only file flag to make the document changeable or could similarly change the checksum number. Therefore, the only technology secure enough to accomplish document integrity is PKC. Similarly, encryption is a necessary element to accomplish authentication and authorization. PKC accomplishes the security goals of document integrity, authorization, and authentication. If a document is encrypted with both the originator's private key and the recipient's public key, then the recipient knows that the document came from the originator accomplishing authentication and the recipient can only read the document if he or she has the correct public key accomplishing authorization. In addition, the document will only be valid if the hashes or signature have not changed so document integrity is accomplished. The most significant impact on the information chain from security will, therefore, be a result of PKC.

Throughout the paper-intensive process of originating a mortgage, documents are gathered and then verified to ensure that the property has the value stated and the loan recipient has the means to repay the loan. The verification process in the information chain is the most time intensive, least automated, and most vulnerable to fraud. If fraudulent loans are inadvertently accepted, then mortgage companies would lose the value of the loan. Having too many loans that were not repaid would impede the mortgage company's ability to sell its mortgages as the default rate would be too high. Other companies would not want to take on the increased risk for little, if any, additional compensation. PKC would address these issues and affect all the steps in the information chain. It acts as an enabler for a paperless mortgage and removes time from the verification step because underwriters would not need to wait for documents to be sent by mail. As stated above, much of the security in the current system is based on trust in human relationships and human verification. This security is not a very tight system. A borrower could sign a document and later someone could modify the document and file it without the borrower's knowledge. Thus, trust establishes the security of document integrity. PKC would provide increased security as the document would become invalid if it were modified. Also, brokers play a major role in determining and establishing the trust. Mortgage banks trust the brokers. The brokers do business with borrowers they trust; and thus, the mortgage companies trust the borrowers. With PKC, trust could develop without the human intervention. As PKC becomes more accepted, the need for brokers will decrease.

8.5.4.3. *Adoption of security technologies*

Security system adoption, specifically public key encryption, has been slow. Until 1999, the algorithm for PKC was under patent protection. The patent owner charged high license fees which made software development and system implementation using PKC cost prohibitive. The patent has expired, so the industry can now implement PKC systems without paying license fees. However, implementation of PKC will take time to implement because companies have scarce resources.

Trust is also a decisive issue. Mortgage companies and other participants in the loan origination process need to develop trust in the security systems. The participants are accustomed to trusting other people, not trusting machines. Social engineering is also contributing to the mistrust. Social engineering refers to the security problem that occurs when people reveal their passwords to unauthorized people or convince systems administrators to give them unauthorized rights to a system. Diligent systems managers are required to keep social engineering at bay, so that trust in the security system can develop.

8.5.4.4. *Document imaging*

Document imaging refers to the set of technologies for converting paper documents into electronic format. The term also includes archival, indexing, and retrieval functions often referred to as "document management". The process involves scanning or electronically converting files into high resolution images which are saved on a storage media. These images can then be organized, stored and retrieved electronically. Optical character recognition (OCR) technology can take scanned text and translate it into character codes. OCR technology gives documents an active content which enables advanced applications such as file retrieval by word or phrase searching.

8.5.4.5. *Document imaging in the mortgage industry*

The mortgage industry is still primarily a paper-driven process. In addition, regulatory requirements regarding archiving of loan files and disclosure requirements add to the paper files. Loan officers are dependent on outside sources for information such as a credit report, employment verification, or tax statements which are often received in various forms and formats. Searching and organizing documents has a significant labor expense attached to it. Mistakes also occur with manual processing which put lenders at risk of losing potential applicants and valuable customers. When the loan is finally approved, the loan documents must be organized and stored which requires expensive physical space. If archived loan documents need to be referenced, a person needs to physically go to the storage warehouse to pull the file. Sometimes, loan files can be misplaced and finding a missing or misplaced file can be time-consuming and expensive.

Document imaging is currently being used to a limited extent in the loan origination process, primarily during the verification process. Many mortgage lenders scan and convert the paper documentation provided by the borrower into an electronic file. Different portions of the file or electronic copies of the file can then be distributed to employees, sometimes in different physical locations, for verification against information gathered from third parties. However, the paper borrower file is usually considered as the source of record and final loan documents are printed on paper, manually signed, and included in the final file for archiving.

8.5.4.6. *Impact of document imaging on the information chain*

Although document imaging is currently in the verification portion of the information chain which requires the most transfer, comparison, and use of paper documents, the technology can affect other portions of the information chain. A fully implemented document imaging system can begin from the time the borrower completes a Form 1003 loan application. Rather than retyping information from a form into a computer, an active, electronic document can be created from the beginning. Similarly in the verification steps, the documents necessary for verification can be purely electronic documents which can be distributed to necessary loan agents quickly and inexpensively which may allow for increased specialization of each item for verification. Also, purely electronic documents may help to automate the process as computers will be able to read the text of the document rather than treating it as a static image. Finally, if combined with electronic signatures, the final loan documentation can be verified and signed electronically without the need for a wet signature by a borrower. The electronic files can be archived which will reduce physical storage space. Also, active electronic files can be searched which can make retrieval of files faster and more efficient.

8.5.4.7. *Adoption of document imaging*

The adoption of document imaging is increasing in the mortgage industry. It allows lenders not only to reduce storage space and costs by eliminating paper, but also to cut labor costs through the network distribution of records which contributes to increased profitability. Less human intervention also reduces the chance of error.

In order to utilize document imaging, each party in the process needs to be equipped with computer hardware such as scanners and software such as e-mail. As many third parties such as appraisers are small businesses, it is unlikely that all parties will be equipped with the necessary tools in the near future. Lack of tools among all parties involved in the loan origination process inhibits the widespread use of document imaging across the entire information chain.

Another hindrance is the industry's difficulty in accepting electronic files. Borrowers are used to having paper in their hands. The average person does not yet trust electronic mortgage files especially with respect to security and are not completely comfortable with its legitimacy. Until consumers and third parties become more comfortable, the adoption of document imaging will be slow. Finally, regulatory issues are not fully resolved. A developed body of law does not yet exist regarding the enforceability of electronic documents. Although electronic documents are encouraged by the federal government, such as through the e-SIGN legislation, companies are not yet willing to risk full reliance on electronic documents without more definite legal precedents.

8.6. Final Conclusions About the Information Chain

The technologies discussed have been shown to affect the loan origination information chain at different points. Figure 8.3 is a diagram that illustrates each step in the information chain for loan origination and where each technology impacts the information chain. The overall effect of each technology on the information chain is more complex than the sum of the impacted steps. By affecting several steps simultaneously, each technology can change the overall loan origination process; it is important to evaluate each of the future trends being affected by the technologies.

While exciting new technology developments hold the possibility of revolutionizing the information chain for loan origination, our research indicates that several helpful and well-developed technologies still have not been adopted.

	Borrower Acquisition	Application & Product Approval	Data Collection	Compare & Reconcile	Underwriting	Fund & Final Docs
XML/ Enterprise System	✓	✓	✓	✓	✓	✓
Intelligent Systems	✓				✓	
E-Signature		✓		✓		✓
Security		✓	✓	✓		✓
Document Imaging		✓	✓	✓		✓

Fig. 8.3. Technology impacts on the information chain.

The major industry trends introduced earlier are revisited and evaluated in light of the five specific technologies discussed.

8.6.1. *The paperless mortgage*

While electronic signatures and document imaging have the ability to significantly reduce the amount of paper in the loan origination process, these technologies currently have not been used to their full potential. Currently, document imaging and electronic signatures are being used by lenders internally during the verification process. We believe that widespread adoption of these technologies with lenders for internal use will occur during the next five years.

However, the goal of the paperless mortgage is very unlikely to occur within the next five years. System integration with the numerous third party information providers during the verification process involves too many entities and too much coordination and agreement on standards that we believe it is unlikely to occur in the near future. Even if MISMO or another central organization could coordinate, set, and enforce industry standards for systems integration, the lack of a body of law regarding electronic documents will also prevent the paperless mortgage from occurring during the next five years. Small lenders which may who consider the paperless mortgage to be a competitive advantage will not have sufficient capital to risk litigation over enforceability of electronic documents in the event of a dispute. Large lenders with sufficient capital to defend potential litigation have loan portfolios too large to risk an uncertain outcome. Finally, personal attitudes about paper and its tangibility will also likely prevent full scale emergence of the paperless mortgage. Because home ownership is such a significant transaction for many borrowers and a mortgage is the largest source of indebtedness for most of the individuals, many individual borrowers may psychologically feel more secure with tangible evidence of their transaction and be unwilling to switch to an intangible electronic documents.

8.6.2. *One-stop shop*

We believe that increasing consolidation will occur in the mortgage industry as there is an industry trend towards increased market power to remain competitive. There is also pressure for companies to broaden their product and service offerings. First, the economies of scale and scope are present and become stronger as loan products in the mortgage industry become commodities. The use of intelligent systems to price complex and specialized loan products for the specific needs of borrowers will make securitization and pricing more efficient. These pricing pressures on an increasingly broader range of loan products will give companies with economies of scale and scope a pricing advantage in attracting borrowers.

Moreover, the ability to retain customers and maintain a customer relationship will become increasingly more important and lenders will be unable to distinguish themselves by their loan product offerings. Therefore, increasing the number of customer contacts through different products is a mean to retain a particular borrower. This includes crossselling of different mortgage and financial products as well as tailoring financial services to individual customers. Also, more information about an individual customer gathered through multiple financial products such as checking accounts or credit cards, can help lenders better gauge credit risk when considering a mortgage application. Advances in data mining and enterprise software will help mortgage lenders and financial institutions develop customer relationships. As a result, there will be a strong movement toward one-stop shops in the next five years — first for home buying and eventually to financial services.

8.6.3. *Automation and outsourcing*

Currently, lenders are re-evaluating their loan origination process to find ways to reduce labor costs through automation or outsourcing. With the loss of jobs in the recent economic recession, offshoring has become a dirty word which many companies do not mention. However, despite the political backlash against sending US jobs to overseas workers, companies, including mortgage lenders, are still quietly and persistently pursuing it. We believe there will be increased outsourcing with significant offshoring in the next five years as competitive pressures in the mortgage industry force mortgage lenders to review their loan processes. Document imaging facilitates the outsourcing of the verification step as images of the loan file can be sent cheaply and quickly to an outside party rather than incurring the costs of shipping physical paper files. Once an image a document in the loan file is in the system, the information can be validated in any location. This makes offshoring a viable alternative for this step. We also believe that automation will increase as it gives lenders more control over the process and does not have the negative public connotations of offshoring.

8.6.4. *Role of broker or representative*

Despite the development of intelligent systems and interfaces with borrowers, we believe that the mortgage broker or lender representative will continue to have a strong position in the loan origination information chain for at least the next five years. First, the increasing number of loan products which can be tailored to a borrower's particular financial situation can overwhelm a home buyer. Also, since home purchases only occur on a few occasions in an individual's lifetime, most individuals do not develop sophisticated knowledge about mortgages and generally do not keep themselves updated on industry developments. The comfort and feeling of security and responsiveness from talking to another human being is important in the mortgage context which we believe will not be replaced by self-service or automation in the next five years.

Also, mortgage brokers and loan representatives play an important role in fraud detection during the loan origination process. The ability of human beings to process subtle and complex signals when meeting a potential borrower and to detect signs for fraud has not been replicated by machines. Even if certain sophisticated borrowers do not need an agent to explain loan product offerings, we believe lenders will still require borrowers to meet in person with a human agent as a means to detect potential fraud.

8.6.5. *Other*

Two other important issues affect the overall business environment in the mortgage industry and the adoption of new technologies. These are changes to regulations and attitudes.

8.6.5.1. *Government regulation*

The changes to regulations in an industry can result in a new prioritization of technology projects especially if there is a deadline for compliance. Technology projects which relate to compliance with the new regulation will have higher priority and increased budgets. Technology projects which relate to other business goals will be delayed. This could impede the adoption of technologies which improve business processes in the industry. Also, a short-term need to comply with new regulations contributes to the piecemeal development of technology solutions at the expense of more efficient long-term strategic planning.

The development of technology is often faster than updates to regulations. Many regulations which have existed for years do not contemplate process changes or paradigm shifts brought about by new technologies. As a result excess resources could be wasted on bringing technologies in compliance with outdated regulations which could otherwise be used for continued process improvement.

8.6.5.2. *Attitudes*

The attitudes of mortgage industry professionals and customers will need to change to accept new technologies and the process changes they bring. Because of the disruptive nature of changes in the industry which result from technology, a complete shift in attitude is often required. However, attitudes do not change quickly especially in an industry with a long tradition. The purchase of a home is a major life event and borrowers need to be completely comfortable with the process, the security of their personal and financial information, and the records of the purchase. Because homeowners have so much at stake, it is likely that their attitude change may be slower than for other industries.

As the industry will change very slowly, especially for the commodity market of conforming loans, the industry will look largely the same to the borrower over the next five years. However, during that time, the technological and legal infrastructure will be developing so that the foundation will be ready when the attitudes catch up.

8.7. Summary and Future Research

The focus of this paper is the loan origination processes within the mortgage banking industry. The most pressing industry trends for the loan origination process which technology can address relate to the reduction in time and paper within the origination process. Future research could be done on the impact of existing and developing technologies in the other two steps in the mortgage information chain, namely, servicing and securitization.

The servicer of a mortgage has a wealth of information about mortgage customers for which they bought the servicing rights, whether or not the servicer originated the mortgage. The number of mortgages serviced can far exceed the number of mortgages originated for an individual servicing company. More research can be done to determine how technology can facilitate the management of the volume of servicing transactions and improve the quality of customer service. Regulatory issues such as privacy regulations and restrictions on marketing through the federal "do not call lists" provide challenges to effective use and management of customer data. Additional research can be done on technologies to evaluate their influence on the servicing information chain.

Securitization is another process on which technology can have an impact, but further research needs to be completed to identify the influential technologies and their effects. One technology that could potentially impact securitization is the development of intelligent systems such as neural networks which could allow for more accurate valuation and risk analysis of MBS.

Even in the loan origination process, other areas for future research remain. For example, even if the mortgage industry successfully implements the paperless mortgage, storage systems to hold all the borrower and loan information will be still required. Although the volume for electronic storage media is much smaller than for paper files, physical storage space will still be a concern. However, the more complicated issue for storage is longevity of the storage media. Because real estate records may need to be stored for decades and sometimes even for generations, the determination of the proper storage media and method of replication is still an unresolved issue. The eventual archiving process needs to ensure document integrity as well as be cost-effective.

Many of the changes analyzed in this paper require changes in attitude. For an industry and a process which has evolved from long tradition, the psychological readiness of mortgage lenders and their customers for technological change plays a significant role in the overall ability of technology to impact the information chain. More research can be done to determine how customers and the mortgage companies will react to and adopt new technologies. This future research could also include an analysis of the features or characteristics that will be needed before a majority of industry professionals and customers will adopt the new technologies.

Acknowledgments

This study was undertaken as an AMR Research Project at the UCLA Anderson School of Management, initiated and supervised by Professor Uday Karmarkar. The study is part of the BIT project undertaken at the Center for Management in the Information Economy, directed by Prof. Uday Karmarkar and Dr. Vandana Mangal.

Bibliography

1. Advantage investors mortgage: Streamlining the closing process. DocumentIQ, 9 February 2004. http://www.documentiq.com/best_practices/161-DocumentIQ%20Best%20-Practices.html.
2. Alexander, M and M Elena (2000). The challenge of intelligent systems. International Symposium on Intelligent Control (ISIC) 2000.
3. Allan, A (2002). Trusted E-signatures through PKI, smart cards and biometrics. Gartner Research COM-17-0295.

4. E-mortgage are becoming reality. Inside mortgage technology. 9 February 2004. e-Original http://www.eoriginal.com/press/articles/030901_imt.html.
5. Fogarty, M (2004). On the road again. *National Mortgage News*. http://www. nationalmortgagenews.com/nmn/onroad.htm.
6. Free D, K Harris, M Kun and S Landry (2001). Emerging XML standards for FSP-transaction enablement. Gartner Research COM-13-9865, 16 August.
7. Fritz, W (1999). Definition of the intelligent system (IS). Intelligent Systems & Their Societies New Horizons Press. http://www.intelligent-systems.com.ar/intsyst/defintsi.htm.
8. Kenney, F and J Thompson (2003). B2B security patterns: Finding the perfect combination. Gartner Research SPA-20-5779.
9. Knox, M (2003). XML and other standards net financial services momentum. Gartner Research T-21-2750.
10. Knox, R and Abrams *et al.* (2003). Hype cycle for XML technologies, 2003. Gartner Research R-19-9727.
11. Kreizman, G (2002). U.S. law and the future of E-signatures in government. Gartner Research COM-16-8533.
12. Kun, M (2001). E-enabling the loan origination process. Gartner Research Tactical Guidelines, TG-13-6030.
13. LaCour-Little, M (2000). The evolving role of technology in mortgage finance. *Journal of Housing Research*, 11 (2).
14. Litan, A, V Wheatman and S Landry (2002). Digital signatures and risk mitigation: A market disconnect. Gartner Research M-17-0621.
15. Mark F (2004). On the road again. *National Mortgage News*. http://www. nationalmortgagenews.com/nmn/onroad.htm.
16. Michael, J (2002). Where do markets come from? Center for the Network Economy CNE WP.
17. Mitchell, HJ (2004). Electronic information — How well is it managed? http://www. ifsam.org/1998/DATA/4.PDF.
18. Mogull, R (2004). When and how to use database encryption. Gartner Research T-20-9876.
19. Mortgage banks in America: Bigger and richer. *The Economist*, 31 October 1992: pp. 85–87. Factiva.
20. Nicolett, M *et al.* (2003). Client issues for security infrastructure. Gartner Research K-20-7781.
21. Noakes-Fry, K (2002). A quick look at digital and electronic signatures. Gartner Research COM-17-1968.
22. Noakes-Fry, K (2003). E-signatures — Digital and electronic: Technology overview. Gartner Research DPRO-91585.
23. Noakes-Fry, K (2003). Public-key infrastructure: Technology overview. Gartner Research DPRO-90693.
24. Originating quality mortgages. Fannie Mae, 12 February 2004. www.efanniemae. com/singlefamily/pdf/qa_best_practices.pdf.

25. Pafenberg, F (2004). The single family mortgage industry in the internet era. Office of Federal Housing Enterprise Oversight, January 2004. www.ofheo.gov/media/pdf/technologypaper12004.pdf.
26. Patrick, B (2003). What happened to the paperless mortgage? *Wall Street Journal*, R4, Factiva.
27. Pescatore, J and R Stiennon (2003). Defining intrusion prevention. Gartner Research TU-20-0149.
28. Rhozwell, C, H Lehong and D Flint (2001). Applying e-business to transform critical processes. Gartner Research COM-13-7435.
29. Richard, B (2002). Housing finance and the role of technology. *Housing Finance International*, Chicago, 16:3 ProQuest Database.
30. Searchexpress document imaging features. Searchexpress, 9 February 2004. http://www.searchexpress.com/g-features.html.
31. Segars, A, A Gold and D Szparaga (2001). The impact of technology and electronic markets on the US commercial mortgage industry. Mortgage Bankers Association of America. White Paper.
32. Segars, A (2002). Transformation of mortgage banking through ebusiness: An overview of contemporary practice and trends. Mortgage Bankers Association of America. http://www.mortgagebankers.org/cref/WhitePaper/PDF/MBAA%20Update.pdf.
33. Sievewright, M (2002). 2003 Info systems guide: Five emerging technologies. *Credit Union Magazine*, 68(12), Factiva.
34. Tichy, L (2004) Paperless mortgage: Possible, feasible, practical. http://www. mortgagebankers.org/present/2002/tichy_0314.pdf.
35. Wheatman, V (2002). Public-key infrastructure Q&A. Gartner Research QA-18-7301.
36. Wheatman, V *et al.* (2003). Hype cycle for information security. Gartner Research R-19-9974.
37. White, J, D Wong and D Latimore (2003). So many borrowers, so little time — Will you be ready when the mortgage boom ends. IBM Business Consulting Services. http://www-1.ibm.com/services//strategy/e_strategy/ibm_mortgageboom.html.
38. Witty, R *et al.* (2001). The price of information security. Gartner Research R-11-6534.
39. Witty, R and R Wagner (2003). The growing need for identity and access management. Gartner Research AV-21-4512.
40. XML implementation guide: General information. Mortgage Industry Standards Maintenance Organization, 15 February 2004. www.mismo.org/mismo/docs/MISMOGeneralGuide2_x(2003-10-16).pdf.

Appendix A: Company Web Sites

ABN Amro Mortgage: http://www.mortgage.com
Broker Universe: http://www.brokeruniverse.com
Countrywide Financial Corp: http://www.countrywide.com/
DignityMortgage.com: http://www.dignitymortgage.com/index.htm
Fannie Mae: http://www.fanniemae.com

Freddie Mac: http://www.freddiemac.com
GMAC Mortgage Corporation: http://www.gmacmortgage.com/home.asp
IndyMac Bank: http://www.indymacbank.com
International Union for Housing Finance: http://www.housingfinance.org
Mortgage Bankers Association: http://www.mbaa.org
Mortech LLC: http://www.mortech-llc.com
Mortgagebot: http://www.mortgagebot.com
Mortgage Banking Mag: http://www.mortgagebankingmag.com
Mortgage Technology: http://www.mortgage-technology.com
Office of Federal Housing Enterprise Oversight: http://www.ofheo.gov
Search Security: http://searchsecurity.techtarget.com
US Department of Housing and Urban Development: http://www.hud.gov

Appendix B: Acronyms

AUS — Automated underwriting systems
B2C — Business to Consumer
e-SIGN — Electronic Signatures in Global and National Commerce Act
HELOC — Home Equity Line of Credit
HUD — Department of Housing and Urban Development
MISMO — Mortgage Industry Standards Maintenance Organization
MBS — Mortgage Backed Security
OCR — Optical character recognition technology
PKC — public key cryptography
RESPA — Real Estate Settlement Procedures Act of 1974
XML — Extensible Markup Language

Appendix C: Research Process

The research process began with secondary research on the mortgage industry and preliminary identification of the information chain for a residential mortgage. An initial identification of key issues in the industry was also accomplished through secondary research. Primary research followed which involved interviewing technology and process improvement executives at local mortgage lenders which were perceived to be leaders in technology adoption or technology innovators in the industry. Further refinement of the information chain was also accomplished through primary research interviews with executives in mortgage lending divisions of mortgage banks.

Through the combination of secondary research and primary research, hypotheses were developed around the major industry issues. Key technologies with the potential to impact the loan origination process were identified. Finally, the hypotheses were tested through additional primary and secondary research. The additional primary research included interviews with executives in the residential mortgage divisions of more traditional commercial banks and interviews with other industry professionals such a mortgage broker.

Appendix D: Brief History of Fannie Mae and Freddie Mac

Since the mid-1980s lenders have financed most of the conforming mortgages by selling them to or swapping them for MBS's guaranteed by Fannie Mae and Freddie Mac, created to provide a secondary market for residential mortgages. Fannie Mae was chartered in 1938 by the federal government to make more money available for the mortgage market by purchasing loans insured by the Federal Housing Administration (FHA) and selling these as securities in the financial markets. The result was a more liquid and efficient market for conforming loans, and a consistent, lending process with the same loan terms, interest rates, and underwriting guidelines applicable nationwide. Also, basic costs of lenders which sold mortgage portfolios to Fannie Mae and Freddie Mac began to converge. Fannie Mae's guidelines and restrictions became uniform principles which lenders needed to follow to sell their loans to the secondary market.

After being re-chartered in 1968 by the US Congress as a private, shareholder-owned and publicly traded corporation, Fannie Mae's focus shifted to conventional loan programs. Nonetheless, its purpose to create a more liquid mortgage market by linking the primary and secondary mortgage markets remained essentially the same. By 1970, Fannie Mae was entirely purchased and owned by private shareholders.

In that same year, the US Congress chartered Freddie Mac with the purpose to increase the supply of mortgage loan funds available to commercial banks, savings and loan institutions, credit unions and other mortgage lenders. Freddie Mac essentially complemented Fannie Mae. Although also not a government agency, but privately owned and publicly traded, Freddie Mac is regulated by the federal government.

Recently, Freddie Mac has encountered accounting and management issues and restated its financial statements for 2000, 2001, and 2002. The problems have damaged its reputation and by association has negatively impacted the reputation of Fannie Mae.

[From "A Brief History of Mortgages," Dignity Mortgage Corporation, 12 January 2004, http://www .dignitymortgage.com/MortgageIndustry/MortgageIndustryHistory.htm.]

Appendix E: Real Estate Regulations Affecting the Mortgage Industry

Laws and regulations of state and federal agencies govern the mortgage industry with the aim to improve consumer protection. These include real estate regulations, banking regulations, and privacy regulations. Some of the principal real estate regulations are described below:

- The Equal Credit Opportunity Act (ECOA) prohibits discrimination by lenders and creditors on the basis of sex, race, religion, color, national origin, age, marital status, whether the applicant receives government assistance and if the person has previously exercised his or her rights under the ECOA. Complaints and violations are monitored by the Federal Trade Commission.
- The Fair Housing Act, administered by the Department of Housing and Urban Development (HUD) focuses on the housing industry and residential real estate. It prohibits real estate industry agents, specialists, and professionals from discrimination on the basis of sex, race, religion, color, national origin, age or marital status.
- The Fair Credit Reporting Act, regulates the reporting of consumer credit and the use of consumer credit reports by creditors and lenders.
- The Home Mortgage Disclosure Act (HMDA), passed by Congress in 1975, addressed public dissatisfaction with the lack of sufficient loans in urban areas. To ensure that mortgage

companies met the credit demands of their neighborhood, information about the loans, property and borrower must be entered in the Loan/Application Register (HMDA-LAR) and reported every year to the government.
- The Real Estate Settlement Procedures Act of 1974 (RESPA) regulates the disclosure requirements for the real estate industry and to protect consumers from undisclosed fees. Two revisions took place in 1990 and 1992. RESPA requires lenders to provide the following disclosure documents: good faith estimate, truth-in-lending disclosure, notice of servicing transfer, escrow disclosure, and HUD-1 Settlement Statement.

Appendix F: Steps to Obtaining a Mortgage

[From Nation's Mortgagebanc, http://www.nationasloan.com/learning_center/mechanics.rad.]

Application

The loan starts when a new homebuyer, also referred to as customer or buyer, approaches a mortgage broker for a home loan. This process could occur in a few different ways such as, the customer filling out an enquiry form on a broker's website or a referral from an existing customer or real-estate agent. The next step in the process is to complete the standard residential loan application form. Most of the brokers or lenders use a standard application form that is accepted by the major secondary market investors, such as Fannie Mae (Federal National Mortgage Association) and Freddie Mac (Federal Home Loan Mortgage Corporation). The form is commonly known as Form 1003 and is divided into sections. Generally, this form is initially completed by the customer and finalized by the lender after verifying the information on the application. It is extremely important that the application contain accurate information. Many loan officers will work with borrowers to help in completing the application and in gathering important documentation.

The following lists the sections of the Form 1003: Uniform Residential Loan Application:

- Type of Mortgage and Terms of Loan.
- Property Information and Purpose of Loan.
- Borrower Information.
- Employment Information.
- Monthly Income and Combined Housing Expenses Information.
- Assets and Liabilities.
- Details of Transaction.
- Declarations.
- Acknowledgment and Agreement.
- Information for Government Monitoring Purposes.

Choosing the right loan requires customers to review their financial objectives. The customer then needs to review their product options and pricing and select the product they want to pursue. Customers depend heavily on brokers and other financial advisors in helping them make this decision.

After customers complete the loan application and choose a loan type, the lender provides several documents to the borrower that discloses important aspects of the loan. These documents are provided within three days of receipt of the application and are required by federal regulations. The documents are:

- Estimated Closing Cost Statement. Lenders provide an estimate of the closing costs incidental to obtaining a loan.
- Truth in Lending Statement — Regulation Z. This statement shows annual percentage rate (APR) on the loan. This rate combines the actual interest paid on the note rate over the life of the loan plus the total costs to obtain the loan. The APR is a measure of the cost of credit expressed as a yearly rate of interest. Because all lenders follow the same rules in calculating the APR, it provides consumers with a good basis for comparing the cost of mortgages.
- Settlement Cost, A HUD Guide. This booklet gives an overview of the lending process and is required by HUD. The booklet is provided to consumers after the loan application is completed.

Underwriting

After the information on the loan application has been validated, the value of the property has been confirmed, and the title search has been completed, the loan is ready to be underwritten. Usually, a trained professional reviews all of the information, analyzes the credit worthiness of the borrower, and renders a decision on the loan request. Increasingly, much of the analytical tasks of underwriting are performed by technology through artificial intelligence and use of databases. There are generally secondary market underwriting guidelines, but many variables are considered in the analysis.

Monthly Housing Expenses and Total Debt Obligations

One of the first things an underwriter determines is the borrower's proposed monthly housing expenses and total monthly debt obligations

Housing expenses

These include the monthly principal and interest payments that are stipulated on the mortgage note. In addition, the monthly housing expenses include a monthly amount for the property taxes and hazard insurance (1/12 of the annual taxes and insurance). There may be other expenses, such as condominium fees, homeowners fees, special assessments, etc. that are included.

Monthly debt obligations

These include monthly credit obligations, such as installment payments, revolving charge cards, or other borrower obligations that will continue longer than 10 months. Usually, 5% of the current balance of a revolving charge account is used for the monthly payment.

Funds to Close

When the proposed loan is being used to finance the purchase of a home, underwriters will determine the source of funds for the down payment and closing costs. The following are acceptable sources of funds for closing:

- *Cash.* Cash in any depository institution or investment company is acceptable.

- *Stocks, bonds, mutual funds, etc.* Cash equivalent investments are acceptable forms of funds. They can be validated through statements from investment companies for the last two months.
- *Sale of existing property.* Many a times the source of funds for the down payment on a home comes from the equity in a property that will be sold. The sales price of the property being sold is indicated on the loan application and any existing loan is verified on the credit report or through a verification of previous mortgage.
- *Gift from family members.* Gifts from family members for the down payment and/or closing costs are acceptable so long as there is no requirement for repayment. Some loan programs limit the amount of gift funds allowed.

Credit Analysis

Another very important part of the underwriting process is determining the credit worthiness of the borrower. Loan underwriters review the borrower's credit report to find evidence of debt repayment behavior. Some of the important areas that are reviewed are:

- Past and existing mortgage debt. The past repayment history on mortgage debt can be a good indication of a borrowers attitude toward mortgage obligations. A good payment history on mortgage debt is very important in the credit analysis. Generally, payments received 30 days past the due date are reflected in the credit report as late. Lenders vary in strictness, and some may not allow any late mortgage payments, while others will allow one or two in the last two years if there is a good explanation.
- Installment and revolving credit. Other items on the credit report can also indicate a borrower's attitude toward credit obligations. Credit reports indicate the outstanding balance, current balance, and terms of payment on the borrower's revolving and installment debt. Underwriters review these credit obligations to determine the borrower's patterns of credit use and repayment behavior. Revolving credit encompasses department store and bank credit cards. Installment credit encompasses longer-term credit with structured payment plans, such as car loans. Generally, underwriters are not concerned over isolated and minor slow payments indicated on the credit report.
- Collections, repossession, foreclosures and bankruptcies. Credit reports also indicate public records such as collections, repossessions, foreclosures, and bankruptcies. Though these items may indicate past credit problems, they sometimes have valid explanations. Underwriters may require a letter of explanation on items noted in the public records. Many a times consumers have re-established credit and have an excellent payment history on their current obligations.

Appraisal

Generally, underwriters are not professional appraisers and do not re-appraise the property. They will review the appraisal to assure that it meets the requirements of the investor and sometimes request additional information to substantiate the value. They may request that a second appraisal or review appraisal be performed. If they believe that the value cannot be substantiated, a review appraisal can be completed from a site inspection or review of the written appraisal. In both the cases, another professional appraiser will perform the review.

Compensating Factors

The underwriters consider many variables in their analysis. No two borrowers have the same credit and income profiles and underwriters use all of the information in the loan file to render a decision. Many a times, borrowers fall outside the guidelines, but have strong compensating factors that reflect low credit risk. Some compensating factors are history of savings, long-term job stability, history of making monthly credit payments that equal or exceed the proposed payments, a substantial down payment, or a large cash reserve after the close of escrow.

Loan Approval

After the underwriter has reviewed the entire loan package, there can be four outcomes:

- *Approval.* If the loan is "picture perfect" and the underwriter has no questions, the loan will be approved with no conditions.
- *Approved with conditions (the most common response).* There are two types of conditional approvals:
    - If the underwriter needs additional documentation before a final credit decision can be made, a "prior to document" conditional approval will be rendered. In essence, the loan documents will not be prepared until the condition has been satisfactorily met. An example of a "prior to document" condition could be a pay stub to validate the borrowers income.
    - If the loan can be approved, but a condition must be met prior to closing, a "prior to funding" conditional approval will be rendered. In this case, the loan documents will be prepared and will be sent to the closing agent, but the lender will not fund the loan until the condition has been met. An example of a "prior to closing" conditional approval could be proof of sale of existing home where the equity will be used as the down payment.
- *Suspended.* Sometimes the underwriter will be unable to make a decision on a loan file because it is either incomplete or there are many unanswered questions. In these cases, the underwriter will ask for additional information from the borrower before an underwriting decision is made. An example of a suspension may be large gaps in the borrower's previous employment history and no tax returns to indicate the place of employment.
- *Denial.* Underwriters will be unable to approve a loan if the loan file has substantial deficiencies and does not meet the minimum standards of the lender or the lender's secondary market investors. Most of the lenders require that a second underwriter review the loan package before a final denial is communicated to the borrower. Denial letters with the reason for denial are sent to borrowers within three days of the final credit decision. The underwriting criterion can be different among lenders and a borrower may find other acceptable alternatives in the market place.

Loan Closing Process

After the borrower has been approved, the legal documents required for the loan closing are prepared by the lender and forwarded to the closing agent. Before funds are released to the closing agent, the borrower must sign the loan documents and meet any conditions required by the lender. The lender will submit instructions to the closing agent that outline the procedure and conditions for loan closing. Closing agents can be title companies, escrow companies and lawyers. Each lender may have its unique instructions (lenders instructions) for loan closing and each state may differ on some of the legal requirements. There are several major documents that are included for all closings.

Required Documents for Loan Closing

Mortgage note. The mortgage note outlines the amount of the debt, the terms and payments, the interest rate, margins and caps for adjustable rate mortgages (ARM's), the name of the lender (beneficiary), the name of the borrower (mortgagor), and any other material item required by the lender. The borrower(s) must sign the note.

Security instrument — Deed of trust/mortgage. A deed of trust is an instrument given by the borrower to a third party (trustee) vesting title to the property in the trustee as security for the borrower's repayment of the mortgage loan. A mortgage is the conveyance of interest in real estate used as security for repayment of a note. Depending on the state and customs within that state, one of these instruments is generally used as security for the mortgage note. In the event a borrower defaults on the note, the security instrument outlines the legal procedure enabling the lender to take ownership of the property. Usually, the security instrument is recorded as a public document.

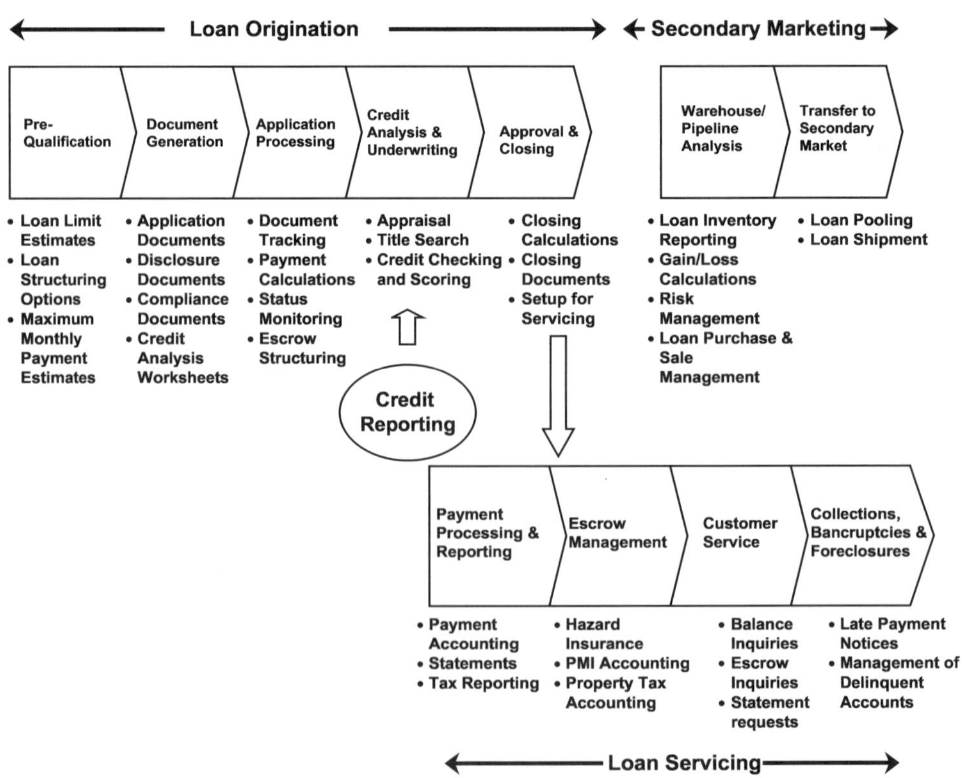

- *Deed of trust riders.* When the mortgage loan is an adjustable rate mortgage, lenders require a rider that is recorded along with the security instrument.
- *Truth in lending statement* — Regulation Z. The lender will provide an updated Truth and Lending Statement to reflect the actual costs of the loan and indicate the annual percentage rate.
- *Closing statement* — HUD 1. After the loan has closed, the closing agent will provide a closing statement document that outlines the final costs of the loan. The borrowers can expect to receive this document within three to five days after loan closing.

Appendix G: Top Loan Originators in 2003

		(in millions)
1.	Wells Fargo Home Mortgage	$470,119
2.	Washington Mutual	435,391
3.	Countrywide Financial Corp.	434,864
4.	Chase Home Finance	284,257
5.	Bank of America	140,937
		(in millions)
6.	ABN Amro Mortgage	124,048
7.	GMAC Residential Holdings	114,455
8.	CitiMortgage, Inc.	108,433
9.	National City Mortgage	105,561
10.	Cendant Mortgage	68,759

[From "Top Mortgage Originators," National Mortgage News, 19 March 2004, http://www.nationalmortgagenews.com/mortgagestats/freedata/orig.htm.]

Appendix H: Alternate Mortgage Information Chain from the Tower Group

Jacobides, Michael, "Where Do Markets Come From?" Center for the Network Economy CNE WP, June 2002.

CHAPTER 9

BUSINESS CONTINUITY AND TECHNOLOGY IN THE RETAIL SECTOR

UDAY S. KARMARKAR and VANDANA MANGAL

Summary

This study examines business continuity in the retail sector. The findings are from a mail survey, case studies and secondary research. An economic framework is also developed for business continuity in retail.

The study found that retail organizations are aware of the need for business continuity, the greater attention being given to information technology. The events of 11 September have not had a major impact on business continuity planning in retail organizations. There might have been a short period when organizations paid greater attention to business continuity. However, that spike has now disappeared.

Retail organizations display certain characteristic features that appear to diminish the incentives for continuity planning. The assets of retailing firms are primarily in the form of inventories, which tend to be geographically dispersed. This provides automatic protection against many kinds of disruptive events. Since the inventories are part of a flow of sales, they do not have long-term asset value. In other words, they are replaceable. Inventories are typically covered by insurance, which adequately protects retail organizations against the monetary impact of losses.

Retail organizations also have some informational assets. The preferred mode of managing informational assets has shifted from paper to telecommunications technologies. As a result, with better telecommunications technologies and lower storage costs, the risk to informational assets has reduced.

9.1. Introduction

Business continuity (sometimes referred to as business continuance) describes the processes and procedures an organization puts in place to ensure that essential functions can continue during and after a disaster http://searchstorage.techtarget.com/sDefinition/0,,sid5_gci801381,00.html.

Disasters can be caused by any of the following:

- Natural causes such as floods, fires and earthquakes;
- System related causes such as network problems, power and telecommunication failures; or,

- Human and malicious causes such as hackers, viruses, terrorism, disaffected employees and theft.

Most of the people think in terms of fire, flood or some other major events when they consider risks from disasters. In reality, it is the small events that have a higher likelihood of interrupting normal business operations. In fact, catastrophes usually start out as small occurrences and if not handled appropriately, end up being major disasters. Some recent examples of disasters are listed below:

- The three-day Microsoft web site outage disaster in January 2001.
- Denial-of-service attacks on various organizations at various times.
- Limited capacity causing spikes in business volumes due to a fashion show event as in the case of Victoria's Secret Retailer.
- Application failure as with the London Stock Exchange outage in April 2000.
- Partner/outsourcer unavailability such as ISP network failure.
- Loss of physical structures such as those due to fire at the Los Alamos National Laboratory.

A Gartner Dataquest research (Wheatman, 2001) on application downtimes found that 40% of downtimes (on an average) occur due to application failures such as performance issues or 'bugs', 40% due to operator error, and about 20% due to system or environmental failures. About 60% of the failures in the latter category are due to hardware problems. Overall, less than 5% of application downtimes are caused by disasters. These are shown in Fig. 9.1.

The question then is why the 5% downtime caused by disasters is of concern. A survey conducted by InformationWeek Research (Eric and Martin, 2001) on downtime and business continuity in organizations reported that 25% of the participating firms had to invoke their business continuity plans in the past year, with 70% reporting the disaster as severe or extremely severe. Therefore, in spite of major disasters occurring infrequently, being prepared for disasters and having a plan for business continuance are critical for all companies.

The downtime in organizations can result in negative media coverage in addition to loss of large sums of money, which can impact a company's image, loss of customer confidence and in some extreme cases, the company's very existence. Losses due to downtime to businesses in some sectors are listed in Table 9.1. These numbers do not take into account effects such as the impact to company reputation and loss of customer confidence.

Given the extensive losses a business can incur due to just 1 h of downtime, it is critical for today's businesses to plan and prepare for business continuity in the event of a disaster. Business continuity planning (BCP) with the focus on technology is discussed in the paper. Whether organizations have begun started paying greater attention to

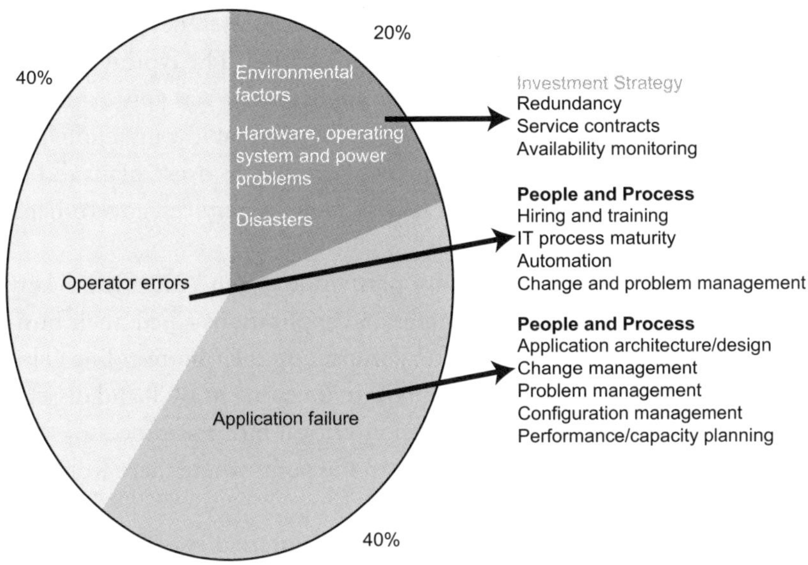

Fig. 9.1. Causes of application downtimes (Source: Gartner Research[9]).

Table 9.1. Cost of downtime for some sectors (Source: Dataquest).

Industry	Business operation	Average cost/hour of downtime
Financial	Brokerage operations	$6.45 million
Financial	Credit card / sales authorization	$2.6 million
Transportation	Airline	$89,500
Transportation	Shipping	$26,000
Retail	Catalog sales	$90,000

business continuity after the events of 11 September or if the attention was just a spike is also considered. An economic framework is developed for BCP and a survey of retail organizations is conducted.

The rest of the paper is organized as follows. Section 9.2 describes BCP. Section 9.3 discusses business continuity in retail. Section 9.4 describes an economic framework for BCP. The results are described in Sec. 9.5 and Sec. 9.6 brings out the conclusions.

9.2. Business Continuity Planning (BCP)

BCP aims to prevent the interruption of mission-critical services, and to return to normal functioning smoothly and as soon as possible. BCP in the early 1990s was focused primarily on disaster recovery. Disaster recovery deals primarily with information technology systems and applications. In the event of a major disaster, networks, applications, systems and data had to be recovered at another location. The typical recovery time objective (RTO — the desired time to recover applications) was approximately three days; the typical recovery point objective (RPO — the acceptable transaction loss) was 24 h. Most of the organizations that implemented disaster recovery plans did so because they were in highly regulated industries such as financial services, government, healthcare or utilities.

BCP gathered momentum in the late 1990s, partly due to the Y2K crisis. Many businesses began to understand that if their systems and applications failed, their business processes would fail along with them, thereby impacting their bottom line. This provided the needed incentive for organizations to begin investing in BCP and disaster recovery between 1997 and 2000. RTOs for mission-critical business processes were reduced to as little as 24 h and RPOs were often set to the point where there would be zero transactions lost.

The growing interdependencies among organizations' internal systems and their contractors' systems began to increase the complexity of recovery in the event of a disaster. In addition, the advent of the internet and e-business in 1999 changed the way businesses thought of BCP. Businesses began integrating their business processes with those of their customers, suppliers and business partners resulting in further reduction of RTOs and RPOs for mission-critical applications.

Business continuity awareness has increased tremendously, since the terrorist attacks of 11 September 2001 in the United States. This caused an increase in disaster recovery and business continuity budgets immediately following the event. Many organizations have assigned dedicated business continuity coordinators or directors and have involved high-level nonIT decision makers in BCP. In a survey conducted for Information Week Research (Encore Consulting Group), of 250 IT and business managers responsible for BCP, Price Waterhouse and Coopers found that over half of the managers reported that their organizations are likely to increase BCP spending. According to Meta Group http://www.equant.com/content/xml/connectonline_june_business_continuity.xml, BCP and disaster recovery budget numbers are expected to approach to 5% of IT budgets by 2005.

However, in spite of increase in BCP awareness since 9/11, studies reported that two-thirds of the thousands of businesses they surveyed did not have BCPs and even among the businesses that did, four-fifths had never tested their plans. Of the companies that had tested their plans, only 17% of the plans had passed.

9.2.1. *What does BCP involve?*

Although companies may follow different processes for BCP, most of the businesses typically use a methodology similar to that listed in Table 9.2. The table shows that

Table 9.2. BCP methodology (Source: http://www.equent.com/content/xml/connectonline_june_business_continuity.xml).

Step 1	*Developing the foundation*
Audit analysis	Identification of the enterprise's assets, which will include, but not be limited to, people, facilities, business applications, processes, and IT systems (hardware, software, files, and communications)
Risk analysis	Identification of the threats, mitigating factors, and dependencies, including the definition of the types and scope of disruptive events
Business impact analysis (BIA)	Measure of the operating, financial, legal, and regulatory impacts of a disruption to an enterprise's operation — identification of the critical business functions and the costs of downtime for each asset. Definition of RPO and RTO objectives for each asset and the prioritization of assets into defined categories, such as critical, vital, sensitive, and noncritical
Step 2	*Developing the plan*
Funding approval	Commitment and financial approval from senior management
Review existing plans	Incorporation and adoption of proven best practices within the enterprise
Recovery strategy	Definition of the continuity model, tasks, processes, technology, roles, and resources required to meet stated RPO and RTO objectives and prioritization levels — forming the plans for disaster recovery, business resumption, business recovery, and contingency
Step 3	*Maintaining the plan*
Training	Creation of awareness and knowledge of the plan
Testing	Continuous testing against the plan, review of results, and modification appropriately
Keeping informed	Update of plan to reflect changes in the enterprise's assets or operational, financial, legal or regulatory environment

BCP is a three-step process that includes analysis, plan execution, and plan maintenance. Business Impact Analysis (BIA) is the most important step during analysis. BCP may be done in-house, by working with consultants who specialize in BCP initially and later managing the plan in-house or by contracting the entire process to an external entity.

9.2.2. *Technology in business continuity*

Although business continuity is important for any business, it may be practical only for the largest organizations to maintain a full functioning plan throughout a disaster crisis. For all other organizations, the first step in BCP should be to decide which of

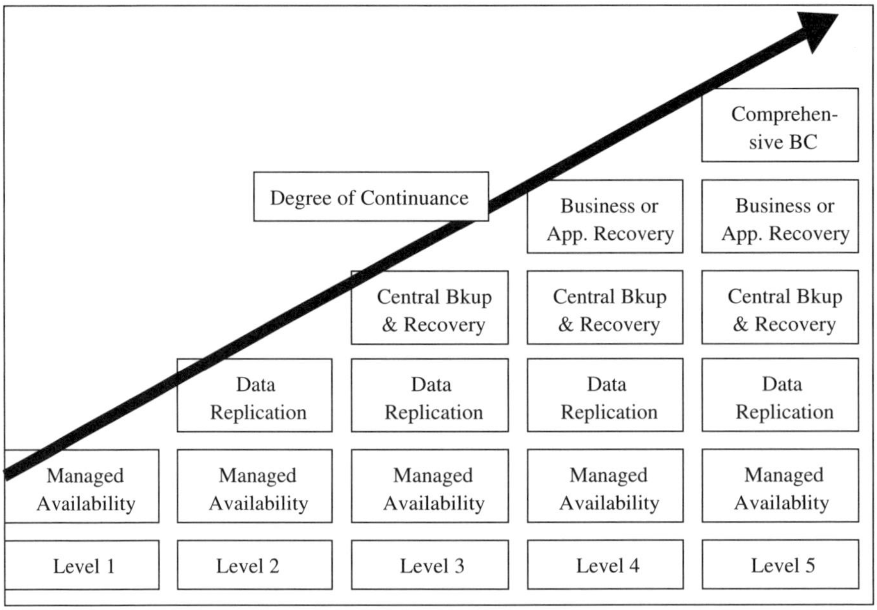

Fig. 9.2. Degree of continuance in the event of a disaster (Source: Erikson, 2002).

the organization's functions are essential, and to assign the available budget for these functions accordingly.

The level of information that will be available after a disaster will be proportional to the degree of continuance an organization has planned for. As shown in Fig. 9.2 above, the degree of continuance is lowest at Level 1 and highest at Level 5.

Several alternatives are available for the recovery of data and applications (information) in the event of a disaster. These are discussed in Sec. 9.2.3 below.

9.2.3. *Recovery alternatives*

The recovery alternatives are listed below. The definitions are from Gartner (Noakes-Fry, and Diamond 2004a,b). Off-site data storage is the most basic solution, which is used by most of the organizations today. Cold and hot sites are also maintained by several organizations today, although these are more expensive to develop and maintain.

- Off-site data storage. Storage on tape or disk to a different physical location. Depending on the budget and geographical risks, off-site storage could be the building next door, a bank safety deposit box, or the branch office across town. A better choice is a secure, climate-controlled, fireproof media vault at a storage facility maintained by a commercial media storage provider.

- Disk-to-disk remote copy. Operates at the disk volume level and is significantly less complex to set up and administer than host-based replication. This is the most popular solution used today. The solution benefits from capturing all application environment changes. A drawback, however, is the lack of transaction knowledge and the potential for data corruption in the event of a disaster. Most of the disk-to-disk remote copy solutions operate in synchronous mode, which degrades the performance of production applications unless the solution can be deployed over fiber link to the recovery site. The distance can generally be from a few kilometers up to about 60 km.
- Cold site. Empty, environmentally conditioned computer room with office space, telephone jacks, etc. ready for the computer equipment to be moved in. The cold site is available on a subscription basis, much more cheaper than a hot site, but because the customer provides and installs all the equipments needed to continue operations, it takes longer to get an enterprise in full operation after the disaster. Often such an equipment is provided through a contract with an equipment leasing company.
- Hot site. Fully equipped, operationally ready data center offering specific hardware platforms ready for almost immediate use when the service provider is notified of a disaster. A hot site has all the equipments needed for the enterprise to continue operation, including office space and furniture, telephone jacks, and computer equipment. Employees report to work at the hot site instead of the usual location. Subscriptions to commercial hot sites are based on the hardware specifications and generally allow hot site use for up to eight weeks in disaster mode.
- Electronic vaulting (or advanced recovery services). Data sent directly from the subscriber site to the hot site. This costly service requires that a direct-access storage device (DASD) be dedicated to the subscriber, preventing the service from being shared with other subscribers. PC/LAN electronic data vaulting is emerging as a popular service.
- Shadowing. Maintains a replica of the database and/or file systems, typically by continuously capturing changes and applying them to the recovery site. Shadowing is an asynchronous process, thus requiring less network bandwidth than synchronous mirroring. The RTO is relatively small, typically 1–8 h, while the RPO is as up-to-date as the last receipt.
- Mirroring. Maintains a replica of databases and/or file systems by applying changes at the secondary site in lock step with or synchronous to changes at the primary site. Due to its synchronous nature, mirroring requires significantly greater network bandwidth than shadowing. The RTO is around 20 min to several hours, while the RPO is reduced to the loss of uncommitted work.

The above recovery solutions can be provided by any of the major BCP players in the market today.

9.2.4. *Major players in BCP*

Today, the major players in BCP are:

- IBM (Noakes-Fry and Diamond, 2004a)
- HP (http://www.hp.com/hps/tech/continuity/)
- Sunguard (http://www.availability.sungard.com/Products+And+Services/Business+Continuity/)

In addition to providing complete solutions, some of them such as IBM also provide consulting services. Several consulting companies that specialize in BCP also exist. Specialized solutions are also offered by the sector. The retail sector is discussed in the rest of the paper.

9.3. Business Continuity in the Retail Sector

The retail industry has traditionally been slower to adopt BCP . This has been in spite of point-of-purchase vulnerabilities prevalent throughout their processes and flow of information in the supply chain. The costs have been considered the biggest barrier to the slow acceptance of BCP in retail. The retail is a business that is mission-critical and its applications need to be available 24/7. The retailers also cannot afford to lose any data.

The supply chain for retail has several points (from store to distribution to Head Quarters) at which disasters can occur. Some of these points include (Encore Consulting Group):

- Credit and debit card systems function so not alienate customers.
- Digital signatures.
- Bar code scanning (pricing errors, customer dissatisfaction, customer alienation).
- Ordering.
- Receiving.
- Moving to shop floor.
- Paperless and wireless warehouse.
- Dispatch.

In retail, downtime can cause an organization as much loss as $100,000/hour on an average (as reported in Table 9.2 above).

9.3.1. *Research methodology*

To understand the business continuity initiatives and practices in retail organizations, a survey was conducted. Each subject in the study was an independent organizational entity which controls its own information technology and information policy and has a CIO or a similar management position within it. It is highly likely that since the subject organization is able to make its own technology decisions (and investments) that it will have profit and loss responsibility, although this is not necessarily always the case. The surveys were addressed to the CIO (or similar position) as the person most likely to be knowledgeable about the subject.

The following steps were followed in the compilation of the survey:

- Issues relevant to business continuity in retail were identified. Some of these issues include whether organizations have BCPs, who implements them, who leads their execution, how they are communicated to the employees and who other than the internal organization is included in the plans.
- A business continuity questionnaire was compiled based on these issues.
- A database containing the names and contact information for the relevant officers in retail organizations was procured. The database contains names and contact information for CIO and similar officers in the retail sector for 2000 organizations.
- A package with the questionnaire and a cover letter explaining the study was mailed to the retail organizations in the United States and Canada.

The survey could be taken on paper or online. An online version of the questionnaire was developed using a survey tool called Zoomerang. The online version was available at http://www.anderson.ucla.edu/bit.xml.

In addition to surveys, a limited number of case studies were conducted to obtain an in-depth understanding of the issues in retail. Executives and Managers who head the major divisions in their organizations were interviewed. The focus was on understanding the critical processes in these retail organizations and on business continuity.

9.4. An Economic Framework for Business Continuity Planning

BCP can be framed in terms of a decision-making process that trades off the potential cost and risk of unforeseen events against the costs of protecting against the consequences of those events. In this sense, BCP is analogous to other forms of risk management including insurance, hedging, or planning against random failures. The frameworks, models, and techniques that are used in these well-developed areas (risk analysis, failure trees and event analysis, reliability methods, insurance, financial risk management) are all applicable to varying degrees. Here, we will not survey all these methodologies and their potential applications. Rather we will outline the major characteristics of BCP, and also consider some of the special aspects of BCP in the retailing sector.

The elements of the problem include, the causative events, the consequences or outcomes, and the losses that are associated with these outcomes for the business. In general, while the causative events can be of many types, they are all characterized by the low probability of occurrence in any given time period, and randomness with respect to the time when the event will occur. Forecasting these events first requires estimating the distribution of time till the next occurrence of each event. Since the events are random low probability occurrences, an exponential distribution is likely to suffice for most of the cases. The complementary information that is required is the cost impact of each event, which may also be a random variable. A typical model for the magnitude of the loss would be a distribution such as the log-normal, reflecting the nature of losses, which are likely to be heavily skewed. On the basis of these, the expected present value of the costs due to the causative events can be estimated, along with the risk (e.g., the variance of costs incurred or other measures of risk).

The next part of BCP analysis would be to list all the protective measures that can be taken with respect to each category of outcome. These measures can include a large variety of possible actions directed towards each kind of event, including approaches for the minimization of costs, and working towards recovery from the event.

This is a very general model. The analytical methods involved are well-known from the disciplines mentioned earlier. Applying it is a lengthy process because of the large number and variety of causative events that might be relevant, and the number and complexity of different outcomes, consequences and costs, which may all be uncertain. Here, we do not go into the technical details of modeling events, consequences, the efficacy of different activities, or the choice problem of which activity to implement. Rather we describe the characteristics of the planning issues for companies in the retail sector.

The losses related to outcomes can be broadly classified into the categories of:

- lost assets (physical, information);
- lost productive time and lost revenues due to the breakdown of systems, or due to damage or danger at retail sites; and
- lost goodwill or lost customers, due to a period in which customers experience either direct costs, or perhaps simply a lack of access to goods and services.

For the retailing sector, the major assets at risk are physical. The large part of these is inventories of goods in transportation pipelines, in storage (warehouses) or at retail locations. For many firms, the inventories tend to be geographically dispersed. As a result, the risk of loss is greatly reduced through diversification, since the causative events (disasters, attacks) are usually geographically localized. Of course, there are some events that can affect all inventory sites (as for example, a national crisis such as a war) but such an eventuality could be considered to lie outside the scope of BCP.

The inventory assets also have the characteristic that they are part of a flow of goods through the company. The implication is that the assets are held temporarily, and that they have no unique long-term value. In other words, they are replaceable, either in kind or in cash. As a result, traditional insurance works to cover company risks.

Retail companies do not tend to have large information assets (unlike say financial services companies, or media companies). However, we note that modern information technologies have resulted in a shift of information storage and processing from paper to electronic form. From a BCP perspective, the result is a centralization of information and information processing assets. However, the same modern technologies also make it very simple to protect against excessive decentralization, through a number of means, including simple duplication of data and systems.

The next major category of risk is that of lost productive time. Over a short-term period, the major operating concerns in retailing (apart from immediate disaster management) have to do with information flows between vendors, inventory and logistics systems, and retail locations, which in turn have value because they relate to physical flows and financial commitments (invoices, purchasing documents, orders). Here, information technologies permit a decoupling between physical working space for staff, and the information systems required. Thus (as illustrated in one case study), all that is necessary to provide a back up working environment is a set of workstations, that can be connected through telecommunications, to the relevant information systems.

The issue of lost retailing time, and temporary loss of access by customers, is a physical issue. For retailers, geographical dispersion is again a saving grace that reduces risks. There are clearly a number of systems and procedures that are required at each retail store location. However, for the most part, the kinds of threats and disruptions that affect these sites are not new to the industry. As a result, we do not see any major change in practice from traditional approaches.

In the future, it is likely that there will be some shift in retailing from bricks and mortar to web-based sales. As this shift occurs, there will be a corresponding centralization of systems, and a concentration of risk in the direction of web sites, and the internet infrastructure. Physical inventories will also become more centralized. As an example, one of our retailers, now sees about 10% of it's sales occurring on the web, which corresponds to about 40 or so physical stores. Overall, this is really a reduction in the magnitude of risk in terms of physical assets, since the increased risk in centralized inventories is offset by the benefits of pooling inventories. There is also a shift of risk from physical events at the level of stores and storage facilities, to the risk of failure of the telecommunications infrastructure and information systems. However, protecting against problems in these systems is much simpler and well organized. In many cases, third party service providers already have many safeguards in place.

In future research, we will be developing a formal model of continuity planning and risk management that can be applied to any industry, to determine the best approaches to BCP for a given company in a given sector.

9.5. Summary of Survey and Case Results

The survey responses were analyzed and compiled. The results are discussed below.

- 45% of the respondents currently have a BCP, 30% are developing plans, and 25% will develop plans. None of the respondents intend to develop any plans.
- E-mails, group meetings, and corporate presentations are the most popular methods of communicating BCPs plans to the employees. Written documentation as in binders is also used by almost 20% of the respondents for communication of plans.
- Most of the respondents develop the requirements for business continuity and network/IT security needs in-house with some of the respondents developing them with the help of a third party.
- CIO's or CFO's generally oversee the BCP process. BCPs are generally implemented by the CIO or the IT Director/Manager.
- Phones/cell phones/pagers are listed as the most popular method of communicating with employees in the event of a disaster followed by e-mail.
- Although most of the organizations review their plans and conduct recovery exercises annually, several respondents have never tested their plans and do not plan to test them in the future.
- Among various technology options for disaster recovery, almost all of the respondents have offsite data storage; the numbers for other technology options are not as high although some of the respondents have mirroring.
- About a third of the respondents involve their IT departments in business continuity recovery. Interestingly, 20% include internal business organizations and 24% include vendors. However, only 12% include suppliers, and 10% include contractors. None of the respondents use offshore contractors for business continuity recovery.
- Most of the respondents use workplace assessment as the risk assessment method (38.2%) followed closely by quantitative risk assessment (35.3%).

The findings from the case studies were also compiled. Mini case studies are described in the Appendix. The review of case studies in retail showed that although most of the organizations agree that business continuity is important, businesses have not allocated large budgets for it. The only aspect of business continuity that has been prepared for in organizations is technology and data retrieval. The most popular method used is offsite backups. Most of the organizations also have cold sites and some also have hot sites. The executives of the three companies discussed on the mini cases as mentioned in the Appendix felt that they were reasonably prepared for a disaster and would be able to have their operations up and running within a short period of time. Two of the three corporations have also been planning to set up backup data warehouses and data centers in different time zones to ensure business continuity in case of a catastrophe. In general, retail companies are somewhat protected in the event of a disaster due to their stores being geographically distributed. The main warehouse is the main concern in terms of physical assets in retail.

9.6. Conclusions

The main conclusions from the survey, case studies and economic framework, are:

(i) The assets of retailing firms are primarily in the form of inventories.
(ii) These assets (inventories) tend to be geographically dispersed which provides automatic protection against many kinds of disruptive events.
(iii) Since the inventories are part of a flow of sales, they do not have long-term asset value. In other words, they are replaceable.
(iv) Inventories are typically covered by insurance, which protects adequately against the monetary impact of losses.
(v) The retail sector has not seen many new developments in the management of these assets. This is partly because recent events such as the terrorist attack of 11 September are not seen as having created any new kinds of risks for retail. However, this may be a somewhat myopic view; were there a disruption of say port facilities due to terrorism, then there would be an impact on the flow of goods, which would be quite significant.
(vi) Retail organizations also have some informational assets. The preferred mode of managing informational assets has shifted from paper to telecommunications technologies. With better telecommunications technologies and lower storage costs, the risk to informational assets has reduced.
(vii) The events of 11 September have not had a major impact on BCP in organizations. There might have been a short period when organizations paid greater attention to business continuity. However, that spike has now disappeared.
(viii) Although disasters such as 11 September are given great importance in the media, 95% of the downtimes in organizations (retail or otherwise) are caused by local factors and events that are not unforeseen. These factors include floods, fires, viruses, disaffected employees, theft, and telecommunication failures.
(ix) Organizations are aware of the need for business continuity. However, although most of the organizations have some sort of disaster recovery plans, they tend to emphasize on the information technology side, other aspects of the organization such as employees and physical structures are not always included.
(x) Even among the organizations that have BCPs, the plans are not tested and updated on a regular basis.
(xi) Among the factors cited as the reasons for the lack of well-developed BCPs, cost is the major issue.

Acknowledgments

The authors of this report would like to thank the AT&T Foundation for their support to this study.

Bibliography

1. Encore Consulting Group. Retail business continuity and disaster recovery. http://www.emc.com/pdf/vertical/retail_bc_dr.pdf.
2. Eric, C and G Martin (2001). Playing for keeps. *InformationWeek*. http://www.informationweek.com/shared/printableArticle.jhtml?articleID=6507804.
3. Erikson, T (2002). Business continuity and disaster recovery. http://www.acmsyr.org/Meetings/Meeting%20Materials%202002/Program_02_10.pdf.
4. http://searchstorage.techtarget.com/sDefinition/0,,sid5_gci801381,00.html.
5. http://www.equant.com/content/xml/connectonline_june_business_continuity.xml.
6. http://www.hp.com/hps/tech/continuity/.
7. http://www.availability.sungard.com/Products+And+Services/Business+Continuity/.
8. Mac, NA (2002). High availability: Views from European end users. Gartner Report. http://gartner.library.ucla.edu/research/108600/108611/108611.html.
9. Noakes-Fry, K and T Diamond (2004a). IBM business continuity and recovery services. Gartner Research. http://gartner.library.ucla.edu/research/90800/90811/90811.html.
10. Noakes-Fry, K and T Diamond (2004b). Business continuity and recovery products and services: overview. Gartner Report. http://gartner.library.ucla.edu/research/100800/100862/100862.html#h6.
11. Wheatman, V (2001). Aftermath: disaster recovery. Gartner Research. http://gartner.library.ucla.edu/research/101100/101102/101102.html.

Appendix: Mini Cases

Two case studies have been conducted. The first is for a teen clothing and accessory retail chain. This is called Company A for the purpose of this report. The second company called Company B in this report is a specialty grocery store chain.

Company A

Company A is a clothing and accessory retailer for male and female teens. It is a growing company. It was started as one store in one mall. The company now has almost 500 stores across the United States. In the 15 years since Company A was started, their revenues have grown from under $1 million to $443 million.

The clothing retailer distinguishes themselves from other teen fashion stores by keeping music as the focal point of their merchandise. Over the years, styles have taken an alternative focus, covering genres like gothic, metal and punk rock, mirroring the tastes of Company A's customer base. The styles are based on the latest bands and their music.

Company A has realized that their customers can help them determine trends. They use several different methods to obtain information from their teen customers. These are listed below:

- report cards are available in all their stores for customers to fill out;
- store employees are encouraged to call in with trends they observe or hearing about from their customers;
- a "Mouth Off" section on their website sends feedback directly to the relevant department in the company; and
- company buyers ensure that they are everywhere the music is, including concerts to see and hear teenagers and bands' clothing and accessories.

In addition to their regular store, Company A also has an internet store which is equivalent to 16 mall stores in terms of the volume they handle. Online, Company A has tried to recreate the community feeling by adding additional features to their site including: streaming music, band reviews, upcoming musical events, polls and a feedback/chat forum called the Mouth Off section. The website is also used for marketing. Registered users receive e-mails of upcoming events as well as new themes and products. The underlying technology is performed entirely in-house including web hosting.

Company A has recently contracted their BCP to a consulting firm. The firm is responsible for putting the systems and processes in place to keep the company running in the event of a natural or man-made catastrophe. This includes communication to and from stores, the distribution network, the electronic network and all other home office functions. Currently, the electronic network is the only segment of the business with any notable contingency planning, having redundant database storage although no offsite redundant web servers. The data center also currently lacks redundant load balancers or routers for the internet operation. This means that if customer traffic significantly increased or servers went down, then company A could temporarily not take orders from customers online. Onsite, motor generators have been installed for the data center which is protected by FM200 fire suppression and an internal air conditioning unit. However, if an event prevented access to the home office, and therefore DC and data center, merchandise orders cannot be processed and products cannot be shipped out.

The scope of their BCP will encompass their headquarters and warehouse/distribution center. A program will also be rolled out to the retail stores throughout the country. The company plans is to determine the risks to the company and to develop a plan that will cover people, technology, warehouse and their computer systems in the event of a disaster. Their plan is to keep all these procedures documented in a manual. This manual will also identify recovery team members, call lists, resources and additional information needed for a successful recovery. Restoration and salvage considerations will also be included.

A crisis communication program to deal with the press and to communicate with employees and their families, key customers, critical suppliers, corporate management and owners/stakeholders is also planned. They also have plans to train staff on the contingency procedures and responsibilities during a disaster for business continuance. Although IT is involved in the BCP process, a special coordinator has been assigned for this purpose.

In summary, Company A has realized the need for BCP. They are working with a consulting group to put together their BCPs and have plans of developing a complete company wide BCP.

Company B

The second case study is for a "natural and specialty foods" grocery store chain. Company B was started over 45 years ago as a chain of convenience stores in Southern California. About 10 years later, to enhance their image, they started carrying boutique wines and gourmet foods at exceptional prices. Now, they have almost 200 stores in 17 states in the United States. The company has been able to develop a large customer base through reputation alone. The retailer targets young, educated buyers by focusing on what is important to them such as natural and organic foods.

Their mission still remains the same — to bring the exceptional wines and fresh, minimally processed foods and beverages to their customers at outstanding prices. Therefore, they do not compete directly with other grocery chains and have been able to carve a niche for themselves. Due to their unique business model, they are often called "store of stores".

They are able to accomplish the above business model by buying directly from suppliers whenever possible hence are able to avoid middleman costs and negotiate better with their suppliers. They buy their products in large quantities. They pay their suppliers in cash and on time so people like doing business with them. All their products are sold under their own brand. A product that is unable to pay its own way is discontinued. They also manage their packaging, distribution and advertising costs in-house. Advertising is minimal — it is done primarily by a radio spot they have or by their magazine which is available online (mailing it out for getting too expensive). All of these allow them to keep their costs low and hence prices of their products low.

They keep their customers coming back by introducing 10–15 new products each week. Taste tests are conducted before any new product is introduced.

Although they have grown to 7488 employees (as of 2001), they still maintain a small company culture that is very casual. Hawaiian shirts are the norm there from employees at the stores to the CEO himself.

Company B has a web presence. However, it does not have sell products by mail order or using e-commerce at this time. Their website is to provide "information" and serves the following purposes:

- educate and inform customers on their products;
- advertise and market their brand; and
- recruit new employees.

Their stores average about 10,000 sq. ft and they carry over 2000 private-label products.

Company B is a privately held company and is very "private". Hence, it is difficult to get their numbers. Hoover's estimates their annual sales at $1,900 million in 2001 and their one-year sales growth is 13.8%.

The business continuity is viewed as a serious issue by Company B, more on the technology front. They have a fully redundant disaster site — a hot site where several applications are minutes away from live — in their own warehouse. It is a "lights-out" facility. Some critical applications are also shadowed. Other applications are backed to tape and are kept in a vault off-site. This process is managed by a third party. These applications would be up and running in 12 h. Their warehouse is 35 miles from their headquarters. It is on a different earthquake fault than their headquarters. They are currently analyzing on how they can have this facility further away than it currently is, perhaps in a different state.

As a part of their BCP, Company B has performed BIA which has included going through various scenarios from not being able to get into their headquarters building even though the building and equipment are fully functional to if the building is destroyed. This has also included identifying the criticality of their applications and assigning RTOs and RPOs based on it. The RTO for critical applications is under 5 min. The systems for buyers are updated every 15 min. In addition to setting up the hot site facility for their systems, they have also created some extra space in the warehouse that can house 18 PCs and phones, etc. This would not be sufficient to accommodate everyone in the event of a disaster. However, it would allow the business to get started and up and running. They also have a facility that houses 30 employees in the Boston area where they will also be creating a backup site. Currently, the company has a server farm where there are redundant systems. All 200 stores are linked through the remote site as well as this site.

Their computer systems include primarily internal applications such as HR, payroll, etc. Merchandising (inventory and warehouse) is their most critical application. They have an internet presence which is primarily informational. The development, maintenance and hosting of the website is currently outsourced. They also have a backup facility. They have been reviewing the idea of bringing it in-house.

Their primarily IT oriented BC plans have been extended to take care of employees by using what they call a "red book". All IT employees carry it at all times. It contains the current phone book, vendor contacts and key employee contacts. It also contains guidelines on what to do in the event of a disaster. Most of the IT crew (including the CIO) is also trained to bring up the system if needed. They also have a PR person for their east coast and one for their west coast to handle press, etc. in the event of a disaster.

The company's view is that 9/11 has not created much change in the business environment on the security side. The occurrence of virus attacks and the impacts they have had in bringing businesses to a halt are more relevant but diverse. For instance, that did not impact business but did impact productivity was from a consultant. Since then, they have changed their practices and do not allow consultants to access their network. They have also installed greater level of security by using Microsoft's new active directory.

Overall, Company B is well-prepared for business continuity in IT and is reasonably prepared for business continuity as far as employees and facilities are concerned. Due to the nature of their business, their stores are geographically dispersed which offers them natural protection. Most of their assets are physical which are covered by insurance. Among their information systems, merchandising is the most important, which they have prepared to recover in negligible time. However, it is the occurrence of viruses rather than the events of 11 September that has caused them to increase their security and pay attention to their BCPs.

Company C

Company C owns a chain of warehouse type stores in California, Arizona, Nevada, and Florida. It sells an assortment of bulk-sized foods and related supplies designed to appeal to businesses, restaurant businesses and household customers. The company was started in the late 1800s as a single grocery store in Los Angeles and grew into a very successful wholesale grocery store chain by the turn of the century. It survived its competition by pioneering the "cash and carry" concept in Los Angeles to cut costs and by locating its stores close to business. Today, the company has 228 stores spread across in Western United States and Northern Mexico and has over $2 billion in annual revenues and provides employment to almost 5500 employees.

Although only about 1.5% of the company's workforce is (information technology) IT and less than 1% of their total budget is devoted to IT, Company C has a strong IT infrastructure, a web site where customers can purchase products online, and have also recently installed digital receipts generation capability.

The company is also prepared for disaster recovery and business continuity. They have off-site data storage (storage on tape or disk to a different physical location) and maintain some cold sites (empty computer facility ready for computer equipment to be moved in). For their critical IT functions, they also do mirroring (maintain replica of their databases/file systems by applying changes at the secondary site in lock step with or synchronous to changes at the primary site) of the data. Company C has also had electronic vaulting (data sent directly from the subscriber to the hot site) to maintain business continuity in the event of a disaster for several years from now. However, the company currently does not maintain any hot sites.

Their business continuity budget over the next few years is expected to remain steady. Company C's perspective is that business continuity awareness among organizations had increased after the happenings of 9/11. However, this awareness has now gone down. Company C believes that this heightened awareness in business continuity after 9/11 was only a spike.

Most of the company's IT functions are currently performed in-house. They have in the past tried outsourcing some of their IT functions overseas. However, that had not worked out favorably for them. However, they have expanded their sales beyond the United States to Mexico as well as Canada.

Overall, the company is very aggressive with their brand. They use various methods to promote their brand awareness. One of the big accomplishments of Company C's IT division is the successful deployment of digital receipts. They can now retrieve any one receipt, which would take them 11 h to retrieve in the manual system in 4 h 30 min. This alone has turned over the company's payment schedule from 34 days to six days. The company has also been able to cut down their labor costs significantly.

CHAPTER 10

IMPACT OF INFORMATION AND COMMUNICATION TECHNOLOGY ON INDIAN BUSINESS SECTOR — REVIEW REPORT

ATANU GHOSH and ABHIJEET KUMAR CHOUDHARY

Summary

Indian businesses during 2002–2003 were poised for a quantum leap in deployment of information and communication technologies in business practices. Computer-savvy employees, at every level, were becoming imperative, need for Decision Support Systems (DSS) and Executive information systems (ESS) were being increasingly felt across the industry. Outsourcing was limited to market research in nonIT, programming, network management, etc. within IT divisions. Functions like payroll, finance, accounting were largely being performed in-house. The advent of e-commerce has underlined the importance of investment in security tools, though advanced techniques like biometry and radio frequency identification were yet to gain a foothold in the industry. Organization websites were largely being used as platforms to provide information, except for in the financial sector, where transaction processing services were also made available through the website.

10.1. Introduction

Information and communication technologies (ICTs) are powerful tools for stimulating economic growth and social change. The quality of, and access to, information is critical to the successful application and adoption of ICTs by society. ICTs cut across all traditional sectors: health, community development, gender, governance, economic growth, and education. It can:

- Reduce business costs while opening access to new markets through electronic commerce, permitting more informed economic decisions.
- Provide access to improved education and health in remote or inaccessible areas through distance learning, telemedicine, and interactive training.
- Improve services to citizens by providing online access to government/public services; enable individuals and communities to make informed choices in the decision-making process.

Enterprise spending on ICT in India is expected to grow at 16.6% as compared to Asia Pacific growth at 7.6% in 2005. In India, $3.34 bln is the projected expenditure on hardware, an increase of 21.1% over 2004; $0.52 bln (a 16.4% increase) on software; and $2.32 bln (a 18.3% increase) on IT services out of the total $22.88 bln. Gartner said that India will remain the highest growth market for telecom with around 35 mln new subscribers in 2005, almost 25% of the new subscribers in Asia Pacific and an 18% increase from 2004.

10.2. A Glance at Information and Communication Technology — Scenario in India

10.2.1. *Information technology*

The IT industry's contribution to the Indian GDP has increased from 1.4% in 1998–1999 to 3% in 2003–2004. The composition of the Indian IT market in the year 2003–2004 is as given below (Fig. 10.1).

According to NASSCOM, the size of the Indian IT industry is around USD 19.6 Bn USD. If we talk of Software and Services alone, the size is around 15.9 Bn USD of which $3.4billion was from the domestic market. It is projected in 2004–2005 that the total revenue would amount to $20.5 billion of which $4.2 billion is expected to be from the domestic market (Fig. 10.2). The industry has recorded a growth of 30.5% in the year 2003–2004 and it is expected to grow at 30–32% in the FY2004–2005 (NASSCOM Strategic Review, 2004).

The financial services sector (IT spending by banks, insurance companies and securities firms) accounted for the largest share of Indian software and services exports at around 40% followed by manufacturing with around 12%. The emerging verticals are: Healthcare, Telecom, Retail and Government (Fig. 10.3). The emerging service

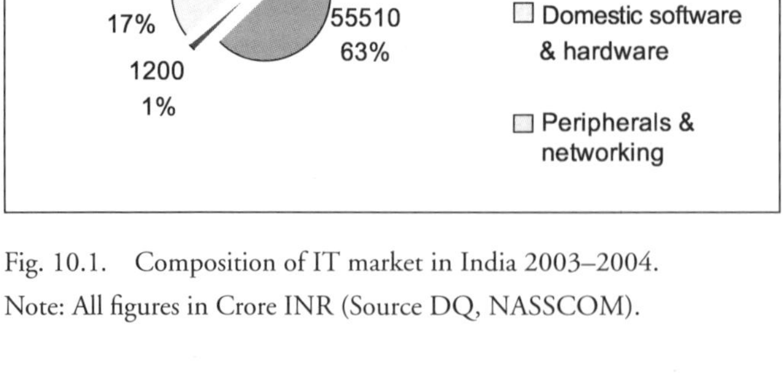

Fig. 10.1. Composition of IT market in India 2003–2004.
Note: All figures in Crore INR (Source DQ, NASSCOM).

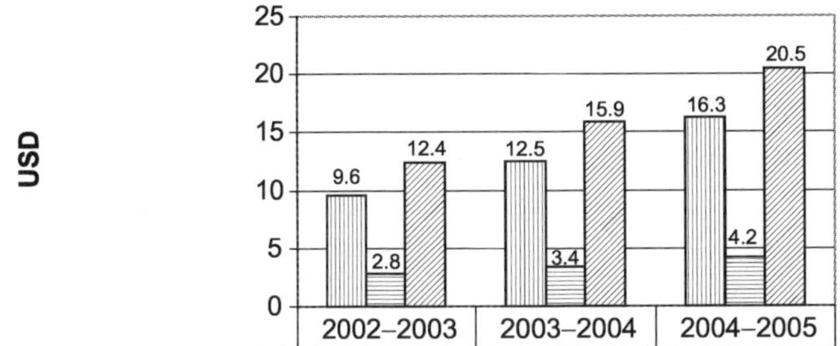

	2002–2003	2003–2004	2004–2005
Software and services exports	9.6	12.5	16.3
Domestic market	2.8	3.4	4.2
Total software and services industry	12.4	15.9	20.5

Fig. 10.2. Indian software and service industry.

lines are: IT Consulting, System integration, Network consulting and integration, Hardware Support and installation, Processing Services and IS outsourcing (UK Trade and Investment, 2003).

10.2.2. *Communication*

Indian Telecom Sector invests a sizeable amount of its revenue on IT services that comes to around 12%. This huge spending is due to revolutionary changes in telecommunication technology and the advent of mobile communications and fierce competition in the global telecom market.

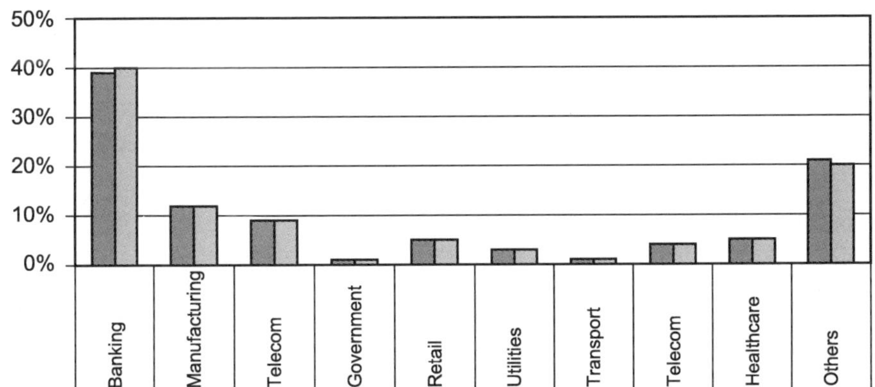

	Banking	Manufacturing	Telecom	Government	Retail	Utilities	Transport	Telecom	Healthcare	Others
2002–2003	39%	12%	9%	1%	5%	3%	1%	4%	5%	21%
2003–2004	40%	12%	9%	1%	5%	3%	1%	4%	5%	20%

Fig. 10.3. Indian IT software services and BPO (ITES) revenues.

The massive growth in the customer base will open the avenues for extensive use of ICT in the communication sector. Bharti's sell-off of its data services to IBM has opened up new avenue of outsourcing in Telecom industry.

The Indian Telecommunication network with 88.46 million telephone connections is the sixth largest in the world and the second largest among the emerging economies of Asia. The present tele-density is 8.24 per hundred (Table 10.1) and the target is to achieve 15 per hundred by 2010. Accordingly, India's 10th five year plan 2002–2007 projects Rs 1750 billion worth of investments in 50 million fixed lines, 30 million cellular lines and 20 million internet connections (UK Trade and Investment, 2003).

In the Telecoms Sector, India boasts the fifth largest network in the world and the second largest, after China, among emerging economies. The annual growth rates in India for "fixed" telephone line users is more than 22%, while mobile and internet usage is growing at over 100%. According to the Gartner Report, the Indian telecom services market will touch Rs 700 billion by 2006.

The private operators have made mobile telephony the fastest growing (over 100% p.a.) in India. Now, they are venturing into more traditional areas such as long distance and international fixed line calling. Three main private groups — Bharti, Tata and Reliance are competing with the public sector incumbents. The consumers, who have been paying among the world's highest tariffs so far, are likely to be the major beneficiary.

According to JM Morgan Stanley, the Telecom services market in India will expand by 9.4% annually for the next five years, with the cellular segment as the key growth driver. The share of public operators in this market is likely to diminish and competition would establish itself faster and get a bigger chunk of the market. This would be led by further liberalization, increasing customer expectations, convergence of technologies and the ability of private players to offer it to the market faster than the incumbent operator (UK Trade and Investment, 2003).

It would be difficult to make in-roads into the semirural and rural areas because of the lack of infrastructure. The sector requires players with huge financial resources. Upfront entry fees and bank guarantees represent a sizeable share. Initially it would be difficult to make in-roads into the semirural and rural areas because of the lack of

Table 10.1. Telephone networks status as of June 2002.

Teledensity	8.24%
Fixed line	43.96 million
Telephone exchanges &	223000
switching capacity*	21.46 million lines
Cellular subscribers	44.51 million

Source: Financial Express, http://www.financialexpress.com/fe_full_story.php?content_id=73662. Date of access: 12 January 2005.
*Source: http://www.indiacore.com/overview-main4.html.
Date of Access: 12 January 2005.

infrastructure. The sector requires players with huge financial resources investments (Table 10.2). The situation is further aggrieved due to reduction in Access Deficit Charges by the present government.

The leading Indian telecom companies are expected to spend Rs 960 bn over next five years. About 73% of the estimated investment is likely to be in the development of an urban network, while the remaining 27% will be invested on rural network. In terms of FDI from 1993 to September 2001, the actual flow has been Rs 81.2 billion with the cellular mobile services attracting the highest inflow of investments (Table 10.2).

According to Voice and Data 100 survey (UK Trade and Investment, 2003), the telecom equipment market grew by 10% in 2002–2003 to touch Rs 282.38 bn, due to the growth in wireless market. The equipment contributed 70% to the total industry size of Rs 282.38 bn, while software contributed 19% and 11% came from turnkey services.

10.2.2.1. *Growth in cellular services*

The cellular industry is strengthening its roots in India. During the first seven months of the financial year ending March 2005, about 11 million mobile subscribers were added, taking the total mobile subscribers in the country to 44.51 million. The biggest churn of all times in the history of Indian mobile industry was initiated by Reliance, one of the largest business houses in India by its Special Offer in the beginning of July'03. The result was simply astonishing. Reliance added 0.5 mn subscribers in 200 cities in just five days.

In October 2005, Bharti added 3.6 lakh new customers, taking its total subscriber base to about 90.63 lakh [9 mn]. BSNL had added highest number of new users of over 4 lakh in October taking its market share at 22.84%. BSNL had added a whopping 6.55 lakh subscribers in September. BSNL's total subscriber base in October stood at 79.41 lakh. Hutch was placed third with a subscriber base of 65.66 lakh and a market share of 18.88%.

Table 10.2. Investment projection over the next five years.

Private players	Investments over next five years (Rs billion)
Reliance	250
Bharti	50
Tata-Birla-AT&T-BPL-Hutchison	20
State owned players	
BSNL	500
MTNL	25
VSNL	25

Source: http://www.tradepartners.gov.uk/telecom/India/profile/ overview.

While in the CDMA category, Reliance Infocomm added 2.86 lakh subscribers taking its subscribers base to 10.3 mn, Tatas lost more than 33,000 subscribers in October 2004. In September 2004 too, Tatas had lost 8000 subscribers.

10.3. Business Sectors and IT

10.3.1. *Banking finance services insurance (BFSI)*

Banking and financial services (BFS) continued to be the domestic IT market's best–loved vertical-pegged at Rs 7231 crore, it accounted for 22% of the total IT spending in FY 2003–2004. The initial cycle of automation was finally over for the banking industry, with the exception of a few laggards. Some of the areas where FY 2003–2004 saw an upsurge were analytics, risk management, business process management (BPM), real-time gross settlement (RTGS), risk management, shared ATM network services and outsourcing in the form of remote infrastructure management.

According to the DQ Top 20, the BFSI segment contributes about 10% of the total IT industry and about 28% of the domestic IT market. In 2002–2003, the BFSI segment alone spent about Rs 7500 crore and, according to DQ estimates, this is expected to increase to a whopping Rs 9800 crore during the 2004–2005 fiscal.

Globalization of economies and financial liberalization within the economies has opened new opportunities of growth for techno savvy institutions. The use of IT in the banking industry in India has, however, been somewhat limited and has as a result, restricted the presence in international operations.

With Basel II norms becoming mandatory to do business with overseas clients, the role of ICT is to witness an increased importance. The use of data warehousing/data mining techniques and risk assessment techniques will be the most used ones. The implementation of core banking solution by PSU banks across the nation will witness an increase in IT expenditure for banks.

Another area of ICT expenditure will be "IT Security". Banks will have to increase the security standards in order to thwart attempts to disrupt normal functioning from hackers/unwanted agents.

With the growing recognition of the need of having in place the financial reforms, the interest in IT application in the banking sector in India has increased. In recent years, the banking industry has been undergoing rapid changes, reflecting a number of underlying developments. The most significant has been advances in communication and information technology, which have accelerated and broadened the dissemination of financial information while lowering the costs of many financial activities.

Another key impetus for change has been the increasing competition among a broad range of domestic and foreign institutions in providing banking and related financial services.

The introduction of the computerization in the Banking industry brought considerable changes in the functioning of clearing house mechanism, which facilitates the exchange of instruments, and processing of payment at a central point among the participating banks. Clearing houses have gradually extended their range of activities to automate and provide electronic means for settlement of payment transaction, electronic clearing service (ECS) emerged as a system/scheme to replace paper instrument.

10.3.1.1. *Computerization in public sector banks/total branch automation*

The Central Vigilance Commission (CVC) and RBI have set a mandate for all PSU banks to be computerized by the end of 2004. Although this target was not achieved by some of the PSUs, yet most of them have achieved more than 90% automation.

10.3.1.2. *Introduction of core banking solution by most of the PSU banks*

The implementation of core banking solutions will enable the banks to give services to customers across the nation like some of the private banks (Table 10.3). This will be a source of competitive advantage to PSU banks because of their sheer reach. But, this will require massive investments in ICT and consulting exercise. The project involves procurement, supply and installation of hardware and the core banking software, customization of the core banking software, implementation, rollout of the software at branches, and training and support.

10.3.1.3. *Cheque clearing*

Magnetic ink character recognition (MICR) based cheque-clearing accounts for about 65% of the value of cheques processed in the country. Magnetic media-based clearing systems account for about 10% additional value, while claim-based processes cover the rest of clearing.

Table 10.3. Core banking solutions in India.

Vendor	Core banking solution
Infosys	Finacle
I-Flex	Flexcube
TCS	B@NCS-24
Polaris	Orbi One Core
Infrasoft Technologies	OMNIEnterprise
Sanchez Capital Services	Profile
ICICI Infotech	Newton
Nucleus Software	FINNONE
Zenith Infotech	Banc724

10.3.1.4. *Introduction of Internet banking*

In India, only selected educated customers use Internet banking. Despite India being one of the leading IT service providers in the world, there is a huge digital divide. The percentage of PC using population at 6.5 per 1000 being very small, the branches where this facility is introduced are carefully selected. A variety of Internet Banking services to both individual and corporate customers are provided by most of the MNC and newly established private banks and a few public sector banks.

10.3.1.5. *BI tools*

There will emerge widespread adoption of business analytics in Banking industry — including business intelligence tools (Table 10.4), which are likely to be integrated with CRM solutions during the year.

While RBI, ICICI Bank, HDFC Bank, IDBI Bank, LIC and Standard Chartered Bank have already gone for BI implementation in 2003, many more like Punjab National Bank, Bank of Baroda are slated to follow.

With retail banking through multiple channels expected to become a norm for the larger banks and insurance companies, BI would be absolutely crucial for them to retain and acquire customers to survive. BI tools help individual banks to know the entire history of the customer, which in turn enables the bank to offer services suited to him.

10.3.1.6. *Antimoney laundering (AML)*

With the Money Laundering Act 2003 likely to come to force, banks in India will have to take prevention of money laundering as a critical business sustaining activity. The bill works out modalities of disclosure by financial institutions regarding reportable transactions, confiscation of the proceeds of crime, declaring money laundering as an extraditable offence and promoting international cooperation in investigation of money laundering. Most of them have realized that they need a comprehensive solution that

Table 10.4. Major BI offerings.

Vendor	BI tool
SAS	SAS Customer Intelligence Solutions
Teradata	Teradata Warehouse 7.0.1
I-Flex	Revelus
Business Objects	Business Objects Enterprise 6
Computer Associates	CleverPath Predictive Analysis Server
SAP	mySAP Business Intelligence
ProClarity	ProClarity Analytics Server
Oracle	Oracle Business Intelligence Solutions
Infosys	FinacleCRM

provides the greatest possible scalability and flexibility. After all, the consequences of failing to detect criminal financial behavior are serious. The only defense is a highly effective antimoney laundering (AML) system.

Only eight PSU banks and private banks like ICICI, which have offshore entities, are in different phases of deploying such systems.

10.3.1.7. *Revolution in ATMs*

Most of the banks in India have their own ATM network. ICICI Bank, will introduce indigenously developed low-cost ATM for rural India and will be supported by biometric authentication. The indigenously developed ATM will be at one-fifth of the international cost and the fingerprinting identification will be the only biometric method used initially.

The Institute for Development and Research in Banking Technology (IDRBT) is in the process of setting-up the National Financial Switch (NFS), which comprises of a National Switch to facilitate connectivity between the Bank's Switches and their ATMs, and interbank payment gateway for authentication and routing the payment details of various e-commerce transactions, e-government activities, etc. The hardware has already been installed and the testing is in progress, and it is expected that the pilot test with the chosen banks would be completed by the mid of August 2004. The switch is expected to start live transactions thereafter. The installed base of ATMs in the country is estimated to be over 15,000 units and it is expected to go up to 30,000 ATMs before December 2005. New private banks have been the biggest deployers of ATMs and more recently public sector banks and old private banks have announced aggressive plans to install ATMs. The Clearing Corporation of India Limited (CCIL) will be the clearing and settlement agency for the switch, which will also facilitate the disaster recovery from its premises at Mumbai.

10.3.1.8. *Real-time gross settlement system (RTGS)*

RTGS is a large value funds transfer system whereby financial intermediaries can settle interbank transfers for their own account as well as for their customers. The system effects final settlement of interbank funds transfers on a continuous, transaction-by-transaction basis throughout the processing day.

There are now a total of 23 banks conducting transactions RBI's online clearing and settlement system, RTGS.

10.3.1.9. *Insurance and IT*

After all these years of being clubbed under the rubric of the ubiquitous BFSI, insurance in FY 2003–2004 merited separate mention, as IT spending in this sector has grown from Rs 270 crore to Rs 668 crore. With the LIC monopoly being finally broken by the entry of nearly 20 private players, this was indeed a sunrise sector for IT adoption, with customer relationship management (CRM) being the most-favored technology, with almost the whole segment taking to it. Insurance companies witnessed unacceptable customer churn levels, which they focused on retaining existing customers.

Bigger players like ICICI Prudential Life Insurance Company adopted CRM in a big way, where the company was earlier using GoldMines (a sales and marketing tool) and HEAT (an operational CRM solution) from FrontRange Solutions, this year it has decided to invest in Teradata's CM3 and SAS's statistical tool for BI. CRM helped ICICI Prudential Life Insurance to capture five lakh customers through effective event-based marketing and lead tracking to cross and up-sell products. CRM also helped Aviva Life Insurance, which catered to close to 100,000 customers with this solution, categorize and segment customers and align them with the products that best suited them.

Another emerging trend has been that of insurance companies joining hands with banks by becoming channel partners for insurance. Tata AIG had a marketing alliance with HSBC, Birla Sun Life had one with Citibank, IDBI and LIC allied with Corporation Bank, while Kotak Life Insurance had an arrangement with Kotak Bank. This strategy helped insurance firms to increase their footprints to cover a larger proportion than they could earlier of the customer base in the 20–30 years demographic profile. CRM helped to connect a bank's high net-worth customers with insurance firms.

Insurance may also see a faster adoption of mobile computing in the year to come. Insurance applications specifically developed for the PDA and interfaced with back-end insurance management software help agents directly log in queries and policy details. Most of the insurance companies also went in for disaster recovery sites.

10.3.1.10. *Highlights of IT spending by BFSI segment in 2002–2003*

(1) Bank of India awarded a 10-year IT infrastructure outsourcing contract valued at $150 million to HP Services. The deal also saw BoI opting for Finacle from Infosys as its core banking solution.
(2) State Bank of India and seven of its associate banks got more than 2500 of their branches connected under the second phase of the $29 million project assigned to Datacraft.
(3) Co-operative banks like Dhanalakshmi Bank and Kerala State Co-operative Bank adopted Flexcube from i-flex, the world's largest selling core banking solution.
(4) State Bank of India launched a mobile ATM, using Reliance CDMA technology, on a boat near Vypeen islands in the Kochi backwaters.
(5) ICICI Bank deployed a mobile ATM using Reliance Fixed Wireless Terminal (FWT) outside the Wankhede Stadium during the India–Australia one-day cricket match.

(6) UTI Bank installed an ATM at Thegu in Sikkim at a height of 13,200 ft. mainly catering to the Army camp located there, while Comsat Max installed India's highest SSALAN VSAT antenna for this ATM.
(7) With over 18 million cards in use, ATMs in India dispensed Rs 55,000 crore during FY 2003–2004. Frauds involving ATM cards in India averaged Rs 30,000 according to the Credit Card Management Consultancy.

The last two years have seen a significant step up in outsourcing of IT services by banks. As compared to 8–12% growth during the year 2001, IT services outsourcing in the banking segment has been pegged by IDC at a CAGR of around 24% from 2001 to 2006. In fact, according to IDC, banking has emerged as the second largest segment, next only to discreet manufacturing, within the IT services gamut.

10.3.2. *Retail*

The Indian retail sector is expected to grow from $180 billion in 2003 to $300 billion by 2010 (NASSCOM Evalueserve Report, 2003). The Indian retail market has been ranked fifth out of 30 developing countries for retail investment attractiveness by AT Kearney and second in Global Retail Development Index. "Organized Retailing" constitutes around 2% ($4.5 billion) and is expected to grow to 15–20% in the coming decade.

The Organized Retail sector is investing on a massive scale in IT to bring about process improvements. Solutions in the order of point of sale (PoS), supply chain management (SCM), CRM, e-business solutions and complex retail enterprise resource planning (ERP) are being implemented.

The Retail industry is being divided into four classes on the basis of IT solutions being implemented:

(1) Large retailers. They have over 30 stores. They use custom built solutions, ERP packages for their back office operations, etc. High-end solutions for retailers with more than 300 stores such as JDA, SAP IS Retail or Retek have takers in India.
(2) Mid-sized retailers. They have around five stores and have the plans to expand to 15–20 stores in the next two years. Packaged IT solutions for PoS, demand forecasting, purchase orders and inventory management are being purchased. Retail Pro is a solution gaining acceptance with stores having 1–50 stores.
(3) Manufacturer–retailer. These involve stores held by manufacturers and their franchisees. They have Retail Pro or other customized software developed by local for back office operations.
(4) Small retailers. They are primarily specialty apparel retailers, discount stores or departmental stores. They also use customized vendor developed PoS systems connected to an inventory system.

The future of IT investments in Retailing would be in the sphere of CRM, ERP packages, online analytical processing (OLAP) tools, B2B software, B2C software, collaborative planning and forecasting (CPFR) tools and other business optimization software.

An IT savvy picture of the retail industry can be drawn from the following instances of retail companies deploying IT (Rediff Business, 2004).

(1) RPG Group. They operate in three formats — Grocery store (Food World), Drug Stores (Health & Glow) and Music Stores (Music World). Food World alone has more than 85 stores as of today, transacts close to 1.5 million bills per month at an average of 10 items per bill across its stores and has invested close to Rs 6 crore for IT infrastructure. RPG group has adopted RetailPro, a widely accepted package for PoS, merchandising and inventory control for speciality retailers. They have thus succeeded in bringing down their inventory from 20 days to a week. Automated indenting, purchasing, billing, distribution and payments, and internal logistics enable strong supply chain. Customer behavior analysis identifies which products to promote to increase the average bill value. They are known to use CRM packages. They are also into e-business through the portals saregama.com, musicworld.com, myfoodworld.com and hamaraCD.com.
(2) ITC lifestyle retailing business division (LRBD) has close to 38 stores across India. Recently they partnered with Intentia to implement PREDATOR (ProActive Demand Accelerator, a fashion and retail management solution, across its stores. This will help increase the efficiency in retail store billing, CRM, distribution and manufacturing operations (CXOToday, 2004). LRBD is implementing collaborative supply chain practices and global standards by adopting the universal EAN barcode. EAN-UCC is being used by major players across the world (EAN India Press Release, 2004).
(3) Shopper's Stop. Shopper's Stop has 15 stores spread all over India. They are the recipients of NASSCOM award of the "Best IT User" in 2003 in the retail vertical. They have implemented the JDA merchandise management system (MMS), warehouse management system (WMS) and perpetual inventory control system (PICS). Their regional distribution systems are connected online. They have thus brought about a reduction in turnaround time by 24 h with a 1 lakh savings per month. They have 150 partners connected to them through Seimens' BconnectB (B2B) solution. Their source tagging initiative has resulted in a reduction in turnaround time from 96 h to 24 h. This has also resulted in manpower cost reduction. This has also resulted in 100% reconciliation of receipts ensuring timely payment to vendors and a reduction in lead-time for distribution.
(4) Westside. Westside has close to 11 stores all over India. They are known to be conservative in their IT spending. They have adopted RetailPro recently for merchandising and inventory management.

(5) Pantaloon Retail India Ltd. PRIL manages Pantaloons, Big Bazaar, Food Bazaar, Gold Bazaar and Central Malls. They have deployed a software tool — automatic replenishment system (ARS), which tracks stock levels in each store and triggers replenishment from the warehouses based on current off takes. It has also installed the WMS. The cumulative effort of a lot of initiatives including IT elements have helped to propel from a sales of Rs 49 crore in 1999 to Rs 441 crore in 2003.

10.3.3. *Automobiles*

There is an increasing use of IT in Indian automobile industry. Almost all major players in this sector have ERP package in place. Now, most of the ERP packages offer SCM module that helps in automating supply chain. Its investments in this sector are restricted to one-time investment of server installation/upgradation and buying new hardware and software for the system.

Tata Motors, through its subsidiary Tata Technologies, pioneers the use of design packages like CAD/Proe for making world-class design. Tata Technologies enjoys patronage of clients like GM, Ford, etc.

The business problems addressed through ERP implementations were:

(i) Data management. With various departments in different places, data generated wasn't managed systematically and information wasn't available on time to the concerned people.
(ii) Inventory. Firm had to keep at least eight days of stock in the materials department, unnecessarily blocking funds. The inventory levels were reduced to two days.
(iii) IT centralization. Due to legacy of islands of information in different departments, closure of financial books always got delayed, which in turn held up auditing. They wanted to automate the processes by connecting all departments, through a web-based environment, so that anyone with authorization could access the required information when they wanted it.

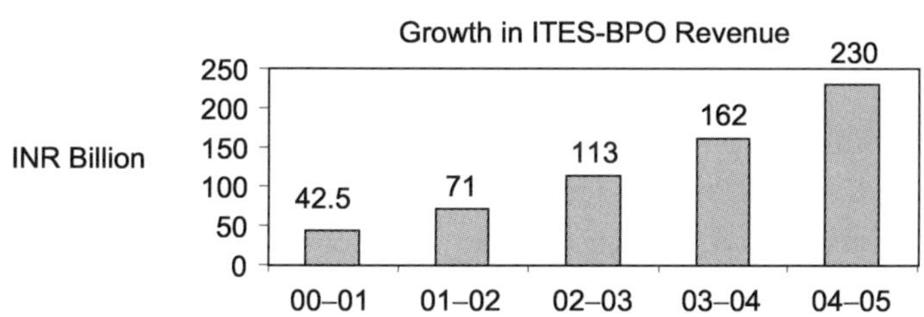

Fig. 10.4. ITES-BPO growth.

Source: NASSCOM Strategic Review, 2003, http://www.rediff.com/money/2004/jun/08bpo2.htm.

(iv) Tracking production. They introduced a bar coding system for engine, chassis and vehicle. As soon as a vehicle is assembled, with chassis and engine, it was recorded in the system. This enabled the company to know the time needed for complete assembly from any stage, any delay in production, and the exact "work-in-progress" level.

10.3.4. *Business process outsourcing (BPO)*

According to NASSCOM, the IT-enabled services-BPO segment contributes 29% of the total IT software and service exports from India and witnessed a growth of 46% to reach $3.6 billion in 2003–2004 from $2.5 billion in 2002–2003 (Fig. 10.4). India has maintained its global competitiveness by providing a winning combination of cost–quality–scalability versus competing destinations such as Philippines and China.

In the last financial year, ITES-BPO companies were the largest recruiters in the IT/ITES sector, adding about 70,000 jobs. This sector is estimated to register a growth of about 40% in FY 2004–2005 to reach revenues of $5.1 billion (230 bn INR).

The ITES-BPO sector continues to gain traction, with more than 80% of the Fortune 500 companies evaluating offshoring of most of the nonstrategic processes now.

The industry is targeting new service lines viz. technical help desks, finance and accounting services, engineering services, equity research, etc. to widen its gamut of services to achieve sustained growth.

The captive units continue to account for 65% of the ITES-BPO industry with one new captive centre being added every week in 2003–2004.

India has become a popular choice for customers seeking outsourced services because it is able to offer a 24 × 7 service and reduction in turnaround times by leveraging time zone differences. In certain Remote Services categories, Indian players have achieved high productivity levels with the emergence of BPO vendors with deep process skills and the ability to offer integrated outsourcing solutions. At the core of India's great attraction as the outsourcing destination is its unbeatable value proposition — (productivity, quality and rate) (PQR) factor.

The key subsegments in the Indian ITES-BPO industry are:

- *Customer care*: includes technical support and monitoring, queries regarding product and services, order status, accounts and services support.
- *Finance*: including billing services, accounting transactions, tax consulting and compliance, risk management, financial reporting, and financial analysis. Finance services are moving up the value chain to offer services such as equity research and insurance claim processing.

- *Human Resources*: includes benefits administration, education and training, recruiting and staffing, payroll services, hiring administration, records management. The growth in HR services in India has been slow due to lack of vendor domain expertise.
- The growth of HR services globally, presents a huge opportunity for Indian vendors. Along with gaining domain expertise, improvement in service quality and enactment of data security regulations by the Indian government are vital for the growth of HR services in India.
- *Payment services*: includes credit/debit card services, cheque processing, transaction processing, electronic data exchange (EDI) database marketing/customer analysis, web sales and marketing.
- *Administration*: includes billing, shareholder services, tax processing, claims processing, asset management, document management, transcription and translation. This is the fastest growing segment within Indian ITES-BPO industry. Despite the successful growth, administration services faced falling billing rates due to intense competition among vendors.
- *Content development*: includes engineering, design, animation, digitization, network consultancy and management, biotech research.

Within the ITES-BPO segment, Customer Care is expected to continue as the dominant segment with both revenues and employment (expected) growing by more than 40% in 2003–2004 over 2002–2003. Other areas that witnessed significant growth were Administration and Finance registering revenue growth (expected) of 74% and 60%, respectively, over 2002–2003. Segments such as Payment services and HR are also expected to register a considerable growth in revenues at 104% and 55%, respectively, in 2003–2004 over 2002–2003. In terms of manpower, Customer Care employs the largest number of people followed by Content Development, Administration and Finance. The number of employees in the Administration and Finance segment is expected to grow 67% and 60% in 2003–2004 over 2002–2003 (Table 10.5).

Table 10.5. ITES-BPO growth by service lines.

Service lines	2001–2002		2002–2003		2003–2004E	
US $ million	Employment	Revenue	Employment	Revenue	Employment	Revenue
Customer Care	30,000	400	65,000	810	95,000	1200
Finance	15,000	300	24,000	510	40,000	820
HR	1500	30	2100	45	3500	70
Payment Service	7000	110	11,000	210	21,000	430
Administration	14,000	185	25,000	310	40,000	540
Content Development	39,000	450	44,000	465	46,000	520
Total	106,500	1475	171,100	2350	245,500	3580

Source: NASSCOM Strategic Review, 2004.

10.3.5. *The key trends witnessed in the Indian ITES-BPO market in 2002*

10.3.5.1. *Market consolidation*

After witnessing a large number of acquisitions in 2002, Indian ITES-BPO industry saw further consolidation in 2003 (Table 10.6). The capital intensive nature of this industry makes it difficult for small players to grow quickly, and a number of IT services companies have added ITES-BPO units to exploit synergies between BPO and IT services offerings. There has been additional impetus to this trend because large customers have become more favorable towards vendors who can provide end-to-end services.

10.3.5.2. *Increase in vendor & BOT contracts*

In a build–operate–transfer model, a vendor sets up and grows a fully functioning center to a desired size and then hands it over to customer at a pre-determined time. The advantages of using multiple vendor strategy include: scalability, vendor de-risking and competitive pricing.

Table 10.6. Recent M&A in Indian ITES-BPO industry.

Company	Acquirer	Seller	Stake	Deal value
Quintant services	Igate	GMR Groups	64.10%	USD 19.9 Mn
Suntech data systems	Zensar	Promoters global technology	50%	NA
I back Office	Polaris	Ventures	NA	NA 21 Crore
IT&T	Mascot Systems	NA Chrysalis capital	NA	INR
Transworks	Indian Rayon	& Promoters	100%	USD 13 Mn
Airline financial support	TCS	Swissair	75.10%	NA
Firstring	ICICI Onesource	Promoters	NA	NA
L&L Services	Ismart	PwC India	NA	4 Crore INR
ClaimsBPO	WNS	NA	NA	NA USD 3.9
C3 (Manila)	Hinduja TMT	Promoters	NA	Mn
Corpay solutions (USA)	Datamatics	NA	NA	USD 9 Mn

Source: Media, company websites.

10.3.5.3. *Continued convergence of supplier models*

Indian vendors will continue to expand services offering in client regions to support a more seamless delivery model. Indian vendors are also setting up centers such as Philippines, China, Japan, with a view to tap these markets.

10.3.5.4. *Vendor polarization*

According to analysts, a large part of the growth in the ITES-BPO may be concentrated with the large vendors. Factors for this include customer preference for size and scalability, delivery capability, track record, client references and management background.

10.3.5.5. *Increase in capacity*

The Indian ITES-BPO industry has witnessed a significant increase in capacity over the last year.

10.3.5.6. *Increased presence of IT services companies*

Many IT service companies expanded their offerings to include ITES-BPO by creating their own capacities (Infosys, Patni, Satyam, HCL, Cognizant, Syntel) or by acquiring ITES-BPO players (Wipro acquiring Spectramind).

10.3.5.7. *Geographical diversification of capacity*

A number of players set up additional centers in new cities drawn by attractive incentives offered by many state governments, and in an attempt to diversify risk of running a single location center and to take advantage of lower labor costs in other cities. The average number of employees in the ITES-BPO sector is 190 but the range is huge and varies from as low as four people to as many as 16,000 people.

10.3.5.8. *Changes in ownership structure*

- Two MNCs have divested part of their stake in their captive units, British Airways in WNS GE in GECIS and Conseco in EXL. They have capitalized on the market value of their firm by bringing in a strategic investor(s). The unit then competes with third party vendors, claiming domain expertise as a differentiator while targeting new customers.
- Venture capital funds such as Oakhill, General Atlantic Partners, Westbridge Capital, Warburg Pincus, among others are reported to have invested close to US$ 300 million in ITES-BPO companies in 2002.
- M&A transactions are on the rise and some IT service companies are choosing to buy rather than build in order to rapidly scale up.

10.3.5.9. *Changing customer behavior*

A number of large customers prefer to outsource business to multiple vendors and also set up a captive unit on their own. In some cases, they are asking the vendor to build a center on a build–operate–transfer model, in which case the vendor would grow the center to a certain size and then hand it over to the customer at the end of the pre-determined period.

Strategic outsourcing is not confined to large corporates. The public sector banks want to outsource their entire IT business to global majors. Strategic outsourcing includes consultancy services, integrated technology solutions, as well as maintaining and running the whole IT environment for an enterprise. Outsourcing the entire IT infrastructure could enable organizations to focus attention on their core activities, improve economies of scale and price performance, and reduce technology risk.

Indian companies are recruiting in large numbers in order to catch up with their BPO demand in outsourcing professionals as well as for domestic BPO business. Due to numerous benefits accrued to the deployment of information technology in business activities, the IT firms in India met with the increase in demand for the firm's human resources.

The most important reason for BPO business (IT) to thrive in India is the abundance of human resources in the field of IT and a cost edge which provides great boost to MNCs to expand their BPO operations in India.

10.3.6. *Employment opportunities in Indian IT industry*

Employment opportunities have increased a lot since the advent of information technology in India. A large number of jobs have been offshored by many MNCs owing to reduced cost structure in India. Outsourcing of IT jobs to India could grow fivefold to $50 billion by 2008 if it can overcome a US labour backlash, as per the pre-report by investment-analyst firm Brean Murray Institutional Research.

From meagre 6800 knowledge workers in 1985–1986, an estimated 6, 50,000 IT software and services professionals were there in March 2003 (NASSCOM Strategic Review, 2004). Out of these, about 2, 05,000 are working in the IT software and services export industry, nearly 1, 60,000 in IT enabled services. The domestic market employs about 25,000 of them and over 2, 60,000 are employed in user organizations.

10.4. Conclusion

The review of the present scenario Internet Technologies in India in terms of its importance to the economy of the country, opportunities for growth and deployment by the various business sectors provides a better understanding of the issues to be addressed for the proposed Business and Information Technologies Study to be carried out in India, by the team from IIT Bombay.

Bibliography

1. CXOToday. http://www.cxotoday.com/cxo/jsp/article.jsp?article id=1356&cat id=908. [Date of Access: 2 April 2005]
2. GSI India (formely EAN India). http://www.gs1india.org/news/Press%20Release%20-%20Garments.doc. [Date of Access: 2 April 2005]
3. NASSCOM Evalueserve Report, 2003.
4. NASSCOM McKinsey Report, 2002.
5. NASSCOM Strategic Review — The IT Industry in India, 2004.
6. Rediff Business. http://www.rediff.com/money/2004/jun/08bpo2.htm. [Date of Access: 12 March 2005]
7. SiliconTaiga. http://www.silicontaiga.org/home.asp?artld=1799. [Date of Access: 12 April 2005]
8. UK Trade and Investment. http://www.tradepartners.gov.uk/telecom/india/profile/overview.shtml. [Date of access: 11 August 2003]
9. Website http://www.dqindia.com/dqtop20/2004/artdisp.asp?artid=60679. [Date of Access: 27 March 2005]
10. Website http://www.expresscomputeonline.com.
11. Website http://www.financialexpress.com/fe_full_story.php?content_id=73662. [Date of access: 12 January 2005]
12. Website http://www.indiacore.com/overview-main4.html. [Date of Access: 12 January 2005]

INDEX